AFRICAN DEVELOPMENT REPORT
2003

AFRICA IN THE WORLD ECONOMY

GLOBALIZATION AND AFRICA'S DEVELOPMENT

ECONOMIC AND SOCIAL STATISTICS ON AFRICA

PUBLISHED FOR THE AFRICAN DEVELOPMENT BANK
BY
OXFORD UNIVERSITY PRESS

OXFORD

Great Clarendon Street, Oxford OX2 6DP
Oxford University Press is a department of the University of Oxford.
It furthers the University's objective of excellence in research, scholarship,
and education by publishing worldwide in

Oxford New York
Auckland Bangkok Buenos Aires Cape Town Chennai
Dar es Salaam Delhi Hong Kong Istanbul Karachi Kolkata
Kuala Lumpur Madrid Melbourne Mexico City Mumbai Nairobi
São Paulo Shanghai Taipei Tokyo Toronto

Oxford is a registered trade mark of Oxford University Press
in the UK and in certain other countries

Published in the United States
by Oxford University Press Inc., New York

The African Development Report 2003 is produced by the staff of the African Development Bank,
and the views expressed therein do not necessarily reflect those of the Boards of Directors
or the countries they represent. Designations employed in this Report do not imply the expression
of any opinion, on the part of the African Development Bank, concerning the legal status of any
country or territory, or the delineation of its frontiers.

British Library Cataloguing in Publication Data
Data available
Library of Congress Cataloging-in-Publication Data
Data available
ISBN 0-19-926283-7
1 3 5 7 9 10 8 6 4 2

Typeset by African Development Bank
Printed in Great Britain
on acid-free paper by
Bath Press Ltd., Bath, Avon

FOREWORD

The 2003 *African Development Report* (ADR) prepared by the staff of the Bank provides an in-depth review of the economic performance of Africa in 2002, viewed from the both the continental and sub-regional perspectives. In particular, the challenges posed by globalization and the strategies that African countries could consider in meeting them are the special focus of this year's Report.

The provisional assessment of the Report reveals that Africa's GDP growth in 2002 declined and is likely to fall below its average trend rate of 3 percent for the first time since 1995. For the year, African economic growth is estimated at 2.8 percent, down from 3.5 percent in 2001. Three strong factors, working in tandem, accounted for this disappointing aggregate outcome. First, the generally weak external environment affected capital flows and exports proceeds, especially from tourism in North Africa; second, drought conditions lowered agricultural production in East and Southern Africa; and, third, civil conflicts depressed economic activity in parts of the continent, particularly in the Western sub-region.

As in previous years, there was, however, considerable variation in the performance of African countries. Fourteen countries experienced growth rates above 5 percent— down from 21 in 2001; another 14 countries had growth rates in the range of 3-5 percent (up from 8 in 2001); 18 countries had growth rates in the range of 0-3 percent; and

5 countries—the same as in 2001—had negative growth rates. Africa's ten largest economies, accounting for over three-quarters of the continent's GDP had an average growth rate of 2.2 percent, contributing to the lower aggregate performance of the continent.

GDP growth is expected to recover modestly to 3.3 percent in 2003, should external and internal conditions improve. In general, however, the aggregate low growth levels and the risks associated with the external environment do not bode well for Africa's quest for reducing poverty and achieving the Millennium Development Goals (MDGs). In this respect, it is becoming clear that while the developing and transition countries of Asia, Eastern Europe, and Latin America and the Caribbean are likely to fulfill many of the MDGs, few African countries, mainly in North African, are likely to meet most of them. It is thus essential that African countries and their development partners redouble their efforts to raise the average growth rate for the continent to the 6-8 percent required to make headway toward the MDGs, and in particular towards halving poverty by 2015.

Such an effort must necessarily include a strategy for Africa to benefit from the process of globalization. On current trends, it is evident that Africa, more than any other region of the world, faces the danger of being left behind by the rapid changes brought about by the forces of globalization. Available statistics reveal clearly the risks facing the Continent. In 1950, for example, Africa delivered a tenth of world exports. Today its share has declined to only 2.7 percent. Similarly, Africa's share of foreign direct investment —and more broadly private capital flows—has fallen to less than 5 percent, despite the enormous surge in such flows to developing countries in the last decade. Moreover, much of the foreign direct investment in Africa is concentrated, geographically and sectorally, in a few countries and in extractive natural resources such as oil and minerals.

Against this background, and as the Report makes clear, Africa's quest for accelerated growth and poverty reduction requires a coherent strategy that seeks to minimize the risks of globalization while maximizing its benefits. To be effective, such a plan must be comprehensive and involve clear strategies at three levels: national, regional, and global.

At the national level, the strategy should be anchored on building the institutions and the enabling environment for a private sector led market economy that is capable of competing at the global level. A critical element of such a strategy must necessarily be building up and diversifying the export sector, and aggressively seeking out export niches and opportunities. Evidently, African countries cannot do well in the global economy if their export revenues continue to depend on one or two primary commodities. Diversification is thus critical and will, in turn, require that countries take steps to improve their investment climate to attract private capital flows. As the experience of developing countries in other regions has shown, foreign direct investment is critical not only for attracting the required capital but also for introducing technological and managerial know-how. It is also proficient at identifying and developing export markets in the industrial countries.

At the regional level, the strategy should seek to enlarge markets and to exploit complemen-tarities, economies of scale, and synergies by deepening regional cooperation and integration efforts. Most African national markets are clearly too small to enable firms, capable of competing on the global market, to emerge. Most are also too small to attract large volumes of foreign capital, except possibly in the extractive sectors. The removal of trade barriers, creating the conditions for market integration, and the free flow of capital and labor across borders would therefore stimulate larger volumes of investments—both domestic and foreign.

The NEPAD initiative holds the promise of giving a new thrust to regional integration efforts and African counties should seek to collectively implement its various components. I may add, in this regard, that at the request of the NEPAD Heads of Sate Implementation Committee, the Bank is providing assistance to NEPAD in the areas of infrastructure and banking and financial standards. A short-term action plan has been developed for regional infrastructure projects, with four projects already approved for financing. The Bank has also developed a framework for improving banking and financial standards, which has been endorsed by African Central Bankers and Ministers of Finance.

National and regional strategies to enable African countries to face the challenge of globalization, if they are to succeed, must be complemented by a global strategy, developed jointly with Africa's development partners. Africa's quest to transform its production structures and to compete globally will necessarily require the support of the industrial countries, in accordance with the pledges they made at important recent fora such as Monterrey, Kananaskis and Johannesburg. Consequently, the donor community will need to increase ODA flows to Africa to help finance investments in infrastructure and key sectors such as health and education, necessary to build a skilled labor force. Similarly, support must continue for debt relief initiatives such as HIPC to help African countries exit permanently from the debt crisis. And finally, Africa's development partners should fully implement the provisions of recent trade initiatives such as the 'Everything but Arms' initiative of the European Union and the African Growth and Opportunity Act (AGOA) of the United States. These are critical for creating a level playing field for Africa's exports, particularly as African countries begin to increase the volume of exports of processed and manufactured goods.

As in the past, the African Development Bank will continue to support the efforts of African countries to develop their economies and thereby take advantage of the opportunities offered by globalization. It will mobilize both concessional and non-concessional resources to finance projects and programs, with the levels of financing now averaging close to $3 billion per year in 2001 and 2002. It will also continue to actively participate in the HIPC debt relief initiative, having already approved $2.2 billion of debt relief for the 22 African countries that have to date qualified.

Its 1999 Vision Statement and the Strategic Plan that it adopted in 2002 will guide the interventions of the Bank Group. Accordingly, in the low-income countries, the focus will be on creating the foundations for long-term growth by giving priority to investments that seek to reduce poverty and develop the human capital base. Priority sectors will therefore be agriculture and rural development and education and health. In the middle income countries, the focus will be on enhancing the competitiveness of their economies by assisting them improve the overall policy environment and strengthening key sectors such as the financial sector, and by providing financing for needed investments.

In both groups of countries, the Bank will continue to support the development of the private sector by helping to improve the investment climate through structural reforms and by directly financing viable projects. A particular focus for Bank support, in this regard, is the development of small and medium scale enterprises. Clearly, the strengthening of the private sector is critical to attract foreign private capital, diversify export baskets, and capture larger trade shares in the international market.

The *2003 African Development Report* provides an in-depth analysis of these issues, the economic trends on the continent, and the many challenges facing African countries in this era of rapid globalization. I am confident that policy makers, as well as the private sector and civil society organizations, both in Africa and in the international community, will find the analysis useful, as well as its policy prescriptions.

Omar Kabbaj
President
African Development Bank

The *African Development Report 2003* has been prepared by a staff team in the Development Research Department under the direction of Henock Kifle.

The research team was led by Mohamed Nureldin Hussain and comprised John C. Anyanwu, Obed Mailafia, Charlotte Vaillant (consultant), Meriem Fergani (consultant) and Barfour Osei (consultant) from the Research Division.

The Economic and Social Statistics on Africa were prepared by the Statistics Division led by Charles L. Lufumpa and comprised André Portella, Beejaye Kokil, Maurice Mubila and Koua Louis Kouakou.

Rhoda R. Bangurah provided production services, Richard Synge editorial services and Maurice K. Kponnou research rssistance.

Preparation of the *Report* was aided by the background papers listed in the bibliographical note. Comments from outside the Bank are noted with appreciation. Kabir Hassan of the University of New Orleans, USA; Christiana Okojie of the University of Benin, Nigeria; Arne Bigsten of Göteborg University, Sweden; Sheila Page of the ODI, United Kingdom; and Charles Chukwuma Soludo of the University of Nigeria, Nsukka, Nigeria; and Farid Ben Youcef, University of Alger, Algeria all made comments and suggestions to improve the *Report*.

ABBREVIATIONS

ACP	African, Caribbean and Pacific
ADB	African Development Bank
ADF	African Development Fund
ADI	African Development Institute
ADR	African Development Report
AEC	African Economic Community
AEF	African Enterprise Fund
AFTA	ASEAN Free Trade Area
AGOA	African Growth and Opportunity Act
AMSCO	African Management Services Company
AMU	Arab Maghreb Union
APDF	African Project Development Facility
APEC	Asia Pacific Economic Cooperation
APRM	African Peer Review Mechanism
ASEAN	Association of Southeast Asian Nations
ATLE	Africa's Ten Largest Economies
AU	African Union
BCEAO	Central Bank of West African States
BEAC	Central Bank of Central African States
BIDPA	Botswana Institute for Development Policy Analysis
BPRS	Botswana Poverty Reduction Strategy
BVMAC	Bourse de valeurs mobilières de l'Afrique centrale
BWIs	Bretton Woods Institutions
CAR	Central African Republic
CDC	Cameroon Development Corporation
CDF	Comprehensive Development Framework
CEMAC	Communauté économique et monétaire de l'Afrique centrale
CEN-SAD	Community of Sahel-Saharan States
CET	Common External Tariff
CFA	Communauté financière africaine
CIP	Competitive Industrial Performance
COMESA	Common Market for Eastern and Southern Africa
CSIR	Council of Scientific and Industrial Research
CSPs	Country Strategy Papers
DCP	Debt Conversion Program
DPIA	Dubai Ports International Authority
DRC	Democratic Republic of Congo
DFID	Department for International Development
DTI	Department of Trade and Industry
EAC	East African Community

EBA	Everything But Arms
ECOWAS	Economic Community of West African States
ECOMOG	Economic Community of West African States Monitoring Group
EERP	Emergency Economic Recovery Programme
EPZs	Export Processing Zones
ERSO	Electronic Research and Service Organization
ESAF	Enhanced Structural Adjustment Facility
EU	European Union
FAO	Food and Agriculture Organization
FDI	Foreign Direct Investment
FTA	Free Trade Area
GATS	General Agreement on Trade in Services
GATT	General Agreement on Tariffs and Trade
GDP	Gross Domestic Product
GEAR	Growth, Employment and Redistribution
GEP	Global Economic Prospects
GNI	Gross National Income
GNP	Gross National Product
GSP	Generalized System of Preferences
GTAP	Global Trade Analysis Project
HCDA	Horticultural Crops Development Authority
HIPC	Heavily Indebted Poor Countries
HIV/AIDS	Human Immunodeficiency Virus/Acquired Immuno-Deficiency Syndrome
ICT	Information and Communications Technology
IDA	International Development Association
IEAP	Interim Economic Adjustment Programme
ILO	International Labour Organization
IMF	International Monetary Fund
IPA	Investment Promotion Agencies
IPRSPs	Interim Poverty Reduction Strategy Papers
ISO	International Standards Organizations
IT	Information Technology
ITRI	Industrial Technology Research Institute
JAI	Joint Africa Institute
KIST	Korea Institute of Science and Technology
LDCs	Less Developed Countries
LIUP	Local Industries Upgrading Program
MAI	Multilateral Agreement on Investment
MAP	Millennium African Renaissance Partnership Program
MDG	Millennium Development Goal
MFA	Multi-Fiber Arrangement
MFN	Most Favored Nation

MNEs	Multinational Enterprises
MRR	Minimum Rediscount Rate
MVA	Manufacturing Value Added
NAFTA	North American Free Trade Agreement
NAMF	New Africa Mining Fund
NASSCOM	National Association of Software and Service Companies
NBFIs	Non-bank Financial Institutions
NEPAD	New Partnership for Africa's Development
NICs	Newly-industrialized Countries
NIEs	Newly Industrializing Economies
NTF	Nigeria Trust Fund
NPV	Net Present Value
OAU	Organization of African Unity
ODA	Official Development Assistance
OECD	Organization for Economic Cooperation and Development
OIC	Organization of Islamic Conference
OPEC	Organization of the Petroleum Exporting Countries
PARPA	Action Plan for the Reduction of Absolute Poverty
PEAP	Poverty Eradication Action Plan
PEEPA	Public Enterprise Evaluation and Privatization Agency
PFP	Policy Framework Paper
PPF	Project Preparation Facility
PRGF	Poverty Reduction and Growth Facility
PRSPs	Poverty Reduction Strategy Papers
RECs	Regional Economic Communities
RISDP	Regional Indicative Strategy Development Plan
RMCs	Regional Member Countries
RTAs	Regional Trade Arrangements
SACU	Southern African Customs Union
SADC	Southern African Development Community
SARS	Severe Acute Respiratory Syndrome
SFM	Supplementary Financing Mechanism
SIRIM	Standards and Industrial Research Institute of Malaysia
SISIR	Singapore Institute of Standards and Industrial Research
SMEs	Small and Medium Sized Enterprises
SOEs	State-Owned Enterprises
SSA	Sub-Saharan Africa
STPs	Software Technology Parks
SWAPs	Sector-Wide Approaches
TAF	Technical Assistance Fund
TLS	Trade liberalization Scheme
TPOs	Trade Promotion Organizations

TSMC	Taiwan Semiconductor Manufacturing Company
TTCL	Tanzania Telecommunications Company
UDEAC	Union douanière des états de l'Afrique centrale
UN	United Nations
UNCTAD	United Nations Conference on Trade and Development
UNDP	United Nations Development Program
UNIDO	United Nations Industrial Development Organisation
US	United States
VAT	Value-added Tax
VLSI	Very Large Integrated Circuits
WAEMU	West African Economic and Monetary Union
WDI	World Development Indicators
WTO	World Trade Organization
WTTC	World Travel and Tourism Council
ZCCM	Zambia Consolidated Copper Mines
ZNCB	Zambia National Commercial Bank

CONTENTS

PART ONE: AFRICA IN THE WORLD ECONOMY

PART TWO: GLOBALIZATION AND AFRICA'S DEVELOPMENT

PART THREE: ECONOMIC AND SOCIAL STATISTICS ON AFRICA

BOXES

TEXT FIGURES

TEXT TABLES

PART ONE

AFRICA IN THE WORLD ECONOMY

Overview

The *African Development Report 2003* reviews Africa's current socio-economic perfor-mance and prospects, and examines in-depth the issue of globalization and development in the continent. Part I of the Report covers two chapters. The first chapter, on "The African Economy in 2002", presents and assesses the continent's economic performance as well as prospects for the medium-term. The second chapter analyses the regional economic profiles, including their recent economic trends, policy developments, privatization, and growth outlook.

Real GDP growth in 2002 was estimated at 2.8 percent, marginally below the 3.5 percent growth rate recorded in 2001. Two powerful factors— the mixed external environment and worsened domestic economic conditions, determined performance in 2002. The momentum of recovery in the industrial countries in the early part of 2002 (engineered in part by the U.S. spending in the aftermath of the September 11 terrorist attacks) fizzled out in the later part of the year. The prices of Africa's major export commodities remained depressed in the year. Also the lingering effects of the September 11 on African econo-mies, especially on the tourism sector in North Africa, affected performance. Although oil prices remained high in 2002, the reduced OPEC quota (designed to shore up prices) reduced the volume and value of exports. Deterioration in economic fundamentals as well as drought in the East and Southern Africa (linked to the El Nino phenomenon) contributed to the dampening of growth.

Africa's real GDP growth in 2002 again reflected performance in the ten largest econo-mies, whose growth slumped from 3.0 percent in 2001 to 2.2 percent in 2002. The number of countries with negative growth rate remained at 5 in 2002, with no change from 2001. An interesting feature of 2002 is that while the number of countries with 3-5 percent growth rate increased from 8 in 2001 to 14 in 2002, the number of countries with growth rate in excess of 5 percent declined from 21 in 2001 to 14 in 2002. This is a worrying feature of Africa's growth that seems to be stabilizing around the 3-4 percent range. The median African country now grows at about 3-5 percent, while an increasing number of countries also fall within the 0-3 percent range. Overall, the median African country's real per capita growth rate falls within 1.5-5 percent range, with a declining number of countries (12 in 2002 relative to 21 in 1999 and 18 in 2001) having a negative growth rate. Sectorally, growth in agriculture, the industrial sector, and services recorded declines in 2002 relative to their 2001 levels. Unlike in 2001 when the agricultural sector recorded growth rate of 5.2 percent, in 2001 it grew by only 3.7 percent; the industrial sector grew by 2.7 percent, down from 3.4 percent recorded in 2001; while the services sector was marginally down from 3.3 percent in 2001 to 3.1 percent in 2002.

In 2002, Central Africa at 5.5 percent recorded the highest economic growth rate among the five sub-regions of Africa, up from 3.4 percent in 2001. Southern Africa followed this at 3.4 percent in 2002, slightly up from 2.9 percent in 2001. East Africa had a growth rate of 2.8 percent in 2002, significantly down from 5.0 percent recorded in 2001. North Africa grew at 2.5 percent in 2002 from 3.5 percent the previous year while West Africa experienced a declined in growth in 2002 to 1.7 percent from 3.4 percent recorded in 2001.

In 2003, the African economy is forecast to grow by 3.3 percent, following expected faster growth in Europe, higher primary commodity export prices, and moderate oil prices. Greater prospects await 2003 as non-oil exporters are expected to see a significant improvement in performance, as commodity markets firm and prices stabilize or even moderately increase in real terms. As in the previous year, these forecasts are based on assumptions of improved weather and hence good agricultural performance as well as improved political and policy stance.

Aside from the non-policy factors impacting on performance, the medium term prospects will, in the final analysis, depend on the deepening of policy reforms in the region. These policies will go beyond political governance and institutional reforms, to broad economic agenda—structural, and sound micro- and macro-economic policy stance. Initiating and sustaining sound economic outcomes depend critically on the policy choices and the commitment of the political leadership to pursue growth-enhancing reforms as exemplified by the experiences of many better-managed African economies in the last two decades. As the African Union (AU) makes important strides in institutionalizing the NEPAD, especially the peer pressure mechanism on good political and economic governance, African countries would come under increasing pressure to deepen and sustain reforms. Complementing these domestic reform measures would be some positive developments in the international community. In particular, there is need to deliver on promises with respect to global actions to provide global public goods, ensure increased ODA flows to the poorest countries, provide market access for the exports of these poor countries, and address several of the systemic defects of the international institutions of governance.

CHAPTER 1
The African Economy in 2002

Growth slumps, as global recovery remains fragile

Growth in Africa decelerated to 2.8 percent in 2002, down from 3.5 percent in 2001 (Table 1.1 and Figure 1.1). Overall, the group of Africa's Ten Largest Economies (ATLE) led the growth deceleration in 2002, with the weighted growth rate at 2.2 percent (see Table 1.2). Aside from Latin America and countries in transition, Africa was perhaps the only region to experience deterioration in growth performance relative to 2001 (see Figure 1.2).

This growth rate leaves growth of per capita income at just 0.4 percent (see table 1.1 and Figure 1.3). Indeed, this increase in per capita income is far below the rate needed to prevent poverty from worsening (5 percent) let alone the rate needed to make a significant dent on poverty (7 percent or more).

Two powerful factors— the mixed external environment and worsened domestic economic conditions, determined performance in 2002. The momentum of recovery in the industrial countries in the early part of

Table 1.1: Africa: Macroeconomic Indicators, 1998- 2002

Indicators		1998	1999	2000	2001	2002[a/]
1.	Real GDP Growth Rate	3.2	3.1	3.3	3.5	2.8
2.	Real Per Capita GDP Growth Rate	0.8	0.6	0.9	1.0	0.5
3.	Inflation (%)	11.0	12.2	13.9	12.7	9.7
4.	Investment Ratio (% of GDP)	20.9	20.7	19.3	19.9	20.8
5.	Fiscal Balance (% of GDP)	-3.5	-2.8	-1.4	-2.1	-2.9
6.	Growth of Money Supply (%)	13.9	16.5	17.3	20.2	13.8
7.	Export Growth, volume (%)	-0.6	2.7	7.2	0.2	1.8
8.	Import Growth, volume (%)	5.4	1.1	2.9	2.8	3.8
9.	Terms of Trade (%)	-10.0	7.4	17.4	-4.6	-1.4
10.	Trade Balance ($ billion)	-15.6	-5.7	22.4	12.3	7.9
11.	Current Account ($ billion)	-22.6	-16.1	4.2	1.3	-7.3
12.	Current Account (% of GDP)	-4.4	-3.1	0.8	0.2	-1.4
13.	Debt Service (% of Exports)	22.2	20.1	17.3	17.3	22.3
14.	National Savings (% of GDP)	16.1	17.5	20.1	19.9	19.4
15.	Net Capital Inflows ($ billion)	23.8	21.1	14.6	20.1	...
16.	FDI ($ billion)	9.0	12.8	8.7	17.2	...
17.	FDI (% of FDI to developing countries)	3.2	2.6	2.5	2.9	...

Notes: a/ Preliminary estimates
      ... Not available
Source: ADB Statistics Division and IMF.

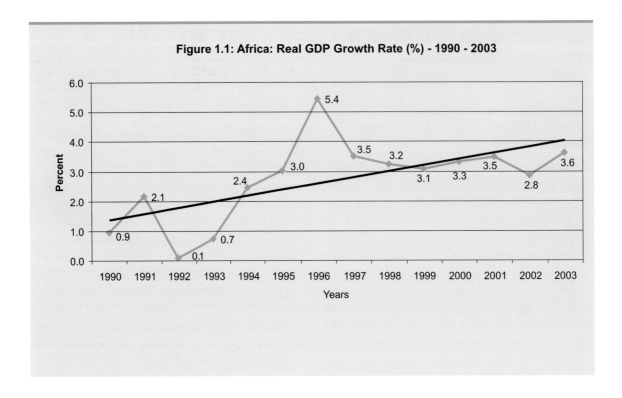

Figure 1.1: Africa: Real GDP Growth Rate (%) - 1990 - 2003

2002 (engineered in part by the U.S. spending in the aftermath of the September 11 terrorist attacks) fizzled out in the later part of the year. The prices of Africa's major export commodities remained depressed in the year. Also the lingering effects of the September 11 on African economies, especially on the tourism sector in North Africa, affected performance. Although oil prices remained high in 2002, the reduced OPEC quota (designed to shore up prices) reduced the volume and value of exports. Deterioration in economic fundamentals as well as drought in the East and Southern Africa (linked to the El Nino phenomenon) contributed to the dampening of growth.

Growth in 2002 was unevenly distributed across countries and too miniscule for poverty reduction (Tables 1.3). The number of countries with negative growth rate remained at 5 in 2002, with no change from 2001. An interesting feature of 2002 is that while the number of countries with 3-5 percent growth rate increased from 8 in 2001 to 14 in 2002, the number of countries with growth rate in excess of 5 percent declined from 21 in 2001 to 14 in 2002. This is a worrying feature of Africa's growth that seems to be stabilizing around the 3-4 percent range. The median African country now grows at about 3-5 percent, while an increasing number of countries also fall within the 0-3 percent range. Overall, the median African country's real per capita growth rate falls within 1.5- 5 percent range, with a declining number of countries (12 in 2002 relative to 21 in 1999 and 18 in 2001) having a negative growth rate. Indeed, Africa

Table 1.2: Africa's Ten Largest Economies (ATLE), 2002

Country	GDP at current US$ (Billions)	Population (Millions)	GDP Growth Rate	Country Weight in total African GDP (%)
SOUTH AFRICA	104.0	44.20	3.0	19.4
EGYPT	87.3	70.28	2.2	16.3
ALGERIA	55.0	31.40	2.5	10.3
NIGERIA	42.6	120.05	-0.9	7.9
MOROCCO	36.9	30.99	4.2	6.9
LIBYA	23.2	5.53	-0.6	4.3
TUNISIA	21.2	9.67	2.0	4.0
SUDAN	13.2	32.56	5.0	2.5
KENYA	11.9	31.90	1.6	2.2
COTE D'IVOIRE	11.6	16.69	0.0	2.2
TOTAL ATLE	**407**	**393**	**2.2**	**75.9**

Source: ADB Statistics Division, UN and IMF.

requires a sustained per capita growth rate of at least 4.6 percent per annum to make a significant impact towards achieving the Millennium Development Goal of halving the incident of poverty by 2015. And this is not yet happening; thereby raising the prospect that Africa might be the only region where the incidence of poverty could worsen by 2015.

Investment ratio (to GDP) improved slightly over the 2001 level, although the impact on growth was more than offset by the dampening of agricultural and industrial output. Inflation rate fell from 12.6 percent in 2001 to 10 percent in 2002 due mainly to the tightening of monetary policy in the region. Growth of broad money was reduced to 14 percent, down from 20 percent in 2001.

Performance also differed across sub-regions

The decisive impact of the group of Africa's Ten Largest Economies (ATLE) on growth performance is reflected on the diverse outcomes for the various sub-regions. Only two sub-regions—Central and Southern Africa—recorded improved performance over the 2001 level. The other three regions experienced worse performance (see Table 1.4).

Growth in the Central African Region was 5.5 percent, up from 3.4 percent in 2001, and this was driven by high oil-linked growth rates in Equatorial Guinea and Chad as well as growth-peace-dividends in post-conflict countries such as Rwanda, Democratic Republic of Congo, and Burundi. The Republic of South Africa and Angola powered the modest recovery in the

Figure 1.2: Developing Countries' vis-à-vis Africa: Major Performance Indicators, 2001- 2002

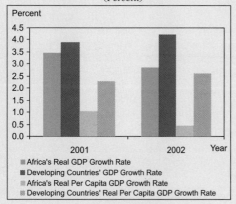

(a) Real GDP Growth and Real Per Capita Growth
(Percent)

■ Africa's Real GDP Growth Rate
■ Developing Countries' GDP Growth Rate
■ Africa's Real Per Capita GDP Growth Rate
■ Developing Countries' Real Per Capita GDP Growth Rate

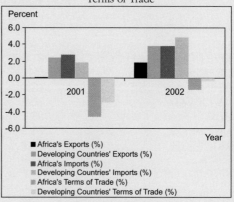

(d) Changes in Merchandise Trade (Volume) and
Terms of Trade

■ Africa's Exports (%)
■ Developing Countries' Exports (%)
■ Africa's Imports (%)
■ Developing Countries' Imports (%)
■ Africa's Terms of Trade (%)
■ Developing Countries' Terms of Trade (%)

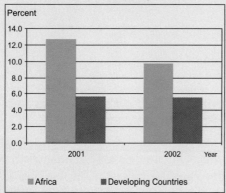

(b) Inflation
(Consumer Price Index, Percent)

■ Africa   ■ Developing Countries

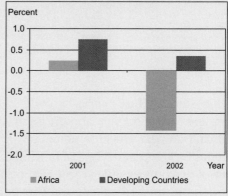

(e) Current Account Balance
as % of GDP

■ Africa   ■ Developing Countries

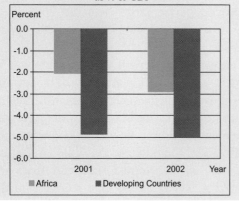

(c) Fiscal Deficits
as % of GDP

■ Africa   ■ Developing Countries

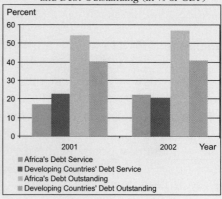

(f) Debt Service (in % of Exports)
and Debt Outstanding (in % of GDP)

■ Africa's Debt Service
■ Developing Countries' Debt Service
■ Africa's Debt Outstanding
■ Developing Countries' Debt Outstanding

Figure 1.3: Africa: Major Economic Indicators, 1998- 2002

(a) Real GDP Growth -Real Per Capita GDP Growth
(Percent)

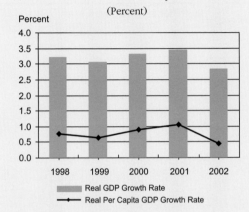

(d) Changes in Merchandise Trade (Volume)
and Terms of Trade

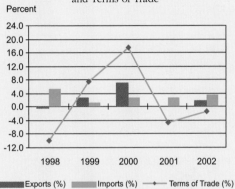

(b) Inflation
(Change in Consumer Price Index, Percent)

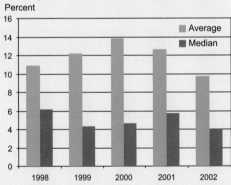

(e) Current Account Balance
(In Billion of US$)

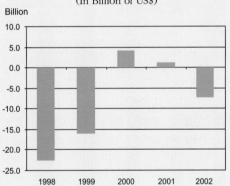

(c) Revenues-Expenditures-Fiscal Deficits
(as % of GDP)

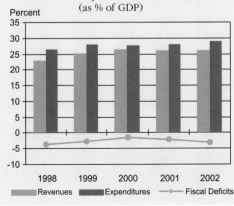

(f) Debt Service (as % of Exports)
and Debt Outstanding (as % of GDP)

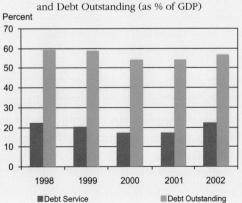

Table 1.3: Africa: Frequency Distribution of Countries According to Real GDP and Real Per Capita GDP Growth Rates, 1998-2002

	Number of Countries				
	1998	1999	2000	2001	2002[a/]
Real GDP Growth Rate (%)					
Negative	8	9	11	5	5
0 - 3	8	14	13	17	18
Above 3 to 5	19	14	14	8	14
Above 5	16	14	13	21	14
Not available	2	2	2	2	2
Total	53	53	53	53	53
Real Per Capita GDP Growth Rate (%)					
Negative	14	21	18	15	12
0 - 1.5	13	9	13	9	13
Above 1.5 to 5	19	17	15	21	22
Above 5	5	4	5	6	4
Not available	2	2	2	2	2
Total	53	53	53	53	53

Note: a/ Preliminary estimates
Source: ADB Statistics Division.

Southern African region to 3.3 percent, from 2.9 percent in 2001. Angola's economy grew by unprecedented 14.5 percent, due mainly to the cessation of the decades-old conflict early in 2002, as well as the coming on-stream of new oil fields. The Republic of South Africa benefited from higher prices for gold and other metals exports and recovery in agriculture. Growth in other Southern African countries was depressed because of drought while Zimbabwe's economy continued its decline due to social instability— with GDP falling by 11 percent.

Growth in Eastern, Northern and Western sub-regions decelerated relative to 2001. Growth in Eastern Africa dropped to 2.8 percent in 2002 (from 5 percent in 2001). This is because, performance in the larger economies in the sub-region (Kenya, Ethiopia, Uganda, Tanzania,

Mauritius) remained relatively unchanged or fell slightly, while Madagascar experienced a major contraction of 12 percent in 2002 compared to the growth of 6 percent in the previous year. The North African region experienced a 1 percentage point drop in its growth rate (2.5 percent in 2002 relative to 3.5 percent in 2001). This was mainly linked to the dwindling fortunes of oil exporters, lower tourist earnings in the aftermath of the September 11 events, and the return to normal trend growth in Morocco, following post drought recovery in the previous year. Growth in the Western region fell from 3.3 percent in 2001 to 1.8 percent in 2002 due mainly to the sharp decline in Nigeria's growth rate from 2.9 percent in 2001 to negative 0.9 percent in 2002, and the continuing deterioration in Côte d'Ivoire due to the conflict in the country.

Table 1.4: Real GDP Growth Rates by Sub-Region, 1998-2002

	Real GDP Growth Rate				
	1998	1999	2000	2001	2002[a/]
ADB Geographical sub-regions					
Central Africa	2.9	0.6	0.4	3.4	5.5
Eastern Africa	2.4	4.2	4.0	5.0	2.8
Northern Africa	4.3	4.0	3.9	3.5	2.5
Southern Africa	1.9	2.3	3.0	2.9	3.4
Western Africa	3.4	2.5	3.1	3.4	1.7
ADB Operational groupings					
ADF-eligible countries (incl. Blend countries)	3.4	3.0	2.7	3.5	3.0
ADF-only Countries	3.8	3.7	2.8	4.1	4.5
Blend countries	2.1	0.6	2.5	1.2	-2.5
Non-ADF countries	3.1	3.1	3.7	3.4	2.7
Regional & economic groups					
AMU	4.0	2.3	2.8	3.4	2.3
CAEMC	5.4	2.9	3.7	7.1	6.7
COMESA	3.5	4.4	3.5	2.9	2.8
ECCAS	3.6	1.1	0.9	3.3	7.4
ECOWAS	3.4	2.5	3.1	3.4	1.7
FRANC ZONE	4.9	3.3	2.3	4.9	4.6
SADC	1.7	1.8	2.6	2.6	3.5
WAEMU	4.6	3.5	1.4	3.5	3.1
Net Oil Exporters	3.4	3.7	4.1	3.1	2.2
Net Oil Importers	3.1	2.6	2.7	3.7	3.3
ALL RMCs	3.2	3.1	3.3	3.5	2.8

Note: a/ Preliminary estimates.
Source: ADB Statistics Division.

The Adverse External Environment Continued to impact

Africa's linkages with the global economy are mostly in the context of trade, capital flows and sectoral/technological interdependence. Subsequently, shocks to the global economy are transmitted to Africa via these channels.

The consequences for specific countries and regions in Africa depend on the production structures, composition of trade, extent of dependence on external finance, and existing economic policy stance, which could amplify or cushion the effects of external shocks. These sources and their effects were manifest in Africa in 2002.

The global economy in 2002 recovered modestly to post a growth rate of 2.8 percent (Table 1.5). This was mostly due to some macroeconomic stimuli occasioned by forceful monetary easing and increased government spending in the United States, and to a lesser extent in Europe. Such a stimuli was complemented by inventory dynamics—a slowing of inventory liquidation which significantly raised the contribution to GDP from the later half of 2001 to the first half of 2002 thereby adding 1.2 percentage points to the GDP growth in Japan and Europe, but a decline in the United States. Also, a powerful recovery in the high-tech markets in the industrial countries helped set the stage for broader global recovery. With increased aggregate demand— and the consequent rise in world trade, firming of commodity prices, and low interest rates facilitated by low inflation—developing countries and Africa faced a more favorable environment in the early part of 2002. But the positive shocks proved temporary as uncertainties beclouding the global financial markets impacted on both investor and consumer confidence. In the wake of large corporate bankruptcies and the accounting scandals in the U.S., the seeming overvaluation of stock markets and underestimation of debts, and falling equity prices, investment pulsed and growth momentum petered out. These had impacts on African economy in 2002.

Trade performance

Despite a slight improvement in the terms of trade, the external sector weakened in 2002 with trade balance and current account balance—all worse than in 2001. Terms of trade improved (but still negative) from –4.6 percent in 2001 to –1.4 percent in 2002; trade balance

deteriorated by $4.4 billion relative to 2001, while current account as a percentage of GDP went into negative (-1.4 percent) after a near zero balance in 2001. Overall, while exports grew by a meager 1.8 percent, imports grew by 3.8 percent.

Much of the subdued trade performance in 2002 was due to the region's export dependence on the European markets—where growth was weak. Demand for Africa's exports was generally weak. The weakness in export volumes was partly offset by the rebound in non-energy commodity prices, which, by August 2002 had gained 26 percent in export-weighted terms. Cocoa gained the most—with 80 percent rise, while others also gained (robusta coffee 20 percent; cotton 33 percent; copper 7 percent; gold 10 percent; and rubber 21 percent). However, because most of the improvements occurred late in the year, the annualized changes indicate that most commodity prices declined in 2002, while most remained below the peak levels of the mid-1990s (see Table 1.6).

Oil exporters, except Nigeria, performed better than expected

Oil exporting countries account for about 15 percent of Africa's GDP. Development in the oil sector is therefore a key driver of African performance. In 2002, oil prices fell slightly relative to 2001, but remained stronger than expected. Oil production increased in some countries (Equatorial Guinea, Angola, and Sudan) due mainly to the on-stream of new oil fields. On the aggregate, oil exporters posted stronger than expected growth outcome (except Nigeria). For example, Equatorial Guinea grew by 30.4 percent, Chad 10.9 percent, Angola 14.5 percent, and

Table 1.5: Selected International Economic Indicators, 1998-2002
(Percentage changes from preceeding year, except otherwise specified)

	1998	1999	2000	2001	2002[a]
Changes in output					
World	2.8	3.6	4.7	2.2	2.8
Advanced economies[b]	2.7	3.4	3.8	0.8	1.7
Developing countries	3.5	4.0	5.7	3.9	4.2
-Asia	4.0	6.1	6.7	5.6	6.1
-Latin American and Caribbean countries	2.3	0.2	4.0	0.6	-0.6
-Africa[c]	3.2	3.1	3.3	3.5	2.8
Countries in transition	-0.7	3.7	6.6	5.0	3.9
Changes in Consumer Price Index					
Advanced economies	1.5	1.4	2.3	2.2	1.4
Developing countries	10.5	6.9	6.1	5.7	5.6
-Asia	7.7	2.5	1.9	2.6	2.1
-Latin American and Caribbean countries	9.8	8.9	8.1	6.4	8.6
-Africa[c]	11.0	12.2	13.9	12.7	9.8
Changes in Merchandise Trade (volume)					
World Trade	4.7	5.7	12.9	-0.6	2.2
Advanced economies					
-Exports	4.4	5.4	12.2	-1.7	1.3
-Imports	6.0	8.8	12.1	-1.8	1.7
Developing countries					
-Exports	4.9	4.4	15.3	2.4	3.8
-Imports	0.5	0.8	16.8	1.9	4.9
Africa[c]					
-Exports	-0.6	2.7	7.2	0.2	1.8
-Imports	5.4	1.1	2.9	2.8	3.8
Changes in terms of trade					
Advanced economies	1.7	-0.1	-2.8	0.6	-0.1
Developing countries	-6.6	5.3	7.2	-2.9	-0.7
-Asia	0.2	-0.7	-3.7	-0.2	0.9
-Africa[c]	-10.0	7.4	17.4	-4.6	-1.4
Countries in transition			9.0	0.2	-0.8
Changes in FDI					
World	45.3	56.7	37.1	-50.7	
Developed countries	80.7	73.0	46.5	-59.0	
Developing countries	-1.8	20.0	5.7	-13.9	
-Asia	-9.2	6.9	30.1	-23.7	
-Latin American and Caribbean countries	10.6	33.0	-12.7	-10.5	
-Africa[c]	-16.0	42.1	-32.2	97.4	
FDI (as percent of global FDI flows)					
Developed countries	69.7	77.0	82.3	68.4	
Developing countries	27.0	20.7	15.9	27.9	
-Asia	13.8	9.4	9.0	13.9	
-Latin American and Caribbean countries	11.8	10.0	6.4	11.6	
-Africa[c]	1.3	1.2	0.6	2.3	

Notes:　a/ Preliminary estimates.
　　　　b/ Comprises the industrial market economies, Israel and four newly industrialized Asian economies.
　　　　c/ ADB Regional Member Countries.
Source: IMF, World Economic Outlook, October 2002 and ADB Statistics Division.

Table 1.6: Selected Commodity Prices Data			
Commodity	Unit	2001	2002
Crude Oil, Brent	$/bbl	24.4	25.0
Agricultural Commodities			
Wheat, U. S., HRW	$/mt	126.8	148.1
Rice, Thai, 5 percent	$/mt	172.8	191.9
Soybeans	$/mt	195.8	212.7
Sugar, world	Cents/kg	19.04	15.18
Coffee, other milds	Cents/kg	137.3	135.7
Coffee, robusta	Cents/kg	60.7	66.2
Cocoa	Cents/kg	106.9	177.8
Tea, auctions (3) average	Cents/kg	159.8	150.6
Cotton	Cents/kg	105.8	101.9
Metals and Minerals			
Aluminium	$/mt	1,444	1350
Copper	$/mt	1,578	1559
Gold	$/toz	271	310
Iron ore, Carajas	cents/dmtu	30.03	29.31
Lead	cents/dmtu	47.6	45.3
Nickel	$/mt	5,945	6772
Silver	cents/toz	438.6	462.5
Tin	cents/kg	448.4	406.1
Zinc	cents/kg	88.6	77.9

Source: Adapted from World Bank, Commodity Price Data (Pink Sheets) (2003), January.

Sudan 5 percent. For Nigeria, the reduced OPEC quota, together with the subdued oil prices and Executive-Legislature logjam that constrained spending led to a stagnation of the economy (estimated at –0.9 percent growth rate). Libya also had a negative growth rate (-0.6 percent) though its performance in 2001 was not significantly better. The higher than expected oil prices impacted negatively on the net oil importers, on balance, there was a positive effect on the African economy.

Tourism in Africa offers a Mixed picture

Tourism represents 11 percent of Africa's exports, and the World Travel and Tourism Council (WTTC) estimates that attack and its effects on Africa's tourism sector has cost 3.2 percent of exports and 1.3 million jobs over the period 2001- 2002. The largest impact was felt in Northern Africa, as the attack on Djerba hurt tourism all over Tunisia, as well as in other parts of Northern Africa. The timing of such attacks is also detrimental for receipts from tourism over the course of the year. For instance, the attack in Tunisia took place in spring, and thus affected the statistics for the entire year and especially the summer season. In contrast, the bombing near Mombassa happened in late autumn, and it had, thus, a small local impact. Based on information from the travel sector and tour operators, tourists have not abandoned Kenya and the sub-region. The performance of the tourism sector by sub-region in 2002 shows a similar contrasting picture, a very mixed picture. While Northern Africa experienced a decrease of 4 percent, Sub-Saharan Africa performed way above average, with an 8.5 percent increase. While countries such as Mauritius continue to experience increased inflow of tourists, tourism in North Africa is still depressed mostly as a result of uncertainties related to a expectation of war against Iraq.

The growth pace of international arrivals to African destinations amounting to 3.7 percent in 2002 is slightly above the world's average (3.1 percent) albeit from a very small base (see Table 1.11). All in all, estimates of 2002 indicate a substantial change in the world tourism map. Europe remains firmly in first place, while Asia and the Pacific claimed the number two spot from the Americas. Africa is gradually enlarging its share in the international market of tourism, from 3.6 percent in 1995 to 4 percent in 2002.

Debt Situation worsened While Capital Inflows Rose Marginally

The overall debt situation in 2002 worsened as debt service to exports ratio increased to 22 percent, up from 17 percent in 2001. This is despite the fact that more than 20 countries have reached the decision point under the Enhanced HIPC as well as better and more effective debt management in several countries. This deterioration in debt service indicates that the impact of the HIPC on debt service burden is heavily dependent on the export performance of these countries and the internal and external factors affecting such a performance. In some countries such as Nigeria, better debt management is producing positive results. Since it came into office in October 2000, one of the accomplishments of Nigeria's new Debt Management Office has been the building up of a comprehensive, computerized inventory of debts, verification of individual loan accounts with creditor statements, and reconciliation meetings with twelve out of the fourteen creditor countries which account for over 95 percent of the country's Paris Club debts. With the completion of the exercise, the Debt Management Office was able to confirm that as at August 31, 2001 Nigeria's debt stock, excluding penalty interests amounted to US$28.42 billion. This contrasts with the World Bank's estimate of $32 billion or the IMF's estimate of $31.94 billion— clearly a difference of more than $3 billion. Furthermore, Nigeria successfully negotiated a non-concessionary long-term rescheduling of its debt, which lengthens the repayment period and also lowers the debt service payment per annum. However, the temporary suspension of debt service payment in 2002 has increased the arrears and penalties. As more countries embark on rigorous verification of their debt data, and with progress on Enhanced HIPC and other concessional financing deals for African countries, the debt situation would continue to improve.

Capital inflows into the developing countries generally increased in 2002. Despite the low international interest rates, the market-based net capital flows into the emerging markets fell from $228.7 billion in 1996 to $24.9 billion in 2001, but estimated to rise to $62.4 billion in 2002—with Africa's rising from $8.2 billion in 2001 to $9.8 billion in 2002. Furthermore, net foreign direct investment (FDI) inflows trended downwards, from $172 billion in 2001 to about $151 billion in 2002, with Africa's share about 7.8 percent or $11.8 billion. This would represent a fall in net FDI to Africa, down from $22.3 billion in 2001. Privatization offerings, which have become major sources of FDI into Africa in recent years, seem to be easing. For example, the expected $2 billion from the privatization of the Nigerian Telecommunications Ltd. did not materialize, as the deal could not be completed. The privatization of Air Madagascar did not also happen. Also, the slow down in global flows of FDI especially to Africa might also be related to heightened uncertainties and insecurity around the region due partly to the September 11 terrorist attacks, uncertainty about Iraq and possible impacts on the North African region, and new conflict in Côte d'Ivoire and tensions in Zimbabwe. Ironically, according to a World Bank (2002) report, FDI in SSA yielded the highest returns in the world in 2002. On a positive note, the slight recovery in the industrial countries improved remittances from the African Diaspora.

The ATLE Countries Dragged growth down

A key feature of the region's growth history is that hardly any of the Africa's ten largest economies (ATLE) is a star performer. But these Africa's ten largest economies (ATLE) constitute about 80 percent of the region's GDP and 55 percent its population. In 2002, ATLE countries' growth slumped from 3.0 percent in 2001 to 2.2 percent in 2002 (see Table 1.7). On almost all major macroeconomic indicators, the aggregate African performance mimics the ATLE outcomes. Except perhaps South Africa, Angola and Algeria, the other seven countries experienced a fall in their growth rates relative to 2001.

South Africa sustained a recovery for the first half of 2002 arising from a boost in agriculture and export-oriented mining and manufacturing, which benefited from the depreciation of the real exchange rate. North African countries—especially Egypt, Morocco, and Tunisia— were generally affected by the external conditions as well as the lingering effects of the September 11 terrorist attacks on the U.S. Deterioration in the external market in the export market growth for diversified exporters such as Egypt, Morocco, and Tunisia as well as declines in the tourism sector contributed to the relative decline of these economies. In Egypt, the tourist inflows fell by 41 percent from the last quarter of 2001 till the end of first half of 2002. Tourism fell 20 percent in Morocco, and exports to the EU also declined (especially Moroccan textiles and electronics). Furthermore, the positive agricultural growth in 2001 in Morocco slowed down in 2002 because of less favorable weather conditions. Nigeria, perhaps presents the greatest decline in growth performance among the ATLE countries. Nigeria's adherence to reduced OPEC production quota more than offset the impact of better-than-expected oil prices, leading to decrease in oil earnings. Furthermore, a budget gridlock between the Executive and Legislative arms of government constrained government spending and thus aggregate demand dipped. Government is still the key driver of economic activity in Nigeria—and much of the private sector activities depend on government patronage.

Economic policy was a mixed mosaic of improved performance and lingering risks

Many African countries are now committed to deepening institutional, governance, and economic policy reforms especially in view of great expectations under new regional initiatives such as NEPAD and the African Union. An increasing number of countries (especially those qualifying for HIPC debt relief) have completed at least the Interim Poverty Reduction Strategy Papers (IPRSPs), which provide a comprehensive action plan for tackling poverty and sustained development.

A major positive development with great promise is the cessation of conflicts in Angola in 2002 as well as in Congo Democratic Republic. Angola has begun to reap the 'peace dividends' immediately as the GDP grew by 15 percent in 2002, up from 3 percent in 2001. In Congo (D.R.) the government is taking strong measures to reverse the disastrous economic policies of the past and promote economic stabilization. An interim economic adjustment program (IEAP) supported by the IMF and World Bank has been put in place since July 2001 following the conclusion of Article IV

Table 1.7: Macroeconomic Indicators for ALTE*, 1998- 2002

Indicators	1998	1999	2000	2001	2002
1. Real GDP Growth Rate	3.0	3.0	3.5	3.1	2.2
2. Real Per Capita GDP Growth Rate	0.6	0.6	1.1	0.7	-0.2
3. Inflation (%)	7.9	5.7	5.2	5.4	4.6
4. Investment Ratio (% of GDP)	20.8	20.7	19.6	19.9	20.9
5. Fiscal Balance (% of GDP)	-2.7	-2.3	-0.7	-2.1	-3.2
6. Growth of Money Supply (%)	12.2	12.3	12.4	15.8	10.5
7. Export Growth, volume (%)	1.3	3.7	9.1	0.9	-1.5
8. Import Growth, volume (%)	7.5	0.3	5.2	1.1	2.2
9. Terms of Trade (%)	-8.0	2.6	19.2	-1.1	-0.8
10. Trade Balance ($ billion)	-12.7	-6.5	10.7	5.8	2.9
11. Current Account ($ billion)	-12.3	-6.4	8.9	8.0	1.3
12. Current Account (% of GDP)	-2.9	-1.5	2.0	1.9	0.4
13. Debt Service (% of Exports)	22.8	21.3	17.7	17.5	...
14. National Savings (% of GDP)	17.0	18.4	20.3	20.6	20.0
15. Net Capital Inflows ($ billion)	8.3	5.7	3.2	6.9	...
16. FDI ($ billion)	4.9	7.8	5.1	13.4	...
17. FDI (% to developing countries)	3.7	5.9	4.0	9.0	...

*   ALTE: South Africa, Egypt, Algeria, Nigeria, Libya, Morocco, Tunisia, Sudan, Kenya and Côte d'Ivoire.
... Not available
Source: ADB Statistics Division and IMF.

consultations. The program, which does not include funding, covers economic reform targets and performance criteria designed to establish macroeconomic stability. If the government succeeds in establishing a track record of performance, it could eventually benefit from the IMF's poverty reduction and growth facility (PRGF) as well as qualifying for debt relief under the enhanced HIPC. On its part, the World Bank also approved a transitional support strategy, which establishes a framework for recovery and social stabilization as well as an emergency economic recovery program (EERP). If successfully followed, the two programs could lead to macroeconomic stabilization and responsible economic policies for the first time

in over 40 years of Congo's independence. Consequently, improved economic policy stance in Congo would improve the aggregate performance of the ATLE countries as well as the continent's outcomes.

A worrisome threat however pertains to eruption of armed conflict in Côte d'Ivoire, which has worsened domestic economic conditions, and the continued social and political crisis in Zimbabwe (leading a further decline in Zimbabwe's growth rate from –7.4 percent in 2001 to –11.4 percent in 2002). The negative consequences of these crisis situations on the quality of economic management in these economies can be enormous. Despite the pressure points, the overall policy stance improved in the year 2002.

Fiscal policy stance remained virtually the same

Fiscal policy stance remained virtually the same in 2002, as the overall fiscal deficit as percentage of GDP recorded -2.9 percent in 2002 compared with –2.1 percent in 2001. The fiscal deficit (less than 3 percent of GDP on average for the last decade) is not unsustainable, and reflects the strengthened capacity for fiscal prudence in much of Africa. This is a positive development especially in view of the high dependence of fiscal revenue on the highly volatile external sector (trade taxes, and grants from abroad).

The aggregate salutary development however masks the individual country and subregional differences. For the CFA franc zone countries, monetary union implies strict adherence to sound fiscal and monetary policies as set and monitored by the regional institutions (regional central bank—Banque centrale des Etats de l'Afrique de l'ouest (BCEAO), UEMOA, and UDEAC). The major challenge faced by the CFA central bank in 2002 has been to dampen inflationary pressures, support the regional currency, and also counter rumours of a possible devaluation of the CFA franc following the introduction of the Euro. A key instrument in achieving these goals was the raising of its rediscount rate.

Other countries had mixed results, with the ATLE countries dominating the aggregate outcomes. Fiscal policy in 2002 oscillated from the extremes of severe stance, with Zimbabwe running a fiscal deficit of about 17 percent of GDP (up from 16 percent in 2001) to moderate surpluses in Sudan, Libya, Equatorial Guinea, etc. Most other countries fell in between the extremes. In Angola, the challenge is to increase transparency and reduce deficit, especially the

extra-budgetary spending. Nigeria instituted a new budget office and a budget monitoring and price intelligence unit in the presidency—with emphasis on due process compliance and adherence to strict procurement procedures—and this, together with the gridlock between the National Assembly and the Presidency over the 2002 budget helped to rein in government capital and other spending. Most other ATLE countries had fiscal deficits in the range of 1- 4 percent of GDP, with the average ATLE fiscal balance at –3.2 percent in 2002.

Although government spending in Algeria increased significantly, it was funded mostly through the oil stabilization fund. Morocco's fiscal system faces immense challenges as it is under pressure to streamline the system, particularly the public sector wage bill that is about 12 percent of GDP as well as the costly subsidy system. The government used the privatization proceeds as current revenues, similar to the situation in Nigeria. The Egyptian authorities set to reduce the fiscal deficit from 3.0 percent of GDP in 2001—to 2 percent by 2003, by rationalizing spending and raising revenue. Revenue is expected to increase by reducing tax evasion, collecting taxes in arrears and bringing more of the sizeable informal sector into the tax net, extension of the general sales tax into a full fledged VAT, program of widening the tax base and familiarizing the citizens with the idea of keeping records and paying taxes. In South Africa, the reappointment (for another three years) of the Finance Minister and the Director-General of the National Treasury, who are both seen as sound positive reformers and assets to the government, was an indication that the prudent fiscal policies of the past and the ANC Government's major economic policy direction embodied in GEAR will be maintained.

Monetary policy was tightened

Monetary policy stance was tightened in 2002 with growth in broad money down to 14 percent, from 20 percent in 2001. The CFA franc zone continued to maintain tight monetary policy, and this moderated inflation and pressures on the exchange rate. The BCEAO introduced a new monetary policy stance in 2002 through a major institutional reform, which bans government borrowing from the BCEAO, and replaced it with the use of Treasury Bills. It is too early to assess how this 'flexibility' will play out in the context of a sub-regional monetary union or how the regional central bank will enforce discipline among member states.

Among the ATLE countries, monetary policy was even tighter than the African average, with a growth rate of broad money at 10 percent. In Nigeria, the monetary authorities yielded to pressures to bring down the lending interest rate. Consequently, the minimum rediscount rate (MRR) was reduced from 22 percent to 18.5 percent and both the Central Bank of Nigeria and the Bankers' Committee reached an agreement that lending interest rates should not exceed the MRR plus 4 percent. In effect, the maximum lending interest has been pegged to no more than 22.5 percent— a very significant reduction from the previous 35- 40 percent lending rates, which prevailed in previous years.

In South Africa, monetary restraint continued in order to counteract the effects of a lax fiscal stance and depreciating Rand. Fiscal and monetary policies were tightened in Tunisia to prevent a potentially steep increase in the current account deficit. This action contained domestic demand pressures and reduced pressures on external balance. Everywhere else in the region, monetary policy remained conservative to rein in price inflation and promote production.

Inflation remain under control positively affecting exchange rate value

The modest fiscal stance and tightened monetary policy further slowed down inflation to 10 percent in 2002 compared to 13 percent in 2001. This also moderated exchange rate fluctuations. Aside from a few outliers, Africa is not generally known for high inflation rates. Indeed, most countries in the region posted single digit inflation rates in 2002, with the average rate for the ATLE countries at 4.6 percent. In Egypt, there remained unresolved problems with the exchange rate regime, which contributed to the slow down of the private sector in 2002. Earlier in 2001, the authorities in Egypt undertook a bold move and devalued the currency by 6.4 percent, thereby bringing the rate below the parallel market rate. In Nigeria, the monetary authorities stabilized both the official and parallel market exchange rates, although the introduction of the Dutch Auction system in official exchange rate determination temporarily depreciated the Naira against major currencies. The parallel market exchange rate to the U.S. dollar has fluctuated between N134 and N140 during 2002.

In South Africa, a major concern in 2002 was the upstick in inflation, which was ostensibly a consequence of nearly 40 percent depreciation of the Rand in 2001. Such depreciation also put pressures on interest rates. The Rand has stabilized around an average of R10.5 to one U.S. dollar after weakening to above R12 to the dollar in late 2001. The Rand is likely to remain vulnerable to external shocks due to South Africa's well-developed financial market (which is integrated into the global market), its low level of foreign reserves and substantial portfolio flows. The high unemployment rate in South Africa (about 30 percent) could be another impetus to pressure the Rand to depreciate even further, although there is evidence that tight monetary policy is holding the forte. For the CFA zone, the relative strengthening of the Euro to which the CFA franc is pegged combined with the sound monetary policy of the regional central bank and continued support from France to prevent a devaluation of the CFA franc meant that the CFA franc significantly appreciated against the dollar in 2002.

Major Sectoral Developments

The performance of the major sectors of the African economy—agriculture, industry (including manufacturing, energy), and services—largely determines the aggregate performance of the economy (see Table 1.8). The two commodity-producing sectors (agriculture and industry) constitute about 52 percent of Africa's GDP—with agriculture 20 percent and industry (including mining and quarrying—energy sector) 32 percent, and both sectors' growth rates significantly dampened in 2002. Over the decades, the shares of both sectors have declined while that of services (48 percent of GDP) has increased markedly.

The share of agriculture has declined slightly over the two decades (1980-2000), from 23 percent in 1980 to 20.4 percent in 2000. Industry's share has declined from about 40 percent in 1980 to 32 percent in 2000, while the share of services soared from 37 percent in 1980 to 48 percent in 2000.

The relative share of the services sector in part reflects the growing size of the informal

Table 1.8: Sectoral Growth Rates, 1998-2002
(Percentage changes from preceeding year)

	1998	1999	2000	2001	2002[a]
Agriculture	4.2	2.2	1.8	5.2	3.7
Industry	2.6	2.7	4.2	3.4	2.7
Manufacturing	2.7	3.3	4.0	4.3	3.6
Services	3.2	3.8	3.5	3.3	3.1
GDP at constant Market prices	3.2	3.1	3.3	3.5	2.8

Note: a/ Preliminary estimates.
Source: ADB Statistics Division.

sector (which is dominated by the services sector) as well as the stagnation of the commodity-producing sectors. African agriculture and industry are largely uncompetitive, and have been losing shares in international markets—even in traditional commodities. Exports are increasingly being concentrated in few primary commodities and de-industrialization occurred in many countries following trade liberalization as the unprepared industrial infrastructure erected under the import-substituting industrialization regime faced stiffer competition from abroad. Indeed, the industrial sector has largely been sustained by the diversified economies of South Africa, North African countries and a handful of other African countries, as well as the activities in the energy (mining) sub-sector.

Agriculture: Millions of Africans in need of emergency food aid

In 2002, agricultural growth was dampened, with a growth rate of 3.7 percent relative to 5.2 percent in 2001. This subdued performance was due mainly to the drought in some East and Southern African countries and also in the case of Zimbabwe and Côte d'Ivoire by political crisis and armed conflicts, respectively.

According to estimates of the FAO, Africa's cereal production in 2002 declined by about five million tonnes, down to 113.1 million tonnes compared with 117.8 million tonnes in 2001 (see Table.1.9). Africa's total cereal imports in 2002 stood at 47 million tonnes, made up 24.8 million tonnes of wheat, 14.9 million tonnes of coarse grains, and 7.3 million tonnes of milled rice. Imports by several countries in North Africa exceeded last year's levels, mainly due to a drop in production due to prolonged dry conditions, especially in Algeria and Tunisia. Total imports by countries in the sub-Saharan region remained unchanged from 2001 levels. In Sub-Saharan Africa (especially in Zimbabwe, Kenya, and Zambia), the serious food supply shortages triggered by production shortfalls and civil conflicts gave rise to even higher import requirements in 2002.

One of the paradoxes of African agriculture is that land is abundant and agriculture is dominated by the food sub-sector and yet hardly any year passes without parts of Africa in need of emergency food aid. One of the major explanations is that agriculture is still dependent on the vagaries of weather including rainfall. Other explanations relate to low productivity as a result of low quality inputs and services including infrastructure and agricultural credit. Civil wars and social conflicts also play an important role, particularly in cases of acute food shortages. In 2002, approximately 30 million Africans were in need of emergency food aid, approximately half of them in southern Africa, which experienced a second successive year of poor harvests. This number is 2 million more than in 2001. The countries badly hit were Malawi, Zambia, and Zimbabwe

Table 1.9: Africa's Cereal Production, 2000-2002 (In million tonnes)

	2000	2001	2002*
North Africa	27.7	33.6	31.8
Eastern Africa	20.7	22.6	20.0
Southern Africa	22.2	17.6	17.5
Western Africa	38.7	41.0	40.8
Central Africa	3.0	3.0	3.0
Africa	**112.30**	**117.8**	**113.1**

* Forecast as of December 2002
Source: Adapted from FAO (2002).

and both incomes and consumption suffered in these countries.

In **East Africa**, cereal output fell to 20 million tonnes, down from the previous year's level of 22.6 million tonnes. In Ethiopia, cereal output was found to be poor due to late and erratic rains and a significant reduction in the use of fertilizer. In Kenya, wheat output was well below average due to erratic rainfall. Also, there was a below average output in the sub-region's aggregate coarse grains crop in 2002 principally due to drought and displacement. In Eritrea, the 2002 harvest was extremely poor due to severe drought. Displacement of farmers from the agriculturally important regions following the border war with neighboring Ethiopia in 1998-2002 has also left large tracts of fertile land uncultivated. In Ethiopia, the coarse grain output was very poor, also reflecting the late and erratic rains. In Kenya, official estimates put the 2002 "long rains" maize crop at 1.89 million tonnes compared to 2.32 million tonnes in 2001. In Somalia, the recently harvested main "gu" season cereal crop in southern Somalia was estimated at about 260,000 tonnes (100,000 tonnes of sorghum and 160 000 tonnes of maize), more than double the relatively poor gu crop in 2001. In Tanzania, following relatively better distributed rainfall during both the short and long rains seasons, the 2002 aggregate coarse grains output was estimated at about 12 percent higher than last year's output of 3.7 million tonnes. In Uganda, erratic rains affected coarse grain crops and displacement hence total output was below that of 2001.

Thus, in 2002, serious food shortages occurred in the East African Region, mainly due to drought. In Ethiopia, poor rains led to severe food difficulties while large numbers of livestock died and unusual population migrations occurred. This put about 11 million people in need of food assistance. Over a third of the population in Eritrea faces food shortages due to drought while assistance was required by displaced people following the 1998-2000 border war with Ethiopia and by refugees who returned from Sudan. In Kenya, despite improved overall food supply, some northern and northeastern districts still faced food shortages in 2002. In Uganda, conflicts in northern areas displaced a large part of the population; while drought induced crop failures in Karamoja aggravated the food supply situation. World Food Programme is currently assisting nearly 1.5 million people. However, the overall food supply improved in Somalia and Tanzania due to good harvests, although localized shortages persisted.

Although cereal production in **Southern Africa** declined only marginally to 17.5 million tonnes in 2002, its level is still far below that of 2000 (22.2 million tonnes). For this sub-region, wheat output was estimated at 2.6 million tonnes, 9 percent lower than the good crop

of 2001 but about the average of the past five years. This reflects a production decline of 9 percent in South Africa, the largest producer, where production was expected to be down to 2.3 million tonnes principally due to lower yields following adversely high temperatures in northern growing areas in October. In Zimbabwe, crop output was put at 213,000 tonnes, one of the lowest in the past decade as a result of lower yields following land reform activities. Coarse grains output was estimated at 14.8 million tonnes, slightly higher than the reduced output in 2001. Despite sharp fall for the second consecutive year in most countries of Southern Africa, these were more than offset by an increase of 22 percent to 9.1 million tonnes in the main producer (South Africa), which was not affected by dry weather during the season. Apart from the minor producer – Botswana - production was reduced in all other countries of the sub-region. Maize output fell by 67 percent to 481,000 tonnes in Zimbabwe, by 24 percent in Zambia, and by 10 percent in Malawi, mainly due to prolonged dry spells that reduced yields. On the other hand, the Republic of South Africa experienced bumper maize harvests—which moderately boosted domestic spending. Agriculture is less than 10 percent of South African GDP, but maize production is a significant economic activity employing a sizeable part of the population, especially the poor. Paddy output was estimated to be 2.4 million tonnes in the sub-region, while in Mozambique; production was put at about 170,000 tonnes. Mozambique has been seriously affected by low rainfall in southern and some central areas, and by excessive rains leading to flooding in the central and northern regions.

In Southern Africa, therefore, after two consecutive years of poor harvests the food and nutrition situation worsened, putting 14.4 million people in need of emergency food assistance in Lesotho, Malawi, Mozambique, Swaziland, Zambia, and Zimbabwe. The situation is particularly serious in Zimbabwe, where half of the population needs relief food. In Angola, 1.9 million people still require food assistance. In Madagascar, food assistance is needed by people affected by the political crisis earlier in the year and those in the south hit by poor harvests. The food situation in Southern Africa has been worsened by the HIV/AIDS pandemic showing that the food crisis and the HIV/AIDS pandemic are closely intertwined. HIV/AIDS has reduced agricultural productivity and increased the demands on a decreasing working population for food provision; at the same time, it has raised the vulnerability of a large proportion of the population to a decline in the level of nutrition. The combination of high HIV/AIDS prevalence and food deficiency is causing an unprecedented dependency on international financial assistance, particularly in the Southern African region.

For **Central Africa**, coarse grains harvest in Cameroon was favorable. In the Central African Republic, harvest was poor due to erratic and below average rains that affected crop development in some regions. In Burundi and Rwanda, crop harvests were poor due to a delay in the start of the rainy season. The escalation of civil conflicts in the Central African Republic and the Democratic Republic of Congo further displaced many people, while in the Republic of Congo food assistance to refugees continued in 2002. In Burundi, emergency food assistance was required due to the deteriorating security situation in that country.

In **West Africa**, the total cereal production of the nine CILSS member countries was estimated at 11.3 million tonnes, 3 percent below 2001 but 11 percent above the average of the last five years. In the coastal countries along the Gulf of Guinea, harvest was generally good in Benin, Nigeria and Togo but less favorable in Ghana, following below-normal rains in September and October. Rice production increased in Sierra Leone but fell in Liberia following renewed civil strife. In Côte d'Ivoire, rice output was estimated at 800,000 tonnes, being 200,000 tonnes less than earlier anticipated and the previous year, due to unfavorable weather and the conflicts that forced many farmers to leave their land and disrupted marketing activities. However, the outcome of the harvest in Nigeria, the largest producer in the sub-region, was good - about 3.5 million tonnes - slightly higher than last year and reflecting generally favorable growing conditions. Food supply difficulties emerged in parts of Cape Verde and Chad, The Gambia, Guinea-Bissau, and Senegal, as a result of below average harvests. In 2002, agricultural activities in Liberia were disrupted by civil unrest, while emergency food assistance was required in Côte d'Ivoire following emergence of civil strife. Food assistance was also needed in Sierra Leone and Guinea as a result of large numbers of internally displaced persons and refugees.

In **North Africa**, production of wheat in 2002 was estimated at 11.7 million tonnes, about 9 percent below production in 2001, but similar to the average of the past 5 years. The fall was mainly due to significant reductions in outputs in Algeria and Tunisia, the result of the late arrival of the seasonal rains and prevailing dry weather during the growing period. Increased wheat production in Egypt and Morocco, mainly in the former country, did not offset the fall. In Sudan, an output of 247,000 tonnes of wheat was harvested, representing about 20 percent below the average for the past five years, due to lower planted area and excessively high temperatures. Also, the production of coarse grains in North Africa in 2002 was estimated at 10.1 million tonnes, close to the 2001 level and about 5 percent above the 5-year average. This increase is mainly the result of a well-above average barley crop in Morocco, which more than offset reduced outputs in Algeria and Tunisia. In Sudan, erratic rains and population displacement due to escalation of conflict negatively impacted on coarse grain production. In Egypt, where maize is the principal coarse grain, production of this cereal decreased by about 240 000 tonnes from 2001 but nevertheless remained slightly above average. Also, Egypt's paddy production was estimated at 6.0 million tonnes, representing 15 percent increase over that in the past year and a record for the country. In Sudan, the food situation deteriorated sharply in the south, while a tight food supply situation persists in parts of the west and the east. Also, the food situation is very serious in parts of Mauritania, following three consecutive years of poor harvests.

Industry, Especially Manufacturing

African industrial sector faced a difficult year in 2002, resulting in the dampening of growth rate from 3.4 percent in 2001 to 2.7 percent in 2002. The manufacturing sub-sector saw its growth rate tumble from 4.3 percent in 2001 to 3.6 percent in 2002. This lackluster performance was mainly due to depressed domestic demand, as well as the sluggish external market conditions. Europe remains Africa's largest market for the exports including industrial products, and the European economy remained depressed in 2002.

UNIDO (2002) estimates show that the growth rate of total manufacturing value added (MVA) increased very marginally from 3.6 percent in 1981-1991 periods to 3.7 percent in the 1991-2001 period. This was however higher than the global average of 3.1 percent respectively for the two sub-periods (Table 1.10). Over the two sub-periods, North Africa's MVA remained unchanged at 4.3 percent while that of Central Africa increased marginally from 1.0 percent to 1.3 percent. MVA growth rate fell in Eastern and Southern Africa during the two sub-periods from 4.1 percent to 3.3 percent while it rose slightly in Western Africa from 3.0 percent to 3.3 percent. For Africa's relatively large economies, there was a marginal increase from 0.8 percent to 1.6 percent for South Africa, a fall from 1.6 percent to 1.1 percent for Nigeria, and a marginal increase from 6.6 percent to 6.9 percent for Egypt. Countries with substantial increases include Equatorial Guinea (from 1.9 percent to 8.3 percent), Ethiopia (from -0.7 percent to 10.0 percent), Rwanda (from 1.2 percent to 5.4 percent), Benin (from 2.2 percent to 5.3 percent), Uganda (from 5.0 percent to 13.5 percent), and Tunisia (from 2.5 percent to 5.5 percent). African countries recording very significant drops in their MVA during the period include Swaziland (from 17.9 percent to 2.9 percent), Somalia (from 3.9 percent to -1.1 percent), Kenya (from 1.2 percent to 1.9 percent), The Gambia (from 7.2 percent to 1.2 percent), Comoros (from 4.3 percent to -1.3 percent), and Zimbabwe (from 3.1 percent to 0.3 percent).

Table 1.10: Annual Growth of MVA, 1981-2001 and Per Capita MVA, 2001[a/]

Country Group or Country/Area	Total MVA						Per Capita MVA						
	Growth Rate Percentage		Index (1990 = 100)				Growth Rate Percentage		Index (1990 = 100)				Value (dollars)
	1981-1991	1991-2001	1998	1999	2000[b/]	2001[c/]	1981-1991	1991-2001	1998	1999	2000[b/]	2001[c/]	2001[c/]
Africa	3.6	3.7	124	130	135	143	0.7	1.2	101	104	105	109	84
North Africa	4.3	4.3	131	139	146	156	1.8	2.3	111	116	120	126	225
UMA	3.7	2.5	116	120	124	133	1.1	0.6	99	101	102	108	258
Central Africa	1.0	1.3	88	92	96	97	-2.0	-1.5	70	72	73	72	42
Western Africa (ECOWAS)	3.0	3.3	127	131	132	136	0.0	0.6	103	103	100	101	40
Eastern and Southern Africa	4.1	3.3	121	123	125	134	0.9	0.6	98	97	96	101	40
Latin America	1.6	2.8	124	123	128	129	-0.4	1.1	108	106	108	108	628
South and East Asia	9.1	8.4	195	213	234	242	7.1	6.8	173	186	202	206	310
West Asia and Europe	3	3.9	119	116	123	124	0.4	1.7	100	96	99	98	619
World	3.1	3.1	119	123	129	131	1.4	1.7	106	108	112	112	1041

a/ At constant 1990 prices.
b/ Provisional.
c/ Estimate.
Source: Adapted from UNIDO Database

For Africa, the growth rate of per capita MVA followed the same trend as the growth rate in MVA, increasing marginally from 0.7 percent in 1981-1991 to 1.2 percent during 1999-2001 periods. North Africa witnessed an increase from 1.8 percent to 2.3 percent while Central Africa's was still in the negative zone of -2.0 percent to -1.5 percent during the period. While Western Africa had a decrease from 1.1 percent to 0.6 percent during the period, Eastern and Southern Africa had their growth in per capita MVA decrease marginally from 0.9 percent to 0.6 percent. Equatorial Guinea (from -2.3 percent to 5.4 percent), Ethiopia (from -3.8 percent to 7.1 percent), Uganda (from 1.6 percent to 10.1 percent), and Tunisia (from 0.2 percent to 4.1 percent) made significant gains during the period, while Swaziland (from 14.1 percent to 1.0 percent) made a very significant loss.

Poor industrial development in Africa is further illustrated by the fact that its share in world total MVA (at constant 1990 prices) remained at 1.0 percent annually between 1998 and 2002. This contrasts 28.2 percent for the European Union (EU), 26.5 percent for North America, 16.9 percent in South and East Asia, and 5.1 percent in Latin America. At current prices, Africa's share in 2002 was estimated at 0.8 percent against 24.8 percent for the EU, 27.9 percent for North America, 16.4 percent for South and East Asia, and 6.2 percent for Latin America.

Performance of the industrial sector (especially manufacturing) since the 1990s has been less than impressive. For a region in urgent need for structural transformation and diversification, the miniscule growth rates ranging from 0—4 percent on the average are likely to keep Africa at a pre-industrial stage for a long time to come if some drastic measures are not taken to reverse the trend. Investment in the sector is too miniscule, and African firms are undergoing the painful adjustments required to be competitive in an increasingly globalizing and competitive world. The somewhat atypically high cost environments in which they operate compound this.

Besides addressing several of the policy, infrastructure and public service delivery bottlenecks to investment and industry, African countries need to pay special attention to strategies to recapitalize the industrial sector. And a major vehicle to achieve this could be through the attraction of FDI. Currently, the largest flows of FDI in Africa—especially Angola and Nigeria— are into the extractive subsectors—oil, and other minerals. FDI into manufacturing, agriculture and services comes a distant second. This needs to change, and there are important lessons to be learnt from a recent UNIDO survey of foreign direct investor perceptions in Sub-Saharan Africa (see Box 1.1).

In today's globalized world, FDI plays a critical role in plugging countries to the global value chains. But FDI should not be a substitute for increased domestic investment. In some cases, policymakers become so obsessed with FDI that they forget to target and encourage domestic investors. This is a mistake that should be avoided. Furthermore, since most African economies are too small to support large-scale investments in industry, efforts must be hastened to fully integrate African economies or at least the sub-regional groupings into customs unions—to enlarge markets. As evident from Box 1.1, the most important consideration of investors— foreign and domestic—is the size of markets, and hence the

profitability of the enterprise. A significantly enlarged African market could become the needed tonic to unleash an investment boom into the African industrial sector.

Services

The services sector grew by 3.1 percent in 2002, from 3.3 percent in 2001. This is a negative growth, reflecting depressed services exports. International tourist arrivals in Africa increased marginally to 28.7 million from its 2001 level of 27.7 million. While international tourist arrivals in North Africa declined from 10.6 million in 2001 to 10.1 million in 2002 due to terrorist fears, Sub-Saharan Africa had an increase from 17.1 million to 18.6 million during the period. While Africa's market share of international tourism rose from 3.6 percent in 1995 to 4.0 percent in 2002, North Africa's share increased only marginally from 1.3 percent to 1.4 percent during the same period. Sub-Saharan Africa's share increased from 2.3 percent to 2.6 percent during the period. It is also significant to note that 2002 reversed the fall in international tourist arrivals' growth rate from 2.5 percent in 2001 to 3.7 percent in 2002. The deceleration of 4 percent in North Africa was more than offset by an increase in growth rate of 8.5 percent in Sub-Saharan Africa (Table 1.11).

Another development of particular interest in the tourism sub-sector is that in Uganda, tourism has overtaken coffee as the country's main source of foreign earnings. For example, in 2001, some 210,000 tourists visited the country leading to the earning of more than $160 million in foreign exchange, compared with less than $100 million from coffee. Also, in 2002, estimated tourists arrivals stood at 300,000, yielding about $245 million in foreign exchange.

Box 1.1: Findings from UNIDO Foreign Direct Investor Perceptions in SSA

In a pilot survey of foreign direct investor perceptions in Sub-Saharan Africa, UNIDO surveyed 430 respondents in four countries—Ethiopia, Nigeria, Uganda, and Tanzania. Among other issues, the survey focused on investors and addressed a number of issues, which are likely to influence the future environment for FDI in each of the four countries.

It found that from an investor perspective there was a strong orientation towards serving the domestic and to a lesser extent local regional markets. These markets were the primary motivations for investor behaviour. The Pan-African market was of only marginal importance. Other factors such as labour availability and cost factors were of secondary importance. The local incentive package available to investors ranked third in order of importance overall, although this varied among the countries.

Investor performance relative to expectations was an important factor. Country analysis indicated that returns were significantly ahead of expectations in two countries—Nigeria and Uganda. Investors in these countries claim to have enjoyed the best relative performance, and were therefore the most satisfied with their returns. In general terms the survey revealed that about 35 percent of investors responding found that returns were in line with expectations, while about 50 percent found that they were below. Favorable market conditions were the primary factors responsible for positive returns. Negative factors, which dragged down performance included, higher than expected overhead costs, material costs associated with the regulatory regime and the costs of services. The survey tracked future investment plans by asking the investors their preferred location for future investment. Generally, they were highly satisfied with their existing location with 70 percent overall claiming it was their favored location in Africa. This is a finding of some importance. This is because the Report also found that existing investors and business contacts transmitted the most significant source of investor awareness of opportunities for new foreign investment. They were responsible for around 50 percent of investor awareness of opportunities. The conclusion is that the best way to encourage new investment, at least under present operating conditions, is through the existing investors or their related base. This implies that national Investment Promotion Agencies (IPA) need to develop close relationships between themselves and existing investors in order to increase investment for the future. This is a low cost exercise especially when contrasted with attempting direct FDI promotion in foreign markets where the costs are high and the yields, at least in the short term, are low. Many country IPAs have been given this advice, but one that is rarely heeded. The survey provides strong empirical evidence that the IPAs should devote more resources and attention to investment promotion through the existing investors.

Source: UNIDO (2002), *Foreign Direct Investor Perceptions in Sub-Saharan Africa,* Vienna, UNIDO.

In South Africa, the black empowerment group, Tsogo Investments has become a controlling shareholder of SABMiller's hotel and gaming interests without having to make cash payments. The $210 million deal is to give Tsogo Investments a 51 percent stake in Tsogo Sun Holdings (TSH), which will in turn hold the entire issued share capital of casino operator Tsogo Sun and hotel group Southern sun Hotels. The deal gives black investors control of a substantial hotel and gaming group, while enabling SABMiller – the world's second largest brewer – to reduce its exposure to hotels and gaming. The second significant empowerment transaction in South Africa involves a consortium of black empowerment companies, which is taking over casino/hotels company, Global Resorts, at a cost of more

Table 1.11: International Tourism Arrivals by Sub-region

	International Tourism Arrivals (million)				Market Share (%)		Growth Rate			Average annual growth (%)
	1995	2000	2001	2002*	1995	2002*	00/99	01/00	02*/01	
Africa	**20**	**27.0**	**27.7**	**28.7**	**3.6**	**4.0**	**3.2**	**2.5**	**3.7**	**6.1**
North Africa	7.3	10.1	10.6	10.1	1.3	1.4	6.8	4.8	-4.0	1.8
Subsaharan Africa	12.7	17.0	17.1	18.6	2.3	2.6	12.0	1.0	8.5	10.0
Americas	**108.9**	**128.3**	**121.0**	**120.1**	**19.7**	**16.8**	**5.0**	**-5.7**	**-0.6**	**3.3**
North America	80.5	91.2	85.0	85.3	14.6	11.9	4.9	-6.8	0.4	2.4
Caribbean	14	71.2	16.9	16.4	2.5	2.3	6.9	-1.9	-3.0	4.2
Central America	2.6	4.3	4.4	4.8	0.5	0.7	8.9	1.6	9.7	9.0
South America	11.8	15.5	14.7	13.6	2.1	1.9	2.4	-5.1	-7.0	7.0
Asia and the Pacific	**85.6**	**115.3**	**121.0**	**130.6**	**15.5**	**18.3**	**12.3**	**5.0**	**7.9**	**7.2**
North-East Asia	44.1	62.5	65.6	73.4	8.0	10.3	13.2	5.0	11.9	8.4
South- East Asia	29.2	37.0	40.1	41.7	5.3	5.8	13.0	8.3	3.9	5.6
Oceania	8.1	9.6	9.4	9.6	1.5	1.3	8.7	-2.1	1.1	6.5
South Asia	4.2	6.1	5.8	5.9	0.8	0.8	5.4	-4.5	2.0	6.8
Europe	**324.2**	**402.8**	**401.4**	**411.0**	**58.8**	**57.5**	**5.8**	**-0.3**	**2.4**	**4.3**
Northern Europe	37.6	44.1	41.5	42.5	6.8	5.9	12.0	-5.9	2.3	4.3
Western Europe	116.7	1412.0	138.9	141.4	212.0	19.8	4.0	-1.6	1.8	22.0
Central and Eastern Europe	67.1	76.8	78.0	81.1	122.0	11.3	4.1	1.6	3.9	5.8
Southern Europe	102.7	140.7	143.0	146.1	18.6	20.4	10.4	1.6	22.0	4.0
Middle East	**13.1**	**22.7**	**21.8**	**24.1**	**2.4**	**3.4**	**13.1**	**-3.9**	**10.6**	**9.7**
World	**551.7**	**696.1**	**692.9**	**714.6**	**100.0**	**100.0**	**6.8**	**-0.5**	**3.1**	**4.3**

Source: World Tourism Organization (2003), January.

than $105 million. Following the take-over, Global Resorts becomes "first significant black-controlled gaming group" in South Africa.

Also, Table 1.12 shows selected African country Internet status as at October 2002. It illustrates the dominance of South Africa, followed by Egypt in the Internet area (see more details in Part 2 of this *Report*).

Mining

Africa is the richest continent in natural resources but ironically the poorest continent. Although under-explored, Africa hosts about 30 percent of the world's mineral reserves, including 40 percent of gold, 60 percent cobalt and 90 percent of the world's PGM reserves - making it a truly strategic producer of these precious metals. The continent produces more than 60 metal and mineral products and is a major producer of several of the world's most important minerals and metals including gold, PGEs, diamonds, uranium, manganese, chromium, nickel, bauxite and cobalt. Its contribution to the world's major metals (copper, lead, and zinc) is less than 7 percent. Consequently, silver production is low (less

Table 1.12: Selected African Country Internet Status Summary by October 2002

Country	Dialup Internet Subscribers	International Bandwidth Kbps Outgoing	Population Millions 2002	GDP/Capita USD 2002	Cities with POPs
South Africa	750000	342000	44.20	2,354	2
Algeria	45000	12000	31.40	1,752	1
Botswana	20000	14000	1.56	3,297	11
Egypt	100000	535000	70.28	1,242	1
Kenya	35000	28000	31.90	372	2
Mauritius	35000	4096	1.18	4,050	1
Morocco	80000	200000	30.99	1,192	1
Nigeria	60000	15000	120.05	355	2
Tanzania	30000	12000	36.82	252	4
Tunisia	70000	75000	9.67	2,195	1
Zimbabwe	25000	11000	13.08	408	4
Africa	**1492535**	**1409100**	**831**	**646**	**283**

Source: Adapted from Jensen (2002).

than 3 percent of the world's production) due to the fact that most silver is produced as a by-product of lead - zinc and copper mining. The increase in exploration and mine development in Africa has been primarily focused on gold and diamond exploration.

In addition, the African continent possesses about 20 percent of the globe's reserves of industrial raw materials, but its respective share of world production has steadily fallen during the past two decades, reflecting low levels of investment in new capacity and continuing geopolitical instabilities in mineral-rich regions of DRC and Angola.

Africa is a major producer of gold, producing an estimated 26.4 percent of the global total in 2002 against Europe's 1.4 percent, North America's 19.1 percent, Latin America's 14.5 percent, Asia's 11.3 percent, and Oceania's 11.2 percent. China, the CIS and other countries accounted for the remaining 16.1 percent. The South African industry, the world's largest gold producer, saw 1998 gold mine production at 15 million ounces, 5 percent less than in 1997. The AIDS epidemic sweeping through the mines is having a severe negative effect on productivity. Although this industry forecast 4 percent increase in production by 2002 (15,581 thousand ounces), this may be optimistic in light of current prices. Production in Ghana was estimated to increase by 11 percent in 2002 while that of Zimbabwe was estimated at an increase of 1.0 percent, same as the global output growth. However, gold output in Mali was estimated to decline by 11 percent in 2002.

In South Africa, Parliament approved the Mineral and Petroleum Resources Development Bill in 2002, which effectively transfers control of all mineral rights from individuals and companies to the State. Among other things, the Bill seeks to redress the results of the past racial discrimination by giving ownership opportunities to black emerging miners. Government would adopt the 'use it or lose it' principle to ensure that new people now had access, as opposed to 'those who always had it and are not evening using it.' It is also important for mining to ensure that economic benefits accrue to society as a whole and more specifically to communities affected by mining. Subsequently, new entrants in mining, local and international, big and small would only need to go to the department of minerals and energy to apply instead of accessing minerals from competitors. The department will facilitate access to technology, which will be provided by Mintek, Miningtek and other sister organizations. The Industrial Development Corporation and the Development Bank of Southern Africa will be in a position to render assistance to small medium and micro enterprises. The government's main priority is to break the existing monopoly (in the minerals sector) in order to stimulate a vibrant and fiercely competitive mining industry.

The mining industry in South Africa received a R1 billion boost in August 2002 with the launch in Johannesburg of the New Africa Mining Fund (NAMF), a Private Equity Investment vehicle focusing on developing the junior mining opportunities in Africa. The NAMF is an outcome of the Bakubung Initiative, an industry stakeholder forum established in 2000, to develop effective and practical solutions to address challenges facing the South African mining industry. The launch of the NAMF is particularly important as it came just a few weeks after the signing of the new mining law and the publication of the Mining Industry Charter, both documents which define the new mining environment in South Africa.

The NAMF's aim is to facilitate the access of capital for junior mining entrepreneurs while providing investors with competitive returns over the period in which their capital is invested. The Fund will invest in junior mining opportunities through the purchase of non-controlling equity stakes of between 10 and 45 percent of each project and aims to build a diversified portfolio of junior mining assets consisting of precious metals and stones, base metals as well as energy and industrial materials. The Fund also aims to promote the development of sustainable junior mining companies and therefore will only consider investing in commercial opportunities that represent prospects of creating real value for both investors and entrepreneurs.

In Ghana, Canada's PMI Ventures has bought up to 85 percent of Goknet Mining's interest in exploration concessions in the Asankrangwa, which lies between the country's two main gold-producing belts, Ashanti and Sefwi. PMI is issuing 3 million shares to Ghanaian firm Goknet, and paying $260,000 in cash. The acquisition will enable PMI to acquire a significant stake in a major established goldfield with only a small initial exploration program.

In Zimbabwe, mining is becoming increasingly difficult for gold companies and smaller mining operations in spite of a 2002 revamped fiscal package intended to stimulate the sector. The revised fiscal package set royalties of 3 percent of total revenues on precious metals producers and a tax rate of 2 percent on base metal producers. Previously, the royalty had not been fixed and there was a lack of certainty, which many investors in the sector had found worrying.

However, mining operators in the country are struggling as inflation hovers near 114 percent and the official exchange rate is held at Z55 to $1, making operating conditions difficult. The parallel market exchange rate is put at about seven times the official rate. For the mining industry operators, who often have to borrow in dollars and import dollar-priced goods and fuel to run their operations, these circumstances adversely affect earnings a great deal. The situation is made worse for the gold mining industry, which does not have special concessions to sell proportions of their production freely on the global market, retaining their dollar revenues.

Producers of gold in Zimbabwe have to sell the metal to the country's central bank, and although the international price of gold averaged $310/oz, producers in Zimbabwe were paid Z$29000/oz, equivalent to an exchange rate of Z$90 to $1. This was well below the blend rate taking into consideration the official rate of exchange and concessions given to exporters of Z$200 to $1 being achieved by normal exporters. It was therefore not surprising that gold production in Zimbabwe dropped from about 29 tons a year to nearer 16 tons by the end of 2002.

Mali has occupied an almost permanent position amongst the list of the 10 poorest countries in the world. Now, the development of gold mines has raised the glimmer of hope that there could be better times ahead. It is in the south that the gold mines are finally being developed after geologists estimated the country had enormous potential for gold discoveries. A number of new mines were opened in 2001, doubling previous production and ranking Mali as Africa's third largest gold producer after South Africa and Ghana. The international mining firm, Anglogold, holds the majority stake in the largest two

mines, but the Malian government also has a 20 percent share.

As a result of the new gold mines, Mali's GDP is grew by 5.2 percent in 2002. That compares to just 1.5 percent economic growth rate in 2001 - a contraction in real terms due to the growing population. But the sudden spurt of growth speaks more of the lack of other components in Mali's economy, rather than a tribute to the amount of gold actually being produced. The World Bank has already warned of Mali's extreme sensitivity to external shocks, with cotton and gold now making up more than four-fifths of all its exports. It leaves the whole country exposed to price fluctuations of these commodities in the international marketplace.

Africa is the world's largest producer of diamonds, producing as much as 50 percent of global production. To date, Africa has produced over 75 percent, in value, of the world's diamonds with more than 1.9 billion carats worth an estimated $158 billion mined. Diamonds are being produced primarily from kimberlite mines (South Africa, Angola, DRC, Ghana, Tanzania, Lesotho and Botswana), followed by alluvial dredging operations (Angola, CAR, Namibia and South Africa) and offshore marine diamond activities (South Africa and Namibia). Most of West Africa's diamond production in the area originates from fluviatile placers and only on a minor scale from eluvial deposits or from altered kimberlite pipes. Almost all these mines are relatively small-scale operations mainly run by artisanal miners, except for the Akwatia mine in Ghana and the Aredor project in Guinea. At the end of 2001, the global diamond production stood at 117 million carats with Botswana producing 25.16 million carats, Congo producing 18.2

million carrats, South Africa producing 11.8 million carrats, and Angola producing 5.2 million carrats.

Most of Africa's copper production comes from Zambia, DRC and South Africa. Reductions in production have come from South Africa and Namibia (in particular). After finally concluding the long awaited privatization of Zambia's Copperbelt, the country is faced with a fresh crisis following the withdrawal of one of the largest investors, Anglo American. The future of Zambia's copperbelt now rests (once again) to a large extent, in the hands of the Zambian Government. However, other smaller foreign and African mining companies continue to rehabilitate other parts of ZCCM. Copper production from the DRC is set to be boosted following the resurrection of many world-class projects.

The government of Zambia is making a last-ditch attempt to save its new mining project, Konkola Deep, the country's best-untapped copper ore body. Multinational mining giant, Anglo American, a veteran of the Copper Belt, is poised to pull out of the new mine, whose operation is crucial to the Zambian economy. The industry has been in decline since its hey day of the early seventies, but the worst may still to come given that Konkola Deep Mine is the only mining project of substance that will replace the aging mines in the Copper Belt. Anglo has taken steps to modernize Zambia's ailing mines. It has already invested more than $300 million in the deep-level mines at Konkola and blames its decision to pull out on the low copper price.

While mining is less than 10 percent of GDP, it is the systemic impact in terms of the contribution to foreign exchange, 70 percent of which comes from mining. Another 11,000 min-

ing jobs are on the line at Konkola after tens of thousands were lost over the past two decades. Zambia faces an economic disaster, unless a new breed of smaller and more nimble mining investors emerge to rescue the Copper Belt.

The latest United Nations report on the Democratic Republic of Congo says rebels and foreign governments are still plundering the country's resources, everything from diamonds to animal skins. It portrays the DRC as a place where rebel movements and foreign armies are using the cloak of war to disguise what has become a blatant exercise in self-enrichment through the illegal plunder of scarce resources. The report says that direct confrontation between rebel groups and the Congolese Government has all but disappeared - but it says that fierce conflict is continuing on the rebel side of the ceasefire line, as different factions compete for access to gold, diamonds and other mineral resources. The report says there are also growing indications that criminal networks, based inside and outside Africa, are becoming increasingly involved. The conflict over resources has an obvious impact on local populations who are often forced to flee fighting. But the report notes that local people also suffer because they are receiving no benefit from the theft of precious minerals from their home areas.

Australia's Argosy Minerals is to restart the development of a new nickel mine in the war-torn Burundi, two years after suspending operations over security fears. A declaration in April 2000 of 'force majeure', which froze a feasibility study, had been lifted at the Musongati nickel project. A United Nations study of the site estimated the nickel deposit contained about 6 percent of the known global supply of the metal. Exploitation has been restricted due to the civil war between the ethnic Hutu majority and the army led by the Tutsi minority which has raged since 1993, killing at least 250,000 people, most of them civilians. Previous studies also suggested the site may contain commercial quantities of platinum group metals. Under a funding deal, the Burundi government would end up owning 15 percent of the mine.

Prices for industrial commodities slumped to historic lows during late 2001. Copper plunged to a 15-year low, zinc to 14-year lows, while nickel and aluminum dropped to three-year lows. During 2001, a year of sagging industrial demand, average prices for major metals was below levels of 1999 and 2000. Nickel recorded falls of 31 percent, zinc 21.5 percent, copper 13 percent, tin 17.5 percent and aluminum 7 percent. Sluggish demand in the industrialized world and excess production capacity of most base metals led to ever larger stocks and plummeting prices. End-2001 aluminum (London Metal Exchange) stocks were reported at 821,850t (up 155 percent over previous year), copper 799,225t (up 124 percent), nickel 19,188t (up 98 percent), tin 30,550t (up 137 percent) and zinc 433,350t (up 122 percent). The price of lead, however, proved resilient rising 5 percent, underpinned by a production deficit of 5,000t and low stockpiles. As table 1.6 shows, in 2002 year, aluminum price averaged $1,350/mt, copper $1,559/mt, gold $310/oz, iron ore 29.31 cents/dmtu, lead 45.3cents/dmtu, nickel $5945/mt, silver 462.5 cents/toz, tin 406.1 cents/kg, and zinc 77.9 cents/kg. Thus, apart from gold, nickel, and silver, all the other metals and minerals recorded price declines from their 2001 levels.

African producers of base metals have had to struggle against tough market conditions over the past year and a half, but now some improvements are on the horizon. As the world's economy improves, so the prospects for Africa's metal resources industries grow more positive. Markets for industrial commodities are finally looking beyond the clouds of global economic slowdown to the blue sky of imminent economic upturn. In essence, the future of metals rests on the strength of global industrial production. Recently, leading economic indicators in North America and Western Europe (the main consuming regions) have turned positive, thus suggesting improved confidence within the manufacturing and services industries. More signs of global recovery may boost base metals consumption in the coming months.

Energy

The estimated volume of world oil demand for 2002 averaged 76.57 million barrels per day (mb/d), compared with 76.35 mb/d the previous year. Africa's oil demand remained a meager 2.46 mb/d (or 3.22 percent of the total) against 2.44 mb/d (or 3.20 percent of world total) in 2001. On the other hand, world oil supply decreased marginally from 77.27 mb/d in 2001 to 76.92 mb/d in 2002 (OPEC, 2003). In 2002, African non-OPEC producers supplied 2.80 mb/d while African OPEC producers (Algeria, Nigeria, and Libya) supplied about 4.28 mb/d, giving a total of 7.08 mb/d or 9.2 percent of the global supply. In terms of metric tonnes, the world crude oil production was estimated to have risen marginally from 3,728.09 million metric tonnes in 2001 to 3,739.02 million metric tonnes in 2002 (Table 1.13).

Algeria, Angola, Egypt, Libya and Nigeria dominate the continent's oil production, accounting for 85 percent of its 2002 total (see Table 1.13). They are followed by a plethora of small-to-medium sized oil producers, the main ones being in order of descending output, Equatorial Guinea, Sudan, Gabon, Congo, Cameroon, and Tunisia. Crude oil production in Nigeria, Libya and Algeria, the three OPEC members in Africa, declined to 7.08 mb/d in 2002, each country slightly exceeding their production quota. Oil production also declined in Cameroon, Congo, Egypt, Gabon, and Tunisia, reflecting depleting reserves in these countries' main fields and diminishing discoveries. Cameroon's oil development prospects could improve following the International Court of Justice's ruling in its favor in October 2002 over the disputed ownership with Nigeria of the oil-rich Bakassi peninsula.

Oil production in 2002 followed an upward trend elsewhere in the region. Crude oil production in Angola rose from 742,000 bpd in 2001 to roughly 900,000 bpd in 2002, as full production began at Girassol. This means that Angola has now overtaken Algeria and Egypt to become the third largest oil producer in Africa. In Equatorial Guinea, oil production has continued its exponential rise, as exploitation at the country's main fields (Zaffiro, Alba, Ceiba) gathered pace. The country has now replaced Gabon as the third largest oil producer in Sub-Saharan Africa, after Nigeria and Angola, with its oil production averaging 258,500 bdp in 2002. Sudanese crude oil production has risen rapidly since the completion of a major oil ex-

Table 1.13: Crude Oil Production, 1994-2002
(In millions metrics tonnes)

Country	1994	1995	1996	1997	1998	1999	2000	2001	2002*
Algeria[a/]	37.24	37.74	40.72	42.21	41.22	37.24	40.22	41.52	44.94
Angola	27.61	30.79	34.27	36.25	36.75	38.29	38.14	36.40	45.69
Benin	0.19	0.12	0.20	0.15	0.15	0.15	na	na	na
Cameroon	6.18	5.40	5.13	5.46	5.94	6.15	5.75	5.47	5.20
Congo	9.04	9.10	10.30	11.60	12.60	13.17	13.06	12.11	12.40
Congo, Dem. Rep.	1.24	1.52	0.53	0.50	0.47	0.43	0.41	na	na
Egypt	44.79	44.20	45.69	45.69	43.90	42.31	40.37	38.06	37.24
Equ. Guinea	0.25	0.31	0.86	3.01	4.10	5.11	5.87	9.71	13.49
Gabon	15.89	17.38	17.83	18.37	17.88	16.88	16.19	14.94	14.40
Libya[a/]	68.53	70.02	69.03	70.52	69.52	67.04	71.01	67.79	66.42
Nigeria[a/]	94.35	95.84	106.77	113.22	105.28	97.83	101.31	103.44	97.46
Tunisia	4.50	4.17	5.31	3.79	3.98	4.03	3.74	3.42	na
Total Africa	309.82	316.60	336.62	350.77	341.78	328.64	336.08	332.86	340.74
OPEC[a/]	1246.91	1266.57	1293.14	1350.75	1383.03	1457.52	1346.28	1352.06	1275.39
World[a/]	3278.35	3341.56	3465.51	3580.48	3648.01	3587.93	3726.48	3728.09	3739.02

na: Not available
* Estimates
a/ Crude oil and Condensates (excluding Natural Gas Liquids).
Sources: Petroleum Economist, December 2002, Economist Intelligence Unit, Etudes et Statistiques BEAC and ADB Statistics Division estimates

port pipeline in 1999. Crude oil production averaged 209,000 barrels per day (bbl/d) in 2001, rising to 227,500 bbl/d in 2002. In August 2001, in recognition of Sudan's growing significance as an oil exporter, OPEC granted the country observer status at OPEC meetings.

Attention in 2002 focused on oil development in Lake Chad and the construction of the Chad-Cameroon pipeline, and new oil findings in Angola (first oil discovery in the country's ultra-deep waters was made in September 2002), Equatorial Guinea, Nigeria, but also in Mauritania, where recoverable oil reserves totalling 60-100 million barrels were discovered in January. Another important development was the start-up of production at Espoir in Côte d'Ivoire in February 2002; this almost doubled the country's crude oil production to an estimated 10,400 bpd.

Global natural gas liquids supply stood at 51.58 mb/d in 2002 against 49.08 mb/d in 2001. Out of these, African producers supplied 3.04 mb/d (5.89 percent of total) in 2002 and 2.50 mb/d (5.09 percent of total) in 2001. The bulk of gas supply projects in Africa have continued to take place in the north, most notably in Egypt and on the Trans-Mediterranean corridor. The main development in 2002, however, was the launch of the construction of Mozambique's first natural gas pipeline in February. The pipeline, which is a joint venture between Sasol and the governments of Mozambique and South Africa, will run from gas fields in southern Mozambique to Secunda, South Africa. The first major contract for the West African gas pipeline development was also signed in 2002. The long-mooted regional pipeline is to supply gas from Nigeria to Benin, Ghana, and Togo, some to be used for electricity generation.

With regard to downstream oil activities in Africa, Egypt, Algeria, South Africa, Libya and Nigeria remain the continent's main refining centres. In May 2002, Libya awarded a contract to upgrade its 120,000 bpd Az Zawiya refinery. Morocco has pre-selected contractors for the expansion of its 125,000 bdp refinery at Mohammedia and Angola has announced that the construction of its second oil refinery will start in 2003. There are also plans to develop Sudan's refining capacity. Chad's Sedigui project, which entails building a refining plant able to meet all domestic petroleum requirements, has suffered some delays.

Africa's great potentials for hydro- and gas thermal- electricity generation remain largely untapped, as the result of lack of foreign funding and the huge costs involved. The year 2002 offered mixed results for Africa's electricity industry. On the positive side, many countries received funding from donors, most notably the African Development Bank, and investment from foreign companies to upgrade their national grid and accelerate their rural electrification programs. Some projects were completed, notably in Angola, where the construction of the Capanda 520 MW hydroelectric dam was completed, with electricity production scheduled to begin in early 2003. The long-delayed 200 MW regional hydroelectric dam in Manantali also came on stream in 2002, its output being shared between Mali, Mauritania, and Senegal. Concerning ongoing structural reforms in this sector, Eskom of South Africa signed a 20-year deal with Uganda in November 2002 to boost the country's energy supply. Little progress was made elsewhere, however. Concerning mega-power sharing projects, the construction of the controversial 2,000 MW Bujagali hydro-electric dam was put on hold in July 2002, when the World Bank decided to suspend its support over environmental concerns. The Bujagali dam is presently East Africa's largest foreign investment project. Some countries, notably Nigeria, Cameroon and Senegal, meanwhile continued to experience serious energy shortages in 2002, as a result of decaying equipment or drought, and/or lack of strategic buyers. Nigeria has announced its decision to divide the electricity giant, NEPA, into 16 smaller companies prior to privatization. Despite substantial oil, gas, and water resources, wood burning remains the main source of energy use in Africa, which raises strong environmental concerns.

Medium-Term Prospects and Sustainability Issues

The Medium-Term Outlook

- **Forces driving the medium-term outlook**

Economic performance in Africa is expected to be better in 2003 following the expected, albeit sluggish, recovery in the OECD countries and subdued oil prices, especially with quick war against Iraq. Growth of the world economy is expected to be moderate buoyed by gradual recovery in industrial countries and Latin America. This increased aggregate demand will significantly increase Africa's external impetus for growth by impacting on both the volume and prices of major exports, as well as continuing to affect capital flows. World trade volume is expected to grow from 2.9 percent in 2002 to an average of 7.2 percent in 2003-4. Despite the lower international interest rates, capital

flows will not likely surge significantly into the developing countries because of continuing fragility and uncertainty in global capital markets. Commodity prices are also likely to be much lower than would be expected.

The major risk to the expected modest global recovery is the possibility of major shocks to the global economy. Some of the risks include: continued financial turbulence in high-income countries that could jeopardize a rebound in investment; and a reversal in capital flows to emerging markets thereby heightening tensions in several vulnerable middle-income countries; (World Bank's GEP, 2002).

Outlook for Africa

Growth in Africa is expected to recover modestly to 3.6 percent in 2003 following the prospects in the international economy and developments in the domestic conditions. On the external front, faster growth in Europe will boost export volumes in Africa, and export prices are likely to trend upwards due to increased demand. Non-oil terms of trade are expected to improve marginally in the 2003-04 period. Assuming away the Iraq factor, some of Africa's oil exporters are projecting a moderate and probably subdued prices of about $20 per barrel. Nigeria, for example, has planned the 2003 budget based on expected average oil price of $18 per barrel. However, OPEC is likely to further cut its quota to members due to expectation of a quick war against Iraq. Also, major new offshore oil is expected to come to production, especially in the Gulf of Guinea (Angola, Equatorial Guinea, and Nigeria). In the event of Iraq-related oil price fall, however, Africa's oil importers could benefit significantly, while Africa's net-oil exporters might face serious current account difficulties if counter adjustment policies are not put in place. Africa's oil importers might thus build larger current account surpluses in 2003.

The accumulated current account and fiscal surpluses in major oil importers would likely fuel large public expenditure program to improve infrastructure, agriculture, and social sectors. This would impact on domestic aggregate demand. Morocco and Tunisia may not rely on such stimulus package in view of the need to pursue fiscal consolidation and keep public sector wage bill and other expenditures under control. Some of the countries such as Morocco and Nigeria would expect to reap substantial revenues from privatization of public enterprises in 2003-04 and these could help to strengthen budget balances.

These forecasts for 2003-04 are based on assumptions of improved weather conditions, which would buoy up agricultural performance, lower spread and effect of the Severe Acute Respiratory Syndrome (SARS) from East Asia, as well as assumptions of, improved political and policy stance. Drought in some Northern, Southern and Eastern countries of Africa is expected to ease, and the expected recovery of agriculture would shore up domestic aggregate demand and investment spending. More favorable conditions in Europe, North America and the Middle East would also lead to improved remittances to the region, and foreign direct investment might recover from the present depressed levels.

Furthermore, the cessation of conflicts in parts of Africa (especially the Congo Democratic Republic, Angola, and Ethiopia-Eritrea conflicts) and the prospects of significant post-conflict reconstruction programs give the hope of possible peace dividends. The successful change of government in Kenya and the promise of fundamental reforms also hold some positive prospects, and send some important positive signals that a new Africa is in the making. These developments would provide impetus for inflows of foreign direct investment.

As with the projections for the global economy, Africa's recovery faces some serious risks. There is the risk that the global economy may not recover as anticipated due to the continuing shocks and uncertainties in the international financial system. It is also possible that the drought in parts of Africa would not cease. Perhaps, the most potent threat to the growth forecast for Africa is the planned military actions against Iraq—which could destabilize much of the Middle East and North African region. Services exports (especially tourism which accounts for 11 percent of Africa's exports) would suffer significantly. If the Iraqi war is quick, for most of the African countries—which are oil importers—this could trigger huge current account surpluses while oil exporters (with high GDP-weights) run huge imbalances. Tangential to possible Middle East crisis is the problem of continuing conflict in several African countries such as Côte d'Ivoire—with the disruption of production activities and high social dislocations affecting all neighboring countries. The prospect for the region also depends on how Nigeria (Africa's most populous country with 8 percent of its GDP) handles the civilian-managed change of government through general elections scheduled for April 2003. Since independence in 1960, Nigeria has never successfully managed a civilian-to-civilian change of government: all previous attempts were marked by political crisis resulting in military coups. Developments in Nigeria would reverberate not only on the Nigerian economy, but also on large parts of Africa especially the West African sub-region.

Aside from the non-policy factors impacting on performance, the medium term prospects will, in the final analysis, depend on the deepening of policy reforms in the region. These policies will go beyond political governance and institutional reforms, to broad economic agenda—structural, and sound micro and macro-economic policy stance. Initiating and sustaining sound economic outcomes depend critically on the policy choices and the commitment of the political leadership to pursue growth-enhancing reforms as exemplified by the experiences of many better-managed African economies in the last two decades. As the African Union (AU) makes important strides in institutionalizing the NEPAD, especially the peer pressure mechanism on good political and economic governance, African countries would come under increasing pressure to deepen and sustain reforms.

Complementing these domestic reform measures would be some positive developments in the international community. Definitely, the various compacts Africa has reached with the international community under the UN system underpin the fact that domestic reforms are not enough. Some of the challenges and risks to the medium term performance— disease, civil strife, poor governance in several countries, erratic weather conditions, the HIV/AIDS pandemic, lack of economic diversification and terms of trade shocks, low savings and investment, dependence on foreign aid and so on— will

not easily be solved through domestic reforms. Two recent initiatives—the United Nations Millennium Declaration on Development and Poverty (September 2000) and the United Nations Conference on Financing for Development (Monterrey, Mexico, March 2002) make clear that the international community (especially the richest industrial countries) must act in concert to lift the poorest regions of Africa and others such as in Asia from poverty. These initiatives reaffirm the need for global actions to provide global public goods, ensure increased ODA flows to the poorest countries, provide market access for the exports of these poor countries, and addressing several of the systemic defects of the international institutions of governance (see Box 1.2).

The international declarations regarding the need for massive international assistance to bail Africa out are legion. The problem however is to effectively implement them and ensure their sustainability. So far, Africa is the only region where the number of people living in absolute poverty (less than $1 per day) is projected to increase by about 30 percent in 2015— a complete negation of the Millennium Development Goal (MDG) of halving incidence of poverty by 2015. To achieve this MDG, Africa's GDP growth rate needs to be sustained at a rate of at least 7 percent per annum until 2015. But the rate for 2002 was just 2.8 percent, and the medium-term prospect in 2003-04 is barely 3 percent— less than half of required growth rate. If the present trend is sustained into the future, Africa will be further marginalized in the world economy. Thus, the challenge facing Africa is not so much how to overcome some short-run cyclical trends. Rather, it is how to overcome the poverty trap, and lay a solid foundation for a virtuous circle of growth and development.

Box 1.2: Global Public Goods and Monterrey Consensus on Financing for Development

The World Bank's *World Development Report, 2000*, argues that a global action is required both to ensure that the opportunities from global integration and technological advance benefit poor people and to manage the risks of insecurity and exclusion that may result from global change. Consequently, the Report recommends five key actions at the international level to make development in the poorest countries possible and sustainable: (a) Promoting global financial stability and opening the markets of rich countries to the agricultural goods, manufactures, and services of poor countries; (b) Bridging the digital and knowledge divides, thus bringing technology and information to people throughout the world; (c) Providing financial and nonfinancial resources for international public goods, especially medical and agricultural research; (d) Increasing aid and debt relief to help countries take actions to end poverty, within a comprehensive framework that puts countries themselves—not external aid agencies—at the center of the design of development strategy; and (e) Giving a voice to poor countries and poor people in global forums, including through international links with organizations of poor people.

This is a laudable agenda. A major missing link is a systematic and adequate set of actions to fully fund the program, including meeting the challenge of the attainment of the Millennium Development Goals (MDGs) which most Sub-Saharan African countries are already sure to miss if current trends continue. Estimates by the African Development Bank reported in the Global Poverty Report 2002, shows that the additional $ 25 billion per annum in ODA would be required (by 31 African countries that have adequate policies and institutions) to meet the MDGs, and Jeffrey Sachs has estimated that to tackle some of the deadly diseases afflicting Africa, additional resources amounting to about $10 billion per annum would be needed. Despite these growing needs, the current flows of ODA are on the downward trend, and Africa is a net loser in terms of FDI flows.

Consequently, the United Nations Conference for Financing for Development (FfD) was held in Monterrey, Mexico (March 18- 22, 2002) to take a comprehensive look at all sources of development finance which, if successfully harnessed and effectively invested would achieve sustainable, poverty-reducing growth and development in poorest countries. The Conference identified the sources of funding to include: domestic, external, public and private, aid and debt relief, as well as, trade and investment. The six major areas of focus include:

a. Mobilizing Domestic Financial Resources for Development

The Heads of State recognized the need to strengthen and develop the domestic financial sector, by encouraging the orderly development of capital markets through sound banking systems and other institutional arrangements aimed at addressing development financing needs, including the insurance sector, and debt and equity markets. An enabling domestic environment was considered necessary for mobilizing domestic resources, increasing productivity, reducing capital flight, encouraging the private sector, and attracting and making effective use of international investment and assistance.

b. Mobilizing International Resources for Development

The Monterrey conference stressed the necessity for countries to deepen reforms to provide a transparent, stable and predictable investment climate, with proper contract enforcement and respect for property rights, embedded in sound macroeconomic policies and institutions that allow businesses, both domestic and foreign, to operate efficiently and profitably. Private international capital especially FDI, together with international financial stability, were accepted as vital complements to national and international development efforts. FDI contributes towards financing sustained economic growth over the long run. The Monterrey conference stressed the importance of providing export credits, co-financing, venture capital and

Box 1.2: (continued)

other lending instruments, risk guarantees, leveraging aid resources and information on investment opportunities. It also recommended increased organization of business development services and fora to facilitate business contacts and cooperation between enterprises of developed and developing countries.

c. International Trade as an Engine for Development

It was agreed that a universal, rule-based, open, non-discriminatory and equitable multilateral trading system, as well as meaningful trade liberalization, can substantially stimulate development world-wide and benefit countries at all stages of development. Consequently, all countries expressed commitment towards trade liberalization. In order to ensure that world trade supported development—for the benefit of all countries, members of the WTO were encouraged to implement the outcome of the Fourth Ministerial Conference, held in Doha, Qatar in November 2001. The Conference also recognized the importance of enhanced and predictable access to all markets for the exports of developing countries. Developed countries, whose markets were not already opened, were advised to work towards the objective of duty-free and quota-free access for all least developed countries' exports, as envisaged in the Program of Action for the Least Developed Countries adopted in Brussels.

d. Increasing International Financial and Technical Cooperation for Development

Official Development Assistance (ODA) was recognized as a critical source of finance, especially for countries with least capacity to attract private foreign investment. Consequently, the conference recognized that effective partnerships, among donors and recipients, and based on recipient leadership and ownership, were needed to enhance the effectiveness of ODA. The conference also urged developed countries, which did not meet the target 0.7 percent of GNP as ODA to developing countries, to make concrete efforts to do so.

e. External Debt

Sustainable debt financing was identified as an important element for mobilizing resources for public and private investment. Debtors and creditors were encouraged to share the responsibility for preventing and resolving unsustainable debt situations. Technical assistance for external debt management and debt tracking was recommended. The enhanced Heavily Indebted Poor Countries (HIPC) Initiative was said to provide an opportunity to strengthen economic prospects and poverty reduction efforts of countries benefiting from it. Speedy, effective and full implementation of the enhanced initiative, which should be fully financed through additional resources, was seen as critical. It was also emphasized that computational procedures and assumptions underlying debt sustainability analysis should be kept under review. In addition, the IMF and the World Bank were called upon to consider any fundamental changes in countries' debt sustainability caused by natural catastrophes, severe terms of trade shocks or conflict, when making policy recommendations, including those on debt relief.

f. Systemic Issues

The conference underscored the need to complement national reform efforts with a more coherent and consistent international governance, monetary and financial as well as trading systems. The conference stressed the need to collectively contribute towards improved global economic governance and strengthening of the United Nations. At the national levels, increased efforts should be devoted to improved coordination among all relevant ministries and institutions.

Sources: World Bank (2000), World Development Report; Report of the UN Financing for Development; CBN, Quarterly Bulletin of International Economic Developments, Jan 2003, the Global Poverty Report 2002, African Development Bank and the World Bank.

The three critical 'C's requiring urgent attention by African policymakers

In the various editions of the *African Development Report*, attention has been drawn to several issues that need to be addressed in order to set Africa on a path to sustainable poverty-reducing growth and development. These issues included adverse external shocks, failure to recapitalize Africa, policy reversal, societal conflicts, private sector development, human capital development, governance and economic management, financing of development, environmental concerns, regional economic integration, infrastructure development, and many others. In 2002, specific attention was focused on issues of structural vulnerability, and NEPAD as a veritable instrument to move African development forward. This year, attention is focused on what we call the three critical 'C's requiring urgent attention— conflict, corruption, and competitiveness— in order to initiate and sustain a stronger base for long-term development.

The synergies among the three 'C's are self-evident. African economies cannot achieve sustainable poverty-reducing growth without laying solid foundations for systemic and international competitiveness. But competitiveness cannot happen where there is no peace and strong institutional infrastructure for resolving societal conflicts. And strong institutions and effective economic management are severely constrained by endemic corruption (see linkage below).

Conflict and Wars

Term development has been the risk or actual occurrence of armed conflicts. Between 1970 and 2002, more than 35 wars have been fought in Africa, with the vast majority of them intra-state in origin. In 1996 alone, 14 out of the 53 countries of Africa were afflicted by armed conflicts, accounting for more than half of all war-related deaths worldwide and resulting in more than 8 million refugees, returnees and displaced persons. The binding constraint of armed conflict on Africa's economic development was recognized by the UN Security Council which, on September 25, 1997 requested the UN Secretary-General to submit a report regarding the sources of conflict in Africa, ways to prevent and address those conflicts, and how to lay the foundation for durable peace and economic growth following their resolution. The Secretary-General submitted his report to both the Security Council and the UN General Assembly in 1998. So far, although some of the gruesome wars—especially in Angola, Liberia, and Mozambique—have ceased, several new ones emerged in countries such as Sierra Leone and Côte d'Ivoire. Several dozen other countries (such as Zimbabwe, Algeria, Guinea, Mali, Nigeria, etc) experience unstable situations that if not managed properly could also explode into armed conflicts.

The literature is replete with several explanations of the causes of these conflicts. For sure, the 53 African countries are as similar as they are diverse—different histories and geographical conditions, different stages of economic development, different sets of public policies and different patterns of internal and international interactions. The sources of intrastate conflicts reflect this diversity. The many causes can be grouped into four key clusters of factors as follows.

Historical legacies of a divided people: This refers to the arbitrary 'creation' of African countries at the Berlin Conference of 1885 by the colonial powers. The outcome was that kingdoms, states and communities were arbitrarily joined together with unrelated areas and peoples banded together. In 1963, the Organization of African Unity (OAU) decided to adopt the inherited boundaries, and the leaders in most countries have had to struggle to weave nation states out of the disparate nationalities and ethnic groups that make up their countries. This challenge was compounded by the fact that the inherited framework of colonial laws and institutions had been designed to exploit local divisions. Many countries have not succeeded in overcoming these legacies.

Internal politics and governance as decisive factor: More than four decades of independence for many countries should have been enough time to sort out the colonial legacies and move forward. Thus, Africa needs to look at itself— especially the nature of political power and governance institutions. In most African countries, the economy is still dominated by the state—with the state as major provider of formal employment, contracts, and patronage while parties are regionally or ethnically based. And politics in most of these countries is such that victory assumes a 'winner-takes-all' form with respect to wealth and resources, patronage, and

the prestige and prerogative of office. If there is lack of transparency and accountability in governance, inadequate checks and balances, non-adherence to the rule of law, absence of credible and peaceful means to change or replace leadership, or lack of respect for human rights, political control becomes excessively important and the stakes dangerously high.

External factors: During the cold war, super-power competition entailed excessive interference in Africa's domestic politics and governance. This intervention has not disappeared in the post-cold war era. The competition has shifted to that for oil, diamond, gold, and other precious metals, and these external interests continue to play critical roles in suppressing or sustaining conflicts. The UN Secretary-General has also candidly acknowledged that while African peacekeeping and mediation efforts have become more prominent in recent years, some African Governments also play active roles in supporting, sometimes even instigating, conflicts in neighboring countries.

Economic factors. Some people obviously profit from conflicts and could have interests in promoting it. Poverty is both a cause and consequence of conflicts. Where a large proportion of the population is unemployed, in deep poverty, and hopelessness pervades, the opportunity cost of being involved in rebel movement is near zero. Indeed, the potential pay-off could be great especially with the prospects of the movement controlling some strategic minerals or resources. The first group that benefits from conflicts is the international arms merchants. The presence of large deposits of natural resources such as diamonds and other raw materials could also provide incentives for armed struggles (see Anyanwu, 2002). For example, in Liberia the control and exploitation of diamonds, timber and other raw materials was one of the principal objectives of the warring factions. In many other countries such as Angola, Congo Democratic Republic, access to such minerals is a key objective as well as the major sustenance of the conflicts.

Whatever the specific weights to be attached to each of these factors in specific cases is an empirical question. A recent study by Anyanwu (2002) shows that African conflicts are significantly caused by GDP per capita growth rate in the preceding period, the amount of natural resources (proxied by primary commodity export-GDP ratio), peace duration, democracy, social fractionalisation, and population size. But whatever the prime cause, the consequences are horrendous in terms of social, human, and physical capital. By 1997, armed conflicts had claimed some 2 million lives in Africa over a five year period, not to mention the millions of refugees and displaced persons who are mostly women and children. As at 2000, there were about 12 million refugees in Africa, over 40 percent of the world's total. In Angola alone, the three decades war is estimated to have claimed over 80,000 lives, created over 500,000 refugees, displaced half of the country's 4.5 million people, and robbed an entire generation of children their future.

A major effect of armed conflicts everywhere in Africa is the reduced opportunity for youths and for productive enterprises. Wars destroy existing capital stock, and the fear of expropriation and safety deny the country of prospective investments—both by domestic and foreign investors. Capital flight is endemic as the elite plunder the State and struggle to keep their loots in safer territories abroad. An aspect that makes conflicts in African countries very costly to the rest of the region is the covariance of the risks and contagion or neighborhood effects. Rebellion or conflict in one country, if not contained, often breeds and re-inforces similar conflicts in other neighboring countries. Also, once there is conflict in one country or sub-region, foreign investors and risk rating agencies generally rate neighboring countries very badly as risky investment sites. Thus, a war in any part of Africa is, in effect, a war on the development of the region as a whole.

Governments facing rebel threats usually divert expenditures away from social and physical infrastructure to the already bloated and ineffective military force. Education system often collapses, unemployment worsens and violent crimes become the defining characteristic of urban cities. Child soldiers, constituting about 10- 15 percent of most rebel movements in Africa are disoriented with a psyche of destruction rather than for productive enterprise, and generally constitute a lost generation. Recent statistics on the HIV/AIDS pandemic in Africa shows that displaced populations and refugees resulting from conflicts are mostly at risk.

What can be done? According to Anyanwu (2002), preventing war outbreak in Africa needs a combination of economic diversification, poverty and population reduction, and political reforms. The Report of the UN Secretary-General to the Security Council and UN General Assembly in 1998 provided a very comprehensive outline of a response action agenda. Each conflict obviously has its differentiating dynamics, which in turn shape the emerging character of post-conflict reconstruction and peace-building (see Box 1.3).

Box 1.3: Responding to Conflict and Post-Conflict Situations in Africa

The essential elements of the transition from conflict to peace are basically the same in most circumstances, including: political commitment of the various warring factions to negotiate an end to hostilities; defining a new security framework for sustaining the peace; elaborating a generally acceptable, inclusive and transparent system of post-conflict governance; and designing and implementing a wide range of post-conflict economic recovery measures. In achieving these measures, the international community and regional bodies have crucial roles to play especially in four areas: peacemaking; peacekeeping; humanitarian assistance; and post-conflict peace-building. In the area of peacemaking, the international community can best help by harmonizing the policies and actions of external actors; avoiding a proliferation of mediation efforts; mobilizing international support for peace efforts; improving the effectiveness of sanctions; and stopping the proliferation of arms. On peacekeeping, there is need for coordinated and consistent approach, ensuring adequate support for Africa's subregional initiatives such as the ECOWAS' ECOMOG force, and mainstreaming the roles of the United Nations in peacekeeping in Africa. Obviously, peacekeeping will be ineffective without responding to humanitarian crisis of the moment—especially the plight of the refugees and displaced persons. Care must also be taken to ensure that the emergency assistance is related to reconstruction and development. Post-conflict reconstruction and peace-building phase is the most complex and most difficult to achieve. Such measures require a coordinated international response and could include measures to: re-establish a framework for governance at all levels; reinforce active involvement of the civil society, institutions of moral persuasion as well as for inculcating civic leadership among the youth; create the conditions for jump-starting the economy by restoring key financial, legal, and regulatory institutions; initiate measures to repair social and physical infrastructure; support health and educational needs; promote measures for reactivating dormant capacity for food production; promote measures targeting war-affected populations through reintegration of internally displaced people as well as demobilized combatants and soldiers; revitalize local communities and create a system of financial intermediation through small grants and micro-credit assistance; promote measures for skills development and job creation through apprenticeship program and labour-based rehabilitation works.

After the post-conflict reconstruction phase, the affected countries and their development partners must move forward to build a durable peace and promote economic growth through two key pillars— good governance, and pursuit of sustainable development. On good governance, programs and policies must be put in place to secure respect for human rights and the rule of law; promote transparency and accountability in public administration; enhance administrative capacity, and strengthen democratic governance. To ensure a sustainable long-term development, the stakeholders must work to create a positive environment for investment and economic growth; emphasize social development; and their international development partners must act to restructure international aid, reduce debt burdens, open international markets, support regional cooperation and integration, and harmonize current international and bilateral initiatives. Most importantly, the global governance architecture needs to be strengthened to ensure a more even development of the regions of the world. Prosperity and good governance around the world is the bulwark against armed conflicts and rebel movements.

Sources: Report of the UN-Secretary-General to the Security Council on the Causes of Conflict and the promotion of Durable Peace and Sustainable Development in Africa, April 1998. Achodo, C.C, 2000 "Conflict and Post Conflict Patterns, Issues, Impact on Economic Development and Poverty Cycle in Countries in Africa", paper presented at Africa Forum on Poverty Reduction Strategies, June 5- 9, Yamoussoukro, Côte d'Ivoire.

Box 1.4: Corruption is a Global Phenomenon

Corruption has several ramifications and a watertight definition is often difficult. But in general, corruption is generally understood as the use of public office for private gain. This includes bribery and extortion, which necessarily involves at least two parties, and other types of malfeasance that a public official can carry out alone, including fraud and embezzlement. Appropriations of public assets for private use and embezzlement of public funds by politicians and high-level officials have several direct and indirect costs to a country's economic development.

Although African countries have been rated more corrupt than others in the Transparency International ratings, it does not imply any conclusion that the more underdeveloped a country is, the more corrupt it is likely to be. After all, Botswana is also in Africa and Italy is not a poor country. Corruption is a global issue. Both the first and third world countries have experienced blatant corruption. Corruption International's ranking shows large variations in the perception of corruption among groups of countries at similar stages of development. In fact and contrary to conventional wisdom, pervasive political corruption can be an entrenched element of highly industrialized, democratic societies. It is not merely a by-product of underdevelopment or authoritarianism. Italy's *Mani Pulite* (clean hands) prosecutions against top politicians and business persons, which began in February 1992, led to the investigation of more than 4000 people, the indictment of 1063 and the conviction of 460, including a former prime minister (Bettino Crax) who held office twice. In the late 1990s, a spell of disgrace engulfed significant numbers of German construction companies and many local officials, while Japan's Finance Ministry, long esteemed as a citadel of virtue, is still paralyzed by scandals involving charges of payoffs and favors from big business.

Corruption cuts across international borders. Many cases of corruption reported in emerging economies involved corporations from the first world. Transnational corruption, for example, is particularly rife in the arms trade. A United States Commerce Department confidential annex to a report on international bribery in July 1998, noted that half of the recorded corruption complaints involved arms sales. The ways of concealing foreign bribes are numerous. One often hears of companies effectively setting up bribery funds to buy favors from the governments of developing countries. For example, the Saudi Ministry of Defence officially bans commissions on arms contracts, but bribes have been channeled via obscure companies in Liechtenstein, into Swiss accounts. Sometimes, middleman companies are designated as local subcontractors for 'support' and lavishly overpaid for their services. For example, middlemen pocketed US $24 million on a $1 billion deal for Bell Canada to modernize Morocco's telecommunications industry, despite the fact that the Canadian government and the World Bank were funding it on the condition that commissions were formally forbidden. A middleman Saudi Company, Eastern Trading Services, simply served as the local subcontractor for 'support'.

Closer to home, alleged bribery in the awarding of contracts for the multinational Lesotho Highlands Water Project recently made headline news in South Africa and Lesotho. The Chief Executive of Transparency International South Africa, Dr. Stiaan van der Merwe commented that *"[c]ross-border bribery of officials by international businesses is the most obvious form of corruption ... [and] ... international bribery and corruption will not disappear if we 'clean up' the public sector in the developing world."* Instead, Van der Merwe points out, corruption mostly involves both public and private parties, across boundaries of the developing and industrialised worlds, conspiring to defraud the public, undermine fair trade, waste resources and frustrate development. In short, *"[t]hose who pay bribes are not, as mostly depicted, innocent parties, forced by ruthless officials to provide kickbacks and special favors in return for business"* This has been acknowledged by the 1998 Organization for Economic Co-operation and Development (OECD) convention against corruption that called on each of the 34 country signatories to enact legislation to *"criminalise foreign bribery"* However, by June 1999, only fifteen of the 34 signatories had

Box 1.4: (continued)

passed national legislation and deposited their instruments with the OECD. This indicates that the definitions of "corruption' and 'corrupt parties' are unclear and that the monitoring of corruption across international boundaries – in recognition of its transnational character – still requires further concerted attention.

Source: Odd-Helge Fjeldstad (1998), "Corruption", CMI Working Paper 8.

Corruption

Corruption is yet another hydra-headed phenomenon that has seriously constrained African development. Corruption is illegal everywhere in Africa, but everywhere it seems to be present. The Transparency International ranks African countries among the most corrupt in the world. For African Heads of State, corruption has reached a crisis point in Africa, and this warranted the commissioning of a study on the problem by the African Union in 2002. In September 2002, the AU considered the report, which estimates that corruption costs Africa some U.S.$148 billion per annum, and the AU has drawn up a convention to fight the menace.

Although corruption is not limited to Africa (see Box 1.4), its costs are enormous. It distorts public spending. These distortions occur in three key ways: from shaping the official priorities of government, by deflecting allocated resources away from their original purpose, and by undermining the tax base of government. It distorts sectoral priorities and technology choices by, for example, creating incentives to contract for large defence projects rather than rural health clinics specializing in preventive car. Corruption undermines efficiency by superimposing informal practices over the proper rules and procedures of government. Corruption discourages investment and growth. It impedes long-term foreign and domestic investment, and misallocates talent to rent-seeking activities. Incidences of corruption deter investment because this is a tax on such investment and implies declining profitability of firms.

Furthermore, corruption undermines the quality of governance by first creating distrust, and the uncertainties associated with arbitrary governance feed such trust. Because of corruption, accountability and transparency could be deliberately obstructed. Corrupt politicians and bureaucrats do not want others to have complete information about resource allocations and the basis for decisions. It also undermines the rule of law. Frisch captures this impact on governance by arguing that *"... corruption kills the development spirit. Nothing is as destructive to a society as the rush to quick and easy money which makes fools of those who can work honestly and constructively"*.

While it may be difficult to completely wipe out corruption of every shade, experience shows that purposive and focused actions can significantly reduce it. Some of the causes, especially in poor and transition economies, are known. And there are some tested remedial actions, which African countries can experiment (see Box 1.5).

Box 1.5: Causes and Cures for Corruption

Corruption is widespread in developing and transition countries especially in Africa, not because their people are different from people elsewhere but because conditions are ripe for it. The motivation to earn income is extremely strong, exacerbated by poverty and by low and declining civil service salaries. Furthermore, risks of all kinds [such as illness, accidents, and unemployment] are high in developing countries, and people generally lack the many risk spreading mechanisms [including insurance and a well-developed labour market] available in wealthier countries.

Not only is motivation strong, but also opportunities to engage in corruption are numerous. Monopoly rents can be very large in highly regulated economies, and, as noted previously, corruption breeds demand for more regulation. Further, in transition economies, economic rents are particularly large because of the amount of formerly state-owned property that is essentially up for grabs. The discretion of many public officials is also broad in developing and transition countries, and this systemic weakness is exacerbated by poorly defined, ever changing, and poorly disseminated rules and regulations.

Accountability is typically weak. Political competition and civil liberties are often restricted. Laws and principles of ethics in government are poorly developed, if they exist at all, and the legal institutions charged with enforcing them are ill-prepared for this complex job. The watchdog institutions that provide information on which detection and enforcement is based – such as investigators, accountants, and the press – are also weak. Yet strong investigative powers are critical; because the two parties to a bribe often both benefit, bribery can be extremely difficult to detect. Even if detection is possible, punishments are apt to be mild when corruption is systemic – it is hard to punish one person severely when so many others (often including the "enforcers") are likely to be equally guilty. And the threat of losing one's government job has only a limited deterrent effect when official pay is low. Finally, certain country-specific factors, such as population size and natural resource wealth, also appear to be positively linked with the prevalence of bribery and corruption.

Can corruption be cured?

Even if they acknowledge many of the costs of corruption, skeptics question whether fighting it is worth the bother. The "fatalist" camp often points out the dearth of successes in anticorruption drives and remarks that it took more than a century for England to bring corruption under control. But Hong Kong SAR and Singapore, for example, have shifted reasonably quickly from being very corrupt to being relatively clean. Botswana has been a model of propriety for decades. Chile has performed well for many years, and Poland and Uganda have recently made some progress toward controlling corruption.

What are the most common features of these successes? Anticorruption watchdog bodies, such as the Independent Commission Against Corruption in Hong Kong and smaller corruption-fighting institutions in Botswana, Chile, Malaysia, and Singapore, are often credited with much of the progress. In contrast, the broader economic and institutional reforms that have taken place simultaneously have not received sufficient credit. The government that came to power in Uganda in 1986 implemented a strategy encompassing economic reforms and deregulation, civil service reform, a strengthened auditor general's office, the appointment of a reputable inspector general empowered to investigate and prosecute corruption, and implementation of a public information campaign against corruption. Botswana is an example of a country with sound economic and public sector management policies that, once instituted, led to honest governance early on; its success has not been principally derived from the more recent advent of its anticorruption department.

Thus, one can surmise that to a large extent, corruption is a symptom of fundamental economic, political, and institutional causes. Addressing corruption effectively means tackling these underlying causes. The major emphasis must be put on prevention – that is, on reforming economic policies, institutions, and incentives. Efforts to improve

Box 1.5: (Continued)

enforcement of anticorruption legislation using the police, ethics offices, or special watchdog agencies within government will not bear fruit otherwise. The following are only some of the major economic policy changes that will unambiguously reduce opportunities for corruption: lowering tariffs and other barriers to international trade; unifying market – determined exchange rates and interest rates; eliminating enterprise subsidies; minimizing regulations, licensing requirements, and other barriers to entry for new firms and investors; demonopolizing and privatizing government assets; and transparently prudential banking regulations and auditing and accounting standards. The reform of government institutions may include civil service reform; improved budgeting, financial management, and tax administrations; and strengthened legal and judicial systems. Such reforms should involve changing government structures and procedures, placing greater focus on internal competition and incentives in complement to these broader reforms, the careful and transparent implementation of enforcement measures, such as prosecuting some prominent corrupt figures, can also have an impact.

A comprehensive list of all possible anticorruption measures might include many not mentioned above. Emphasis should be placed on selecting the key measures to be implemented, in line with a country's implementation capabilities, during the first and subsequent stages of an anticorruption campaign. The entrenched nature of systemic cor-

ruption requires boldness in implementation – incrementalism is unlikely to work. Since windows of opportunity to take action against corruption have recently opened up in many countries, reformers will want to move quickly beyond the general first principles usually listed in the literature on corruption and instead demand practical, country – specific advice. After careful country assessments are prepared, specific policy and institutional advice will need to be provided. For instance, technocratic lessons are beginning to emerge as to how different privatization methodologies may contain greater or lesser opportunities for corruption, how the strengthening of banking regulations needs to reflect the particular lessons the country has learned about dealing with perverse political influences, and how specific innovations in procurement and bidding methods can reduce opportunities for corruption.

In parts of Africa, efforts are being made to confront this problem. The AU convention contains some 'best practice' rules and action agenda for corruption eradication and countries that sign up for it are required to conform to the tenets of the convention. In much of Southern Africa, efforts are targeted at four levels—prevention, investigation, prosecution and civic awareness. Several improvements have also been observed in some countries since the Lima Declaration— which highlighted the need for a global coalition targeted at the institution of transparency, accountability and integrity.

Source: C.W. Gray and D. Kaufman (2002), "Corruption and Development", in Finance and Development, IMF.

Competitiveness as key to long-term sustainability

With appropriate responses to prevent and resolve conflicts, and also significantly reduce corruption, attention must begin to be focused on long-term prosperity of the economies through competitiveness—to develop ca-

pabilities and increase productivity through concerted innovation and learning. Industrial competitiveness (especially manufacturing) is the potent engine of sustainable growth in developing countries in today's globalizing world. Industry is the main source, user and diffuser of technological progress, drives innovation; diffusing innovation, developing new skills and attitudes, leading institutional development, generating dynamic comparative advantages, stimulating modern services, and modernizing enterprises. Part of Africa's quest for diversification away from dependence on few primary commodities with volatile terms of trade must embrace industrial competitiveness (especially labour-intensive manufactures) as the key.

The United Nations Industrial Development Organization (UNIDO) has developed the competitive industrial performance (CIP) index that measures the ability of countries to produce and export manufactures competitively. The index is constructed from four indicators: manufacturing value added per capita, manufactured exports per capita, and the shares of medium- and high-tech products in manufacturing value-added and in manufactured exports. A ranking of 87 countries in the world (based on availability of data for cross country comparisons) shows that African countries weigh heavily at the bottom of the league table. It is not only that low-income economies remained at the bottom in the CIP index but also that the gap between them and other economies widened during the period 1985- 1998. Evidence indicates that 42 developing countries had a technology structure in 1998 similar to that in 1985. The top 5 countries account for about 60 percent of developing country industrial output and 61 percent of exports, whereas the bottom 30 countries account for only 2 percent of output and 1 percent of exports. These shares indeed declined during the 1985- 98 period. Particularly for Africa, the continuous loss of global market shares in both traditional and non-traditional products is a worrisome phenomenon.

The reasons for the woeful performance of African economies are legion and cannot be fully elaborated upon here. They range from factors related to geography and demography, conflicts and corruption, bad governance and institutions, poor policies, external shocks, including constraints imposed by global trading and financial system.

Whatever the causes, Africa needs to diversify and be competitive. There is really no real alternative. The challenges of becoming competitive in an increasingly globalizing world, especially for latecomer industrializers in Africa are enormous but not insurmountable. Useful lessons could be learnt from other countries' experiences, and innovative approaches need to be crafted to respond to the changing world (see Box 1.6). In the last decade, better-managed African economies are seeing their exports of non-traditional products soar by more than 30 percent per annum, albeit from a low base. This demonstrates the possibilities that exist, and the difference which sound policy reforms can make.

Box 1.6: Strategy and interventions to promote competitiveness

The recent UNIDO's Industrial Development Report 2002/03 shows that successful developing countries have used widely differing strategies to build industrial capabilities and compete in world markets: building capabilities through domestic research and development (R&D), through foreign direct investment or through a combination of the two. Some, but relatively few, have succeeded by drawing in foreign technology largely at arm's length while building strong technological and innovative capabilities in local firms. Others, a large number, have gone some way by plugging into global value chains, becoming suppliers of labour-intensive products and components, without having strong domestic capabilities. Of these economies, a few have managed to combine their reliance on foreign direct investment with strong industrial policy, targeting the activities they wish to enter and the functions they wish to upgrade. Others have tapped the potential of foreign direct investment by more passive policies, benefiting from sound economic management, pro-business attitudes, attractive locations and plain good luck. The less successful countries have not managed to follow any of these strategies effectively.

It might seem that the best strategy for countries without strong technological capabilities is to find their way into the production systems of global value chains and let local capabilities develop slowly. While recent experience of global production systems shows that this works, some caution must be exercised. Latecomers entering global production system might find it difficult to sustain growth as wages rise— unless they can raise their skill, technological and institutional bases. Plugging into global value chains does not by itself ensure that participants will upgrade their capabilities. Yet such upgrading is essential. Moreover, global production systems are highly concentrated, and the concentration rises with the sophistication of the technology.

With globalization and liberalization on the rise, economies must be internationally competitive to prosper and grow. Production across national boundaries is being integrated under common ownership or control—often in the hands of a small number of large private companies—making it even more difficult to isolate economies from world market forces. Technical change is underpinning these processes. The result is that enterprises are exposed to global competition with an immediacy and intensity rarely seen before.

Can African governments provide support institutions to help their firms compete? The UNIDO Report is affirmative. It details how support institutions can help firms meet the information, skill, finance and other needs that are difficult to satisfy in open markets. Thus, a nurturing environment is what is required to foster vibrant industrial services. Many of these services are supplied through the market in industrial countries, but even these countries find it necessary to augment what is supplied through the market with subsidized services. Some of these services might include:

Basic industrial services (promote inward investment, provide export services, provide management services such collecting marketing information, managerial consulting, etc)

Technology information centers (provide information technology to firms, including networks, software, internet capabilities, intranet, and databases; provide training in information technology applications

Metrology, Standards, Testing, and Quality Control Centres—define domestic standards, assist firms in meeting international organization for standardization compliance standards, help firms with calibration of instruments.

Productivity centers—improve quality, productivity, efficiency, provide training

Technological Extension Agencies— provide information on available technology, promote cooperation of small and medium-size enterprises with larger research and cluster initiatives

Research and Development Laboratories—design new processes and products, train businesses through demonstration, participation and extension, implement new technologies.

Source: UNIDO (2002), Industrial Development Report 2002/2003, Competing Through Innovation and Learning, UNIDO.

CHAPTER 2
Regional Economic Profiles

Introduction

This chapter focuses on economic performance in Africa in the framework of the five sub-regional groupings into which Bank Group operations are classified namely, Central Africa, East Africa, North Africa, Southern Africa, and West Africa. The analysis of the regional economic performances are intended to deepen the general analysis of the economic performance of the continent given in Chapter 1. For each of the sub-regions, in addition to an overview of the sub-regional performance, the chapter discusses in some detail the country performances, highlighting the major changes that occurred during the year. The analysis focuses on the recent economic trends, policy developments, and outlook for the years immediately ahead.

Table 2.1 summarizes the sub-regions' real GDP growth rates, as well as share in Africa's GDP, exports, and population. It shows that growth in Eastern, Northern, and Western Africa decelerated in 2002, compared with their respective average year trend in 1998-2001. By contrast, Central and Southern Africa recorded the highest and second highest growth rates on the continent in 2002, at 5.5 percent and 3.4 percent, respectively. Northern Africa remains by far the largest wealth contributor in Africa, accounting for 44.6 percent of its GDP in 2002, while more than 70 percent of Africa's exports originated in North and Southern Africa. This highlights the many disparities that exist across Africa's sub-regional groupings.

Table 2.1: A Sub-Regional Overwiew of African Economies

	Average Real GDP Growth 1998-2001	2002[a]			
		Real GDP Growth	Share in Africa's GDP	Share in Africa's Exports[b]	Share in Total Population
Central Africa	1.8	5.5	5.6	6.7	12.3
Eastern Africa	3.9	2.8	8.2	6.5	23.2
Northen Africa	3.9	2.5	44.6	35.3	22.1
Southern Africa	2.5	3.4	26.1	35.5	14.4
Western Africa	3.1	1.7	15.5	16.0	28.1
Franc Zone	3.8	4.6	9.6	17.5	13.1
Net Oil Exporters	3.6	2.2	48.3	67.8	32.7
Net Oil Importers	3.0	3.3	51.7	32.2	67.3
ALL RMCs	**3.3**	**2.8**	-	-	-

Notes: a/ Preliminary estimates
         b/ Exports of Goods & Nonfactor Services at Current Market Prices
Sources: ADB Development Research and Statistics Divisions.

Central Africa

Ten countries constitute Central Africa: Cameroon, Central African Republic (CAR), Chad, Congo, Equatorial Guinea, and Gabon (which are all CFA zone countries) and Burundi, the Democratic Republic of Congo (DRC), Rwanda and Sao Tome and Principe. Military and civil conflicts, most notably in the Great Lakes region, have long prevented Central Africa to fully exploit its abundant natural resources and rich agricultural land. As a result, Central Africa's contribution to continental GDP is the lowest amongst the sub-regions, accounting for 5.6 percent of the continental gross output in 2002. The strengthening of the peace process in the DRC since 2001 has nonetheless improved the region's economic prospects.

Cameroon, Congo, Gabon and Equatorial Guinea are major oil exporters in the sub-region. The DRC has great export potentials in minerals, including copper, cobalt, and diamonds. Other main exports in the sub-region include timber, coffee, cocoa, and cotton. Central Africa's exports made up 6.7 percent of the continental total in 2002.

Economic growth in the region has failed to match that of the population, leading to a continuous decline in GDP per capita. Total population in Central Africa represented 12.3 percent of the continental total. The region's GDP per capita averaged $292 in 2002, against a continental average of $646. This hides wide disparities, however, with GDP per capita in Gabon and Equatorial Guinea reaching $3923 and $4461, respectively in 2002.

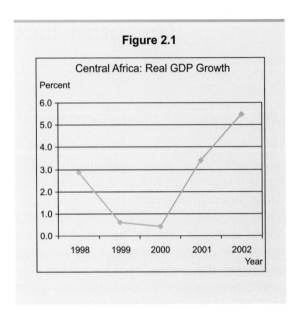

Figure 2.1

Central Africa: Real GDP Growth

Recent Trends in the Domestic Economy

Growth in Central Africa accelerated from 1.8 percent in 1998-2001 to 5.5 percent in 2002, fuelled by post-war economic recovery in DRC and fast oil development in Equatorial Guinea and Chad (Table 2.2 and Figures 2.1 and 2.2). This compares favorably with the continental growth average of 2.8 percent in 2002. All countries fared better than in 2001, but for Cameroon, Gabon, and Rwanda. The gross domestic investment-to-GDP ratio for the region as a whole averaged 21.1 percent in 2002 (Figure 2.3), with Chad securing the highest investment rate in the region that year. Inflation in Central Africa averaged 4.3 percent in 2002, down from 5.4 percent in 1998-2001 (Figure 2.4). This reflects tight monetary and fiscal policies in CFA zone countries and successful macroeconomic stabilization in DRC. Inflationary pressures nonetheless mounted

Table 2.2: Central Africa: Gross Domestic Product and Export Performances

Country	Real GDP Growth Rate (%)		GDP Per Capita (US$)		Real Exports[c] Growth (%)		Exports[b] Per Capita (US$)	
	Average 1998-2001	2002[a]	Average 1998-2001	2002[a]	Average 1998-2001	2002[a]	Average 1998-2001	2002[a]
BURUNDI	1.3	3.0	116	97	23.3	36.2	9	8
CAMEROON	4.7	4.4	590	607	5.5	1.2	169	145
CENTRAL AFRICAN REP.	2.3	4.0	272	272	-9.5	15.7	51	43
CHAD	4.9	10.9	202	230	-2.3	8.4	33	23
CONGO, DEM. REP. OF	-4.1	3.0	91	86	-6.9	18.7	21	20
CONGO, REPUBLIC OF	3.0	3.9	860	943	2.5	13.5	676	712
EQUATORIAL GUINEA	31.4	30.4	2471	4461	6.4	4.7	2279	4360
GABON	-1.2	1.0	3902	3923	-9.0	-1.3	2373	1943
RWANDA	7.3	6.5	259	215	11.4	-5.2	18	17
SAO TOME & PRINCIPE	3.0	5.0	332	356	11.0	30.2	114	140
CENTRAL AFRICA	**1.8**	**5.5**	**283**	**292**	**3.2**	**12.2**	**107**	**106**

Notes: a/ Preliminary estimates
  b/ Exports of Goods and Nonfactor Services at Market Prices
  c/ Real Exports of Goods and Non Factors Services Growth
Sources: ADB Development Research and Statistics Divisions.

Figure 2.2

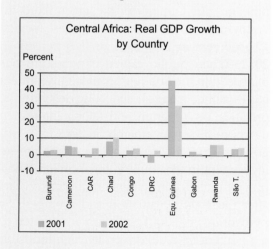

Central Africa: Real GDP Growth by Country

Figure 2.3

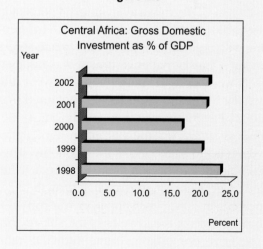

Central Africa: Gross Domestic Investment as % of GDP

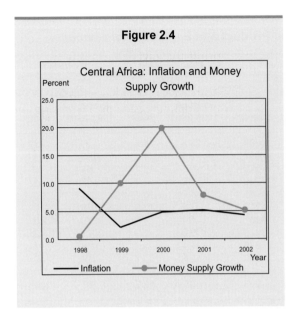

Figure 2.4

Central Africa: Inflation and Money Supply Growth

in 2002 for some countries, because of strong demand and food shortages.

Almost a decade of civil war has destroyed much of **Burundi**'s administrative capacity, basic infrastructure and manufacturing base. As a result, growth has been either low or negative, with real GDP growth averaging 1.3 percent in 1998-2001 (Table 2.2 and Figure 2.2). In keeping with the August 2000 Arusha peace agreement, a transitional government was installed in November 2001, but fighting between the regular army and Hutu rebels continued into 2002. Favorable weather conditions nonetheless stimulated the output in agriculture, which is the backbone of the economy. This, combined with buoyant construction activity, led an acceleration in real GDP growth to 3.0 percent in 2002. Investment in war-torn Burundi is one of the lowests in the sub-region. The gross domestic investment-to-GDP ratio averaged 8.5 percent in 1998-2001, rising to 12.0 percent in 2002. A drop in domestic pro-

duction, increased import costs, notably fuel, and rapid monetary expansion led to high inflation rates through most of the 1990s. Inflation has fallen since 2001, as a result of a recovery in food production and tighter fiscal and monetary policy. Overall, consumer prices rose by an average of 12.4 percent in 1998-2001, before declining by 2.7 percent in 2002, as a result of bumper harvests.

Cameroon has had post a robust economic growth since 1996, a result of a stronger commitment to reforms following the CFA franc devaluation in 1994. Economic growth averaged an annual 4.7 percent in 1998-2001, which is above population growth. Cameroon has developed a well-diversified economy outside its oil sector. Real GDP growth nonetheless decelerated to 4.4 percent in 2002, largely because of a fall in domestic oil production. Growth was mostly driven by good performance in agriculture (bad weather had disrupted cash and food crops in 2001), and a dynamic construction sector (with notably, the construction of the Chad-Cameroon gas pipeline). In Cameroon, the gross fixed investment-to- GDP increased from an average 17.6 percent in 1998-2001 to 18.6 percent in 2002. While public capital expenditure has increased in the last years, private investment has remained sluggish, reflecting delays in the privatization program and falling interest in the non-oil sector, notably in forestry. Poor governance is the main impediment to private investment in the country. Inflation in Cameroon returned to single digit numbers two years after the 1994 devaluation and averaged 2.4 percent in 1998-2001. Inflation accelerated to 4.0 percent in 2002, driven by high foodstuff prices, as a result of poor agricultural performance the previous year.

Weak economic management and political instability have hindered economic progress in **Central African Republic (CAR)**. Real GDP growth notably turned negative in 1996, as a result of violent political and social unrest. There was an energy crisis in 2000, followed by another damaging period of political instability in 2001. As a result, GDP grew by a low 2.8 percent a year in 1998-2001, before accelerating to 4.0 percent in 2002, as improved security in the country, and the region as a whole, spurred transportation and trade activities. Mining and agriculture are the mainstay of this landlocked economy. Already low by regional standards, the gross domestic investment-to-GDP ratio in CAR has declined continuously since 2000, owing to rising political instability and falling capital spending by the government. CAR inflation has remained subdued by virtue of the country's membership to the Franc Zone, averaging 1.1 percent in 1998-2001 and 3.0 percent in 2002.

Development prospects in **Chad** have improved dramatically with the construction of the Chad-Cameroon gas pipeline and the Dolba oil project, with real GDP growing by 8.5 percent in 2001 and 10.9 percent in 2002. While unprecedented, growth in 2002 was somewhat dampened by the decline in the world price of cotton, Chad's main export commodity. Oil and gas production is due to start in early 2004. Gross domestic investment in Chad jumped with the Dolba and oil pipeline project from an average 22.5 percent of GDP in 1998-2001 to 58.8 percent of GDP in 2002. Poor harvests and the surge in domestic demand emanating from oil workers pushed inflation up to 12.4 percent in 2002, against a yearly average 3.8 percent in 1998-2001.

Economic growth in the **DRC** turned positive in 2002, ending six years of continuous decline during the civil war, with real GDP falling by an average 4.1 percent a year between 1998 and 2001. Beside continued progress in consolidating peace and fostering the inter-Congolese dialogue, donor confidence was further boosted by the IMF approval of a Poverty Reduction and Growth Facility (PRGF) in June 2002. The resumption of public investment and donor-funded projects has underpinned the reconstruction process, with real GDP rising by 3 percent in 2002. The gross fixed investment-to-GDP ratio in DRC started to rise since 2000, as a result of peace consolidation. It was estimated at 10.7 percent in 2002. Inflation has slowed down as a result of tighter fiscal and monetary policy and fell to a two-digit number for the first time in 2002, when it averaged 25.0 percent. This compares with an annual average inflation rate of 322.2 percent in 1998-2001.

The non-oil sector in **Congo** suffered a substantial setback from the 1997-99 civil war, while the oil sector continued to grow. This helped to sustain economic activities and finance public spending. The normalization of the political situation in 2000 led to a strong recovery in the non-oil sector, but oil production started to decline that year, which dampened the overall growth performance. Lower oil production coupled with resumed rebel activities in the Pool region also slowed economic recovery in 2002, with real GDP still growing by 3.9 percent. Congo benefited from relatively high rates of investment despite the civil war in 1997-1999, because of continued foreign interest in the oil sector. Investment in this sector has slowed down in recent years. This has been partly offset by the resumption of public investment under the government's post-war reconstruction program. Congo's inflation averaged 2.7 percent a year in 1998-2001, rising to 7.6 percent in 2002.

By far the most impressive economic performance in the region remains that of **Equatorial Guinea**. The country has enjoyed phenomenal rates of growth since large oil reserves started to be exploited in the mid-1990s. Real GDP growth averaged 31.4 percent a year in 1998-2001. In 2002, real GDP grew by a further 30.4 percent, the fastest rate of growth in the world. The oil discovery has fuelled activities in construction and services, but the economy has stagnated elsewhere, most notably in agriculture. Fuelled by continued activity in oil exploration and construction, the investment-to-GDP ratio averaged 62.9 percent in 1998-2001, before dropping to an all time low of 18.9 percent. Inflation in Equatorial Guinea, which is a Franc Zone member, averaged 4.4 percent a year in 1998-2001 and 6.0 percent in 2002, which is remarkably low in the context of strong economic growth.

Gabon, which is the second most important economy in the region, relies heavily on oil. Domestic oil production has fallen since 1997, because of depleting reserves. Growth averaged a negative 1.2 percent a year between 1998 and 2001, as a result. Real GDP grew by an estimated 1 percent in 2002, mostly reflecting investment in the timber industry. Momentum to diversify the economy away from the oil sector has been slow, the country still having one of the highest GDP per capita in Africa. Gross domestic investment in Gabon was at its peak in the 1970s and 1980s, as a result of fast oil development and large public spending. The gross fixed investment-to-GDP ratio fell to an average 25.8 percent in 1998-2001 and was

estimated at 22.7 percent in 2002. Inflation in Gabon averaged 1.1 percent a year in 1998-2001 and 2.3 percent in 2002, reflecting economic stagnation and Franc Zone membership.

Economic prospects in **Rwanda** have steadily improved since the end of the military and civil conflict in 1995, as strong external assistance spurred activities in manufacturing, construction, and services. The agricultural sector also performed relatively well, notwithstanding the slump in the world prices of coffee and tea, Rwanda's main exports. Real GDP growth was put at 6.5 percent in 2002. Gross domestic investment in Rwanda has resumed in recent years, largely reflecting an expansion in public investment. Its ratio to GDP was estimated at 18.8 percent in 2002, against an average 17.0 percent in 1998-2001. Stringent fiscal and monetary policy since the end of the civil war has led to a continued fall in inflation from 48.2 percent in 1995 (when the Rwandan franc was devalued) to 3.4 percent in 1998-2001 and 3.5 percent in 2002.

Economic growth in **Sao Tome and Principe** has lagged behind population growth through most of the past decade. Strong expansion in food and cash crop production, construction, and trade, nonetheless pointed to a marked acceleration in real GDP growth in 2002, while also largely reflecting a joint settlement with Nigeria over oil exploration and improved macroeconomic stability. Sao Tome and Principe's investment rate is high by regional standards, accounting for 44.8 percent of GDP in 2002, against a regional 21.1 percent. A tightening in monetary policy since 1998 has brought inflation down from 19.6 percent in 1998-2001 to a higher than projected 9.0 percent in 2002, reflecting adjustments in water and electricity that year.

Recent Policy Developments

Poverty alleviation strategy

All countries but medium income **Gabon** and **Equatorial Guinea** have sought to formulate their poverty reduction programs within the framework of the Enhanced Heavily indebted poor country (HIPC) debt relief initiative sponsored by the IMF, World Bank and African Development Bank. Rwanda released its final Poverty reduction strategy papers (PRSP) in 2002, through conducting wide-ranging household surveys and seeking the participation of the civil society and donors. The Rwandan government has set ambitious and well-documented goals for poverty alleviation, identifying six priority areas, namely, rural development, human development, economic infrastructure, good governance, private sector development, and institutional capacity building.

In **Cameroon**, the final version of the PRSP was expected by mid-2002, but it has yet to be completed. In keeping with the 2000 interim PRSP, the main priorities of the program are to improve the quality and access to public services in health and education, rehabilitate infrastructures, and pursue reforms to strengthen public administration and fight corruption. The completion process has also been delayed in **CAR**, **Chad**, and **Sao Tome and Principe**, which all released an interim version of their PRSPs in 2000. Although governments in **Burundi** and **Congo** have made some progress in drawing a national poverty reduction program as part of their negotiations for a financial deal with the IMF, the DRC was the only country in the region to publish an interim PRSP in 2002. The document centers the country's poverty alleviation strategy on peace consolidation, economic stabilization and post-war reconstruction.

While not qualifying for HIPC debt relief, the **Gabon** government has also started to work on the formulation of a national poverty alleviation strategy since 2000; a first draft was presented to donors in 2001. The government in **Equatorial Guinea** has no poverty alleviation program. Income inequality is particularly high in this country, most citizens living well beyond the reach of the average per capita GDP of US$4461.

Privatization

Privatization in Central Africa is progressing slowly. Many countries in the region have notably recorded very little privatization activity in recent years, owing to a combination of factors, ranging from political instability, lack of foreign interest, low government commitment, or simple lack of viable state-owned enterprises (SOEs).

Privatization is not on **Burundi**'s immediate agenda, peace consolidation being the utmost priority. There are more than 50 public enterprises in the country. While on the reform agenda since 1990, privatization in **Cameroon** kick-started in the late 1990s, as the government previously favored public enterprises restructuring. A number of state-owned enterprises in banking and insurance, agro-industry, forestry and transport were sold between 1997 and 2000. Public utilities were meanwhile added to the list of enterprises to be privatized, and Sonel (electricity) was sold in 2001. The government has since encountered difficulties in meeting its privatization targets. Cameroon Development Corporation (CDC) was the only state-owned enterprise to be sold in 2002. Negotiations with strategic investors over their participation in Camtel (telecommunication) and SNEC (water) broke down, and there was further delay in the preparation for sale of Sodecoton. Other enterprises likely to be privatized include Cameroon airlines, SCDP (petroleum storage facility) and the commercial side of the port of Daoula.

The pace of privatization in **CAR** has been slow. In the oil sector, Petroca, the public company responsible for petroleum distribution and storage, was liquidated in 2000 and replaced by private interests. Two commercial banks were privatized in 1999. Enterprises currently reviewed for privatization include BARC (freight), Sogesca (sugar), Enerca (electricity), Socatel (telecommunication), and SNE (water). In Chad, a tender for the sale of DHS, the oil and soap unit of Cotontchad, was issued in May 2002 and a study looking into the privatization options of Cotontchad has been commissioned. The main enterprises that have been privatized since the program was launched in the early 1990s are STEE (water), Sonasut (sugar) and SNER (road maintenance).

In **Congo**, the civil war halted the divestiture program started in the mid-1990s. A new program, which included the sale of five major utilities (petroleum distribution, transportation, telecommunications, power and water distribution), was launched in 2000. In 2002, the management of SNDE (water) was handed over to a private company, while petroleum distribution, previously under the monopoly of Hydro-Congo, was privatized. Other state-owned utilities earmarked for sale include CFCO (railway) and Coraf (oil refinery). The **DRC** had plans to establish a privatization timetable by end-September 2002. The government in Equatorial Guinea has made a nominal commitment to privatization but has yet to draw a program.

Only a handful of state-owned enterprises have been sold in **Gabon**, since the privatization program was initiated in 1997. In fact, the program has been stalled for more than two years, the last divestiture being that of Cimgabon (cement) in 2000. Other enterprises privatized include SEEG (power and water, 1997) and Sosuho (sugar, 1998). The government has failed to find any buyer for Hevegab (rubber), Gabon Telecom (telecommunication) and Air Gabon, reflecting poor market conditions and the companies' poor financial state.

Some 72 state-owned enterprises were slated for privatization in **Rwanda**, when the program was launched in 1996. All were due to be sold by end-2001, but this has proved over-ambitious, with only 23 enterprises divested so far. Focus in 2002 was on the preparation of the sale of Electrogaz (electricity), Rwandatel (telecom), Rwandex (coffee and hide exports), and tea state-owned factories and estates. Two bidders have been short-listed to take over the management of Electrogaz, with a final decision expected in 2003.

In **Sao Tome and Principe**, the focus switched from land redistribution from the state to farmers in the mid-1990s to privatization of major utilities from 1999 onwards. The government has sold 40 to 50 percent of its shares in ENCO (petroleum distribution), CST (telecom) and Air Sao Tome and Principe. EMAE (water and electricity) is also due to be privatized.

Fiscal developments

The region's fiscal position largely reflects fluctuations in government earnings from the oil sector. Overall, the region achieved a small fiscal surplus (1.37 percent of GDP) in 2002 (Figure 2.5), as a result of firm oil prices. This

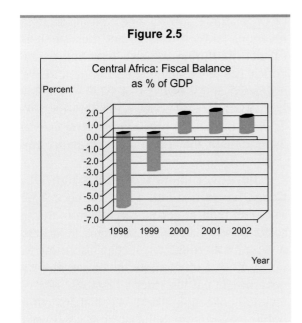

Figure 2.5

Central Africa: Fiscal Balance as % of GDP

compares with an average deficit of 1.4 percent of GDP during 1998-2001 (Table 2.3).

The government's fiscal position in **Burundi** deteriorated with the onset of the civil war, because of a drop in revenue collection and increased military spending. Tax revenue collection has nonetheless strengthened in recent years, which, coupled with the timid resumption of donor support, has helped to maintain the average fiscal deficit at a still high 4.8 percent of GDP in 1998-2001, rising to 5.3 percent of GDP in 2002.

Cameroon's fiscal position has improved with the CFA franc devaluation. On the revenue side, lesser tax and customs exemptions, the strengthening of administrative capacity and the introduction of a value-added tax in 1999 have helped to increase the domestic

Table 2.3: Central Africa: Macroeconomic Management Indicators

Country	Inflation (%)		Fiscal Balance as % of GDP		Gross Domestic Investment		Gross National Savings	
					as % of GDP			
	Average 1998-2001	2002[a]	Average 1998-2001	2002[a]	Average 1998-2001	2002[a]	Average 1998-2001	2002[a]
BURUNDI	12.4	-2.7	-4.8	-5.3	8.5	12.0	2.9	3.7
CAMEROON	2.4	4.0	-0.2	1.7	17.6	18.6	14.9	12.6
CENTRAL AFRICAN REP.	1.1	3.0	-0.8	-1.3	10.2	10.0	6.3	4.3
CHAD	3.8	6.0	-5.1	-12.7	22.5	58.8	3.3	5.3
CONGO, DEM. REP. OF	322.2	25.0	-4.6	-3.2	10.5	10.7	8.7	4.5
CONGO, REPUBLIC OF	2.7	7.6	-5.9	0.8	25.7	29.3	17.7	28.9
EQUATORIAL GUINEA	4.4	6.0	5.4	22.4	62.9	18.9	5.6	18.1
GABON	1.1	2.3	0.9	4.8	25.8	22.7	20.8	14.2
RWANDA	3.4	3.5	-1.9	-0.6	17.0	18.8	10.6	12.8
SAO TOME & PRINCIPE	19.6	9.0	-22.6	-6.3	42.3	44.8	22.6	25.4
CENTRAL AFRICA	**5.4**	**4.2**	**-1.4**	**1.37**	**20.1**	**21.1**	**13.4**	**12.6**

Note: a/ Preliminary estimates

Sources: ADB Development Research and Statistics Divisions.

revenue-to-GDP ratio. Recent measures have also been taken to improve public expenditure management and increase the share of expenditures towards social sectors. Cameroon's overall government balance has been in surplus since 2000, as a result of strong revenues from the oil sector, rising to 1.7 percent of GDP in 2002. This is to be compared with a fiscal deficit of 3.2 percent of GDP in 1999, in the context of depressed world oil prices.

Improving the domestic tax efforts has proved slow in **Central African Republic**. A value-added tax was introduced in 2001, but there is still great scope for lesser tax and customs exemptions and fighting fiscal evasion. The government has been relatively successful in reining in recurrent expenditures, by notably trimming public sector employment. It is, however, still struggling to settle months of salary arrears. Budget support has nonetheless helped to maintain an overall government deficit of less than 1 percent of GDP in 1998-2001, rising to 1.3 percent of GDP in 2002, as a result of rising political unrest.

Although a value-added tax was introduced in 2000 and measures have been taken to strengthen revenue collection, most notably customs, the domestic revenue-to-GDP ratio in **Chad** continues to be one of the lowest in Africa. The country's fiscal deficit is largely structural. It surged from an average 5.1 percent of GDP in 1998-2001 to 12.7 percent of GDP in 2002, indicating rising public investment in the context of oil development and strong external borrowing. The deficit is set to fall, as the government starts receiving proceeds from the oil sector.

The government in **DRC** has made some progress in rehabilitating public finances since 2000. Military spending, the collapse

of expenditure control, and a slump in fiscal revenues had led to large and persistent fiscal deficits during the civil war. The overall deficit has since fallen significantly and was estimated at 3.2 percent of GDP in 2002. A key aspect of fiscal policy is to fight a plethora of extra-budgetary procedures, centralize all expenditures and receipts, and enhance revenue collection.

The government's overall balance in **Congo** has turned into a surplus since 2000, as higher than projected receipts from the oil sector more than offset shortfalls in non-oil revenue collection. Oil receipts account for up to a third of domestic revenues, but the government has also tried to increase non-oil revenue collection. There was a sharp cut in public expenditure in the late 1990s, owing to reduced military spending and wage-cutting measures. The cost of organizing the national dialogue was nonetheless higher than planned in 2001 and domestic payment arrears have continued to pile up as a result. The fiscal surplus was put at 0.8 percent of GDP in 2002.

Despite rapidly growing oil revenue, the overall government balance in **Equatorial Guinea** was in deficit through most of the last decade, as the government went on a spending spree. Beside lacking fiscal discipline, there is a problem of transparency, with notably the multiplication of extra-budgetary procedures. The overall balance has nonetheless been in surplus since 1999 and amounted to 22.4 percent of GDP in 2002, owing to strong oil revenues.

The overall government balance in **Gabon** was in surplus until 1998, when a slump in world oil prices, combined with extra-budgetary expenditures, led to a sharp deterioration in public finances. The government has since cut down on recurrent expenditures and stepped up its efforts to increase non-oil tax revenue, by notably strengthening tax and custom administration. The overall balance returned into a small surplus in 1999, rising to 4.8 percent of GDP in 2002.

Helped with strong donor support, the **Rwanda** government has maintained a sound fiscal stance through most of the last decade. The overall government deficit averaged an annual 1.9 percent of GDP in 1998-2001, falling to 0.6 percent of GDP in 2002. This partly reflects generous grants and the government's efforts to strengthen custom and tax administration. Recent fiscal measures included the introduction of a value-added tax in 2001 and the lowering of import tariffs. Concerning expenditures, attention has switched to social spending allocation and monitoring. Priority expenditure as a ratio to GDP has almost doubled in the last five years and was equivalent to 5.3 percent in 2002.

The fiscal situation in **Sao Tome and Principe** is still fragile, although the government has made some progress in broadening the tax base in recent years. Improving public expenditure management, increasing outlays for education and health, and reducing the number of civil servants, are all part of the government's agenda. Over-spending is still frequent, however. The overall government deficit was estimated at 6.3 percent of GDP in 2002, down on 22.6 percent of GDP in 1998-2001.

Monetary and exchange rate developments

Monetary policy in the Central African CFA zone is dictated by the regional central bank, Banque des Etats d'Afrique Central (BEAC). In 2002, money supply growth declined to 5.1 percent from 7.8 percent in 2001 (Figure 2.4). All CFA countries share the same currency, the CFA franc, which is pegged to the euro at a rate of CFAfr656: 1. Foreign reserves are pooled together in an operation account held at the French Public Treasury, which in turn guarantees the stability and convertibility of the regional currency. The CFA franc is by far the most stable currency in the region and in Africa as a whole. The external value of the CFA franc was devalued by 50 percent in 1994, the first parity re-adjustment in 49 years of existence. An inter-bank and money market was set up in the wake of the CFA franc devaluation in a bid to modernize BEAC's monetary policy, but it has lacked effectiveness, because of the region's excess liquidity and poor regional financial integration. Statutory reserve requirements for commercial bank have become effective since September 2001. Interest rate adjustments remain rare. The BEAC cut its rediscount rate from 6.5 percent to 6.35 percent in April 2002, in the context of falling world interest rates. The BEAC has plans to introduce government bonds by 2004. At a country level, bank credit to the private sector has been roughly in line with the level of economy activity, while some countries have set ceilings on net bank credit to the central government as one of their quantitative benchmarks. Safeguard measures underpinning the Franc Zone monetary arrangements reduce the risk of slippage: the BEAC is required to maintain 20 percent foreign exchange to cover its sight liabilities and governments are only allowed to draw a maximum of 20 percent of the previous year's budget receipts from the central bank. The CFA franc lost up to 25 percent of its dollar value after the launch of the European currency in January 1999. The depreciation of the currency slowed in 2001 and by the end of 2002, the CFA franc had recovered some of its external value. The exchange rate averaged CFAfr680:$1 in 2002, against CFAfr733:$1 in 2001 and CFAfr712:$1 in 2000.

The Bank of the Republic of **Burundi** (BRB) relaxed its monetary stance with the onset of the civil war to finance growing fiscal deficits. Credit to the government has since been markedly reduced. The BRB's lending policy to commercial banks was lax until late 2000, when a ceiling on bank refinancing was introduced, rules on reserve requirements re-inforced, and the refinancing rate increased from 12 percent to 14 percent. This tighter monetary stance was roughly maintained in 2001 and 2002. As a result, there has been a marked slowdown in money supply growth. Although interest rates are still negative in real terms, the BRB intends to make greater use of indirect instruments and set up a money market. The Burundi franc is pegged to a weighted basket of currencies. Despite successive devaluations, the gap between the official and parallel exchange rate remained wide through most of the 1990s. The government has adopted a more flexible exchange rate policy since 2000, by introducing foreign exchange auctions market and liberalizing change transactions. Deteriorating terms of trade nonetheless prompted a 20 percent devaluation of the Burundi franc in August 2002.

Lacking independence, the Banque centrale du Congo (BCC) had to print money through most of the 1990s to cover growing central government and public enterprises deficits. A new currency, the Congolese franc was introduced in the **DRC** in 1998 to replace the nouveau Zaire, introduced in 1993. Parity with the dollar was fixed. But excess money supply led to renewed hyperinflation, a free fall in the new currency, and the dollarization of the economy. A floating exchange rate system was finally introduced in May 2001. Inflation and the depreciation of the franc have since slowed down, as bold steps were taken to make monetary policy more effective. In 2002, lower inflationary pressure prompted a cut in the rediscount rate from 140 percent in June 2001 to 90 percent in January 2002. New BCC statutes that enshrine its independence in the conduct of monetary policy were published in 2002. The bank is currently undergoing a financial audit to improve its financial position and internal management, but it is the whole banking system that needs restructuring.

Rwanda has a well-developed money and inter-bank market. The National Bank of Rwanda uses interest rates, reserve requirements, and money market interventions as its main policy instruments. T-bills auctions were introduced in 1998. The bank temporarily relaxed its stance around mid-year in 2001 and 2002 to revitalize the inter-bank market. Monetary policy has been tight otherwise and efforts to strengthen banking supervision and improve loan compliance and enforcement are being undertaken. Inflationary pressures in 1995 were fuelled by a 54 percent fall in the dollar value of the Rwandan franc, as the authorities switched to a floating exchange rate and proceeded with the liberalization of the foreign exchange market. Previously pegged to the SDR, the Rwandan franc had already been devalued by 40 percent in November 1990 and by 15 percent in June 1992. The currency has since never lost more than a yearly 5 percent in external value, despite deteriorating terms of trade.

On the verge of bankruptcy, the central bank in **Sao Tome and Principe**, which then combined central and commercial lending activities, was liquidated in 1993. Monetary policy still proved ineffective between 1994 and 1997, as the central bank continued to finance growing fiscal deficits and the discount rate remained negative in real terms. There has been a marked improvement in money aggregates since 1998, as a result of a tightening in reserve requirements, greater fiscal discipline, and a substantial fall in net bank credit to the government. The discount rate was gradually reduced from 43 percent in end-1997 to 15 percent in end-2002, as a result of lower inflation. Lax monetary and fiscal policy led to a sharp depreciation of the Dobra until 1997. The currency has since stabilized.

Recent Trends in Globalization

Trade liberalization and regionalization

Central Africa as a whole is relatively open by continental standards, with an average trade-GDP ratio standing at 76.0 percent in 2002 (Table 2.4 and Figure 2.6). All countries, but Equatorial Guinea, and Sao Tome and Principe, are members of the World Trade Organization, which means that they are nominally committed to multilateral trade liberalization and must grant Most Favored Nation treatment to all their trading partners. Trade openness in Central Africa, however, reflects more the importance of oil exports in the region's main economies, than real progress made towards trade liberalization and regionalization. Indeed, countries in Central Africa that support the highest trade-to-GDP ratios are economies that are heavily dependent on oil exports, notably Congo, Equatorial Guinea, and Gabon, as well as Sao Tome and Principe, the latter bearing the characteristics of a small island economy. By contrast, the trade-to-GDP ratios in the region's landlocked countries, notably Rwanda and Burundi, remains low by regional and continental standards, at less than 40 percent. The importance of trade has grown with oil development in Chad.

Six of the countries- Cameroon, CAR, Chad, Congo, Gabon and Equatorial Guinea- belong to the Communauté économique et monétaire de l'Afrique centrale (CEMAC), which is part of the CFA Franc Zone. Three countries - Burundi, DRC and Rwanda - are members of the Common Market for Eastern and Southern Africa (COMESA).

In terms of trade reforms, CEMAC countries have agreed to liberalize their trade regime, by notably adopting a common external tariff structure and lifting intra-regional import barriers. There have been some delays in the implementation of the tax reforms, however. CEMAC countries have recently committed to reduce further the common external tariff to a maximum rate of 20 percent and the number of non-zero tariff bands from four to three. CEMAC intra-regional trade is poorly developed. According to the African Development Bank statistics, exports to the region accounted for 1.2 percent of all exports, and imports from the region accounted for 3.1 percent of all imports in 2000. This largely indicates the lack of product diversification and poor road infrastructure between countries. Some cross-border trade goes largely unrecorded, however, especially between coastal and landlocked countries.

Table 2.4: Central Africa: The External Sector

Country	Trade*		Trade Balance as % of GDP		Current Account		Terms of Trade (%)		Total External Debt as % of GDP		Debt Service as % of Exports	
	Average 1998-2001	2002a/	Average 1998-2001	2002a/	Average 1998-2001	2002a/	Average 1998-2001	2002a/	Average 1998-2001	2002a/	Average 1997-2000	2001
BURUNDI	29	36	-7.9	-12.8	-13.7	-19.9	0.6	-0.4	164.7	209.4	82.9	132.1
CAMEROON	55	55	4.7	2.1	-2.7	-3.8	5.9	-9.8	88.9	78.1	20.2	9.6
CENTRAL AFRICAN REP.	44	41	1.9	1.8	-3.9	-5.8	1.3	-4.7	82.6	68.5	4.9	5.7
CHAD	53	81	-7.7	-32.9	-18.6	-56.9	3.6	-11.6	68.9	71.7	5.3	20.9
CONGO, DEM. REP. OF	46	53	7.6	1.9	-4.8	-4.3	8.9	-9.4	274.5	184.9	72.8	79.3
CONGO, REPUBLIC OF	135	138	50.0	54.0	-6.5	5.2	7.3	-13.0	214.2	215.0	10.9	7.9
EQUATORIAL GUINEA	193	165	34.7	103.4	-57.3	2.6	6.8	29.4	31.8	14.6	12.3	5.5
GABON	100	93	33.1	26.7	-6.6	-3.9	10.0	-7.7	70.5	57.0	13.9	22.5
RWANDA	31	33	-9.3	-10.3	-7.1	-11.5	-7.5	-5.4	68.2	72.7	9.2	6.9
SAO TOME & PRINCIPE	117	132	-37.9	-40.7	-40.5	-29.5	-13.6	-5.2	673.0	593.5	31.9	45.9
CENTRAL AFRICA	70.9	76.0	13.9	14.8	-7.6	-6.7	5.0	-9.5	125.9	108.8	20.6	18.1

Note: a/ Preliminary estimates
*: (Exports & ports) of Goods and Non Factors Services at Market Prices
Sources: ADB Development Research and Statistics Divisions.

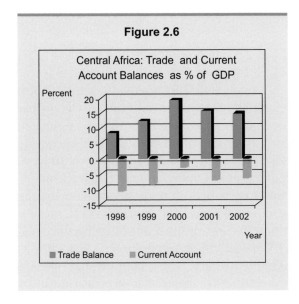

Figure 2.6

Central Africa: Trade and Current Account Balances as % of GDP

As part of the reforms agreed under COMESA, DRC, Rwanda and Burundi have agreed to lower import tariffs ahead of the adoption of the common external tariff in January 2004 (see East Africa regional section for more details on COMESA).

Trade performance and export diversification

The region's external position improved in 2002, with the current account deficit standing at 6.7 percent of GDP, compared with 7.6 percent of GDP in 1998-2001 (Table 2.4). Export diversification is poor in Central Africa. Only Cameroon has a relatively wide export base, although this mostly entails low added-value agricultural products. This has helped the country to successfully weather external shocks in the past. Years to come will bring dramatic changes to export performance in some countries, notably in Chad, with oil soon replacing cotton and livestock as the country's main export, and in DRC, as peace brings formerly smuggled commodities into the fold of the formal economy.

The terms of trade of oil exporting countries in Central Africa have greatly improved since world oil prices rebounded from their historical low of $12.8 per barrel in 1998. World oil prices stayed firm in 2002, averaging $24.86 a barrel, up 1.5 percent on 2001. Trends are roughly reversed for oil-importing countries in the region, which mostly export soft primary commodities and minerals such as manganese, diamond and cobalt. The world price of cocoa beans has post a strong recovery since 2001, but prices have remained depressed for most other commodities.

The 1996 coup in **Burundi** triggered the imposition of economic sanctions by neighboring countries. The sanctions were eased in April 1997 to allow emergency assistance to reach vulnerable groups. The recovery in imports, which was welcomed in this crippled economy, led to a widening in the current account deficit through the late 1990s, as rising tea and coffee export volume failed to compensate for plunging world prices. Burundi's current account deficit widened to 19.9 percent of GDP in 2002, owing to the continuous fall in coffee export revenue. This compares with an average 13.7 percent of GDP in 1998-2001.

Cameroon's current account balance is marginally negative by regional standards. The country, which exports oil as well as agricultural commodities (coffee, cocoa, bananas and timber), has traditionally enjoyed a healthy trade surplus. Yet, earnings from non-oil exports have stagnated since 1995, reflecting depressed world prices, disruptions in the cocoa and coffee sectors and more recently, the banning of unprocessed timber. The current account deficit widened for the second consecutive year in 2002 to 3.8 percent of GDP, reflecting rising outflows of goods and services emanating from the construction of the Cameroon-Chad oil pipeline and falling oil revenues.

Net trade in goods and services has traditionally been negative in **CAR**, because of heavy freight costs. Export earnings, mostly from diamond, timber, and to a lesser extent, cotton, are nonetheless high enough for the country to occasionally post a small trade surplus in fob terms. Political instability is reflected in the current account balance movements. Falling net official transfers contributed to a widening in the current account deficit in 2001, rising further to 5.8 percent of GDP in 2002.

Cotton and livestock, **Chad**'s main sources of export earnings, received an initial boost from the CFA franc devaluation. Export earnings started to decline again in 1999, following a fall in the world price of cotton. Imports have surged with the purchase of capital and intermediary goods for the Dolba project. As a result, the current account deficit peaked to an unprecedented 36.3 percent of GDP in 2001, rising further to 56.9 percent of GDP in 2002. This external gap was matched up by rising capital inflows. The trade deficit is expected to turn into a surplus by 2004, as oil fields come on stream.

Available data on the **DRC**'s external sector have to be treated with extreme caution, given the scale of smuggling activities in the Great Lakes region (the country's mineral resources were major plunders during the war). The country, which is awash with natural resources, has a well-diversified export base, comprising diamond, crude oil, copper,

cobalt and coffee. The current account deficit widened to 4.3 percent of GDP in 2002, up from 2.8 percent of GDP in 2001, as a result of post-war reconstruction efforts.

Largely reflecting fluctuations in oil export earnings, the current account in **Congo** has been in surplus since 2000 and was estimated at 5.2 percent of GDP in 2002. The country enjoys a healthy trade surplus, with up to 90 percent of its export earnings coming from oil. Because of the CFA franc devaluation and the war, the demand for imports was depressed through most of the 1990s, barring the occasional years when oil equipments was shipped into the country. Non-oil imports have picked up since 2000, as a result of post-reconstruction efforts.

Equatorial Guinea's trade balance has turned into a surplus since 1997, with fast growing oil production leading to an exponential growth in exports earnings. Imports of consumer and capital goods have also surged, reflecting investment in the oil sector, government capital outlays, and rising standards of living. Freight and insurance costs, profit remittances and external borrowing by private oil investors have also increased significantly. Taken together, these factors contributed an average current account deficit of 57.3 percent of GDP a year between 1998-2001. The current account balance, however, recorded a small surplus equivalent to 2.6 percent of GDP in 2002, as less capital equipment was imported in the country.

Gabon enjoys a relatively modest import bill because of its small population, but its trade surplus is slowly eroding, as a result of falling oil production. Oil export earnings contribute up to 80 percent of the country's export receipts. Prospects for the development of tropical wood and manganese, the country's other main exports, remain limited. The country's heavy dependence on oil was striking in 1998, when the current account balance turned into a deficit equivalent of 18.7 percent of GDP, as a result of the oil price crash. The recovery in 2000 was short-lived, with the current account balance slipping back into a deficit in 2001 and amounting to - 3.9 percent of GDP in 2002. This contrasts with most of the 1990s, when the trade surplus was high enough to pay for services and income outflows (mostly external debt servicing and profit remittances).

Rwanda's terms of trade have deteriorated sharply, as a result of falling tea and coffee prices and a sharp reduction in mining receipts (mostly cobalt). Swings in the current account balance are wide, although falling petroleum prices and bumper harvests have somewhat reduced the trade deficit in some selected years. The country is also heavily dependant on aid to finance its external sector. The current account deficit, including grants, was estimated at 11.5 percent of GDP in 2002, against an average 7.1 percent of GDP in 1998-2001.

Sao Tome and Principe's export base is very narrow (mostly cocoa beans), while imports comprise essential goods, such as food, oil and capital equipment. Freight and insurance freights are also high in this island economy, which has yet to fully develop its tourism industry, also a main source of foreign exchange earnings. The current account deficit averaged 40.5 percent of GDP a year during 1998-2001, as a result, before declining to 29.5 percent of GDP in 2002, mostly reflecting recovering world cocoa prices.

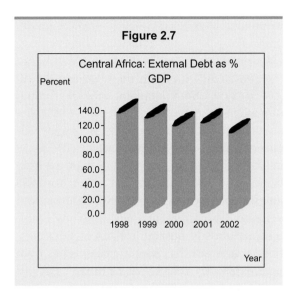

Figure 2.7

Central Africa: External Debt as % GDP

External debt and foreign direct investment

Central Africa's external debt burden is the highest in Africa, amounting to 108.8 percent of the region's GDP in 2002, down an average 125.9 percent of GDP in 1998-2001 (Table 2.4 and Figure 2.7). The stock of external debt, which is mostly made of public and publicly-guaranteed loans, was mostly contracted in the 1970s and 1980s as governments launched major infrastructure projects. Oil-exporting countries formerly classified as middle-income countries, like Cameroon (and still today Gabon and Equatorial Guinea), did not have access to concessional assistance until the late 1980s. This has contributed to higher debt service payments. Only four countries out of ten have so far qualified for debt relief under the HIPC initiative.

Foreign direct investment, another source of external financing, has increased significantly in some countries in recent years, but it remains largely confined to the oil sector, political instability being the main hindrance to FDI elsewhere. According to UNCTAD's *World Investment Report 2002*, FDI inflows to the region totaled US$ 551 million in 2001. Central Africa CFA zone countries have plans to install a regional stock exchange market, Bourse de valeurs mobilières de l'Afrique centrale (BVMAC), in Libreville, Gabon, in 2003, but there are little hopes to attract substantial foreign portfolio investment, because of slow privatization and because the large companies operating in the area are already quoted in Paris or Johannesburg. Cameroon has recently opened its own national stock exchange in Daoula.

Total debt in **Burundi**, which is mostly multilateral, amounted to a high 209.4 percent of GDP in 2002. The debt service ratio was at 132.1 percent in 2001, the last year for which data is available. While current with the World Bank, its main lender, the country is in arrears with other multilateral institutions, including the African Development Bank, and a number of bilateral creditors. Donors agreed in December 2000 to set up a multilateral debt trust fund to help the government clear its stock of payment arrears, and eventually qualify to HIPC assistance.

Cameroon's stock of debt stabilized in the second half of the 1990s, with the government negotiating debt relief deals with the Paris Club of bilateral, official creditors in 1994, 1995 and 1997. The last debt relief deal with the Paris Club was in January 2001. In October 2000, the country qualified for the enhanced HIPC initiative. This will lead to a nominal $2bn in debt relief in nominal terms at completion point. The deals, combined with the government's improved fiscal position and prudent borrowing policy, has led to a continuous

decline in the country's external debt-to-GDP ratio. The debt service ratio has also declined, notwithstanding fluctuations in export earnings. It stood at 9.6 percent in 2001, the last year for which data is available, compared with 20.3 percent in 1997-2000. According to *UNCTAD World Investment Report 2002*, FDI inflows to Cameroon totaled US$75 million in 2001. Corruption and delays in the program of privatization have act as major deterrents to foreign investment in the country.

CAR's external debt rose continuously through the 1980s, as a result of heavy government borrowing. Bilateral debt stopped rising in the 1990s, when highly-concessional, multilateral, long-term loans became the main source of financing. There were two Paris Club deals in 1994 and 1998. Today, multilateral debt accounts for about two-third of the country's total debt stock. The government has continued to run up arrears on its debt service obligations, including to the World Bank and the African Development Bank. The debt service ratio was estimated at 5.7 percent in 2001. CAR has yet to qualify for debt relief under the enhanced HIPC initiative, reflecting delays in the economic program supported by the IMF. FDI in CAR is largely confined to the mining sector.

The nominal stock of debt in **Chad** has doubled in the past decade amounting to 71.7 percent of GDP. The HIPC initiative, for which Chad qualified in May 2001, will lead to an estimated $260m in debt relief. The debt service ratio, which surged to 20.9 percent in 2001, was expected to decline in 2002, as a result of Paris Club debt relief deal in June 2001 and HIPC interim assistance. FDI in Chad has surged since 2001, as the oil pipeline and Dolba project kicked off following the World Bank's approval of the project.

Total debt in **DRC** surged in the 1970s and 1980s, but was roughly constant in the 1990s, when the debt burden nonetheless increased, because of the declining economy, and arrears piled up. The situation with external creditors was normalized in 2002, when total debt stock represented 184.9 percent of GDP. Payment arrears owed to the IMF were cleared, while the African Development Bank approved in June 2002 a mechanism for the clearance of the country's arrears. The World Bank, which had suspended its financial assistance in 1993, approved two new loans in 2002, totaling $900m. Paris Club creditors agreed to a debt rescheduling deal in September 2002, leading to the immediate cancellation of about $4.6 billion of the country's external debt. The country hopes soon to qualify for HIPC assistance. The DRC government aims to boost DFI, following the adoption of a new investment and mining code in 2002.

The debt burden in **Congo** is very high, because of excess borrowing against future oil earnings in the 1970s and 1980s. External debt continued to rise in the 1990s, albeit at a slower pace, representing 215 percent of GDP in 2002. The government defaulted on its debt though most of the 1990s, leading to misleadingly low debt service ratios. Although the government is committed to reduce gradually its stock of arrears, including those vis-à-vis the African Development Bank, and normalize its relations with creditors, arrears continued to pile up in 2002, with the debt service ratio (paid) estimated at 7.9 percent in 2001. FDI in Congo has declined in recent years, because of diminishing discoveries in the oil sector.

Equatorial Guinea is not eligible for concessional assistance, being a middle-income economy. Most of the country's external public debt has been contracted on a bilateral basis, as a result. The debt burden is low: owing to remarkable growth rates and rising oil export earnings, total debt amounted to less than 15 percent of GDP in 2002 and the debt service ratio stood at 5.5 percent in 2001. The government has nonetheless been reluctant to clear principal and interest payments arrears contracted by previous administrators. After averaging US$ 88 million a year between 1998 and 2001, FDI inflows in Equatorial Guinea slowed down in 2002, as a result of lower activity in oil exploration.

The government in **Gabon** has pursued a relatively prudent external borrowing policy since the mid-1990s, with the debt-to-GDP ratio falling to 57.0 percent in 2002, compared with an average 70.5 percent between 1998 and 2001, despite poor economic performance. The debt service ratio has meanwhile failed to decline, instead rising to 22.5 percent in 2001, as a result of falling export earnings. The accumulation of external payment arrears prompted three debt-rescheduling deals with the Paris Club in 1994, 1995, and 2000. But the country contracted new payment arrears in 2001 and 2002. Gabon does not qualify for the HIPC debt relief initiative, since it is classified as a middle-income economy. Like Cameroon, its debt is mostly bilateral. FDI in the oil sector represent the bulk of Gabon's investment and amounted to US$ 200 million in 2001

Rwanda's external debt was estimated at 72.7 percent of GDP. The debt service ratio averaged 9.2 percent in 1997-2000 and was estimated at 6.9 percent in 2001. The structure of the debt is heavily weighted toward multilateral debt. Debt management is satisfactory and the government has started to clear the stock of payment arrears it owes to bilateral creditors. A new debt rescheduling and relief deal is due to be signed with the Paris Club in 2003. The last Paris Club deal was in 1998. The country qualified for debt relief under HIPC in May 2001, which will lead to a nominal $ 810 million in debt relief at completion point.

The government in **Sao Tome and Principe** pursued a lax borrowing policy through most of the 1980s and early 1990s. At 593.5 percent of GDP, the country's stock of debt is one of the highest in Africa. Sao Tome qualified for the HIPC initiative in December 2000, which will lead to a nominal debt relief of $ 200 million at completion point. About 65 percent of the country's debt is owed to multilateral lenders. The debt service ratio rose to 45.9 percent in 2001, despite a Paris Club debt rescheduling deal in May 2000 and HIPC interim debt relief, owing to falling export earnings that year. FDI in Sao Tome and Principe has risen timidly in recent years, as a result of development projects in oil exploration and the development of a free trade zone.

Outlook

In 2003, Central Africa GDP is forecast to grow higher than its 2002 rate of 5.5 percent. Growth in **Burundi** is expected to pick up in 2003, as a result of peace consolidation, rising donor assistance (the country is currently negotiating a post conflict recovery program with the IMF), a boom in construction and resumed activity in manufacturing and trade.

A continued decline in oil production and lesser activities in construction and services following the completion of the Chad Cameroon pipeline will meanwhile challenge **Cameroon**'s growth targets. Annual rates around 5 percent

could nonetheless be achieved, providing an acceleration in structural reforms and the implementation of poverty alleviation measures.

Economic recovery in **CAR** will hinge on success in fostering peace and stability under the aegis of the regional grouping, CEMAC. Growth is set to remain strong in **Chad** in 2003, at around 9 percent, as development in the oil sector continues, with petroleum production expected to start in early 2004.

Growth in **DRC** will accelerate to a projected 5 percent in 2003, driven by an increase in externally financed investment, macroeconomic stabilization, and the implementation of structural and sectoral reforms. GDP in **Congo** is expected to rise by 4-5 percent, on the back of activity in the non-oil sector. Growth performance will remain exceptionally strong in **Equatorial Guinea**, although it is set to decelerate to 16.4 percent, as some of the country's main oil fields reached maturation. Meanwhile, growth in **Gabon** will remain subdued or negative, as activity in the private sector fails to compensate for falling oil production.

In **Rwanda**, the ongoing program of privatization, notably in the commercial agricultural sector, and strong external assistance will help to achieve annual rates of growth of around 6 percent. Continued investment in petroleum exploration and development will drive economic performance in **Sao Tome and Principe**.

East Africa

Eleven countries make up the East Africa region: Comoros, Djibouti, Eritrea, Ethiopia, Kenya, Madagascar, Mauritius, Seychelles, Somalia, Tanzania and Uganda. None of these countries possesses significant mineral or energy resources by African standards, but the region is a major destination for tourism. It is a region of great contrasts- from mostly-desert Somalia in the north to the lush vegetation in southern Kenya. East Africa's GDP accounted for 8.2 percent of the continental output in 2002. Kenya is the largest economy of the zone, followed by Tanzania, Ethiopia, and Uganda.

The region has become more politically stable in recent years, following the end of the hostilities between Eritrea and Ethiopia, peace talks in neighboring DRC and the national reconciliation process launched in Comoros since February 2001. Somalia is still at war, however, whereas Madagascar experienced a severe political crisis in 2002, following contested presidential election in December 2001. The landslide victory of opposition leader, Mwai Kibaki in the December 2002 presidential election in Kenya marked the end of 24 years of rule under President Daniel arap Moi.

Beside tourism, most countries in East Africa still thrive on the exports of primary commodities, notably tea and coffee. Other countries, like Mauritius, have been more successful in diversifying their export base away from traditional products. East Africa's exports made up 6.5 percent of the continental total in 2002. The East African Region is a net importer of oil.

The population of East Africa was esti-

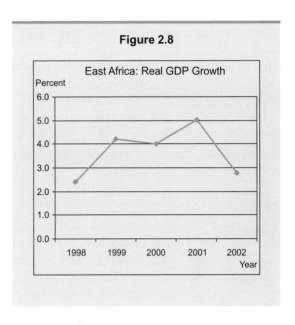

Figure 2.8

East Africa: Real GDP Growth

mated to represent about 23 percent of the continent's population in 2002. Seychelles and Mauritius are middle-income countries, their GDP per capita being estimated at $ 7486 and $ 4050 respectively in 2002. By contrast, Eritrea and Ethiopia are among the poorest countries in Africa, their per capita income being below $ 100. Overall, and despite some of the countries' strong performance in the last decade, the region's GDP per capita remains the lowest in Africa, averaging $ 241 in 2002 (Table 2.5).

Recent Trends in the Domestic Economy

East Africa was the best performer in Africa between 1998 and 2001, with the region's GDP growth averaging 3.9 percent. There was a reversal of fortunes in 2002, however, with growth decelerating to 2.8 percent, as a result of a growth deceleration in Eritrea, Ethiopia,

Table 2.5: East Africa: Gross Domestic Product and Export Performances

Country	Real GDP Growth Rate (%)		GDP Per Capita (US$)		Real Exports[c] Growth (%)		Exports[b] Per Capita (US$)	
	Average 1998-2001	2002[a]	Average 1998-2001	2002[a]	Average 1998-2001	2002[a]	Average 1998-2001	2002[a]
COMOROS	1.0	3.0	309	335	-22.2	30.8	74	66
DJIBOUTI	1.3	2.5	874	921	8.5	1.5	392	375
ERITREA	0.3	8.8	-	-	5.9	-15.2	-	-
ETHIOPIA	4.5	5.0	102	87	8.8	4.3	16	14
KENYA	1.0	1.6	361	372	2.1	0.4	92	89
MADAGASCAR	4.8	-11.9	253	266	13.4	-16.5	66	67
MAURITIUS	5.8	4.0	3783	4050	6.8	9.3	2279	2361
SEYCHELLES	-3.2	-2.4	7486	7423	4.7	0.9	5577	5586
SOMALIA	-	-	-	-	-	-	-	-
TANZANIA	4.4	5.9	255	252	5.5	0.5	37	39
UGANDA	5.7	5.7	258	243	6.9	9.3	29	24
EAST AFRICA	**3.9**	**2.8**	**246**	**241**	**4.0**	**2.5**	**56**	**55**

Notes: a/ Preliminary estimates
    b/ Exports of Goods and Nonfactor Services at Market Prices
    c/ Real Exports of Goods and Non Factors Services Growth
Sources: ADB Development Research and Statistics Divisions.

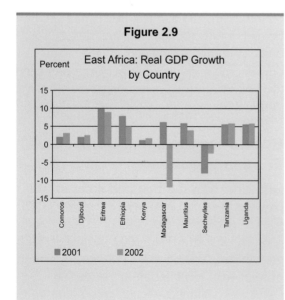

Figure 2.9

East Africa: Real GDP Growth by Country

Mauritius, and Madagascar (see Table 2.5 and Figures 2.8 and 2.9). The investment-to-GDP ratio stood at 17.1 percent in 2002, against 17.3 percent in 1998-2001, notwithstanding low and declining savings in Kenya, but also in Seychelles and Uganda (Figure 2.10). Inflation in East Africa averaged 3.1 percent in 2002, down 6.3 percent a year during 1998-2001, notably reflecting tighter monetary and fiscal policy in Kenya, Tanzania, and Uganda (Figure 2.11).

Resumed donor support, high export prices and the lifting of an embargo on the island of Anjouan have spurred some economic activities in **Comoros**, with the economy growing by 3.0 percent in 2002, up from 1.0 percent in 1998-2001. This is the first time in five years that economic growth matches that of the

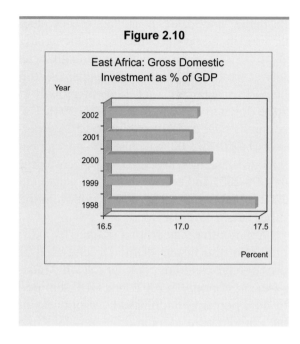

Figure 2.10

East Africa: Gross Domestic Investment as % of GDP

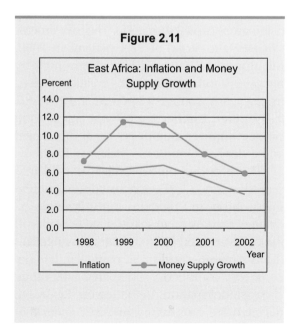

Figure 2.11

East Africa: Inflation and Money Supply Growth

population. The investment-GDP ratio surged to 12.5 percent in 2002, up from an average 11.6 percent in 1998-2001. Strong price stability has prevailed in the islands economy, its currency being firmly pegged to the euro. Consumer prices rose by an average 3.0 percent in 2002.

Growth in resource-scarce **Djibouti** accelerated to 2.5 percent in 2002, reflecting a rise in services associated with its port activities and the presence of foreign troops on its territory. Public administration is meanwhile characterized by huge cross-debts, an over bloated civil service, and weak capacity, all major hindrances to investment. Djibouti's currency board with the US dollar has helped to keep inflationary pressures under control. Inflation was estimated at 2.0 percent in 2002.

The threat of famine and falling world coffee prices have dealt a blow to **Ethiopia**'s impressive economic recovery since the end of the conflict with Eritrea. Strong donor support (the country is currently one of the largest recipient of external grants and loans in Africa) has nonetheless continued to spur some economic activities, with real GDP growing by 5 percent in fiscal year 2001/02. The resumption of foreign assistance, bumper crop harvests and a rebound in tourism had previously led to an acceleration in growth to 7.7 percent in 2001. But the country's economy remains fragile, being mostly based on weather-dependent activities in agriculture and livestock. On a more positive side, the GDP share of gross capital formation has continued to rise, reaching 17.1 percent in 2002. Inflation, which turned negative in 2001, as a result of bumper crop harvests, was also negative in 2002, at –7.2 percent, notwithstanding the food crisis that hit the country in the later part of the year.

Growth recovery in **Eritrea** started in 2001, reflecting the end of the hostilities with Ethiopia and a rebound in crop production. Post-war reconstruction, soldiers' demobilization, and population resettlement helped to maintain economic growth at 8.8 percent in 2002, despite poorer performance in agriculture that year. This compares favorably with the yearly average 0.6 percent during 1998-2001. Inflation in Eritrea mostly reflects the availability of food products. It remains high by regional standards and amounted to 14.1 percent a year in 1998-2001.

Long one of Africa's more vibrant and dynamic economy, **Kenya** has born the brunt of weak economic management, inefficiency in the public sector, and strained relationships with donors, since the mid-1990s. As a result, the state of infrastructure has deteriorated sharply and investor's confidence has been lost. Economic growth fell behind that of population for the sixth consecutive year in 2002, with real GDP growing by a sluggish 1.6 percent, as the government's program with the IMF remained unstuck over governance issues. The declining rate of capital formation, which stood at 13.9 percent of GDP in 2002, has been a major contributory factor to low growth performance. Inflation in Kenya has moved down to single-digit rates since the late 1990s (barring 1997 an election year and despite a drought and high oil prices in 2000), reflecting tighter monetary and fiscal policy. Consumer prices rose by 1.8 percent in 2002, against a yearly average 5.0 percent in 1998-2001.

Mauritius remains one of the best performers of the region, although the general context of moroseness in Europe and the US and the country's eroding comparative advantages have somewhat dampened growth per-

formance since 2001. A rise in sugar production and in the output of the Export Processing Zone (EPZ), combined with growing financial services and a recovery in the tourism sector, helped to maintain a 4.0 percent growth in 2002, down from 5.8 percent in 1998-2001. The country's GDI-to-GDP ratio rose to 25.9 percent of GDP in 2002, which is high by regional standards. Inflation averaged 5.8 percent a year in 1998-2001 and accelerated to 6.4 percent in 2002, notably reflecting a depreciation in the rupee and a VAT rise.

A 6-month political crisis sparked by a dispute over the results of the December 2001 presidential elections took its toll on **Madagascar**'s economy in 2002. Real GDP slumped by 11.9 percent, roadblocks by supporters of the outgoing president and the general strike in the capital being particularly damaging to services and activity in the industrial sector. Economic growth had markedly accelerated between 1997 and 2001, fuelled by the development of the EPZ (notably clothing) and rising gross capital formation. The investment-to-GDP ratio stood at 22.4 percent in 2002. Inflation in Madagascar is relatively high by regional standards. In 2002, inflation picked from a yearly average 9.2 percent in 1998-2001 to 15 percent, reflecting the scarcity of food products and consumer goods in the capital and a depreciation of the Malagasy franc.

The economy in **Seychelles** has slid into recession since 1999. Extensive government intervention and rigidities in the foreign exchange market have created bottlenecks in the economy and led to negative savings and disinvestment. Tourism, in particular, has become less competitive, compared with other, cheaper, destinations in the region. Real GDP declined by 2.4 percent in 2002. Consumer prices in Seychelles are administered, with annual inflation averaging 5.3 percent in 1998-2001 and 6.4 percent in 2002.

The economy in war-torn **Somalia** has suffered from the anti-terrorist campaign that the US launched after the September 11th attacks. In addition, the transitional government in place since August 2000 has little control over the country's territory. Weather conditions in south Somalia improved in 2002, but the agricultural sector has yet to recover from years of severe drought and insecurity, whereas the import ban on the country's livestock has not been lifted. This gloomy picture contrasts with that of Somaliland, north of the country, where a relatively peaceful self-sufficient economy has been established. Inflation in Somalia remains at two-digit rates.

Economic growth in **Tanzania** accelerated for the third consecutive year to 5.9 percent in 2002, on the back of improved overall crop production and a consolidation in macroeconomic stability. Tanzania is the second largest economy of the region, after Kenya. The country's performance still largely hinges on agriculture, which accounts for a bit less than half of its GDP. Mining (led by gold) and tourism are growing fast, however, and so is their annual contribution to GDP (tourist trade stagnated in 2002 following the events of September 11th 2001). Gross capital formation reached 16.9 percent of GDP in 2002, up from an average 18.6 percent in 1998-2001. Inflation in Tanzania has been subdued since 1999, reflecting tighter monetary policy and the use of a cash budget by the government; it stood at 4.6 percent in 2002, against a yearly average 7.8 percent in 1998-2001.

Uganda was the fastest growing economy in the region through most of the 1990s, as a result of successful macroeconomic stabilization policy, strong donor support and increased interest from foreign investors after the end of the civil war. While manufacturing and services have expanded over the past decade, agriculture remains the largest sector of the economy. Recent years have seen a slight deceleration in the country's growth, because of unfavorable external conditions, notably drought and depressed world coffee prices. Improved weather conditions helped to maintain a 5.7 percent economic growth in 2001/02 (as reported in our 2002 database). Activity in telecommunications, construction (the World Bank withheld its assistance to the Bujagali dam construction project in June 2002), and government services were also buoyant. The private sector continued to lead gross capital formation, which rose to 19.9 percent of GDP in 2002. Inflation in Uganda turned negative in 2002, at –2.2 percent, reflecting a slowdown in monetary expansion and increased availability of food products.

Recent Policy Developments

Poverty reduction strategy

Seven East African countries but Mauritius, Seychelles, Tanzania, and Kenya, are classified as Least Developed Countries by the United Nations. Reducing poverty is therefore at the forefront of their governments' domestic policy programs. Most countries have adopted the participatory process that the IMF, World Bank and African Development Bank support to formulate national poverty reduction strategies, as part of the Enhanced HIPC debt relief initiative.

Three countries, **Ethiopia**, **Tanzania**, and **Uganda**, have released their final PRSPs. Ethiopia released its final PRSP in July 2002. The strategy, which builds on the interim PRSP presented in March 2000, was well received by multilateral organizations. Ethiopia's poverty reduction program concentrates on agricultural development, since the sector is the source of livelihood for 85 percent of the population, and water resource utilization. Other priorities consist of strengthening private sector and export growth, undertaking major investment in education, deepening the decentralization process, and improving governance. More specific policy measures are in the process of being elaborated. At $87, Ethiopia's GDP per capita is the second lowest ratio on the continent, after DRC. Tanzania completed its final PRSP in October 2000. The first year of its implementation has focused on enhancing budget support for the priority sectors, carrying out a new household budget survey, and elaborating strategies for education, agriculture, and cross-cutting areas (HIV/AIDS, governance, gender, environment). Some social and income indicators have improved since the adoption of the PRSP. Uganda adopted a Poverty eradication action plan (PEAP) in March 2000. The PEAP entails four main components: sustainable economic growth; good governance and security; income opportunities for the poor (especially in agriculture); and the quality of life. The government has sought to reallocate public resources towards primary education, health care and water resources, but the capacity of the public sector to deliver services has remained weak. Progress has also been slow in fighting corruption and tackling security issues.

The countries that have released an interim PRSP in the region are **Djibouti**, **Kenya**, and **Madagascar**. Djibouti adopted an interim PRSP in November 2001, based on income-generating growth, increased access to social services, administrative capacity building and good governance. Kenya's interim PRSP was released in June 2000. There have been some delays in the preparation of a full PRSP, originally announced for May 2001. Madagascar released its interim PRSP in November 2000. The thrust of the program consists of access to essential services (education, health, and sanitation), administrative capacity building, and rural development. The final document is now to be released in the first quarter of 2003.

Elsewhere, **Comoros**, which does not have a program with the IMF and thus, does not qualify for HIPC assistance, is also in the process of drawing up a national poverty reduction program, under the aegis of the UN Development Program. **Eritrea** has yet to develop a nationwide strategy to fight poverty, although multilateral donors support a string of emergency reconstruction programs. With a GDP per capita of $4,050, **Mauritius** is classified as an upper middle-income country. Income disparity is low and the bulk of the population has access to reasonable income and social welfare, safe water, electricity, education and health services. There are still some pockets of poverty, however, and unemployment is rising. Hence, one of the key objectives of the government's Economic Agenda for the New Millennium (NEA, 2000) is to fight social exclusion. Social exclusion is also a problem in **Seychelles**.

Privatization

The recent transaction that took place in the energy sector in Uganda has mitigated Central Africa's poor record in privatization in recent years. Yet many divestitures have continued to be challenged, some even cancelled, because of a lack of transparency in the bidding process or in the regulatory framework of the sector concerned.

In **Comoros**, the difficult process of political reconciliation has switched the focus away from reforms. The last privatization to take place was that of the water and power utility in 1998. Handling activities at the port of Moroni were handed over to a private company in mid-2002, on a temporary basis, in replacement of the now defunct Socopotram. There are also plans to privatize the postal service and state telecommunication company.

The government in **Djibouti** has worked towards privatizing four main public utilities (water, electricity, telephone and airport). A contract to manage Djibouti's international airport was awarded to Dubai Ports International Authority (DPIA) in June 2002. DPIA has been in charge of managing Djibouti's port since June 2000. The **Eritrea** government proceeded with the sale of some hundreds small units in the early 1990s. A more comprehensive program of privatization was launched in 1997, but has remained stalled since.

The privatization of some 200 state-owned enterprises and units in **Ethiopia** has proceeded in fits and starts. Some hotels, small retail trade outlets, industrial plants and state farms were brought to the point of sale in 1999 and the government resumed its divestiture program shortly after the end of the hostilities with Eritrea in 2000. The response has been poor, however. The government sold 7 public enterprises, put three entities under private management contract, and completed the preparation for the privatization of 36 others in 2000/01. Some enterprises were meanwhile returned to the state, pending the result of some corrup-

tion investigations. The foreign firm that signed a management contract with Commercial Bank of Ethiopia (CBE) in June 2001 withdrew in January 2002, as managers of the CBE were arrested for corruption charges.

While privatization in **Kenya** started in earnest in the early 1990s, most enterprises handed over to the private sector were small businesses, with the exception of Kenya Airways, which was privatized in 1996. The government subsequently adopted a more comprehensive and far-reaching program of privatization in 2000, including telecom, railways, and port authorities, electricity and oil refiner. Kenya's current record with restructuring and privatization of public enterprises remains an issue of contention between the government and its major development partners. In 2001, the government promised to table a Privatization Bill aimed at streamlining and accelerating the implementation of the program. The draft Bill was only ready in mid-2002 after extensive consultations with a broad section of stakeholders. The privatization of Telcom Kenya (TK), which first went out to tender in April 2000 fell through for several reasons. At the start of 2002, the government re-affirmed its determination to privatize the utility but subsequent negotiations with Mount Kenya Consortium proved unsuccessful. The last divestiture to take place was in 2001, when the government sold 30 percent shareholding in Mumias Sugar Company. The government has nonetheless made some progress with the preparatory process for the privatization of Kenya Reinsurance Corporation, and Kenya Commercial Bank.

Some 15 out of a total of 46 state-owned enterprises mooted for privatization in **Madagascar** have been sold. The program came to a standstill in 2002, as efforts towards political reconciliation and economic reconstruction became the main priorities. The new government is committed to privatization. The sale of the oil distribution company, Solima, which was awarded to a consortium of foreign firms in late 2001, was confirmed in June 2002. Other enterprises soon to be divested include Telecom Malagasy, the sugar company, Sirama, and the cotton companies, Hasyma and Sumatex.

The only privatization to take place recently in Mauritius, was that of **Mauritius** Telecom in 2000. Although the government in **Seychelles** has privatized some small state-owned enterprises in the fishing and tourism sector, the public sector continues to play a prominent role in the economy.

In **Tanzania**, more than 250 state-owned enterprises have been liquidated or sold to the private sector since the late 1980s. In 1996, the program of privatization was extended to include all major utilities and infrastructure (water, energy, rail, port, transports, telecommunications), as well as banking and mining. In 2000, the management of the Tanzania harbor was handed over to a foreign consortium. The National Bank of Commerce was also privatized. First bids for Dar Es Salaam Water and Sanitation Authority (Dawasa) were meanwhile rejected, prompting an extensive rehabilitation program for the company (now to be leased for an initial period of ten years). In 2001, a 35 percent share in the electricity utility, Tanzania Telecommunications Company (TTCL), was sold to a strategic buyer. No privatization took place in 2002. The lack of transparency in the bidding procedures is being dealt with.

In **Uganda**, more than one hundred state-owned businesses have been opened to private participation since a program of divestiture was first launched in the early 1990s. The second wave of privatization engaged in 2000 has proceeded at a slower pace, reflecting the complexity of the sale for medium-to-larger scale public enterprises. The main enterprises that have been sold recently include Uganda Telecom, in June 2000 and Uganda Commercial Bank, in October 2001. There has been some delays elsewhere. Uganda Airlines was liquidated in mid-2001, after a botched privatization. In January 2002, two pre-qualified bidders for a share in the Uganda Electricity Board (UEB)'s generation and distributions divisions withdrew, citing confusion in tariffs and concerns over political interference. An independent power regulator, the Electricity Regulatory Authority, became operational in 2002. UEB (generation) was finally taken over by Eskom of South Africa in November 2002. Other enterprises yet to be privatized include Uganda Railway Corporation, Dairy Corporation Limited, and Kinyara Sugar Works.

Fiscal Developments

The measures adopted by governments to enhance revenue and tighten expenditure control have helped to improve East Africa's fiscal position over the years, although the overall regional deficit continues to stand above other regions' deficits, partly reflecting continued expansionary policies in countries like Seychelles, and partly because the tax base in politically instable countries like Comoros, Ethiopia and Eritrea has yet to be fully worked out. East Africa's deficit rose to 5.4 percent of GDP in 2002, against a yearly average 3.3 percent in 1998-2001 (Table 2.6 and Figure 2.12).

The fiscal situation in **Comoros** mirrors political developments over the past decade.

Table 2.6: East Africa: Macroeconomic Management Indicators

| Country | Inflation (%) | | Fiscal Balance as % of GDP | | Gross Domestic Investment | | Gross National Savings | |
| | | | | | as % of GDP | | | |
	Average 1998-2001	2002[a]	Average 1998-2001	2002[a]	Average 1998-2001	2002[a]	Average 1998-2001	2002[a]
COMOROS	3.8	3.0	-2.3	-3.9	11.6	12.5	8.9	7.8
DJIBOUTI	2.0	2.0	-0.9	-2.3	12.9	17.1	8.3	4.8
ERITREA	14.1	.	.	.	.	.	.	.
ETHIOPIA	1.6	-7.0	-7.7	-9.9	16.7	20.2	11.9	11.4
KENYA	5.0	1.8	-0.9	-5.3	15.9	13.9	12.7	10.2
MADAGASCAR	9.2	15.0	-3.9	-6.0	15.8	22.4	9.7	13.0
MAURITIUS	5.8	6.4	-4.2	-6.5	25.9	25.9	24.9	27.4
SEYCHELLES	5.1	...	-12.9	-10.4	33.2	20.3	16.4	10.7
SOMALIA	12.8	20.0	-	...	-	-	-	-
TANZANIA	7.8	4.6	-2.4	-4.3	16.3	16.9	12.1	10.7
UGANDA	3.1	-2.2	-2.7	-4.1	18.6	19.9	11.5	10.5
EAST AFRICA	**6.3**	**3.7**	**-3.3**	**-5.4**	**17.3**	**17.1**	**12.7**	**11.6**

Note: a/ Preliminary estimates
*: (Exports & Imports) of Goods and Non Factors Services at Market Prices
Sources: ADB Development Research and Statistics Divisions.

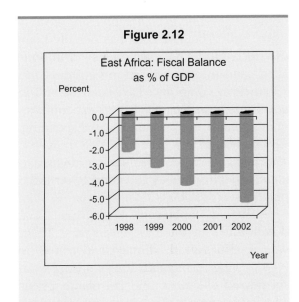

Figure 2.12

East Africa: Fiscal Balance as % of GDP

Revenue performance deteriorated with social unrest, the 1999 coup, and lower donor support. The government meanwhile made some limited progress in containing expenditures (and notably reducing the public sector wage bill) and continued to pile up domestic and external payment arrears. The central government deficit widened to 3.2 percent of GDP in 2001, owing to the change in administration and the costs of the national reconciliation process, rising slightly to 3.9 percent of GDP in 2002, when elections were held.

Djibouti ran large fiscal deficits until the mid-1990s. Measures to trim down the public sector wage bill and push through with the demobilization program helped to improve the country's fiscal position in 1996-2001.

A cash-flow management system was adopted in April 2001 to improve expenditure control. This helped to improve the fiscal situation in 2002. The reduction of budgetary payments arrears remains one of the government's highest priorities. The fiscal deficit rose to 2.3 percent of GDP in 2002, against a yearly average of 0.9 percent in 1998-2001.

There was a sharp deterioration in public finances in **Ethiopia** with the outbreak of the war with Eritrea in 1998. Poverty targeted expenditures have now largely substituted military spending. In fact, social and capital spending, which come under special, donor-funded, demobilization and reconstruction programs, largely explain the rise in public expenditures since 2001. Budget preparation and expenditure tracking have meanwhile improved. On the revenue side, the government has taken some important measures to strengthen revenue collection and widen the tax base (a VAT is to be introduced in January 2003). The fiscal deficit averaged 7.7 percent in 1998-2001, rising to 9.9 percent of GDP in 2002.

Eritrea has little up-to-date fiscal and monetary data available. There was a strengthening in the government fiscal position before the introduction of the national currency in 1997, followed by a relapse during the war with Ethiopia, as a result of military spending and a drop in public revenue. The bulk of public expenditures has now been redirected towards demobilization and reconstruction.

The government in **Kenya** has made major efforts to switch away from "stop-and go" macro-economic policies and curb non-essential public expenditures over the past decade. The central government balance strengthened to turn positive in 1998-1999, but there was some slippage in 2000. Overall, the deficit averaged 0.9 percent of GDP in 1998-2001, and widened to 5.3 percent of GDP in 2002 (an election year). Lower than budgeted revenue performance in 2002 are due to poor economic performance, failure in carrying through the privatization Telkom Kenya and the continued suspension of international assistance. The high public sector wage bill, the domestic debt burden, lack of transparency and poor governance, have rendered Kenya's fiscal situation particularly fragile and proved detrimental to public investment. Recent expenditure control and revenue enhancing measures entail the introduction of a medium-term expenditure framework, and the strengthening of the office of the controller and auditor-general.

The public deficit-to-GDP ratio in **Madagascar** has decreased with economic growth since 1997. The deficit widened to 6.0 percent in 2002, as a result of the political crisis and the drop in domestic revenue and grants. Tax revenue efforts have overall improved, with the domestic-revenue to GDP ratio rising steadily since 1997. The VAT base has notably been extended (and VAT exemptions on imports lifted) and measures to reform customs and reinforce tax compliance have been taken. The government has meanwhile kept expenditures under control and prioritized social spending. Civil service reforms have been slow, however. The new government is strongly committed to increased transparency and good governance practices.

Public finances in **Mauritius** have deteriorated in the past two years. There was a shortfall in domestic revenue in 2001, owing to financial losses arising from subsidized electricity and petroleum prices and lower trade tariffs. Corrective measures were subsequently taken, with notably a rise in the VAT rate (introduced in 1998) and the broadening of the tax base. In keeping with its ambitious Economic Agenda for the new Millennium, the government engaged in an expansionary fiscal policy in 2002. Revenue enhancing efforts led to a slight rise in the domestic revenue-to-GDP ratio, but the fiscal deficit nonetheless widened with rising capital expenditures to 6.5 percent of GDP, against a yearly average of 4.2 percent in 1998-2001. The bulk of the deficit was financed through domestic borrowing.

Easy access to foreign financing has traditionally permitted the **Seychelles** government to run wide fiscal deficits. The sustainability of such policy has been challenged since the economy fell into recession in 1999. Although the government has reduced transfers to parastatals and strengthened expenditure management in recent years, its involvement in the economy remains impressive. Taken together, public revenue and expenditures account for 100 percent of GDP or more. The fiscal deficit stood at 10.4 percent of GDP in 2002, against a yearly average 12.9 percent in 1998-2001.

Tanzania's government maintained a prudent fiscal stance through most of the past decade. The central government deficit averaged 2.4 percent of GDP a year in 1998-2001, rising to 4.3 percent of GDP in 2002. The tight expenditure management system based on monthly cash budgeting is been gradually replaced by a more flexible, quarterly cash-flow planning and management system. High priority has been given to social sectors spending in recent years. Whereas nominal public revenues have increased with economic growth, the revenue-to-GDP ratio has risen only slightly. Measures to widen

the VAT base, reduce tax exemptions and strengthen tax administration are being taken to reduce Tanzania's dependence on external assistance.

Fiscal adjustment in **Uganda** concentrates on reinforcing domestic tax efforts; strengthening expenditure management; curbing non-essential public expenditures; and rising spending in priority sectors. Fighting corruption is also essential. The tax base has been widened, with notably the introduction of a value-added tax in 1996, and measures to strengthen the capacity of the Uganda Revenue Authority have been taken. Yet, the domestic revenue-GDP ratio remains low and the government still relies heavily on external support to finance its budget. Fiscal policy was expansionary in 2002, with the central government deficit rising to 4.1 percent of GDP, up from an average 2.7 percent of GDP a year in 1998-2001.

Monetary and Exchange Rate Developments

In 2002, money supply growth in East Africa declined to 5.9 percent from 8.0 percent recorded in 2001 (Figure 2.11). Monetary rules in **Comoros** are tight, as the Banque Centrale des Comores conducts its policy within the framework of the Franc Zone. As a member of the Franc Zone, Comoros has its currency pegged to the euro. The external value of the Comorian franc was devalued by 33 percent in January 1994, with inflation surging to 15 percent that year.

In **Djibouti**, negative broad money growth reflects depressed economic activity and the Djibouti franc's unchanged peg to the US dollar since 1973. Eritrea has pursued an independent monetary policy since 1997. The Bank of Eritrea's policy framework consists of reserve requirements and interest rate adjust- ment. A money market is being developed. In November 1997, Eritrea introduced its own currency, the nafka, to replace the Ethiopian birr. The currency has lost some external value since its adoption.

The National Bank of **Ethiopia** has pur- sued its efforts to enhance the use of indirect monetary instruments and reduce excess li- quidity since the end of the war, by inciting commercial banks to increase their holdings of T-bills, while keeping interest rates stable in order to boost lending activities. The banking sector, which the Commercial Bank of Ethiopia dominates, needs restructuring. The govern- ment has plans to strengthen the supervisory capacity of the central bank, make provi- sions for non-performing loans, and increase competition in the financial sector. Ethiopia switched to a floating exchange rate in 1992. Since then, change transactions have been gradually liberalized and in 2001, an inter-bank foreign exchange market became operational. The external value of the birr has since been relatively stable, depreciating against the US dollar by 2.9 percent in 2001.

The Central Bank of **Kenya** (CBK) has gained greater monetary autonomy since 1997, as a result of the central bank's financing of the government's deficits. The CBK has since maintained a tight monetary policy. Open market operations, discount rate adjustments, and reserve requirements are its main policy instruments. Money growth has slowed in recent years, reflecting tight monetary policy, but also weak economic activity and reduced government borrowing on the domestic mar- ket. Provisions establishing a minimum de- posit rate and a maximum lending rate (the 2000 Donde Act) were dropped in 2002. The

high level of non-performing loans renders the whole banking sector particularly fragile. Kenya has adopted a flexible exchange rate system since 1995. The Kenyan shilling has remained remarkably stable against all major currencies, a reflection of the mix of fiscal and monetary policy, as well as weak demand for imports owing to weak economic activity.

The Banque centrale de **Madagascar** made important progress towards restoring monetary stability in 1997-2001. Interest rates were con- sequently reduced with inflation. The BCM regulates the liquidity of the economy through T-bill auction and reserve requirement ratios. Its discount rate, which is market-determined since August 1999, is regularly adjusted to signal changes to the monetary policy stance. During the 2002 political crisis, two central banks were established, and open market interventions were brought to a halt. T-bills auctions finally resumed in late October, after an 8 months gap. There was a strong devaluation of the Malagasy franc in 1994, when a floating exchange rate was pushed through. The currency, whose value is market- determined, has been relatively stable since. There is no restriction on change transactions and the central bank only intervenes on the inter-bank foreign exchange market to reduce short-term volatility.

Mauritius was one of the first countries in the region to implement tight monetary policy. The Bank of Mauritius has used the Lombard rate to signal its monetary policy stance since December 1999. The Lombard rate was re- duced to 11.75 percent in August 2001 and 11.5 percent in November 2001, in the context of falling world interest rates. Money growth accelerated in 2002 for the first time since 1998, fuelled by a rise in commercial bank lending to the government and a rise in net foreign assets. Exchange rate control in Mauritius was abolished in 1994. The rupee has been implicitly anchored to the US dollar since 1999/2000, following a speculative attack against the currency in 1998. A real depreciation of the currency occurred in 2002, reflecting the strengthening of the euro against the US dollar.

Like prices and the exchange rate, interest rates in **Seychelles** are administratively set. The Central Bank in Seychelles also use reserve requirements as a policy tool. Trade and change transactions in Seychelles are tightly regulated. The currency is pegged to a pre-determined basket of currency. There is a central bank in Somalia (Somaliland). Although the Somaliland shilling has become legal tender since 1995, its external value is largely approximate.

The Bank of **Tanzania** (BoT) has had a successful track record in controlling the growth of money supply over the past 5 years. Broad money grew by an estimated 11.5 percent in 2002. The BoT liberalized its interest rates, developed open market operations, and pegged its discount rate to average T-bill yields in 1993-94. The bank's financing of budget overruns led to a rapid expansion of broad money until 1995. The deceleration in money growth and inflation has since led to a decline in interest rates. Change transactions in Tanzania were liberalized in 1993. The exchange rate is now market-determined. The Tanzanian shilling came under pressure in 2001, as a result of delays in export earnings, and lower than anticipated tourism receipts. The dollar value of the shilling depreciated by an average 14 percent that year. The rate of depreciation has since slowed down, with the shilling depreciating by only 2 percent against the US dollar during the first half of 2002.

The Bank of **Uganda** has switched to market-determined interest rates since 1995. Open market operations (interventions on foreign exchange markets, T-bills auctions, and since August 2001, repurchase operations (REPOs)) have become its main policy tools. Attention in recent years has focused on mopping up excess liquidity and deepening financial intermediation. Excess liquidity stems in part from bank closures in the late 1990s and in part from government spending of donor aid for poverty alleviation. The Ugandan shilling has been market-determined since 1993. The Central Bank occasionally intervenes on the inter-bank foreign exchange market to maintain exchange rate stability. The currency has maintained relative stability since 2001.

Recent Trends in Globalization

Trade liberalization and regionalization

The majority of countries in East Africa have adopted across the board liberalization and export-orientated development strategies since the late 1980s and early 1990s. As a result, external trade in the region as a whole has grown in importance and stood at 55.4 percent in 2002, which is low by continental standards (Table 2.7 and Figure 2.13). Paradoxically, as many as 5 countries in the region (Comoros, Eritrea, Ethiopia, Seychelles and Somalia) have no membership with the World Trade Organization. This indicates wide differences across countries. In Djibouti, Seychelles and Mauritius, exports and imports of goods and non-factor services amounted to more than 100 percent of GDP in 2002. By contrast, Ethiopia, Uganda and Tanzania bear the characteristics of relatively close economies, their trade-to-GDP ratio standing at less than 45 percent in 2002 (Table 2.7).

Table 2.7: East Africa: The External Sector

Country	Trade* as % of GDP		Trade Balance as % of GDP		Current Account		Terms of Trade (%)		Total External Debt as % of GDP		Debt Service as % of Exports	
	Average 1998-2001	2002a/	Average 1998-2001	2002a/	Average 1998-2001	2002a/	Average 1998-2001	2002a/	Average 1998-2001	2002a/	Average 1997-2000	2001
COMOROS	57.5	56.1	-13.7	-14.8	-7.4	-8.4	22.6	-25.7	99.9	96.4	3.7	8.4
DJIBOUTI	106.6	106.9	-34.1	-35.0	-3.1	-8.2	-0.5	1.3	66.6	72.9	5.5	5.3
ERITREA	.	.	.	.	.	.	.	.	.	.	.	.
ETHIOPIA	44.3	48.6	-16.0	-20.5	-4.8	-7.0	-3.6	-6.6	84.3	102.5	22.1	19.7
KENYA	59.5	59.4	-10.2	-10.7	-3.2	-4.6	-2.4	0.2	48.7	38.7	25.0	19.8
MADAGASCAR	59.8	55.6	-3.4	0.5	-6.0	-3.6	-4.5	-0.9	97.4	83.8	12.6	5.0
MAURITIUS	124.3	125.2	-8.9	-6.6	-1.0	1.3	-0.4	-2.5	26.0	22.0	5.0	9.2
SEYCHELLES	163.8	185.7	-31.9	-32.7	-17.3	-23.1	-4.1	-3.1	60.9	88.2	7.3	17.7
SOMALIA	.	.	.	.	-4.7	-3.4	-0.1	0.0	119.0	.	117.6	103.2
TANZANIA	40.0	43.1	-8.5	-8.9	-3.9	-4.9	-0.4	-0.8	85.6	82.0	34.5	29.6
UGANDA	38.3	37.1	-8.6	-10.4	-11.5	-12.4	-8.3	-2.0	58.9	63.8	20.7	22.8
EAST AFRICA	**55.1**	**55.4**	**-14.9**	**-14.4**	**-5.6**	**-5.7**	**-2.7**	**-1.4**	**75.9**	**75.2**	**20.1**	**18.2**

Note: a/ Preliminary estimates

Sources: ADB Development Research and Statistics Divisions.

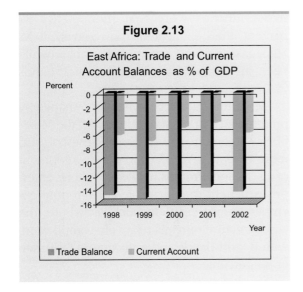

Figure 2.13

East Africa: Trade and Current Account Balances as % of GDP

■ Trade Balance   ■ Current Account

Trade liberalization in East Africa has gone hand in hand with efforts to foster regional trade integration. All East African countries but Somalia and Tanzania are members of the Common Market for Eastern and Southern Africa (COMESA). They account for 9 out of a total of 20 member countries. Tanzania withdrew from COMESA in September 2001 in favor of its membership to the tri-partite East African Community (Kenya, Uganda and Tanzania, EAC was re-launched in 2000). Tanzania, Mauritius and Seychelles are also members of the Southern African Development Community (SADC). Mauritius, Madagascar and Comoros form the Indian Ocean Commission, with France (Réunion).

Intra-regional trade within COMESA accounted for 5.2 percent of the region's exports to all Africa and 3.4 percent of the region's imports to all Africa in 2000. This does not account for informal cross-border trading. Kenya dominates intra-regional trade within EAC. The

EAC has in fact become the largest outlet for Kenya's exports, after the European Union. Kenya is in turn the first largest source of imports for Uganda, and the fourth largest source of imports for Tanzania. The three member countries have agreed to an 80 percent tariff discount among them and are in the process of devising a CET structure. By contrast, intra-regional trade within the OIC is relatively small, although trade between Madagascar and Mauritius has markedly increased since the mid-1990s, owing to the vertical integration of their EPZs.

The COMESA states were to remove all internal trade tariffs and barriers by end-2000 and establish a common external tariff structure by end-2004. Only nine countries, among which Djibouti, Kenya, Madagascar, and Mauritius, have implemented free trade policy within COMESA. Other COMESA countries have nonetheless greatly reduced their import tariffs on goods originated in the region. All member countries, but Seychelles, have also made some progress towards adopting the agreed common external tariff (CET) structure. The CET structure entails a four tariff bands, with rates ranging from 0 percent on capital goods to 30 percent on final goods.

Except for rice and petroleum products, which state trading monopolies import, there is no quantitative restriction on imports in **Comoros**. The external tariff regime was streamlined in 1996-97 to a system of three non-zero bands, with an average tariff rate of 30 percent. A significant number of goods are nonetheless subject to specific import taxes. Import licensing is still used in Djibouti, its cost varying with the volume and the category of products imported. Regular import taxes range from 5 percent to 40 percent. Djibouti is one of the nine countries to have joined COMESA's Free Trade Area (FTA) of zero tariffs.

Eritrea has committed itself to adopting the COMESA common external tariff structure by 2004. This implies streamlining its tariff regime from a cumbersome 12 to 4 rates and slashing the present maximum rate from 200 percent to 30 percent. Ethiopia has made some significant progress in liberalizing its external sector since the mid-1990s. All export taxes and non-tariff barriers have been eliminated and custom duties have been reduced for a wide range of imports. The government plans to reducing the average import tariff from the present 19.5 percent to 17.5 percent, lowering the maximum tariff rate from 50 percent to 30 percent, and reducing the number of bands from 7 to 4.

Kenya has simplified its trade regime over the years. A complex structure of *ad valorem* tariff rates and stand-by duties (mostly on food products) contributed to an average tariff rate of 18 percent (20.7 percent, when import fees are included). All stand-by duties have now been suspended and switched to an adjustment in tariff barriers. The number of tariff bands has since been gradually reduced from 13 to 9. This has led to a reduction in the average tariff rate to 17.2 percent. By virtue of its membership to COMESA and CBI, Kenya plans gradually to reduce the number of its non-zero tariff bands to 3 and the maximum *ad valorem* rate to 40 percent (except for tariff on sugar, which is 100 percent) to 25 percent.

Madagascar has agreed to special trade arrangements with Comoros and Mauritius, the other two members of the Indian Ocean Commission. Tariffs on goods with at least 45 percent value added originated in these two countries were first reduced by 80 percent, then eliminated from January 2000. Madagascar's tariff structure has meanwhile been streamlined from six to four tariff bands (5, 15, 25, and 30 percent).

Mauritius trade regime has been shaped by preferential market access (notably, the Multi-fiber Agreement, the EU Sugar Protocol, and more recently, AGOA) and the development of its Export Processing Zone, where enterprises benefit from sizeable custom duty exemptions and tax reduction. Elsewhere, the tariff structure remains relatively complicated, with 8 tariff bands and a maximum tariff rate of 80 percent.

Seychelles pursues a restrictive import licensing system, although the number of goods for which the Seychelles Marketing Board (SMB) has exclusive import rights have been reduced. All imports are subject to quotas.

Tanzania long used non-tariff barriers to protect its domestic industry. Tariffs have now become its main trade policy instrument; all import and export licenses have been abolished. Its two EAC partners, Kenya and Uganda, benefit from a reduction in import duty of 80 percent. The country is also committed to streamline and reduce its import tariff structure in concordance with the trade preferential agreements of SADC. The number of bands has recently been reduced to 3.

Uganda has pursued a liberalization of its trade regime since the late 1980s. At 9 percent, its average import tariff rate is the lowest in the sub-region. The tariff structure was simplified in 1995, with a reduction in the number of non-zero tariff bands from four to two and the lowering of the maximum *ad valorem* rate from 60 to 15 percent. Special protection is given to the sugar and textiles industry. Some imports are still subject to an import license commission of 2 percent and a 4 percent withholding tax. EAC originating imports are charged a preferential 20 percent of the country's most favored nation tariff.

Trade performance and export diversification.

East Africa's current account deficit widened in 2002 to 5.7 percent of GDP, compared with an average 5.6 percent of GDP in 1998-2001 (Table 2.7 and Figure 2.13). Some countries like Mauritius, and to a lesser extent, Madagascar, have succeeded in widening their export base to include manufactured goods, through the development of Export Processing Zones. Other countries that already have a small manufacturing base, notably Kenya, Tanzania, and Uganda, hope to take advantage of the US African Growth and Opportunity Act and progress towards regional integration to boost the export of their manufactured products in the coming years. All Eastern Africa countries, but Comoros, Eritrea, and Somalia, qualify for the Africa Growth and Opportunity Act-II (AGOA-II), as signed in August 2002. In addition, all the beneficiaries in the region, but middle income Mauritius and Seychelles, are eligible under the apparel Special Rule, which means that their apparel articles can enter the US duty free, regardless of origin of fabric and yarn. All Eastern Africa countries have also privileged access to the EU, as members of the African Caribbean and Pacific (ACP) group of countries.

Tourism is a vital source of foreign currency in East Africa. Kenya, Tanzania, Uganda and Mauritius account for the bulk of the region's tourism receipts. The impact of the September 11th attack on the region tourist industry was relatively small compared to other regions. There was no sharp drop in the number of tourists, but rather a stagnation in tourism receipts, owing to the world economic slowdown in 2001. Domestic political instability, security concerns and poor inadequate international air links remain the main hindrance to tourism development in the region.

One of the main realities of globalization for East African countries is that the price of their primary commodity exports is determined by global supply and demand conditions on which they have little control. After a steep recovery in 1996-1997, the world price of coffee, which is produced in Uganda, Ethiopia, Kenya, Tanzania, and Madagascar, has declined continuously since 1998, owing to over-supply on the world market. The last months of 2002 pointed towards a timid recovery in prices. The world prices for tea, a main foreign exchange earner in Kenya, Tanzania, and Uganda, and for cotton, which Tanzania and Uganda export, have also followed a downward trend since the mid-to-late 1990s. This, coupled with rising world oil prices in 1999-2000, has put pressure on the region's terms of trade. Gold, Tanzania's main export, was the only primary commodity exported in the region that experienced a price recovery in 2002

In contrast with the region as a whole, **Comoros**'s terms of trade improved between 1998 and 2001, indicating bullish world prices for vanilla and cloves, its main exports. The trend was reversed in 2002, with the growth of imports outpacing that of exports. The current account deficit increased to 8.4 percent of GDP in 2002, from an average 7.4 percent in 1992-2001, as a result. Rising private transfers and travel receipts from the exiled Comorian community and rising donor assistance partly compensated for the widening in the country's trade deficit.

Djibouti's current account deficit widened to 8.2 percent of GDP in 2002, down an average 3.1 percent of GDP in 1998-2001. The country's main source of foreign exchange earnings is transit trade with Ethiopia and Somalia. Non-factor services inflows from the airport and port activities declined in line with the switch in transit activities from Djibouti to the port of Assab in Eritrea.

With coffee exports accounting for two-thirds of the country's export, **Ethiopia** has borne the brunt of the continued decline in world coffee prices. Resumed economic growth fuelled the demand for imports in the meantime (despite a lower fuel bill in 2001-2002). Private transfers from the exiled community and resumed external assistance have nonetheless matched the trade deficit since 2000. Tourism receipts have also resumed since the end of the war. This has helped to maintain the current account deficit at a reasonable 7.0 percent of GDP in 2002.

Post-reconstruction activities in **Eritrea** have replaced military spending as the imports' main driving force. Given the country's narrow export base, consisting of salt, hide and skin and livestock, and despite resumed trade with Ethiopia, the trade deficit has widened since 1998, which rising external assistance and private transfers, and a small recovery in Assab port transit activities have failed to compensate.

Despite a continued slump in the world price of some of its major export crops, **Kenya**'s terms of trade only slightly declined by a yearly average 2.4 percent between 1998 and 2001, before stabilizing in 2002. This reflects a relatively wide export base and lower crude oil and petroleum products prices. Whereas tea, horticulture, petroleum products and coffee have suffered declined in receipts, earnings from exports of lesser importance, notably tobacco products, fish, and soda ash, have increased. The trade deficit remained largely unchanged in 2002, as a result. This, coupled with a continued decline in current transfers and sluggish tourism receipts, contributed to a slight deterioration in the current account deficit to 4.6 percent of GDP in 2002, against an average 3.2 percent of GDP in 1998-2001. The country's export base is dominated by agriculture, but Kenyan hopes to take advantage of AGOA and EAC to boost the exports of its manufactured products.

Madagascar expected the poor global economic performance in 2002 to have a dampening impact on its Export Processing Zone and tourism activities. With the political crisis, both Madagascar's exports and imports dropped drastically, as the EPZ was brought to a halt, access to harbors for traditional exports, such as vanilla, clove and coffee, were blocked and tourists cancelled their trips. There was a timid resumption in the second half of the year, when donors returned with generous aid pledges. The current account deficit stood at 3.6 percent of GDP in 2002, against an average 6.0 percent of GDP in 1998-2001.

Earmarked as a major success story of Africa, **Mauritius** was the first country on the continent to develop an EPZ. EPZ manufactured products (mostly clothing) now account for almost two-third of the country's exports. Tourism is the second largest source of foreign exchange earning, followed by sugar, Mauritius's traditional exports. The trade deficit averaged 8.9 percent of GDP in

1998-2001 and was estimated at 6.6 percent of GDP in 2002, mostly reflecting movements in the EPZ exports and imports. The services surplus was lower in 2002, reflecting a slight fall in tourism receipts (financial services are still at early stages). As a result, the current account surplus fell from 1.8 percent of GDP in 2001 to 1.3 percent of GDP in 2002, which still compares favorably with previous years. Mauritius's external competitiveness, which rising labor costs have started eroding, could be dealt with a major blow, once preferential trade agreements, such as the EU Sugar Protocol, come to an end in 2004 and competition for AGOA-eligible products intensify.

The surge in export earnings that characterized **Seychelles** in the 1995-2000 period, owing to the expansion of its canned tuna industry, ended in 2001. Tight foreign exchange regulations and a depressed economy led to a slight decline in the trade deficit in 2002. But the current account deficit stood at 23.1 percent of GDP in 2002, as a result of a sluggish tourist industry (tourism receipts, the country's biggest foreign exchange earner, have roughly remained unchanged since the mid-1990s) and rising external debt payments.

Mineral (mostly gold) and cash crops (notably coffee, cotton and tea) constitute the bulk of **Tanzania**'s exports. The commencement of gold production by Kahama Gold Mining Corporation in the second half of 2001 and rising world gold prices in 2002 compensated for poor export performance in the agricultural sector. There was an encouraging rise in manufacturing exports (mostly textile), owing to increased private interest in the industrial sector. Imports of capital and intermediary goods increased for the same reason. This led to slight rise in the country's trade deficit in 2002. The services account, which is negative owing to expensive freight, meanwhile suffered from sluggish tourism receipts. As a result, the current account deficit widened to 4.9 percent of GDP in 2002, down 3.9 percent of GDP in 1998-2001.

Despite a relatively successful strategy of export-led economic growth, **Uganda**'s export base remains poorly diversified, mostly consisting of weather-dependent agricultural products, such as coffee, tea, tobacco, and cotton, whose prices and volume can fluctuate widely. Uganda's terms of trade have continuously declined with world coffee prices since 1999. Despite being supported by strong private and official transfers inflows, the current account deficit rose from less than 11.2 percent of GDP in 1998-2001 to 12.4 percent of GDP in 2002. This mostly reflects a widening in the trade deficit, high freight and transport costs (owing to the country's landlocked position and firm world oil prices), and depressed tourism receipts.

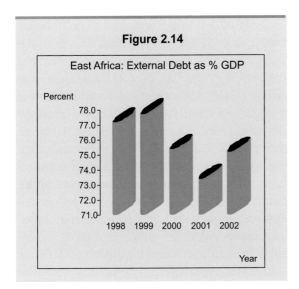

Figure 2.14

East Africa: External Debt as % GDP

External debt and other capital flows

The region's access to external financing is largely limited to official lending. The region's external debt burden has stabilized in recent years, due to prudent borrowing policies and the positive impact of the HIPC initiative. East Africa's debt stock stood at an equivalent 75.2 percent of GDP in 2002, against a yearly average 75.9 percent in 1998-2001 (Figure 2.14).

The process of globalization involves the removal of restrictions in both trade and capital flows. The region has little access to international capital markets and private lending and many countries have taken the decision to open their economies to foreign capital flows unilaterally. Yet, the lack of sophisticated domestic stock exchange markets restrains the potential for inflows of portfolio foreign investment. Foreign investors participation is nonetheless relatively high in Mauritius and Kenya exchange markets. Efforts to attract direct foreign investment (FDI) have concentrated on opening public enterprises to strategic investors, simplifying investment procedures by creating one-stop investment shops, offering tax incentives, and permitting outward income transfers (when the profits and dividends on investment are repatriated). The perception of corruption in the region is a major hindrance for FDI, however. Uganda, and Kenya are among the most 10 corrupt nations, according to *Transparency International.* In 2000, net foreign direct investment brought in US$ 493m to the region, according to UNCTAD's *World Investment Report 2002.*

Comoros has failed to attract foreign direct investment, mostly because of the country's endemic political instability. Comoros' debt burden stands above the regional average. Its debt GDP ratio was 96.4 percent in 2002. Multilateral debt makes up more than 70 percent of the total debt stock. The country remains current on its obligations with the World Bank, its main lender, but significant payment arrears are owed to the African Development Bank. A donor roundtable in July 2001 prompted a surge in debt service payments that year. The islands have never benefited from Paris Club rescheduling deals.

Djibouti's debt-to-GDP ratio followed an upward trend through most of the last decade, owing to a combination of sluggish economic growth and a continued rise in the nominal debt stock, especially in recent years. External debt totaled $400 million in 2002, 90 percent of which being publicly guaranteed official loans. The country's debt-to-GDP ratio rose to 72.9 percent of GDP in 2002, whereas the debt service ratio rose slightly to 5.3 percent in 2001. The small size of the economy has limited FDI inflows to port and airport activities, now under private management.

Half of Ethiopia's external debt is being owed to multilateral creditors. The nominal stock of debt was slashed by half in 1999, as a result of the cancellation of its Soviet debt. The debt-to-GDP ratio nonetheless still amounted to 102.5 percent in 2002. Ethiopia reached decision point under the enhanced HIPC initiative in November 2001. A Paris Club deal ensued in March 2002. Falling export earnings have mitigated the impact of debt relief under the enhanced HIPC initiative. FDI inflows in Ethiopia surged to US$ 136 million in 1998/99, an equivalent 2.1 percent of GDP, before subsiding to less than 1 percent of GDP in subsequent years.

After a surge in FDI inflows to US$ 127 million in 2000, investors confidence in the **Kenyan** economy reached rock-bottom, owing to economic mismanagement and strained relationships with donors. The stock of the country's external debt meanwhile continued its downward trend reflecting a lack of new lending to the country from both bilateral creditors and multilateral lenders. The government has pursued a relatively prudent borrowing policy since the early 1990s, mostly contracting loans on a long-term, concessional basis. The debt burden also subsided following the November 2000 debt rescheduling agreement with the Paris Club. Kenya is not eligible for debt relief under the Enhanced HIPC initiative. According to IMF estimations, the country's external debt appears sustainable. The nominal debt-GDP ratio declined to 38.7 percent in 2002, compared with a yearly average 48.7 percent in 1992-2001.

Madagascar reached decision point under the HIPC debt relief initiative in December 2000, paving the way for interim debt relief and a new Paris Club deal in March 2001. A Paris Club deal in March 1997 had previously helped to clear the payment arrears that Madagascar had accumulated over the years. Borrowing activities were brought to a halt through most of 2002 because of the political crisis. The stock of debt declined slightly as a result, to an equivalent of 83.8 percent of GDP. The government managed to remain current on its obligations to multilateral lenders, after some initial delays in payments. The country's EPZ development has drawn in significant FDI inflows in recent years, especially in 2001, when they netted US $ 108 million.

Mauritius's external debt profile bears the characteristics of that in an upper middle-income economy. Both the government and the private sector have access to foreign private lending, which makes up 45 percent of the country's total external debt. The government has tightened its external borrowing policy since 1997, instead preferring to finance its fiscal deficit from domestic sources. The debt-to-GDP ratio averaged 26.0 percent in 1997-2001, falling to 22.0 percent in 2002, whereas the debt service ratio rose to 9.2 percent in 2001. The bulk of FDI in Mauritius took place in the late 1980s. There was nonetheless a surge in FDI in 2000, as a result of the privatization of Mauritius Telecom.

Seychelles's external debt has increased continuously since 1999, reflecting the large fiscal deficit and increased public commercial borrowing, often at a premium. The government has continued to pile up principal and interest payment arrears. The debt-GDP ratio rose to 88.2 percent in 2002, whereas the debt service ratio stood at 17.7 percent in 2001. Seychelles attracts a small, albeit regular, stream of FDI each year, equivalent to about 5 percent of its GDP, mostly reflecting off-shore investment opportunities.

FDI in **Tanzania** took off in the mid-1990s, some being privatization-driven. Capital inflows have since kept up with GDP growth, gently rising from US$ 134 million in 1996 to US$ 400 million in 2001, both figures being roughly equivalent to 2 percent of GDP. The country reached the HIPC completion point in November 2001, giving rise to $3.0 billion of debt service relief in nominal terms over a 20-year period. The African Development Bank has agreed to $ 190.7 million of debt service relief. The Paris Club creditor countries followed up with a debt cancellation worth $737 million in NPV terms in January 2002. This, coupled with previous debt relief schemes and the government's prudent borrowing policy, helped towards a continuous decline in the debt-to-GDP ratio to 82.0 percent in 2002. The debt service ratio also fell to a still high 29.6 percent in 2001.

Uganda's debt structure indicates that multilateral creditors accounted for more than 70 percent of the total debt, bilateral creditors for less than a third, and private creditors for the remaining 2 percent. Uganda was the first country to reach completion point under the enhanced HIPC debt relief initiative in May 2000. Bilateral and multilateral debt relief is to total $ 2 billion over time under the initiative. The fall in the debt service ratio has been lower than expected as a result of a sharp drop in coffee export earnings and delays in securing bilateral agreements. The debt stock to GDP ratio also rose in 2002 to 63.8 percent, against an average 58.9 percent in 1998-2001. FDI in Uganda has surged since the end of the civil war, the net FDI inflows-to-GDP ratio standing at 4 percent in recent years.

Outlook

Economic growth in East Africa is expected to accelerate in 2003, with real GDP projected to rise by over 5 percent, up from 2.8 percent in 2002. The food crisis that **Eritrea** and **Ethiopia** are facing since summer 2002 will nevertheless dampen growth prospects in the sub-region. Whereas rates of growth were projected to exceed 6 percent in 2003 in these two countries, the drop in agricultural production could prove to be a major set back for these fragile economies in the medium term.

Elsewhere, the mixed success of the national reconciliation process in **Comoros** renders economic recovery fragile, although international support is still expected to rise. Growth will equally remain subdued in **Seychelles, Djibouti** and **Somalia**. In the meantime, growth in **Mauritius** will be restrained by declining external competitiveness and modest world growth. On a more positive side, a slight acceleration in Kenya's growth is projected for 2003, as confidence in the economy grows with the change in administration. Both the IMF and World Bank have said they were ready to release some of the suspended funding for economic and public sector reforms, if the new administration shows strong commitment to reforms of parastatals, macroeconomic stability, reforms in the judiciary and legal system, the privatization of Telkom Kenya and the introduction of anti-corruption bills.

A strong economic recovery is also expected in **Madagascar**, with real GDP growing by 8 percent, on the back of resumed activity in the EPZ, tourism, construction, mining, and possibly higher agricultural production. Growth will remain above 6 percent in **Tanzania**, assuming satisfactory weather conditions and continued strong activity in the mining sector. Economic prospects in **Uganda** will be mixed, as rising world coffee prices boost the agricultural sector, while activity in construction, a major source of growth in 2002, slows down, following withheld assistance for the Bujagali dam construction project.

North Africa

North Africa, which comprises seven countries – Algeria, Egypt, Libya, Mauritania, Morocco, Sudan and Tunisia - is the largest contributor to the continent's wealth, accounting for 44.6 percent of its GDP in 2002. It is a region of great disparities. Three countries are mostly oil producers (Algeria, Libya, and Sudan), while others depend on agriculture, mining, and/or tourism.

On the political front, the Sudanese government and the Sudan People's Liberation Movement signed a peace agreement in Kenya in July 2002, after 19 years of civil war, but commitment to the ceasefire has been shaky. Security in Algeria has improved since the signing of the Civil Concord in 1999, but the social and political situation has remained tense, notably in the region of Kabylia and during the period surrounding the May 2002 legislative elections. The region is relatively politically stable elsewhere, although terrorist fears following the September 11th events have seriously affected Tunisia, Morocco, and Egypt, all major tourism destinations.

Oil and natural gas exports, low value added manufactured products, non-oil minerals (phosphate and iron ore) and soft commodities (fish, cotton) dominate the region's merchandise exports. Libya and Algeria are the second and third largest oil producers in Africa, after Nigeria. North Africa's exports made up 35.2 percent of the continental total in 2002, the bulk of which being crude oil and gas.

North Africa's population represents about 22.1 percent of the continent's total. The region's per capita GDP averaged $1298 in 2002, which is more than double the continental's average. All countries are classified as middle-

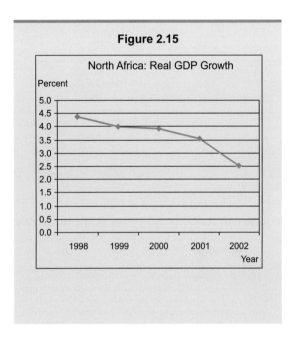

Figure 2.15

North Africa: Real GDP Growth

income countries, except for Mauritania and Sudan, where per capita GDP is less than $410. Sparsely populated Libya is the wealthiest country, with an income per head above $4000 (Table 2.8).

Recent Trends in the Domestic Economy

North Africa's growth performance has followed a downward trend in recent years. Real GDP growth slowed from a yearly average 3.9 percent in 1998-2001to 2.5 percent in 2002, which is 0.3 percentage point below the continental's average (Table 2.8 and Figure 2.15 and 2.16). This mostly reflects a slowdown of the Egyptian economy. Growth in the region has traditionally been underpinned by strong domestic investment, with the investment/GDP ratio standing at 24.7 percent in 2002 (Figures 2.16 and 2.17). Inflation in North Africa has

Table 2.8: North Africa: Gross Domestic Product and Export Performances

Country	Real GDP Growth Rate (%)		GDP Per Capita (US$)		Real Exports[c] Growth (%)		Exports[b] Per Capita (US$)	
	Average 1998-2001	2002[a]	Average 1998-2001	2002[a]	Average 1998-2001	2002[a]	Average 1998-2001	2002[a]
ALGERIA	3.2	2.5	1695	1752	2.8	-0.4	551	582
EGYPT	4.8	2.2	1361	1242	4.3	0.3	223	244
LIBYA	0.5	-0.6	5991	4192	.	.	.	.
MAURITANIA	4.3	5.1	372	342	-0.3	5.1	146	127
MOROCCO	3.8	4.2	1168	1192	9.0	-0.9	356	332
SUDAN	6.3	5.0	363	407	27.0	18.3	.	52
TUNISIA	5.2	2.0	2129	2195	8.4	1.4	935	931
NORTH AFRICA	**3.9**	**2.5**	**1375**	**1298**	**8.5**	**4.0**	**293**	**310**

Notes: a/ Preliminary estimates
         b/: Exports of Goods and Nonfactor Services at Market Prices
         c/: Real Exports of Goods and Non Factors Services Growth
Sources: ADB Development Research and Statistics Divisions.

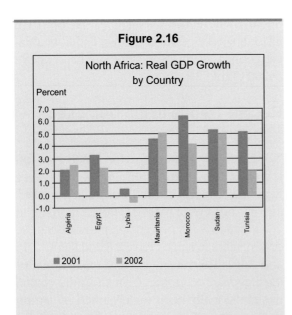

Figure 2.16

North Africa: Real GDP Growth by Country

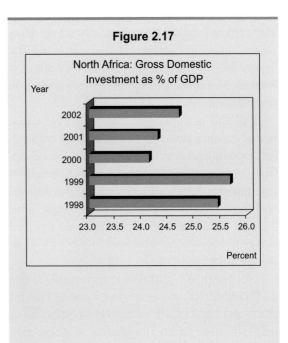

Figure 2.17

North Africa: Gross Domestic Investment as % of GDP

remained roughly stable in recent years, and averaged 3.4 percent in 2002, against an average 6.0 percent in 1998-2001 (Table 2.9 and Figure 2.18).

Despite sustained adjustment efforts following the oil price crash in 1986, economic recovery has been slow in **Algeria**. The Algerian economy is poorly diversified, with growth subject to large fluctuations caused by weather and oil price vulnerability. Real GDP grew by a moderate 2.5 percent in 2002, reflecting a mix combination of higher added value in the oil industry, sluggish activity in manufacturing and a slight contraction in agriculture. This is below the 1998-2001 annual average of 3.2 percent. Unabated political violence and civil unrest have continued to hamper private investment. The gross capital formation-to-GDP ratio nonetheless rose to 28.2 percent in 2002, reflecting rising public investment under the Economic Recovery Plan (2001-04). Sound fiscal and monetary policy and a stabilization in

the external value of the domestic currency brought inflation down from double digit rates in the mid-1990s to a yearly average 2.4 percent in 1998-2001 and 3.0 percent in 2002.

Economic performance in **Egypt** has followed a downward trend since 2000. Growth was robust in 1995-99, as austerity measures introduced in the early 1990s helped to create a more stable, macroeconomic environment. In 2002, economic growth decelerated to 2.2 percent, partly reflecting the impact on tourism and services of war against terrorism and escalating violence in the Middle East. Growth was supported by rising production in food crops, manufacturing, gas and electricity. Despite rising public capital outlays, the investment-to-GDP ratio declined in 2002, to 22.3 percent of GDP. The lack of access to credit, red tape and foreign currency shortages have continued to hinder private sector investment, after a boost in 1995-99 emanating from privatization and construction. Inflation in Egypt has markedly de-

Table 2.9: North Africa: Macroeconomic Management Indicators

Country	Inflation (%)		Fiscal Balance as % of GDP		Gross Domestic Investment		Gross National Savings	
					as % of GDP			
	Average 1998-2001	2002[a/]	Average 1998-2001	2002[a/]	Average 1998-2001	2002[a/]	Average 1998-2001	2002[a/]
ALGERIA	2.4	3.0	2.2	1.7	26.6	28.2	33.5	35.5
EGYPT	3.1	2.8	-3.3	-5.8	24.3	22.3	22.7	22.3
LIBYA	17.5	1.0	.	.	11.9	13.0	.	.
MAURITANIA	5.4	3.0	0.3	8.9	23.3	24.7	22.9	17.7
MOROCCO	1.5	3.0	-4.6	-6.3	22.8	24.4	23.5	28.3
SUDAN	10.6	8.5	-0.7	-1.0	17.7	18.2	.	.
TUNISIA	2.6	2.8	-2.6	-2.1	27.0	27.1	23.5	21.8
NORTH AFRICA	**6.0**	**3.4**	**-2.0**	**-3.5**	**24.9**	**24.7**	**25.7**	**26.7**

Note: a/ Preliminary estimates
Sources: ADB Development Research and Statistics Divisions.

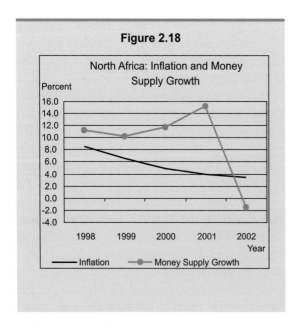

Figure 2.18

North Africa: Inflation and Money Supply Growth

Inflation — Money Supply Growth

celerated since the mid-1990s, reflecting a mix combination of stop-and-go fiscal and monetary policies and the Egyptian pound's peg to the US dollar. In an indication of the country's low import penetration ratio, consumer prices rose by a subdued 2.8 percent in 2002, against an average 3.1 percent in 1998-2001, despite the rise in import prices that stemmed from the depreciation of the Egyptian pound in 2001 and 2002.

Growth performance in **Libya** fluctuates with world crude oil prices. Whereas oil production has remained roughly unchanged, real GDP growth peaked to 4.4 percent in 2000, before slumping to 0.6 percent in 2001 and turning negative at –0.6 percent in 2002. Subsidized prices for food, housing and social services have kept inflation relatively low despite the international sanctions.

Mauritania's economy has successfully weathered external shocks, because of sound macroeconomic policy, sustained structural

reforms, and strong donor support. Real GDP grew by a yearly average 4.3 percent in 1998-2001 and accelerated to 5.1 percent in 2002. Private and public investment in telecommunication, energy, mining, social services, and infrastructure, have been buoyant, with the investment-to-GDP ratio standing at 24.7 percent of GDP in 2002. Tight fiscal and monetary policy has kept inflation under control, with price variations largely reflecting food availability and energy costs. Consumer prices rose by 3.0 percent in 2002.

Growth recovery in **Morocco** slowed down in 2002. A rebound of agricultural production and strong performance in tourism, telecommunication and construction spurred real GDP growth to 6.5 percent in 2001, after two years of drought-induced economic stagnation (agriculture's contribution to growth was negative through much of the last decade). In 2002, agricultural production grew by an estimated 11 percent, reflecting satisfactory weather conditions. The economy also performed well in the construction, mining and energy sectors. There was nonetheless a drop in tourism activities and other related services, as a result of the September 11th attack. All in all, the economy grew by 4.2 percent in 2002, which is still above the region's average. Public investment, notably in infrastructure, housing and water resources, spurred gross capital formation in 2002, with the investment-to-GDP ratio rising to 24.4 percent. Inflation meanwhile remained subdued, at 3.0 percent, against a yearly average 1.5 percent in 1998-2001.

Oil development largely explains **Sudan**'s robust economic growth since 1993. Harsh weather conditions and 19 years of civil war have hindered the development of the non-oil sector, notably in agriculture, which remains the main livelihood of the population. Real GDP growth averaged 6.3 percent a year between 1998 and 2001, before declining to 5.2 percent in 2002. The investment-to-GDP ratio has stagnated around 18 percent in recent years. Annual inflation followed a downward trend from 3 digit figures in the mid-1990s to a yearly average 10.6 percent in 1998-2001 and 8.5 percent in 2002, in large part indicating that money is no longer printed to finance fiscal deficits.

Growth in **Tunisia** has been strong in all sectors through much of the past decade, with the exception of agriculture. Real GDP grew by an average 5.2 percent a year in 1998-2001. In 2002, real GDP growth decelerated to 2.0 percent, reflecting a drought-induced drop in agricultural production, reduced tourism flows after the September 11th events, and sluggish export activities owing to a depressed demand in Europe. Private investment, mostly in services and export orientated manufacturing, and public investment in social and physical infrastructure inched down to 27.1 percent of GDP in 2002. Price stability has been maintained by a prudent monetary policy, with inflation down to a yearly average 2.6 percent in 1998-2001. Inflation rose to 2.8 percent in 2002, partly reflecting the government's decision to raise the price of subsidized food items.

Recent Policy Developments

Poverty reduction strategy

North Africa as a whole has the least poverty rate among all developing regions in the world, with only 2 percent of its population living under the poverty line of one dollar per day and 22 percent of its population living under the poverty line of two dollars per day. This hides wide disparities across countries, however.

Rising per capita GDP and improving the living standards of the population in terms of access to water, education and health constitute the main poverty reduction goals in Mauritania and Sudan, which are both on the list of the UN's least developed countries. **Mauritania**'s poverty reduction strategy program has been shaped by the Enhanced heavily indebted poor country (HIPC) initiative, to which it qualifies. A report was released in April 2002, which review progress made in the first year of the implementation of the Poverty Reduction Strategy Paper (PRSP, December 2000). An up-to-date poverty profile demonstrates a decline in the country's average poverty rate in recent years but mixed progress in the PRSP's five priority areas, namely rural development, urban development, universal education, health and water supply. Sudan was due to finalize a first draft of its interim PRSP by end-2002, with special reference to war-affected areas. Rising oil receipts will support the country's programs for poverty alleviation and rural development.

Algeria, Egypt, Morocco and Tunisia, which the World Bank classifies as lower middle income economies, are expected to reach most Millennium Development Goals by 2015. These countries boast the lowest HIV/AIDS prevalence rates in Africa. While Tunisia has achieved an impressive record of poverty reduction, the social situation has threatened to deteriorate in other countries, indicating a stagnation, if not decline, in GDP per capita and rising unemployment. Unemployment and lack of housing are acute problems in **Algeria**, where 30 percent of the active population is jobless (mostly the result of the liquidation of some thousands SOEs in the 1990s). Whereas education standards remain satisfactory, access to health services has deteriorated in this country. Education and health indicators in **Egypt** continue to be among the highest on the continent, with social programs concentrating on eliminating gender inequality and pockets of poverty and illiteracy in rural areas. Education policy and rural development are main priorities in **Morocco**, where the illiteracy rate is 50 percent. Poverty reduction strategy in **Tunisia** has largely focused on promoting professional training, creating jobs and fighting social exclusion. Tunisia runs an impressive, but costly, social protection system.

In **Libya**, the only upper middle income country in the region, income disparity is high. The Libyan authorities are in the process of mapping development indicators throughout the country, with the assistance of the UN Development Program.

Privatization

Akin to other African regions, privatization in North Africa slowed down in 2002, mostly reflecting bearish world market conditions. This contrasted with the successful privatizations of 2001, especially in the telecommunication sector. Attention has focused on Algeria, where the government has made some progress in devising a comprehensive privatization program.

While privatization has been part of **Algeria**'s economic reform program since 1995, previous efforts largely focused on restructuring public enterprises until new regulations were introduced in 2001. The privatization and investment codes were streamlined and some progress was made towards liberalizing key sectors of the economy, including telecommunications and mining. The first major divestiture to take place was that of the steel complex, SIDER, in 2001. The privatization program remained stalled in 2002. In October 2002, the ministry in charge of privatization announced that a first group of privatization announced that a first group of 70 small-to-medium SOEs will be auctioned within the next six months. A draft law aimed to liberalize the hydrocarbon sector meanwhile encountered strong domestic resistance, notably within the trade union movement.

Egypt's privatization program was launched in the early 1990s, involving the divestiture of some 314 state-owned companies. More than half of these enterprises have been fully or partially privatized (including six in 2002). The pace of privatization, which was particularly intense in 1996-99, has somewhat decelerated, largely reflecting time-consuming restructuring, a sluggish stock market, and political concerns that further job losses may spark strong domestic opposition. The government has notably been reluctant to privatize the banking sector. Attention has switched to the privatization of strategic utilities, most notably in telecommunications and electricity. The government has recently decided to postpone the 20 percent sale of Egypt Telecom, pending improved global market conditions.

Privatization in **Mauritania** has been extended to include major public utilities. The Banque de l'habitat de Mauritanie and Air Mauritanie were sold in 2000. The sale of a majority share in telecommunication utility, Mauritel, was completed in 2001. The bid for the electricity and water utility, Société nationale d'eau et d'électricité, was unsuccessful in 2002, reflecting the financial tightness of multinationals in this sector.

Morocco has privatized some 65 state enterprises (including 28 hotels) out of a total of over 110 since its public sector program was launched in 1990. The most significant recent privatization was the 35 percent sale of Maroc Telecom in 2001, which brought in an equivalent 59 percent of all proceeds between 1993 and 2001. The sale was allied with deregulation of the entire telecommunication sector, which also led to the sale of the country's second GSM license in 1999. In 2002, the government anticipated to sell the automotive plant, Somaca, the tobacco firm, Régie des Tabacs (a bid was subsequently launched in February 2003), and another 16 percent stake in Maroc Telecom. Progress was made in drafting a liberalization framework in the petroleum sector. Bids for a concession in the Rabat zoology park, two sugar processing plants (SURAC and SUNABEL) and for a second fixed-telephony license were unsuccessful. Three state banks are also due to be restructured and privatized.

The **Sudanese** government has drawn up a program of privatization, which includes the sale of public utilities, notably the post office, Sudan Air and the electricity parastatals.

The government in **Tunisia** has engaged in the gradual liberalization of the economy, since the 1986 collapse of oil prices. A total of 163 state-owned enterprises were sold between 1987 and November 2002. Focus switched from small, loss making companies to larger public firms in the mid-1990s. In 1995, a 20 percent share in Tunis Air was sold through public offering on Tunis Stock Exchange. The sales of cement plants in 1998 and 2000 were the largest privatization to date. The pace of privatization has slackened since 2001, reflecting the global economic slowdown and a genera lack of interest from international investors. Of the 41 enterprises scheduled for privatization in 2001, only 15 small companies were sold. Similarly, few of the 28 enterprises mooted for privatization in 2002 have gone through. These include Tunisie Telecom, which is in keeping with the liberalization of the telecommunications sector (a second GSM license was sold in March 2002).

Some state-owned financial institutions are also due to be opened to private participation, as part of the government's move to strengthen the banking sector.

Fiscal developments

The fiscal position in North Africa is relatively healthy compared with the rest of the continent. This has permitted to adopt pro-cyclical policies and delay unpopular civil service reforms. The regional fiscal deficit rose to 3.5 percent of GDP in 2002, from a yearly average of 2.0 percent of GDP during 1998-2001 (Table 2.9 and Figure 2.19).

With earnings from the oil sector accounting for as much as 60 percent of all annual receipts, the **Algerian** government's budget balance largely follows fluctuations in world oil prices. Fiscal policy has taken an expansionary stance since 2001, which is in line with the Economic Recovery Program. This notably involved a nominal rise in public sector salaries

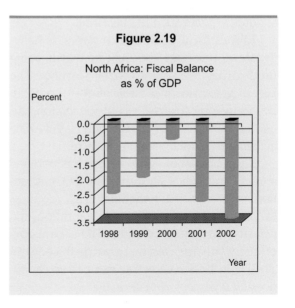

Figure 2.19

North Africa: Fiscal Balance as % of GDP

in January 2001 and higher capital and social spending, especially in infrastructure. A surge in oil revenues brought a positive fiscal balance of 9.8 percent of GDP in 2000, before falling to 3.4 percent in 2001 and 1.7 percent in 2002. Higher-than-budgeted oil revenues in 2002 nonetheless continued to feed the oil receipt stabilization fund established in 2001.

The fiscal deficit in **Egypt** has widened since 1999 to reach 5.8 percent of GDP in 2002. This partly reflects improved reporting of fiscal data, notably for capital outlays. The government has also sought to provide a fiscal stimulus to the economy, by increasing public investment, social spending and wages, and paying over-dues. The domestic revenue-to GDP ratio has nevertheless declined in recent years, owing to lower earnings from the oil industry and the Suez Canal Authority. Measures are being taken to strengthen revenue collection, reform the personal and corporate income taxes, and reduce tax exemptions. The government is also in the process of gradually converting the general sale taxes into a value-added tax, which should help to widen the tax base.

Libya's fiscal performance depends heavily on oil revenues, the bulk of which being used to pay the wages of civil servants. The Libyan government controls almost the entire economy, private activities outside the foreign-owned oil sector being restrained to low-scale activities in retailing and agriculture.

The **Mauritanian** government has pursued a tight fiscal policy since the mid-1990s. Attention has focused on strengthening tax revenues (a VAT was introduced in 1995), and boosting poverty-alleviation spending. The central government balance averaged a yearly 0.3 percent of GDP in 1998-2001 before rising to an exceptional 8.9 percent of GDP in 2002.

Despite a strong track record in tax administration, revenue performance in **Morocco** has weakened over the years, reflecting a proliferation of tax exemptions and external tariff reduction. The government has instead relied on substantial revenues from privatization to pursue an expansionary fiscal policy. There was a fall in the fiscal deficit in 1999 - when the country's second GSM license was sold - and in 2001 - when Maroc Telecom was privatized - despite rapidly rising recurrent expenditures (notably wages) and capital outlays (under the Hassan II Development Fund). Other sources of revenue, however, have failed to match the rise in public spending. The fiscal deficit notably widened to 6.3 percent of GDP in 2002, as a result of lower-than-expected privatization proceeds, and despite a 24 percent fall in subsidy costs, lower debt service payments and a 11 percent rise in direct tax revenues. The country's deteriorating fiscal stance calls for further revenue consolidation and a reduction in the public sector wage bill, currently at a high 13 percent of GDP.

The government in **Sudan** has embarked into a program of fiscal consolidation since 1997, as a result of which the pace of spending has declined and revenue generation has strengthened. Slippages remain frequent, however, notably indicating a heavy dependence on oil revenues and the cost of food insecurity. The fiscal deficit stood at 1.0 percent of GDP in 2002.

Fiscal consolidation has helped to maintain **Tunisia**'s budget deficit at a yearly average 2.6 percent of GDP in 1998-2001. Measures have notably been taken to widen the income, corporate and value-added tax base and strengthen revenue collection. This has helped to compensate for falling custom revenues following the trade agreement with the European Union. Structural rigidities exist on the expenditure side, with wages accounting for about 12 percent of GDP. The budget deficit declined to an equivalent 2.1 percent of GDP in 2002. The authorities have recently agreed to a general pay rise, following negotiations with trade unions in 2002. In return, the government has postponed a number of investment projects and continued to limit net hiring in civil service.

Monetary and exchange rate developments

Monetary policy in North Africa is characterized by its strong focus on maintaining competitive exchange rates. Public domestic borrowing and limited access to foreign currencies have often created tight liquidity situation. The region witnessed a drastic fall in money supply growth from 15.1 percent in 2001 to -1.5 percent in 2002.

The Central Bank of **Algeria** has used open market operations and discount rate adjustments since reforms in the mid-1990s. Money supply growth has been contained since 2000, despite rising net foreign assets. There has been an improvement in the banking sector's liquidity, as a result of reduced government borrowing, which prompted the Central Bank to reintroduce compulsory reserve requirements in 2001. Interest rates have meanwhile declined in the context of low inflation. The Central Bank notably cut its rediscount rate from 8.5 percent in 2000 down to 5.5 percent in 2002. After a sharp depreciation between 1993 and 1996, the Algerian dinar has achieved relative stability in recent years.

Pressure on the Egyptian pound has mounted in recent years, owing to the appreciation of the US dollar, to which the currency is pegged,

and the severe lack of foreign currencies resulting from a drop in tourism receipts. In January 2001, the Central Bank of Egypt formally abandoned the peg to the US dollar in place since 1991, to adopt a more flexible fixed exchange rate system. This resulted in a cumulative exchange rate depreciation of about 25 percent. In January 2002, the currency was fixed to the US dollar at a reduced rate of 4.51 LE/$. The resulting improvement in foreign currency liquidity was short-lived, however, and activities on the black market soon resumed. The Central Bank finally adopted a floating exchange rate system in January 2003, by eliminating exchange rate bands. After being expansionary in 1998-99, the restrictive monetary policy adopted in 2000 to defend the exchange rate led to a liquidity squeeze in the domestic economy. The Central Bank has reversed to an expansionary monetary policy since 2001, by notably lowering the rediscount rate and the reserve requirement ratio, in an attempt to boost economic activity.

There are tight foreign exchange regulations in **Libya**, with often, large premium between the black market and the official rate. The Libyan dinar, which is pegged to the SDR, was devalued by 51 percent in December 2001. Slashed import tariffs, administered prices and non-tariff barriers greatly reduced the inflationary impact of the devaluation. The central bank in **Mauritania** has adopted an accommodating stance, by notably lowering its discount rate in the context of low inflation. The country has allowed the ouguiya to float against other word traded currencies since 1995. The external value of currency has remained relatively stable in recent years.

The Bank Al-Maghrib in **Morocco** has eased its monetary stance in recent years, without threatening price stability. The Bank has favored the use of indirect instruments since 1993 and interest rates were deregulated in 1996. Advances to commercial banks were reduced and almost the totality of the central bank's T-bonds sold in 2001, to sterilize excess liquidity resulting from the sale of Maroc Telecom. The monetary stance was loosened in 2002 to support economic recovery and notably, encourage private investment. Interest rates have consequently followed a downward trend, with the inter-bank money rates standing at 2.6 percent in November 2002, against an average 4.4 percent in 2001. The authorities adjusted the fixed exchange rate for the first time in 11 years in April 2001. The currency basket, to which the Dirham is pegged, was adjusted to reflect the growing importance of the euro area in Morocco's trade and there was a 5 percent devaluation. The currency has since roughly maintained its parity against the US dollar.

Monetary developments in **Sudan** in the late 1990s focused on consolidating the independence of the central bank and unifying the exchange rate. A foreign exchange auction market was introduced in December 2001, paving the way for a managed floating exchange rate system.

The Central Bank of **Tunisia** has pursued a sound monetary policy, while gradually abolishing credit control and constantly upgrading and widening its range of monetary indirect instruments. After tightening its stance in 2001 in response to demand pressure on the external balance and depleting foreign reserves, the Central Bank injected some liquidity in the money market in 2002. The central bank's main objective is to maintain a constant real exchange rate, through regular intervention on the foreign exchange market. The convertibility of the dinar is limited. A slight depreciation of the nominal

exchange rate against the US dollar and the euro has helped to maintain the country's competitive edge in recent years.

Recent Trends in Globalization

Trade liberalization and regionalization

The region as a whole is moderately open, with the merchandise trade-to-GDP ratio standing at 53.5 percent of GDP (Table 2.10). This is because Egypt, the main economy of the zone, has traditionally been inward looking, having the largest domestic market in the region. The country's trade-to-GDP ratio was 40.8 percent in 2002, although Egypt is the main economy of the Common Market for Eastern and Southern Africa (COMESA, see East Africa). By contrast, Mauritania, which heavily depends on imports, and Tunisia, which has actively promoted greater integration with the global economy since the mid-1990s, are the most open economies of the region, with a trade openness ratio above 90 percent of GDP.

North Africa has tended to favor North-South co-operation over regional integration. Maghreb countries (Algeria, Morocco, Tunisia) and Egypt, in particular, have pursued trade liberalization under the so-called Barcelona Process (or Euro-Mediterranean Partnership). Signed in 1995, the Barcelona process seeks to intensify bilateral, multilateral and regional cooperation between the European Union and its 12 Mediterranean partners. Association Agreements, under which reciprocal, preferential partnerships are formally established with a view to creating a free trade zone by 2010, have come into force in Tunisia and Morocco; the agreement with Egypt, which was signed in 2001, has yet to be ratified, whereas negotiations were completed with Algeria in December 2001, with the association

Table 2.10: North Africa: The External Sector

Country	Trade* Average 1998-2001	2002[a/]	Trade Balance as % of GDP Average 1998-2001	2002[a/]	Current Account Average 1998-2001	2002[a/]	Terms of Trade (%) Average 1998-2001	2002[a/]	Total External Debt as % of GDP Average 1998-2001	2002[a/]	Debt Service as % of Exports Average 1997-2000	2001
ALGERIA	54.9	57.7	12.5	12.9	6.8	8.1	13.1	-7.3	52.9	42.3	36.7	22.1
EGYPT	40.2	40.8	-12.4	-9.0	-1.5	-0.2	6.0	-5.1	30.3	33.6	11.8	11.8
LIBYA	.	.	.	.	.	.	.	.	.	.	.	.
MAURITANIA	91.6	94.2	0.9	-5.4	-0.4	3.8	-0.9	-7.2	221.6	196.0	29.2	23.0
MOROCCO	65.3	65.7	-8.0	-8.1	0.6	1.3	3.8	3.3	53.5	45.0	21.1	16.5
SUDAN	.	.	-3.5	2.5	-14.0	-9.9	.	.	.	.	.	.
TUNISIA	90.9	96.0	-11.1	-11.5	-3.5	-4.6	-0.9	-0.5	58.4	59.9	19.9	15.6
NORTH AFRICA	**50.8**	**53.5**	**-2.4**	**-0.8**	**1.1**	**1.5**	**5.0**	**-3.3**	**45.3**	**48.6**	**24.2**	**18.3**

Note: a/ Preliminary estimates
*: (Exports & Imports) of Goods and Non Factors Services at Market Prices
Sources: ADB Development Research and Statistics Divisions.

agreement subsequently singed in April 2002. The agreements commit the four countries to gradually liberalizing trade in EU manufactured and agricultural products and EU services, in return for duty free access to EU markets. The EU is by far the region's main trading partner. Exports to the EU account for 70-80 percent of Tunisia, Algeria, and Morocco's exports, while imports from the EU account for 60-70 percent of their imports.

The Barcelona process also seeks to implement free trade among the Mediterranean signatories. Recently revived by Tunisia and Morocco in 2001, the Arab Maghreb Union (AMU), which is made up of Algeria, Libya, Mauritania, Morocco and Tunisia, aims to foster regional economic and cultural co-operation (involving notably the harmonization of custom procedures, and the reduction in intra-regional trade barriers) and to promote common defense. There are also plans to create a regional investment bank. In July 2002, the European Parliament adopted a resolution in favor of a EU-UMA partnership, seeking to establish a privileged partnership between the two regions. But the continuing deadlock between Algeria and Morocco over the status of Western Sahara has hindered the union's revival. In addition, intra-AMU trade remains marginal, contributing to 2.3 percent of the regional grouping's exports and 3.3 percent of its imports. A head-of-state AMU summit was due to take place in Algeria in June 2002, but was subsequently postponed. Perhaps more promising are plans for an Arab-Mediterranean free-trade zone, as initiated by Morocco, Tunisia, Egypt and Jordan in 2001, which is in keeping with the Barcelona initiative. Experts from the four countries met in 2002 to draft the agreement.

Morocco and Tunisia's decision to become members of the Community of Sahel-Saharan States (CEN-SAD) in 2001 has further weakened AMU's viability. CEN-SAD entails the broadest regional integration arrangement in the region. The regional organization was established in 1998 in Tripoli, Libya. The fourth summit was held in Syrte, Libya, in March 2002, when Togo's and Benin's memberships were accepted but that of Liberia adjourned. This brings the CEN-SAD community to 18. All countries in North Africa, but Algeria and Mauritania, are now represented. The objective of the organization is to promote trade, development and regional integration (with notably the development of economic infrastructure), and to secure peace, stability and security in the region. African Union is its ultimate target. The African Bank for Development and Trade, a regional investment bank financed by CEN-SAD, recently opened a branch in Dakar, Senegal, and there is also a Special Fund for Solidarity. CEN-SAD plans to create a regional airline, a conflict watchdog, and a university hospital.

All North African countries, but Algeria, Libya, and Sudan, are members of the World Trade Organization. Algeria is actively negotiating its WTO membership and discussion on terms of entry has started. Sudan applied for membership in 1994, but negotiations have yet to start. Note that the General Agreement on Trade in Services (GATS), which was signed under the Uruguay Round, is of special relevance for countries, like Tunisia, Morocco, and Egypt, where tourism is a main source of foreign exchange revenue.

There has been a marked acceleration in **Algeria**'s trade liberalization program over the past 2 years. This has entailed the discontinuation of minimum duty values (now replaced by temporary additional duties); the lowering in the maximum MFN rate from 45 to 30 percent; and the establishment of three non-zero tariff bands. The country's external tariff structure was previously characterized as complex, uncertain and inequitable. The average MFN tariff rate was down 25 percent by 2002. The authorities are next to streamline the number of goods subject to temporary additional duties and proceed with preferential tariff dismantlement with the EU. Membership with WTO will probably be concluded in 2003.

Egypt has initiated trade policy reforms under the Most Favored Nation clause since 1995, when it acceded to the WTO. Main achievements include the discontinuation of import licensing requirements (formerly banned imports are now subject to tight quality control requirements); the reduction in the maximum MFN tariff from 100 percent to 40 percent (with exceptions in alcoholic beverages, textiles, and some motor vehicles); the reduction in the average tariff from 42 percent to 27 percent; and the streamlining of the custom duties structure. There is still a strong anti-export bias in trade policy, however. The Association Agreement with the EU, which has yet to be ratified, will provide the country's exports with immediate and unlimited duty-free access to EU markets; some agricultural exports will nonetheless remain subject to quotas. In return, Egypt is committed to gradually reducing tariffs on EU agricultural and industrial goods.

Libya has become candidate to join the WTO since December 2001. The country also takes part in the Barcelona Process as an observer, with the view to soon becoming full partner of the initiative. Import controls remain tight, despite the lifting of international sanctions. Custom duties were significantly reduced in 20002, in an attempt to mitigate the price impact of the December 2001 devaluation.

Mauritania has eliminated barriers to international trade and liberalized its exchange rate system since the early-1990s. In line with its participation in the multilateral trading system, import licenses and other non-tariff measures have been abolished (including the former rice quota system, which was discontinued in 1999)., the number of custom duties was reduced from 13 in 1997 to 4 in 2000 and the maximum MFN rate feel from 30 to 20 percent. The average MFN rate stood at a low 10.6 percent in 2002. The export regime has also been liberalized.

Despite substantial trade liberalization since the mid-1980s, import duties in **Morocco** are general high, with an MFN average tariff rate above 30 percent. Health and security standards and the use of reference prices also apply to certain categories of products. Measures recently taken include reducing the number of tariff bands to 8 in 2001 and transforming quantitative restrictions (most notably on agricultural goods) into tariff equivalents. There are plans to reduce the number of tariff bands down to 5 and reduce e the maximum MFN tariff rate from 50 to 40 percent. Trade liberalization under the Association Agreement with the EU, which came into force in 2000, has progressed as planned. A further 6.5 percent in custom duty revenues has been budgeted for 2003.

Sudan is in the process of devising a trade reform program to streamline and rationalize its custom duty structure. There are few quantitative restrictions. There was a temporary increase in the average tariff rate to 19.9 percent in 2001, which is low by continental standards. A 2 percent defense tax is imposed on imports since January 2002.

Tunisia was the first country in the region to pursue preferential trading with the EU. The dismantlement of import tariffs with the EU has been phased over a 12 year period (1996-2008) and across four categories of products (non-competitive equipment goods, primary and semi-finished products, home-substituting equipment goods and consumption goods). Specific agreements have been signed with the EU on agricultural trade and fisheries. At the same time, the MFN average tariff for non-EU products is relatively high, at 28.3 percent in 2001. The authorities intend to simplify and modernize custom procedures, deemed cumbersome.

Trade performance and export diversification

The region's external position remains comfortable. The current account balance was in surplus in 2002, at 1.5 percent of GDP, against a yearly average 1.1 percent of GDP in 1998-2001 (Table 2.10 and Figure 2.20).

All North African countries, but Mauritania and Morocco, are crude oil exporters. Whereas merchandise exports from Algeria, Libya and Sudan are almost entirely oil and gas related, export composition vary greatly in other countries. Despite being the second largest economy on the continent after South Africa, Egypt has a relatively narrow and unsophisticated export base, dominated by petroleum products, agricultural goods (mostly cotton), and the spinning and weaving industry. This is because growth has been inward looking, with the bulk of investment taking place in the non-tradable sectors. By contrast, Morocco and Tunisia have been more successful in diversifying their export base away from traditional products. In Tunisia, the importance of traditional exports, mostly crude oil and phosphates, markedly declined in the 1990s, as the authorities pursued an active

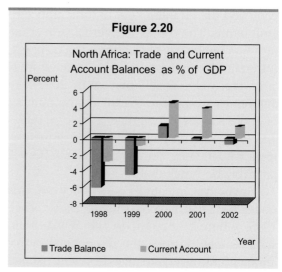

Figure 2.20

North Africa: Trade and Current Account Balances as % of GDP

diversification policy. Manufactured exports, particularly textiles, and electronic and mechanical equipment, nowadays constitute the bulk of the country's exports. Likewise, export earnings from finished products (consumption and equipment goods) constitute roughly 40 percent of all exports in Morocco. The export share of phosphate and phosphate-derivated products remain relatively high, however.

Export diversification makes North Africa as a whole less sensitive to external shocks. As a result, the sub-region has been relatively sheltered from the sharp downward trend in prices that has characterized many non-oil primary products in recent years. While world cotton prices have slumped since the late 1990s, the Egyptian cotton is high-grade and is thus sold with a premium. In addition, world markets for fish, phosphate rock, and iron ore, the region's main commodity exports, have held up relatively well to the global demand slowdown, compared to other commodities.

Outside oil and merchandise exports, tourism is a major source of foreign exchange earnings in North Africa. Tourism figures in Egypt,

Morocco and Tunisia dropped sharply in the fourth quarter of 2001, following the aftermath of September 11th. Egypt is particularly sensitive to the security situation, especially since the Luxor terrorist attack on tourists in 1997. While 2001 as a whole was a relatively good year for tourism in Tunisia and Morocco, tourist arrivals fell by 16 percent in Egypt. The tourism industry in North Africa was depressed in 2002 reflecting an overall crisis of the tourism industry in the Moslem world and poor growth performance in Europe (North Africa is the region to attract most tourists from Europe on the continent).

Despite preferential access to the EU markets, many North African producers are likely to face rising competition for their export markets, with notably the dismantling of the Multi-Fibre Agreement, but also domestically, as the free trade provisions of the association agreements with the EU are gradually implemented. Morocco and Egypt have also faced rising competitive pressure over the years, as the result of an appreciation in their real effective exchange rates. Both countries have recently proceeded with a devaluation of their national currency.

Hydrocarbons earnings account for 98 percent of total exports in **Algeria**. Given the stagnation in gas production in recent years, the trade surplus and current account balance have mostly reflected fluctuations in world oil prices and changes in OPEC oil production quotas. The oil price recovery in 1999-2000 largely explains the strengthening of the current account balance over this period. The current account surplus fell to 12.4 percent of GDP in 2001, owing to a 14 percent fall in world oil prices. Despite relatively firm oil prices, lower oil exports led to a further fall in the current account surplus, to 8.1 percent of GDP in 2002, which is still above the 1998-2001 average.

Egypt's trade deficit shrank in 2002, because of a fall in imports brought about by a tight dollar liquidity situation, restrictions on the public sector's imports, and the decline in the dollar value of the Egyptian pound. The performance of non-oil manufacturing exports meanwhile remained lukewarm, whereas oil exports declined slightly with production. The fall in the trade deficit was enough to compensate for the 21 percent drop in tourism receipts in 2002, with the current account deficit narrowing to 0.2 percent of GDP. This is an improvement on the 1998-2001 period, when it averaged 1.5 percent of GDP.

Libya is also heavily dependent on oil, which accounts for over 95 percent of export revenues. The country's trade surplus fluctuates with world oil prices, in the context of restrictive trade rules and OPEC production quotas. The current account balance frequently moves from deficit to surplus, given uncompressible outflows in oil-related services and income.

Mauritania's trade performance is vulnerable to external shocks, being dependent on only two major exports, fisheries and iron ore, with its import mostly consisting of oil and food products. High freight and transport costs have largely contributed to the external gap, the trade balance occasionally reaching equilibrium. Strong donor support nonetheless helped to turn the country's current account deficit into a surplus equivalent to 3.8 percent of GDP in 2002.

Morocco's export growth outpaced that of imports in 2002, with notable increases in the exports of electrical goods, phosphates and phosphate-derived products. Imports stagnated, as a result of sluggish domestic demand and a roughly unchanged fuel import bill. As a result, the trade deficit was maintained at 8.1

percent of GDP in 2002, against an average 8.0 percent in 1998-2001. The country's current account deficit is smaller in comparison and even turned into a surplus in 2001, as a result of exceptional workers remittance inflows and rising tourism receipts. The current account surplus fell to 1.3 percent of GDP in 2002, largely reflecting the slowdown in the country's tourism industry.

The profile of **Sudan**'s external sector has changed dramatically since oil came on stream in mid-1999. Whereas the trade balance has turned into a healthy surplus since 2000, invisible outflows have surged, reflecting oil-related transport expenses and profit remittances by foreign oil companies. The current account deficit averaged 14 percent of GDP in 1998-2001, falling to 9.9 percent of GDP in 2002.

Tunisia's trade deficit was maintained at 11.5 percent of GDP in 2002, despite lower performance in manufacturing exports and rising food imports. This is because the demand for equipment and semi-finished imports emanating from exporting companies and that for consumption goods lost momentum, owing to a deceleration in economic growth. Yet the country's current account deficit rose slightly to 4.6 percent of GDP in 2002, owing to a sharp fall in services resulting from falling tourism receipts and lower air transport revenues. Success in boosting tourism had given rise to large services surplus in previous years. Tourism receipts notably rose by 7.5 percent in 2000 and 6 percent in 2001, before falling by 18.5 percent in the first half of 2002.

External debt and other capital flows

The structure of North Africa's capital account differs greatly from that in Sub-Saharan African regions. Firstly, many North African countries have easier access to international capital markets. Egypt, Morocco, and Tunisia have secured favourable ratings from several credit rating agencies, which has enabled the Egyptian and Tunisian governments to raise money through sovereign bonds, while the Moroccan government has converted part of its external debts into Brady bonds. Note that most countries nonetheless favor official, concessional long-term lending. Secondly, North Africa is a main pool for foreign investors on the continent. In 2001, according to UNCTAD *2002 World Investment Report*, FDI inflows in the region totaled US$5.5 billion in 2001. The rich natural endowment of crude oil continues to be a major attraction, while there has been strong international support from some privatization transactions. Foreign equity investment has also begun timidly, since Morocco and Egypt open their stock exchange markets to foreign investors. Finally, the region's external debt burden is overall low by regional standards. The total debt stock equivalent to 48.6 percent of regional GDP in 2002 (Figure 2.21).

Whereas **Algeria** continues to attract substantial foreign investment in its hydrocarbons sector, FDI is minimal in the non-oil sector, because of the perceived risks associated with the country's unstable political situation and more recently because investors have adopted a wait-and-see attitude pending changes in the investment code and restructuring of the public sector. The external debt stock in Algeria is mostly made of rescheduled bilateral loans from the 1994-98 period and multilateral credits. The government has refrained from borrowing or guaranteeing commercial loans, to which the country has access at a premium, and has focused on concessional lending instead. The external debt stock has followed a downward

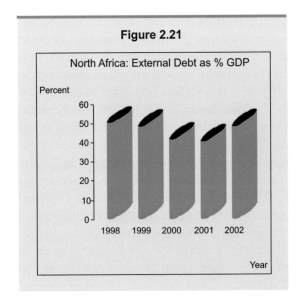

Figure 2.21

North Africa: External Debt as % GDP

trend since the mid-1990s, equivalent to 42.3 percent of GDP 2002. While more erratic, the debt-service ratio also greatly reduced through the 1990s and stood at 22.1 percent of GDP in 2001, reflecting firm oil prices.

Egypt is the largest recipient of private capital flows and official lending in the region. Yet, much more could be done to attract investors, given the country's potentials (the net FDI-GDP ratio stands at less than 2 percent of GDP). Egypt has considerably liberalized and simplified its investment regime since a new code was passed in 1997. The country has opened its domestic stock exchange market to foreign portfolio investment since the early 1990s, but the slow pace of privatization, depressed global financial markets, and the tight liquidity situation has hindered progress in recent years. Generous debt relief deals in the early 1990s, coupled with the government's prudent borrowing policy, slashed the country's external debt stock from 90 percent of GDP in the early 1990s to 33.6 percent in 2002. The debt service

ratio was maintained at 11.8 percent in 2001. Greater integration into global capital markets was achieved in June 2001, when Egypt successfully issued Eurobonds, worth US$1.5bn.

Libya is poorly integrated to the world financial markets, having little needs for external financing. **Mauritania** reached completion point under the Enhanced heavily indebted country initiative (HIPC) in June 2002, paving the way for debt service relief equivalent to $ 1.1 billion. This is expected to reduce the debt-service/government revenue from 35 percent in 1998 to 11 percent over 2002-11. Also reflecting HIPC debt relief, the debt-GDP ratio declined to a still high 196 percent in 2002.

The government in **Morocco** has pursued to reduce its external debt burden since the mid-1990s, by notably negotiating debt-for-equity swaps with its major official creditors and buying back some of its commercial debt. The stock of external debt consequently declined from roughly 75 percent of GDP in the early 1990s to 45 percent of GDP in 2002, as a result. Privatization proceeds occasionally inflate FDI inflows in Morocco. There was notably a surge in foreign investment inflows in 2001 to US$2.3bn (an equivalent 6.6 percent of GDP), as a result of a 35 percent sell in Maroc Telecom. A small amount of foreign equity investment is raised on the Bourse des Valeurs de Casablanca.

Sudan is heavily indebted, but the oil export boom in the country has greatly alleviated the country's debt burden, whereas rising FDI in the oil sector has helped to diversify the balance of payment financing sources. Whereas the government in **Tunisia** frequently draws on international capital markets, the external debt stock is in large part owed to official creditors, on a long-term, concessional basis. The debt-

GDP ratio has followed a gently downward trend since the mid-1990s and stood at 59.9 percent in 2002. Tunisia's net FDI-GDP ratio is the highest in the region, hovering between 3 and 4 percent. The bulk of FDI takes place in manufacturing. There were more than 2,000 foreign capital enterprises implemented in the country by end-2000. The capital account has yet to be fully liberalized, however, by notably permitting overseas portfolio investments within a ceiling.

Outlook

Economic growth in North Africa is forecast to accelerate slightly to about 3.6 percent in 2003, from 2.5 percent in 2002. There are significant risks linked to a possible deterioration in the international political environment, however. Security concerns stemming from the war in Iraq could notably affect both investment and tourism in the sub-region.

Growth in **Algeria** is forecast to accelerate in 2003, driven by rising oil production, reinforced co-operation with the EU, a dynamic telecom industry and improved conditions in agriculture. Growth rates in Algeria could nudge 5 percent in the medium run, depending on the pace of structural reforms, notably with regard to the privatization program and the restructuring of the banking sector.

Egypt's economic outlook will be mostly driven by natural gas development, as the government successfully promotes new export options, including a pipeline to Jordan and liquified natural gas trains to feed European market. The country's business climate is also set to improve in 2003, following the authorities' decision to adopt a floating exchange rate system and, in so doing, restore foreign

exchange liquidity. The anticipated recovery in tourism activity, which slumped in 2002, as a result of the September 11th, 2001 attack, has become increasing uncertain, however, as tension in the Middle East is set to escalate.

In **Mauritania**, the economic deceleration evidenced in the later part of 2002, on accounts of droughts and a drop in fish and iron ore exports, is likely to continue into 2003. The government in **Morocco** projects growth to rise to 5.5 percent in 2003, as a result of a good agricultural season, a dynamic construction sector and rising business confidence as reforms proceed at a satisfactory pace. Yet, as much as one percentage point growth could be lost in the event of a war in Iraq, as a result of a higher energy bill and lower tourism receipts.

Likewise, **Tunisia**'s growth is projected at between 2.7 and 3.6 percent in 2003, driven by a pick up in exports and tourism and by a recovery in agricultural production, but this is assuming no external shocks and a modest recovery in demand in Europe. Economic prospects in **Libya** and **Sudan** will meanwhile be brighter, as both world oil prices and their respective domestic oil production are set to remain favorable.

Southern Africa

Ten countries make up Southern Africa –Angola, Botswana, Lesotho, Malawi, Mozambique, Namibia, South Africa, Swaziland, Zambia, and Zimbabwe. The sub-region is well endowed with natural resources, notably minerals. In 2002, Southern Africa contributed 26.1 percent of Africa's GDP, making it the second largest wealth contributor on the continent after North Africa. The region is dominated by South Africa, which accounts for about 76 percent of the sub-region's GDP.

The March 2002 presidential election in Zimbabwe has dominated recent political news in the region. The Zimbabwe president, Robert Mugabe, whose re-election has been condemned by the international community, has received the support of neighboring countries. Another equally important development was the signing of a peace agreement between the Angolan government and the military wing of UNITA in April 2002, following the death of Jonas Savimbi. Namibian and Zimbabween troops have meanwhile started to withdraw from neighboring DRC.

In 2002, Southern Africa's exports accounted for 35.5 percent of the continental total, with South Africa contributing more than a half. Southern Africa is heavily reliant on exports of primary products – oil, gold, diamonds, copper, platinum, and agricultural products including tobacco, cotton, horticulture and fruit. The more developed economies in the region also export labor-intensive manufactured products.

The population in Southern Africa represented 14.4 percent of the continent's total in 2002. The region's per capita income stood at $1169 in 2002. But this average hides considerable disparities between middle income

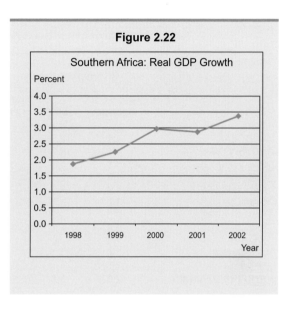

Figure 2.22

Southern Africa: Real GDP Growth

countries– Botswana, Namibia, South Africa and Swaziland – where per capita GDP ranges between $1200 and $3300, and some of the world's poorest – Mozambique, Malawi, and Zambia - where per capita incomes range between $150 and $350 (Table 2.11).

Recent Trends in the Domestic Economy

Whereas continental growth slowed down in 2002, GDP growth in Southern Africa accelerated from an annual average of 2.5 percent during 1998-2001 to 3.4 percent in 2002 (Table 2.11 and Figures 2.22 and 2.23). The regained economic activity during 2002 was mostly driven by improved performance in South Africa. Economic performance was diverse elsewhere, ranging from growth of 14.5 percent in Angola to an estimated decline of 11.4 percent in Zimbabwe. A defining characteristic of Southern Africa's growth performance is the decline in domestic investment. Gross domestic investment declined

Table 2.11: Southern Africa: Gross Domestic Product and Export Performances

Country	Real GDP Growth Rate (%)		GDP Per Capita (US$)		Real Exports[c/] Growth (%)		Exports[b/] Per Capita (US$)	
	Average 1998-2001	2002[a/]	Average 1998-2001	2002[a/]	Average 1998-2001	2002[a/]	Average 1998-2001	2002[a/]
ANGOLA	4.1	14.5	584	728	1.1	25.2	467	511
BOTSWANA	7.4	5.1	3171	3297	1.9	0.4	1823	1709
LESOTHO	0.1	4.0	423	323	12.9	38.9	96	132
MALAWI	1.9	1.8	157	153	0.8	0.7	44	36
MOZAMBIQUE	8.9	9.0	211	243	27.4	-0.8	40	50
NAMIBIA	3.1	3.1	1928	1571	0.7	2.5	924	869
SOUTH AFRICA	2.3	3.0	2950	2354	3.1	0.9	813	908
SWAZILAND	2.6	1.6	1464	1243	0.8	0.0	1096	977
ZAMBIA	2.3	2.8	321	340	3.5	11.6	89	100
ZIMBABWE	-2.6	-11.4	481	408	-5.8	-18.3	228	137
SOUTHERN AFRICA	**2.5**	**3.4**	**1399**	**1169**	**4.6**	**6.1**	**449**	**474**

Notes: a/ Preliminary estimates
         b/: Exports of Goods and Nonfactor Services at Market Prices
         c/: Real Exports of Goods and Non Factors Services Growth
Sources: ADB Development Research and Statistics Divisions.

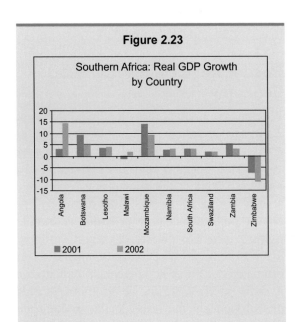

Figure 2.23

Southern Africa: Real GDP Growth by Country

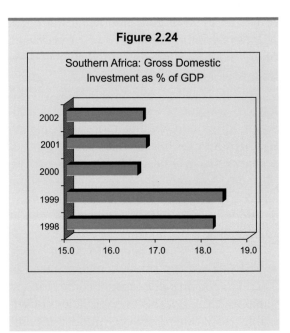

Figure 2.24

Southern Africa: Gross Domestic Investment as % of GDP

from an average of 17.4 percent of GDP during 1998-2001 to 16.7 percent in 2002 (Figure 2.24). Domestic investment has nevertheless remained strong in some countries, notably Mozambique and Namibia. The severe food crisis that has gripped the sub-region heightened inflationary pressures in the later part of 2002, with the rate of inflation averaging 10.4 percent that year (Table 2.12 and Figure 2.25).

Angola registered an exceptional growth of 14.5 percent in 2002, as a result of higher oil output and massive foreign investment in the oil sector. The country continued to face hyper inflation, underlying a loose fiscal and an accommodating monetary stance. The inflation rate nonetheless decelerated from an average 212.7 percent in 1998-2001 to a promising 109 percent in 2002.

Growth in **Botswana** decelerated to 5.1 percent in 2002 as a result of lower diamond production. Growth in the non-mining sector, notably services, has helped to compensate for poor performance in the mining sector. The GDI-GDP ratio declined from an average 24.8 percent in 1998-2001 to 14.0 percent in 2002, because of lower foreign direct investment. Exchange rate depreciation drove inflation to a yearly average of 7.3 percent in 1998-2001, before decelerating to 5.6 percent in 2002. There was a marked rise in consumer inflation in the later part of the year, as a result of the regional food shortage.

Lesotho experienced a relatively strong growth performance in 2002, on the back of export-oriented manufacturing growth. Real GDP grew by 4.0 percent, against an average

Table 2.12: Southern Africa: Macroeconomic Management Indicators

Country	Inflation (%)		Fiscal Balance as % of GDP		Gross Domestic Investment as % of GDP		Gross National Savings	
	Average 1998-2001	2002[a]	Average 1998-2001	2002[a]	Average 1998-2001	2002[a]	Average 1998-2001	2002[a]
ANGOLA	212.7	109.0	-11.4	9.8	35.7	29.0	25.2	33.0
BOTSWANA	7.3	5.6	0.9	-2.9	24.8	14.0	32.9	32.7
LESOTHO	6.7	10.0	-6.8	-1.6	41.8	36.4	23.1	31.5
MALAWI	32.8	16.7	-5.8	-5.2	12.9	11.1	7.6	-2.5
MOZAMBIQUE	9.1	9.5	-3.1	-6.7	33.2	53.3	15.2	19.3
NAMIBIA	8.4	11.3	-4.3	-5.5	24.8	26.9	28.8	31.6
SOUTH AFRICA	5.8	5.9	-2.0	-2.1	15.8	14.9	15.3	15.7
SWAZILAND	8.5	11.8	-1.3	-5.1	20.2	19.1	17.8	20.0
ZAMBIA	24.7	.	-5.4	-6.2	18.2	18.4	0.3	-1.8
ZIMBABWE	54.5	98.0	-11.3	-14.7	7.1	0.3	5.7	1.4
SOUTHERN AFRICA	**16.5**	**10.4**	**-2.8**	**-2.1**	**17.4**	**16.7**	**16.0**	**16.9**

Note: a/ Preliminary estimates
Sources: ADB Development Research and Statistics Divisions.

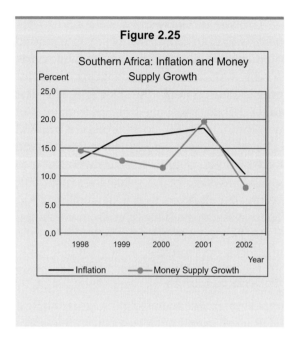

Figure 2.25

Southern Africa: Inflation and Money Supply Growth

0.1 percent in 1998-2001. Inflation in 2002 accelerated to 10.0 percent with food shortages and imported inflation from South Africa, the source of nearly 90 percent of Lesotho's imports.

Malawi's economy remained depressed for the third consecutive year in 2002, as a result of a drought-induced fall in agriculture. Growth stood at a low 1.8 percent in 2002, against a yearly average 1.9 percent in 1998-2001. Preliminary estimates pointed to a deceleration in inflation to a still high 16.7 percent in 2002, notably reflecting the acute food shortage that the country experienced in the last months of the year.

Mozambique has registered a remarkable rate of economic growth over the last five years, notably reflecting successful macroeconomic and structural reforms. The country is still vulnerable to external shocks, however, as demonstrated in 2000, when floods brought growth down to 1.6 percent. Economic grew

by 9 percent in 2002, reflecting buoyant activity in agriculture, construction and manufacturing. Private foreign direct investment in mega-projects and development corridors has been the catalyst for economic growth. The GDI-GDP ratio has more than doubled in the past five years, reaching 53.3 percent in 2002. Public investment has also risen with development expenditures. Tighter monetary policy has greatly reduced inflationary pressures since 1997. Inflation nonetheless surged to double-digit rates in 2000, as the result of the floods, and stood at 9.5 percent in 2002, partly reflecting a steep depreciation in the exchange rate the year before.

In **Namibia**, real GDP grew by 3.1 percent in 2002, against an average 3.1 percent in 1998-2001, with good performance in mining and meat processing offsetting the decline in crop production. Inflation rose to 11.3 percent, against a yearly average 8.4 percent in 1998-2001. Growth in South Africa has failed to accelerate since the advent of democratic rule in 1994. The economy grew by 3.0 percent in 2002, which is above the yearly average of 2.3 percent in 1998-2001. All sectors benefited from competitive gains in 2002, as a result of the sharp depreciation of the exchange rate in late 2001. This helped to compensate for lackluster world growth and weak international demand in 2002. South Africa is still characterized by relatively low levels of investment: the investment-GDP ratio decreased from 15.8 percent in 1998-2001 to 14.9 percent in 2002, owing to delays in the privatization process and slower-than-expected public capital outlays. Inflation averaged 5.8 percent in 1998-2001, accelerating to 5.9 percent in 2002, in response to the rand depreciation in late 2001 and rising food prices.

Swaziland's growth decelerated for the third consecutive year in 2002 to 1.6 percent, as a result of depressed food and cash crop production. Inflation accelerated to 11.8 percent, as a result of higher food prices and imported inflation from South Africa. The government's financial difficulties and heavy dependence on copper have hindered economic performance in **Zambia**. Real GDP grew by an exceptional 5.2 percent in 2001, owing to a 20 percent rise in the production of recently privatized mines. Mining production rose by a further 8 percent in 2002, despite Anglo-American Corporation's withdrawal from the country's largest mining company, but a drought-induced drop in agricultural production brought economic growth down to 2.8 percent that year. The GDI-GDP ratio stood at 18.4 percent in 2002, partly reflecting privatization-induced foreign investment since the mid-1990s. Zambia inflation is high by regional standards, averaging an annual 24.7 percent in 1998-2001, as a result of heavy government borrowing and exchange rate volatility. Rising food prices contributed to an acceleration in inflation in 2002.

After a period of sustained growth, **Zimbabwe** has been facing an ever-deepening economic crisis since 1998. Real GDP, which already shrunk by 2.6 percent in 1998-2001, contracted by 11.4 percent in 2002. Political uncertainty and negative publicity following the launch of the land resettlement program in 2000 and the disputed re-election of President Robert Mugabe in 2002; the drought that hit the country in 2002; the disorganizational problems associated with land reforms; and an acute shortage of foreign currency and skilled labor are the main factors underlying the general downturn of the economy. Growth in all major economic sectors (agriculture, manufacturing, mining,

and tourism) was negative in 2002. A drop in domestic savings and investment likewise characterizes the country's economic crisis, with the GDI-GDP ratio slumping from an average 7.1 percent in 1998-2001 to 0.3 percent in 2002. Inflation reached 98.0 percent in 2002, as the result of excessive monetary expansion, currency devaluation on the parallel market and the steep increase in food prices. The government has sought to introduce direct price controls on selected items in a vain attempt to contain inflation.

Recent Policy Developments

Poverty reduction

By far the main challenge for Southern African countries is to fight the spread of HIV/AIDS. South Africa, Swaziland, Zambia and Botswana have the highest prevalence rates in the world. The spread of the illness constitutes a serious restriction for development efforts. Life expectancy is decreasing fast and the general health of the active population has worsened, with strong negative impacts on health costs and labor productivity, notably in agriculture, education and healthcare. Concerning growth prospects, the Botswana Institute for Development Policy Analysis (BIDPA) predicted that annual GDP growth in Botswana will be 2.5 percentage points lower than it would have been in the absence of the epidemic over the period 1996-2021. Another immediate challenge for Southern Africa is the food security situation. The region has been hit by another major food crisis in 2002/03. Lesotho, Malawi, Mozambique, Swaziland, Zambia and Zimbabwe are the six most affected countries. The World Food Program is projecting that up to 14.4 million people will be at risk.

Most governments in Southern Africa have put in place a poverty alleviation strategy that embraces the Millennium Development Goals. Malawi, Mozambique, and Zambia are heavily indebted poor countries that qualify for debt relief under the HIPC initiative. Their governments have therefore adopted a broad-based participative framework, as sponsored by multilateral institutions, and so has less-indebted Lesotho.

Despite being classified as an upper middle income country, with social indicators including free primary health care and primary education for all, **Botswana** still suffers widespread poverty, high unemployment rate, and unfair income distribution. In addition, HIV/AIDS has offset much of the country's impressive health progress in the last decade, with notably a higher incidence of related diseases, such as respiratory diseases (including tuberculosis) and gastro-intestinal infections. The supply and quality of teaching and secondary school attendance have also greatly suffered from the spread of the illness. The National Strategic Vision aims to eradicate poverty by 2016. The first Draft Botswana Poverty Reduction Strategy (BPRS), which was prepared in October 2001, aims at enhancing the accessibility of the poor to social investment and strengthening the capacity of local government institutions.

Lesotho released its interim PRSP in December 2000, but progress towards completion has been delayed, owing to a number of factors; in particular, the government has yet to set up an official measure of poverty and finalize its first household survey.

Malawi produced its final PRSP in April 2002. Poverty, which affects 65 percent of the population, is to be achieved through promoting agricultural development and economic diversification, developing human capital (education, health, and training), addressing problems of governance, and fighting HIV/AIDS.

The government in **Mozambique** finalized its *Action Plan for the Reduction of Absolute Poverty* (PARPA) in April 2001, the overall objective being to reduce the incidence of absolute poverty from 70 percent to less than 50 percent by 2010. In order to achieve this goal, the government is pursuing policies aimed at promoting sustainable growth in sectors with the broadest impact on the poor, including agriculture, transportation and commerce. PARPA constitutes the country's final PRSP under HIPC.

Formidable challenges face **South Africa** as unemployment, HIV infection rates and income inequality continue to rise. Almost 8 years after the democratic government, there are still major pressures for fairer income, as exemplified by a range of policy initiatives to promote black economic empowerment. Education expenditures in South Africa currently comprise approximately 8 percent of GDP. This partly reflects government's commitment to addressing the apartheid education backlog. The New Partnership for Africa's Development (NEPAD), initiated in October 2001 is of special importance for South Africa, as the country and its president are central to the conception and sustainability of the initiative.

The poverty situation in **Zambia** has dramatically worsened with the country's poor economic performance. Around 73 percent of Zambians are classified as poor. Completed in early 2002, the PRSP has placed agriculture as first priority, although the document sets out goals and policy actions in other vital economic sectors, such as industry, mining and tourism. Objectives are also set to promote equitable and efficient health and education services in the country. Both the education and health systems have worsened over the last thirty years, due to economic decline, lack of resources and institutional inefficiencies.

Zimbabwe enjoys a well-educated population by developing country standards. Primary education is now free and universal and more than half of the 15-19 age group was enrolled in secondary schools in 1999. Adult literacy rate has increased accordingly from 70 percent in 1980 to 88 percent in 1999. Nevertheless, current political and economic difficulties, HIV/AIDS, and population displacement have hindered progress, and drop-outs, especially in the age group 15-19 years, are increasing.

Privatization

The pace of privatization in Southern Africa has lagged behind that in other regions. The second generation of privatization, which includes larger and more attractive SOEs, such as utilities in mining, energy, and telecommunication, has barely begun. Performance varies greatly across countries, however, Malawi and Mozambique being the best performers in 2002.

Privatization in **Botswana** is still in its infancy. The Public Enterprise Evaluation and Privatization Agency (PEEPA), which was established in 2001 to draw up a privatization master plan, is currently evaluating the performance of the main SOEs and investigating the potential gains from privatization. The national carrier, Air Botswana, is the first SOE to have been earmarked for privatization. Most of the privatizations will go through the stock market.

35 out of about 100 SOEs have been sold in **Malawi** since the establishment of a Privatization Commission in 1996. The privatization program was temporarily suspended in 2001 but resumed under donor pressure. Enterprises that were privatized in 2002 include Chemicals and Marketing and the Malawi Lake Services. Attention has focused on preparation for the sale of Malawi Telecommunications and Air Malawi in recent years, but progress has been slow.

The government's restructuring program is nearing completion in **Mozambique**. More than 1,200 state-owned enterprises, including all state owned manufacturing companies, have been restructured or privatized since the program was launched in 1991. The program also entailed the deregulation and concessioning of railways, ports, and water services. The main utilities yet to be privatized include Telecommunication of Mozambique and the national airline. A second mobile telephone license was sold in 2002. Banco Austral was privatized in December 2001.

The government of **Namibia** has re-iterated its commitment to privatization, although details of its program have yet to be released. The sale of SOEs will likely remain partial and on an *ad hoc* basis. The privatization process in **South Africa**, which was launched in 1996, has been slow. Attention has recently focused on selling equity shares, or offering concessions, in public utilities, such as Telkom (telecommunication), Eskom (energy), and Transnet (air, maritime, and road transport). The process has entailed unbundling some parastatals into different units and restructuring the state defense corporation, Denel. Only two small bids were received for a 51 percent stake in the country's second line fixed operator, SNO, after Telkom lost its monopoly in May 2002. The public listing of the second tranche of Telkom's shares was meanwhile delayed, owing to adverse market conditions. In May 2002, the government announced it would "fast track the concessioning of the Durban Container Terminal, despite trade union protest. Full privatization in South Africa has been rare and limited to holiday resorts and broadcasting.

Privatization is progressing slowly in **Swaziland**. Only the Royal Swazi National Airways and the commercial arm of the Swaziland Dairy Board have been privatized so far. Although a substantial number of companies have been privatized in **Zambia** (257 out of a portfolio of 280 SOEs), some strategic utilities are still state-owned and the mines, which represent the country's greatest asset, were only privatized in 2000. After incurring substantial losses, Anglo American Corporation, pulled out from Konkola Copper Mines (KMC) in early 2002. The new government, elected in December 2001, has promised to accelerate the privatization program, involving the sale of Zambia National Commercial Bank (ZNCB), ZAMTEL (telecommunication), ZESCO (electricity), and state-owned oil refineries, mostly through public flotation or concession agreements.

Although the government's decision to privatize public enterprises was announced in 1991, the Privatization Agency of **Zimbabwe** was not established until 1999. The privatization process still lacks a regulatory policy framework and sales are conducted on a case by case basis. A *fast track* divestiture of firms already listed on the stock exchange took place in 2001, with notably the sale of the Cotton Company of Zimbabwe (Cottco), the Zimbabwe Reinsurance Company (ZimRE), and the Zimbabwe Development Corporation (ZDC). Public utilities due to be privatized include the domestic airline and railways. Four companies were short-listed for a majority share in Tel One and Net One (telecommunication) in 2002.

Fiscal developments

Fiscal developments in Southern African countries have been mixed. Most countries have tightened fiscal policy in recent years, with the result that the regional deficit fell from an annual average of 2.8 percent of GDP during 1998-2001 to 2.1 percent in 2002. (Table 2.12 and Figure 2.26). Some governments, especially in Zimbabwe, have nonetheless continued to run large fiscal deficits, which they finance through excessive domestic borrowing.

Budget transparency is lacking and expenditure control is lax in **Angola**. The government has plans to introduce a value-added tax and modernize tax and customs administration. The budget balance turned positive in 2002, at 9.8 percent of GDP, as a result of exceptional oil proceeds, against an average deficit of 11.4 percent of GDP in 1998-2001.

The government in **Botswana** has pursued a prudent fiscal policy, by notably anchoring budget spending to a medium-term framework, as currently outlined by the eighth National Development Plan (1997-2003). Mineral taxes,

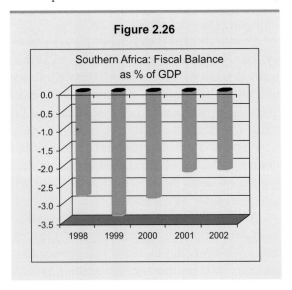

Figure 2.26

Southern Africa: Fiscal Balance as % of GDP

royalties and dividends, which constitute the bulk of domestic revenues, have allowed budget surpluses in all but two years since 1982/83. The budget registered a deficit of about 2.9 percent of GDP in 2001/02, mainly on account of a drop in mineral revenue. The government has worked hard to diversify its sources of revenue, and strengthen the tax collection system. The domestic sales tax was replaced by a value-added tax (VAT) in July 2002.

Lesotho maintained a tight fiscal policy in 2002, despite being an election year. Donor assistance helped to pay part of the food security expenses, with the fiscal deficit rising from an average 6.8 percent of GDP in 1998-2001 to 1.6 percent of GDP in 2002. Expenditure slippage has been reported in **Malawi** in recent years, prompting delays in IMF disbursements. The fiscal deficit stood at 5.2 percent of GDP in 2002, against an average 5.8 percent in 1998-2001.

Fiscal consolidation has continued in **Mozambique**, where the financing of the government budget still heavily depends on external assistance. The fiscal deficit nonetheless rose to 6.7 percent of GDP in 2002, against a yearly average 3.1 percent in 1998-2001. Expenditure management has improved, since the government adopted a medium term expenditure framework in 1997, which entails reducing non-essential expenditures and raising social spending. Measures to strengthen tax collection have been taken, with a view to raising domestic revenue to 15 percent of GDP by 2005. The VAT introduced in 1999 has been consolidated, and a new fiscal incentive code was introduced in 2002. A new income tax law is to be implemented in 2003.

Namibia has recently established a medium-term expenditure framework. The central government deficit nonetheless widened to 5.5 percent of GDP in 2002, as a result of sluggish tariff revenue from the Southern African Customs Union (SACU), a larger-than-projected wage bill and transfer to Air Namibia. The government in **South Africa** has maintained a strict fiscal discipline since 1994. The fiscal deficit averaged 2.0 percent of GDP over the period 1998-2001 and stood at 2.1 percent of GDP in 2002. The low deficit in fiscal year 2001/02 reflects in part improvements in revenue collection to roughly 24 percent of GDP, with notably a sharp rise in company tax receipts and, in part, capital under-spending, owing to the weak absorption capacity of provinces and local governments. The authorities have adopted an expansionary fiscal policy in 2002/03, which aims to increase spending on social services and foster economic growth by effecting income tax cuts and promoting business tax incentives.

Swaziland's custom revenues have followed a downward trend, as a result of a gradual decline in SACU common external tariffs. Relatively tight control over expenditure helped to contain the rise in the budget deficit from an average 1.3 percent of GDP in 1998-2001 to 5.1 percent of GDP in 2002. **Zambia**'s fiscal deficit rose to 6.2 percent of GDP in 2002, against a yearly average 5.4 percent in 1998-2001. Total revenues as a percentage to GDP have followed a downward trend, reflecting a reduction in external budget support, tax exemptions for the newly privatized mines and the withdrawal of the Anglo-American Corporation in 2002. The government, which has resorted to heavy domestic borrowing to finance its deficits, has continued to miss its payment obligations.

Zimbabwe's fiscal deficit has deteriorated in recent years, because of lax spending policy and a freeze in external assistance. The deficit notably peaked to 21.7 percent of GDP in 2000 (an election year), partly on the account of significant unbudgeted increases in civil service wages and military spending. A forced restructuring of the government's domestic debt slashed the fiscal deficit to 8.1 percent of GDP in 2001. In 2002, in response to acute food shortages, a supplementary budget law was approved at mid-year, bringing the annual budget deficit to 14.7 percent of GDP.

Monetary and exchange rate developments

Monetary and exchange rate developments in Southern Africa closely follow developments in South Africa, the largest economy of the zone. Three countries, Lesotho, Namibia, and Swaziland, have their currencies pegged to the South African rand at parity under the Common Monetary Area. The rand is also a currency of reference in Botswana. In 2002, the region's money supply growth declined to 8.2 percent from 19.8 percent recorded in 2001 (Figure 2.25).

Despite some commitment in recent years, the Central Bank in **Angola** has at large continued to accommodate large fiscal deficits, leading to excessive broad money expansion. Hyper inflation, currency instability (under a new floating exchange rate since 1999) and negative interest rates have contributed to the dollarization of the economy.

The Bank of **Botswana**'s tight monetary policy is anchored to a pegged exchange rate system. The BOB has improved the effectiveness of its open market operations by moving from monthly to weekly auctions and shortening maturities (91 days). An inflation target within the 4-6 percent range was announced

in 2002, as a mean to achieve general stability in the real effective exchange rate. The external value of the pula is pegged to a currency basket comprised of the South African Rand and the SDR. The BOB carefully balanced the objectives of price stabilization and export competitiveness in 2001, when the rand depreciated sharply against the major international currencies. Despite concerns over competitiveness, the Bank of Botswana failed to adjust the exchange rate basket that year. As a result, the pula appreciated by 21.8 percent against the Rand in 2001.

Monetary policy in **Lesotho** is limited, given the peg per par of the Loti to the South African rand. The central bank tightened its stance in 2002, to reflect rising interest rates in South Africa. The central bank in **Malawi** pursued a relatively tight monetary policy in 2002, in the context of rising food prices and fiscal slippage. The Central Bank rates remain excessively high, at 43 percent. The kwacha, which was floated in 1994 and lost 97 percent of its US dollar value by end-1997, continued gently to depreciate against all the currencies of its major trade partners in 2002.

Mozambique has taken some bold monetary measures to curb inflation and stabilize the domestic currency under a flexible exchange rate system. This notably entailed raising the rediscount rates, strengthening the reserve requirements, and stepping up foreign currencies and T-bills auctions. In line with reduced inflation, the metical regained some stability in 2002, after depreciating by 33-36 percent against the US dollar in 2001.

Monetary policy in **Namibia** is geared towards maintaining the 1:1 parity between the domestic currency, the Namibian dollar, and the South Africa rand. Interest rates were increased in 2002, in line with monetary developments in South Africa. The **South African** Reserve Bank, which has adopted an inflation targeting strategy since 2000, tightened its monetary stance in 2002 to counter inflationary consequences of the 2001 exchange rate depreciation. Beside weekly interventions on the money market to mop up excess liquidity, the repurchase rate of the Reserve Bank was increased on four occasions in 2002, each time by 100 basis points. The exchange rate in South Africa is flexible. The weighted exchange rate of the rand depreciated by 34 percent during 2001, mostly in the final two months of the year, owing to a combination factors, including sluggish economic performance and concerns over regional instability. The South African currency had regained 24 percent of its external value by end-2002.

Akin to the currencies in Lesotho and Namibia, the lilangeni in **Namibia** is pegged to the South African rand. The monetary authorities closely follow developments in South Africa as a result. The government's high domestic debt burden has restrained room for monetary manoeuvre in **Zambia**. The Bank of Zambia (BoZ) accommodated government borrowing requirements in 2000, before tightening its monetary policy in 2001, by notably increasing reserve requirements ratios, stepping up its open market operations, and temporarily re-introducing foreign exchange controls. This led a sharp increase in real interest rates, however, and in 2002, the BOZ adopted a pro-cyclical stance, with T-bills yields declining from 50 percent in end-2001 to 32 percent in November 2002, as a result. The kwacha's external value has followed a downward trend, after strengthening by 7 percent against the US dollar in 2001.

Monetary policy in **Zimbabwe** has continued to accommodate the rapid surge in liquidity re-sulting from excessive government borrowing and the forced restructuring of the government domestic debt. The Reserve Bank of Zimbabwe (RZB) has also implemented a targeted reduction in interest rates since 2001 to help alleviate the government's debt burden. This, coupled with galloping inflation, has led to sharply negative real interest rates. Both inflation and money supply growth were maintained at three digit levels in 2002. The Zimbabwe dollar has been officially pegged to the US dollar at Z$55 to US$1 since the currency was devalued by 31 percent in August-October 2000. But the parallel exchange rate continued to register steep premium, prompting the government to tighten control on bureaux de change activities.

Recent Trends in Globalization

Trade liberalization and regionalization

Southern Africa is strongly trade-orientated, with a trade-GDP ratio of over 75 percent (Table 2.13 and Figure 2.27). The economies of Botswana, Lesotho, Namibia, Swaziland, and oil-exporting Angola, are the most open. In comparison, South Africa is relatively close, with a trade openness ratio of 66.5 percent. South Africa's large domestic market and the relatively recent lifting of international sanctions explain the country's relatively low trade integration. All 10 countries in the region are members of the Southern African Development Community (SADC), formed in 1980. Angola, Malawi, Namibia, Swaziland, Zambia and Zimbabwe also belong to COMESA, while Botswana, Lesotho, Namibia, and Swaziland (commonly referred to as the BLNS states) form the Southern Africa Customs Union (SACU) with South Africa.

Intra-regional trade in SADC accounted for 12.2 percent of the region's exports and 10.9

Table 2.13: Southern Africa: The External Sector

Country	Trade* Average 1998-2001	Trade* 2002[a]	Trade Balance as % of GDP Average 1998-2001	Trade Balance as % of GDP 2002[a]	Current Account (%) Average 1998-2001	Current Account (%) 2002[a]	Terms of Trade Debt as % of GDP Average 1998-2001	Terms of Trade Debt as % of GDP 2002[a]	Total External as % of Exports Average 1998-2001	Total External as % of Exports 2002[a]	Debt Service Average 1997-2000	Debt Service 2001
ANGOLA	154.5	137.0	36.6	38.9	-12.7	5.1	12.6	-3.5	134.6	68.0	32.2	30.3
BOTSWANA	93.6	93.8	11.6	13.6	8.5	6.2	4.4	1.6	22.1	24.6	17.4	2.6
LESOTHO	124.7	161.9	-59.3	-40.4	-18.6	-10.7	4.9	-3.1	68.9	69.7	17.8	11.4
MALAWI	67.4	68.8	-3.6	-11.5	-5.4	-11.2	3.1	6.1	150.0	146.5	14.6	19.4
MOZAMBIQUE	56.4	88.1	-17.4	-27.1	-18.0	-35.9	0.7	3.5	60.8	41.6	15.5	21.6
NAMIBIA	108.5	114.6	-7.9	-7.8	3.9	3.3	1.0	0.9	2.3	2.6	13.2	1.4
SOUTH AFRICA	52.9	66.5	3.1	6.0	-0.7	0.8	-1.4	2.7	28.5	.	14.2	19.7
SWAZILAND	164.2	162.6	-7.9	-3.2	-2.3	-3.5	-1.1	1.4	24.1	36.1	12.4	0.0
ZAMBIA	68.2	76.6	-6.2	-8.6	-17.9	-17.5	-2.4	-2.5	182.9	136.6	12.9	21.0
ZIMBABWE	94.1	77.4	3.1	2.1	-1.1	-3.8	-2.8	-1.4	82.1	126.9	13.4	4.3
SOUTHERN AFRICA	63.7	75.5	3.6	6.2	-1.7	-0.4	0.0	2.3	40.0	39.9	17.6	16.3

Note: a/ Preliminary estimates
*: (Exports & Imports) of Goods and Non Factors Services at Market Prices
Sources: ADB Development Research and Statistics Divisions.

Figure 2.27

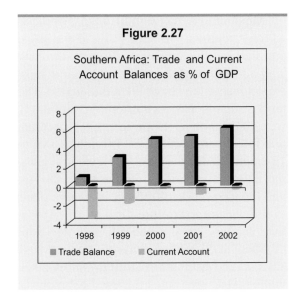

Southern Africa: Trade and Current Account Balances as % of GDP

■ Trade Balance   ■ Current Account

percent of the region's imports in 2000. A similar level of integration has only been achieved in West Africa. South Africa, which is by far the largest supplier of intra-SADC imports, enjoys a significant trade surplus with the rest of the region.

Southern African countries are all members of the World Trade Organization. They are committed to multilateral trade liberalization and grant Most Favored Nation treatment to all trading partners. In addition, Malawi, Mozambique, Namibia, Swaziland, Zambia and Zimbabwe, are active participants of the Cross-Border Initiative, which the African Development Bank supports.

There are two main regional trade agreements in the region. SACU, the oldest custom union in Africa, provides for a common external tariff and a common excise duty, while allowing free movement of goods and the right of transit within the union. All customs and excise collected are paid into South Africa's National Revenue Fund. A new revenue-sharing formula

was agreed in October 2001.The new deal, which was due to come into force in April 2002, has yet to be ratified by the parliaments in the five member states before it becomes effective. The SACU heads of state formally agreed to the new deal in October 2002. The main aim is to ensure that both revenue and development consideration are balanced. The introduction of a development component raises the revenue shares of the poorer SACU member states and should help to stabilize future flows to the BLNS. New institutional arrangements for setting tariffs within SACU are being implemented. Negotiations on a free trade area between the US and SACU started in 2002.

The main objective of SADC is to achieve poverty reduction, development and economic growth, through deeper, outward-oriented, regional integration. Trade being the most prominent form of integration within SADC, a protocol establishing the SADC Free Trade Area was signed in September 2000. Over 85 percent of SADC trade is expected to be duty free by 2008. The remaining tariffs on sensitive products will be removed over the period 2008-2012. The SADC least developed countries (including Malawi, Mozambique, and Zambia) are to phase out tariff reduction over the 8 year period, while the relatively more developed SACU countries have removed tariffs more rapidly. Not all member countries have passed legislation to ratify the free trade agreement and rules of origin remain an outstanding issue.

Traditionally working under the principle of decentralized co-operation, SADC has decided to move towards a more centralized institutional set-up since the March 2001 Head of State Summit. This aims to make the organization more effective. Progress was reviewed during the 2002 summit, held in Luanda, Angola in October. Among the task completed are the establishment of three out of four directorates (Trade, Industry and Finance; Food Agriculture and Natural Resources; Social and Human Development); and the commencement of work on the Regional Indicative Strategy Development Plan (RISP). RISP will make SADC Common Policy Agenda operational, by notably consolidating, and merging, the organization's sector-based protocols.

South Africa has undertaken extensive trade liberalization, since international economic sanctions were lifted in 1994. A main priority for the government is to reduce the level of dispersion of tariffs and make the tariff structure more uniform. South Africa concluded a bilateral Free Trade Agreement with the EU in January 2000. The agreement has continued to be implemented provisionally, pending ratification by all EU member states. After much contention, the wines and spirits agreement was signed in January 2000. A fisheries agreement is still pending. The EU is South Africa's largest trade partner, accounting for 31.3 percent of exports and 39.7 percent of imports in 2000.

BLNS countries have brought their trade liberalization policy in line with that of South Africa. Average tariffs in the union fell from 30 percent in 1990 to 7 percent presently, as South Africa proceeded with lowering its external tariffs with the European Union and SADC.

Angola adhered to the SADC Trade Protocol in February 2002, which has yet to be ratified by parliament. **Malawi** has embarked in trade liberalization since 1996. Foreign exchange controls have been relaxed; import and export licensing has been removed; and non-tariff barriers have been eliminated. The maximum custom rate has been reduced to 25 percent.

Mozambique has significantly liberalized its trade regime, with exception in the sugar and cashew nut industries. Import licensing was abolished in the early 1990s and most export restrictions have been eliminated. The tariff structure has recently been simplified, with rates ranging from zero to 30 percent and the average MFN tariff brought down to 13.8 percent. Excise taxes are levied on automobiles, luxury goods, alcoholic beverages, and tobacco products. The government plans to reduce the maximum tariff to 25 percent from January 2003. **Zambia** has ratified both COMESA and SADC customs unions. COMESA aims at establishing a custom union by 2004, while SADC envisages the establishment of a free trade area by 2008. A task force was established between the two unions in 2001 to harmonize custom procedures.

Despite major efforts pursued in the last ten years to liberalize trade, **Zimbabwe** is still characterized by a restrictive trade regime, particularly on the capital account. The foreign exchange allocation system relaxed at the beginning of the decade has been recently restored in the form of stringent foreign exchange controls as a measure to regulate the growth of imports. A system of permits and monopolies for some exports is still active. In March 2001, the authorities raised the effective level of protection by increasing tariff rates on certain processed items that have domestically produced substitutes, such as food, and reducing rates on some raw material and capital goods, mostly machinery. However, in mid 2002, in order to reduce the cost of maize to alleviate the sufferings caused by the drought, duty on maize and wheat imports have been suspended.

Trade performance and export diversification

The external position of the sub-region improved in 2002 compared with 1998-2001, with the current account deficit falling from a yearly average 1.7 percent of GDP to 0.4 percent of GDP (Table 2.13 and Figure 2.27). Southern African countries are traditionally mineral exporting economies. This includes precious metals, notably gold and platinum in South Africa, diamond in Botswana and copper and cobalt in Zambia. All but Angola are net crude oil importers. Angola is the second largest oil exporter in Sub-Saharan Africa, after Nigeria, while Botswana is the world's largest producer of diamond.

Export-oriented development strategies, the opening of new markets, and rising foreign direct investments have boosted the region's manufacturing exports in the past decade. For example, the manufacturing share of total exports in South Africa has increased from 35 percent in 1994 to over 50 percent, as a result of the lifting of international sanctions and improved access to EU markets. Manufacturing export activities have also expanded strongly in Botswana and in Lesotho, principally in the clothing and footwear sectors, and for Botswana, in the motor vehicles assembly industry. In Mozambique, the establishment of an export processing zone regime, and the launch of mega-projects in the Maputo-Johannesburg corridor have boosted exports away from traditional agriculture and fishery products since the late 1990s.

All Southern Africa countries, but Angola and Zimbabwe, qualify for the Africa Growth and Opportunity Act-II (AGOA-II), as signed in August 2002. In addition, all the beneficiaries in the region (including Botswana and Namibia,

since 2002) but South Africa, are eligible under the apparel Special Rule. AGOA-I has strongly benefited the region's textile industry since 2000. All Southern Africa countries have also privileged access to the EU, as members of the African Caribbean and Pacific (ACP) group of countries (the arrangements with South Africa being on a reciprocal basis).

Angola's trade surplus surged to 38.9 percent of GDP in 2002, driven by rising oil export earnings. This largely compensated for the high interest obligations on the country's external debt and remittances on profit and dividends by oil companies, with the current account balance turning into a surplus equivalent to 5.1 percent of GDP in 2002, against an average deficit of 12.7 percent in 1998-2001.

The expansion of diamond production has given rise to healthy trade surpluses in **Botswana** in the last 20 years, despite a strong demand import. The country's external position deteriorated in 2001, because of sales quotas imposed by the Diamond Trade Corporation in the context of depressed global markets. Garment sales are slowly increasing under AGOA, but diamond still constitute more than 80 percent of the country's exports. Lower diamond production in 2002 contributed to a fall in the current account surplus from an average 8.5 percent of GDP in 1998-2001, to 6.2 percent of GDP in 2002.

Lesotho's trade deficit remained high in 2002, at 40.4 percent, as a result of a rising import bill from South Africa and weak economic growth in the US and the EU, the main outlets for its export-oriented manufacturing industry. Strong workers remittances helped to maintain the current account deficit at 10.7 percent of GDP, against an average 18.6 percent of GDP in 1998-2001. **Malawi** is heavily dependent on commodity exports, tobacco, tea, sugar and cotton, although textile exports have grown rapidly in recent years. Transportation costs are high, given the country's landlocked position. The current account deficit widened to 11.2 percent of GDP in 2002, from an average 5.4 percent of GDP in 1998-2001, as a result of falling tobacco exports and a higher food import bill.

Aluminum and electricity have become **Mozambique**'s main sources of export growth in recent years. Export earnings notably doubled in 2001, following the start-up of the Mozal aluminum smelter in late 2000. There was a sharp increase in imports in 2002, related to further large-scale foreign investments, including a gas pipeline to South Africa and Mozal II. Net official transfers and workers remittances continue to be a vital component of the country's current account, whose deficit rose to 35.9 percent of GDP in 2002, against an average 18.0 percent of GDP in 1998-2001. **Namibia**'s current account balance was in surplus in 2002, equivalent to 3.3 percent of GDP. This reflects strong export growth in recent years, especially diamonds and beef.

South Africa's export performance remained robust in 2002, despite the relatively slow recovery in global economic activity and the weak international demand. Manufacturing exports increased on the back of the sharp rand depreciation in late 2001 and privileged market access to the EU, while the value of mining exports increased marginally, spurred by a rise in world gold and platinum prices. Import demand meanwhile remained subdued. The trade surplus rose to 6.0 percent, against an average 3.1 percent in 1998-2001. The current account balance registered a small surplus of 0.8 percent of GDP in 2002, against an average

deficit of 0.7 percent of GDP in 1998-2001, also reflecting a decline in net investment income and increased tourism receipts (with the hosting of the UN World Summit on Sustainable Development in August 2002).

Swaziland's current account deficit rose to 3.5 percent of GDP in 2002, against an average 2.3 percent of GDP in 1998-2001, the growth in workers' remittances and sugar and textile exports failing to compensate for the rising demand for food imports. **Zambia**'s export earnings from the mining sector, which constitute roughly 70 percent of total exports, continued to rise in 2002, despite the withdrawal of the Anglo-American Corporation from the mining conglomerate, Zambia Consolidated Copper Mines, partly reflecting a recovery in world copper prices. After surging by 29 percent in 2001, as a result of a boom in the demand for imports of intermediate and capital goods in the mining sector, the value of merchandise imports declined slightly in 2002. As a result, the current account deficit fell to 17.5 percent of GDP in 2002, down from an annual average of 17.9 percent of GDP during 1998-2001.

Zimbabwe's external position has seriously deteriorated since 1999. The volume of agriculture, manufacturing, and mining exports continued to decline in 2002. Foreign exchange shortage and the overvalued exchange rate meanwhile continued to severely limit the country's ability to import, keeping the overall trade balance in surplus. Rising food imports necessary to compensate the decrease in staple food production in 2002 further reduced resources available for other critical imports such as raw material and capital goods. The slump in tourism receipts combined with the freeze on foreign assistance contributed to a widening in the current account deficit to 3.8 percent of

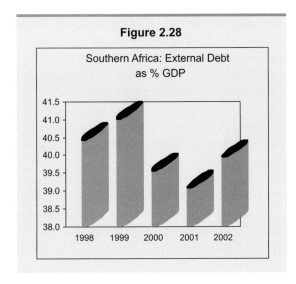

Figure 2.28

Southern Africa: External Debt as % GDP

GDP in 2002, against a yearly average 1.1 percent of GDP during the 1998-2001 period.

External debt and other capital flows

Southern Africa's external debt had been on the downward trend, reflecting the impact of HIPC as well as reduced inflows to the region. The debt burden also declined, with the debt/GDP ratio falling to 39.3 percent in 2002 (Figure 2.28), making Southern Africa the lowest indebted region in the continent. There are wide disparities across countries, however. Malawi, Mozambique, and Zambia, are all classified as heavily indebted poor countries. By contrast, the stock of external debt in Botswana, Namibia, South Africa and Swaziland stand below 30 percent of their respective GDP in 1998-2001. Angola, Malawi, Mozambique, and Zambia are the only four countries to have negotiated debt rescheduling deals with the Paris Club of official, bilateral creditors.

Most countries in Southern Africa have been successful in boosting foreign direct investment over the years, because they are richly endowed

in mineral resources, and/or because they have actively pursued broad-based economic reforms. This is the case of Mozambique, where an active privatization program has been pursued and numerous tax incentives are provided to foreign investors. The country also benefits from political stability, low cost labor, cheap sources of energy, and improved infrastructure. Private flows to the region also consist of portfolio foreign investment. According to UNCTAD *World Investment Report 2002*, the region hosted an exceptional $ 8.2 billions in FDI inflows in 2001, 80 percent of which going to South Africa. The JSE Securities Exchange South Africa (JSE) in South Africa is by far the largest and most developed bourse on the continent. Stock exchange markets in Botswana and Zambia are relatively well developed, while those in Malawi, Namibia, Swaziland, and Zimbabwe, are small, but thriving. Access to non-residents is regulated and there are ceilings on foreign ownership in all countries but Zambia. There are plans to link SADC stock exchange markets to that in Johannesburg. The government of South Africa and Botswana has also access to international capital markets at a relatively low premium, being credit rated by leading rating agencies.

The stock of external debt in **Angola** is relatively high, reflecting the government's frequent use of oil-back finance. Buoyant oil revenues since 2000 have reduced the pace of borrowing, with external debt declining to 68.0 percent of GDP in 2002, as a result. Great oil potentials have continued to fuel strong FDI inflows in the country. **Botswana**'s sizeable foreign exchange reserves limit external borrowing needs. In 2002, the stock of external debt, represented 24.6 percent of GDP. The bulk of the debt is owed to official creditors, indicating the government's reluctance to borrow on commercial rates, despite being favorably graded by leading credit ratings agencies. Almost 80 percent of FDI in Botswana takes place in the mining sector, although the government has succeeded in attracting export-oriented investment in textiles, auto and the beef industry in recent years.

Lesotho's external debt-to-GDP ratio was maintained at 69.7 percent of GDP in 2002, as a result of prudent borrowing policy. The country's external debt burden is deemed sustainable and the country does not qualify for debt relief under HIPC. Foreign investment, notably under the Lesotho Highland Water has played an important role in Lesotho. Many multilateral firms established their subsidiaries in Lesotho when South Africa was under international sanctions. FDI has remained robust in recent years, fuelled by Asian and South African investment in the textiles and clothing industry.

Mozambique was included in the HIPC initiative in 1998, reaching completion point in June 1999. The country was granted additional relief under the enhanced HIPC at completion point in September 2001. The debt-to-GDP ratio now stands at 41.6 percent. FDI has come to play a central role in Mozambique since the mid-1990s. The privatization of firms in the tourism, industry and banking sectors largely characterized FDI until 1996. Since then, FDI has mainly been directed towards the exploitation of natural resource, and large-scale, capital-intensive projects.

Namibia is Africa's least-indebted countries, with a foreign debt equivalent to 2.6 percent of GDP. FDI inflows to this well-endowed country have increased over the years, owing to macroeconomic stabilization and an investor-friendly environment. **Swaziland**'s external debt stood at 36.1 percent of GDP in 2002. Like Lesotho, Swaziland has long been a preferred choice of location for multinational firms, because of its proximity to South Africa. The creation of a one-stop investment shop in 1998 and qualification under AGOA in 2000 has boosted FDI inflows in recent years.

South Africa's external debt rose beyond its 2001 level of $32.3 billion, as a result of new borrowing by the government in international capital markets and a rise in the dollar value of the rand-denominated and euro-denominated debt. The absence of external borrowing before international sanctions were lifted in 1994 explains the low debt burden (28.5 percent of GDP in 1998-2001). According to UNCTAD, FDI inflows to South Africa alone totaled an exceptional US$6.7bn in 2001, representing 39 percent of total FDI inflows on the continent. South Africa is also a pool for foreign portfolio investment, non-residents taking a keen interest in the country's financial markets, which are well-developed and liquid. In return, South African interests are very active on international equity markets and are also involved in a large number of direct investment projects in other parts of Africa, including the Mozal smelter in Mozambique, retailing in Botswana. South Africa's investment in Africa at the end of 2000 exceeded R24 billion. Net portfolio investment flows reached a small surplus in 2002, but net direct investment changed from inflows to outflows.

In late 2000, **Zambia** reached the decision point under the Enhanced HIPC initiative. The stock of debt declined less rapidly than expected in 2001, as a result of delays in agreeing on a debt relief deal with the Paris Club of official bilateral creditors. In 2002, external debt equivalent to a high of 136.6 percent of GDP. Falling export earnings brought a rise in the debt service ratio to 21.0 percent in 2001. Foreign direct investment also declined in 2001, as a result of bearish prospect in the recently privatized mining sector.

Although the stock of **Zimbabwe**'s foreign debt has remained unchanged since 1997 reflecting the cutback in aid inflows, the country's offshore obligations have risen sharply with the built-up of foreign arrears. The stock of total external debt – excluding arrears - rose to 126.9 percent of GDP in 2002. Half of the public external debt is owed to multilateral institutions, notably the World Bank and the IMF. In June 2002, the IMF suspended its technical assistance to the country, in response to the accumulation of arrears. FDI inflows, which peaked to $ 444 million in 1998, have now reached rock-bottom.

Outlook

Because of South Africa's dominance and the influence it has on the other Southern Africa economy, the outlook for the region depends very much on the performance of the region's biggest economy. GDP in **South Africa** is set to accelerate for the second consecutive year, to 3.3 percent, as falling interest rates support consumption and investment growth and government spending remains strong. Higher commodity prices (particularly for gold and platinum) will meanwhile enhance South Africa's export earnings. These will, however, be moderated by the poor performance in Zimbabwe and the continued adverse effects of drought and HIV/AIDS pandemic. Overall, therefore growth in Southern Africa in 2003 is forecast to remain unchanged at its 2002 level.

The exceptional economic performance that **Angola** experienced in 2002, on the back of rising oil production, is unlikely to be repeated in 2003, when oil production is nonetheless expected to top 1 million bbp. Attention will focus on development in the non-oil sector, as it is hoped that 2003 will mark the beginning of the country's economic and social recovery following the April 2002 peace agreement. Growth in **Botswana** will remain robust, reflecting stable mineral production. The drought in 2002/03 will keep crop production low, but this will have little impact on overall growth, agriculture accounting for less than 2 percent of the economy.

By contrast, **Lesotho**, **Malawi**, **Swaziland** and **Zambia**, will be strongly affected by food security issues, growth recovery largely hinging on a return to normal weather conditions in time for the next harvests in April-June. The high incidence of HIV/AIDS on some of these countries' productive capacity make an economic rebound unlikely in the medium term. Growth will nonetheless rise in 2003, as economic recovery in South Africa provides some support to their output and assuming agricultural output returns to normal levels. The economic situation in **Zimbabwe** will meanwhile continue to deteriorate, as disorganizational problems associated with land reforms and disinvestment continue.

Economic performance in **Mozambique** will remain buoyant in 2003, with industry being the main source of growth, as FDI flows in to finance the country's megaprojects. The government will meanwhile remain committed to increasing social spending in education, health, agriculture and basic infrastructure, while maintaining macroeconomic stability and pursuing structural reforms.

West Africa

West Africa is made up of fifteen countries, divided into two distinct groups: the CFA zone comprising eight countries – Benin, Burkina Faso, Côte d'Ivoire, Guinea Bissau, Mali, Niger, Senegal and Togo – and the non-CFA zone, consisting of Cape Verde, Ghana, Guinea, the Gambia, Nigeria, Liberia, and Sierra Leone. The sub-region is dominated by Nigeria, which accounts for some 54 percent of the region's output. In 2002, regional GDP constituted 15.5 percent of the continent's total, a contribution roughly equivalent to those of Central and East Africa combined. Unlike in the previous year, the CFA zone outperformed the CFA in terms of real GDP growth: 3.1 percent against non-CFA zone's 0.9 percent (Figure 2.29).

The onset of a civil war in Côte d'Ivoire in September 2002 has dealt a major blow to the West African region. Côte d'Ivoire is the second largest economy in the sub-region. Despite remarkable progress in Sierra Leone's peace process, the civil war in Liberia, which is Côte d'Ivoire's direct neighbor, has continued to threaten stability in the sub-region. The year 2002 was an election year for Burkina Faso (legislative), Mali (presidential and legislative), Sierra Leone (legislative and presidential) and Togo (legislative). Attention in Nigeria has focused on preparations for the 2003 presidential and legislative polls.

Nigeria is the region's chief exporter, accounting for about two thirds of total exports in the sub-region – a reflection of its rich endowment of crude oil and gas. Other mineral resources that the region exports include bauxite, gold, diamond and phosphate. Agricultural exports, to which many countries in the sub-region depend, include cocoa, coffee,

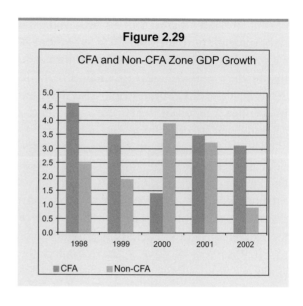

Figure 2.29

CFA and Non-CFA Zone GDP Growth

■ CFA   ■ Non-CFA

timber, nuts, fisheries, livestock and cotton. West Africa's exports represented about 16.0 percent of the continental total in 2002 (Table 2.14).

Population of the region was estimated at 228 million, or 28.1 percent of the continent's total. Nigeria, which is the most densely populated country in continental Africa after Rwanda and Burundi, alone accounts for 51 percent of the region's total. With GDP per capita of $355, West Africa ranks far behind the Northern and Southern Regions in terms of living standards, but ahead of the Central and Eastern Regions.

Recent Trends in the Domestic Economy

Growth in West Africa decelerated from a yearly average of 3.1 percent between 1998 and 2001 to 1.7 percent (Table 2.14 and Figure 2.30), reflecting two main external factors: a tightening in OPEC quotas for Nigeria oil production; and the impact of Côte d'Ivoire's

Table 2.14: West Africa: Gross Domestic Product and Export Performances

Country	Real GDP Growth Rate (%)		GDP Per Capita (US$)		Real Exports[c] Growth (%)		Exports[b] Per Capita (US$)	
	Average 1998-2001	2002[a]	Average 1998-2001	2002[a]	Average 1998-2001	2002[a]	Average 1998-2001	2002[a]
BENIN	5.0	5.3	375	405	6.2	22.5	60	51
BURKINA FASO	4.2	4.5	213	208	7.7	15.3	25	21
CAPE VERDE	6.4	3.0	1329	1373	7.4	-1.5	295	289
COTE D'IVOIRE	1.2	0.0	738	693	2.0	2.5	292	256
GAMBIA	5.4	6.0	324	244	5.3	7.6	157	145
GHANA	4.3	4.4	339	324	4.8	3.9	129	114
GUINEA	3.5	4.2	406	373	7.1	4.4	94	98
GUINEA-BISSAU	-3.2	0.5	178	172	13.9	6.4	44	42
LIBERIA	-	-	-	-	-	-	-	-
MALI	4.2	5.2	234	247	10.3	17.3	63	65
NIGER	4.0	2.7	185	187	6.3	-0.2	32	27
NIGERIA	2.5	-0.9	339	355	-1.3	-18.3	143	120
SENEGAL	5.5	4.9	495	529	6.9	6.3	148	134
SIERRA LEONE	0.1	6.6	156	168	3.3	10.9	24	23
TOGO	0.3	3.0	299	290	-3.0	19.5	98	84
WEST AFRICA	**3.1**	**1.7**	**351**	**355**	**5.5**	**6.9**	**129**	**112**

Notes:　a/ Preliminary estimates
　　　　b/ Exports of Goods and Nonfactor Services at Market Prices
　　　　c/ Real Exports of Goods and Non Factors Services Growth
Sources: ADB Development Research and Statistics Divisions.

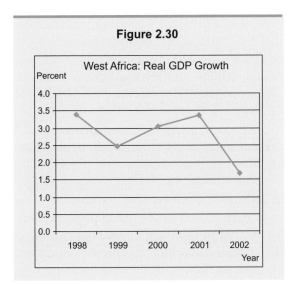

Figure 2.30

West Africa: Real GDP Growth

crisis on the sub-region. Domestic investment stood at 21.8 percent of GDP in 2002 (Figure 2.31), although performance was mixed on an individual country basis. Tight monetary and fiscal rules have kept inflation in CFA countries low by continental standards (barring the post-1994 devaluation period), hence the regional inflation average was 5.4 percent in 2002 (Figure 2.32).

Benin has experienced robust growth since the devaluation of the CFA franc in 1994. The economy grew by an average 5.0 percent in 1998-2001, accelerating to 5.3 percent in 2002. Despite a bumper cotton production (from 337,000 tons in 2000/01 to 412,000 tons in

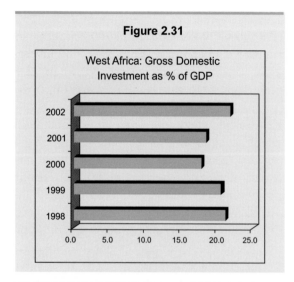

Figure 2.31

West Africa: Gross Domestic Investment as % of GDP

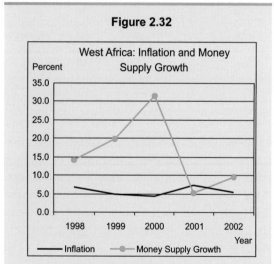

Figure 2.32

West Africa: Inflation and Money Supply Growth

— Inflation   — Money Supply Growth

Growth in **Burkina Faso** is highly sensitive to external shocks. The export and food crop sector performed well for the second consecutive year in 2002, owing to satisfactory weather conditions, but the crisis in Côte d'Ivoire took a heavy toll on the landlocked economy in the fourth quarter of 2002, border closures notably paralyzing transportation services and hindering activity in the secondary sector. Preliminary estimates suggest a 4.5 percent growth in 2002, which is still above the yearly average of 4.2 percent during the 1998-2001 period. The investment-GDP ratio rose gently to 32.1 percent in 2002, a rate fuelled by government capital outlays that is well above the region's average. Inflationary pressures accelerated in the later part of the year, as a result of the scarcity of products previously imported from Côte d'Ivoire. On average, however, inflation decelerated to 1.1 percent, as a result of satisfactory harvests, and despite an increase in the price of petroleum products that resulted from the adoption of a new tariff system.

The economy in **Cape Verde** grew by 3.0 percent in 2002, against an average 6.4 percent in 1998-2001 (when bumper harvests were recorded), fuelled by improved macro-economic stability and resumed donor support. The investment-GDP ratio declined slightly to 21.2 percent. Cap Verde's inflation accelerated to 3.0 percent in 2002, against an average 2.3 percent in 1998-2001, reflecting tighter food supplies.

Côte d'Ivoire was on the path to recovery in 2002, after three years of economic decline or stagnation. The semblance of political stability, the return of donor assistance, and rising domestic consumption had fuelled secondary and tertiary activity in the first three quarters

2001/02), growth performance in 2002 was somewhat dampened by the sharp decline in world cotton prices and its impact on export performance. Gross domestic investment as a percentage to GDP was maintained at 19.3 percent in 2002, reflecting activity in construction and public works. Inflation in Benin decelerated in 2002 to 1.6 percent, reflecting good harvests and stable food prices.

of the year, although construction was slow to resume. Performance in agriculture was mixed, preliminary estimates pointing towards a small decline in export crops but a rise in food crops. All sectors suffered from the fighting in the fourth quarter of the year. Revised estimates point to a 0 percent GDP growth in 2002, against an initially projected 3 percent. Trade, transportation and other services have been the most affected by the crisis. The initial growth projection was based on the assumption that public and private investment would rebound in the second part of the year, with the investment to GDP ratio rising to 13.4 percent in 2002. This figure may need to be revised downwards, in view of recent events. Inflationary pressures, which decelerated in the first part of 2002, notably as a result of lower petroleum prices, have re-emerged with the crisis.

Economic growth in **The Gambia** was estimated at 6 percent in 2002, against a yearly average 5.4 percent in 1998-2001. Recent developments, notably poor agricultural performance in the 2002/03 season (with, notably, a 25 percent fall in cereal crop and a 52 percent drop in groundnut production), border problems with Senegal and lower tourist arrivals, paint a darker picture, however. Fresh donor support has continued to fuel public investment, the investment to GDP ratio rising to 27.3 percent in 2002. Exchange rate depreciation and food scarcity fuelled inflation in 2002 to 5.5 percent, against an average 2.5 percent in 1998-2001.

Growth in **Ghana** has taken an upward turn since 2001, on the back of a recovery in world cocoa and gold prices and improved macroeconomic stability. Trade diversion away from Côte d'Ivoire also fuelled port and trans-

port activities in the latter part of 2002. Real GDP grew by 4.4 percent in 2002, against an average 4.3 percent in 1998-2001. The investment-to-GDP ratio increased slightly to 22.9 percent in 2002, as a result of a rise in public capital outlays under 2002-05 Ghana poverty reduction strategy. The average inflation rate, which peaked at 32.9 percent in 2001 as a result of the sharp exchange rate depreciation, decelerated to 14.5 percent in 2002, as a result of tighter fiscal and monetary discipline.

Rising external assistance and reasonable performance in agriculture and mining contributed to an acceleration in growth in **Guinea** to 4.2 percent in 2002, against an average 3.5 percent in 1998-2001. Government poverty alleviation spending was the main source of investment in 2002. Inflation in 2002 decelerated to 6.0 percent against an average 6.5 percent in 1998-2001. Economic performance in **Guinea-Bissau** deteriorated sharply in 2001, as a result of a freeze in external assistance, and a drop in the world prices of cashew nuts. An 11 percent drop in cereal production, coupled with poor economic management and elusive political stability kept real GDP growth subdued in 2002. The investment-to-GDP ratio remained low, at 7.8 percent, as a result of delays in the post-war reconstruction program. Inflation meanwhile decelerated to 4.0 percent, against an average 4.9 percent in 1998-2001.

The crisis in Côte d'Ivoire and depressed world cotton prices somewhat dented **Mali**'s good growth performance in 2002. Real GDP growth nevertheless accelerated to 5.2 percent (albeit from a low base), as a result of resumed activity in the cotton sector and improved food crop production. Farmers had boycotted the previous cotton season to protest against low farm-gate prices. This combined with poor weather conditions had slashed economic growth to 1.5 percent in 2001, despite a doubling in gold production that year. Inflation in Mali accelerated to 4.5 percent in 2002, against a yearly average 1.8 percent in 1998-2001, notably reflecting higher water and electricity tariffs and rising import prices.

Niger's economic activity heavily hinges on climatic conditions. After two years of recession, real GDP growth rebounded to 7.6 percent in 2001, as a result of bumper cereal harvests. Despite satisfactory weather conditions, agricultural output failed to rise in 2002. Transport bottleneck caused by the Ivoirian crisis, coupled with the impact of an army mutiny in August and continued strikes by public workers, also contributed to a deceleration in growth in 2002, to 2.7 percent. In an indication of rising external assistance, Niger's investment ratio rose to 13.3 percent in 2002, which is still low by regional and continental standards. Inflation decelerated from 4.0 percent in 2001 to 3.0 percent in 2002, as a result of good harvests and cheap food products.

Nigeria, which is the leading economy of the zone, is strongly oil-dependent. Oil production was constrained by a tightening in OPEC quotas in 2002, leading to a -0.9 percent growth in 2002, despite strong performance in agriculture. Although the investment ratio has increased with the return to civilian rule in 1998 and the 2000 surge in oil prices, institutionalized corruption, security issues, high energy costs, and decaying infrastructure are major deterrents for investment in the non-oil sector. Inflation declined to 14.2 percent in 2002, down from an average 10.5 percent in 1998-2001, reflecting a tightening in monetary policy but continued fiscal expansion.

Senegal's economic growth decelerated slightly to 4.9 percent in 2002, against an average 5.5 percent in 1998-2001. Notwithstanding marketing problems in the groundnut sector, other sectors performed well, notably in mining and manufacturing, with the expansion of the Industries chimiques du Sénégal, and in energy, with the start-up of electricity at the Manantali dam. Public works continued to drive investment, which stood at 18.8 percent of GDP in 2002. The marginal increase in inflation that followed the introduction of a single-rate VAT and the liberalization in petroleum prices in 2001 subsided in 2002, with average inflation decelerating to 3.0 percent.

Sierra Leone's 10-year civil war was declared over in January 2002, paving the way for peaceful legislative and presidential elections in April. Improved security situation and increased donor support contributed to accelerating economic growth to 6.6 percent in 2002, against an average 0.1 percent in 1998-2001. Public and NGO investment has meanwhile gathered pace under the post-war recovery program. Increased domestic supply in Sierra Leone led to a fall in inflation from a yearly average 17.9 percent in 1998-2001 to 1.0 percent in 2002.

Togo's economic performance has remained below its potential since the early 1990s in the absence of external assistance. The country nonetheless experienced a 3 percent economic growth in 2002, as a result of rising production in phosphate and cement, bumper cotton harvests and boosted port activity with the onset of the civil war in Côte d'Ivoire. This compares with an average 0.3 percent in 1998-2001. Togo's consumer prices rose by an average 2.8 percent in 2002, against a yearly average 0.8 percent in 1998-2001.

Recent Policy Developments

Poverty alleviation strategy

West Africa hosts the highest number of countries that qualify for debt relief under the enhanced debt relief poor country initiative. The conditions attached to the initiative have incited some 12 West African countries to adopt a broad-based participative approach to their drafting of a national poverty alleviation strategy. **Liberia** and **Togo** are the only heavily indebted countries in the region that have not released an interim poverty reduction strategy paper (PRSP). **Nigeria**, which does not enter the heavily indebted poor country category, has no nationwide poverty alleviation strategy either, instead favoring a sectoral approach. Four countries, The Gambia, Guinea, Niger, and Senegal, completed their full PRSP in 2002. Ghana produced the final draft version of its poverty reduction strategy (GPRS) in February 2002. Côte d'Ivoire's full PRSP was on the verge of completion, when the civil war broke out in September. The program will no doubt need revising to account for the impact of the fighting on the poor and most vulnerable. In March 2003, **Mali** released its final PRSP.

Burkina Faso released its final poverty alleviation strategy program in 2000. Two progress reports have since been compiled. There has been some progress in increasing social spending and improving health and education indicators. School enrollment, literacy rates, immunization coverage rates, and health center staffing, have improved. The government, which adopted a ten-year basic education plan in 2001, hoping to achieve primary education for all by 2015, is in the process of devising a nationwide rural development strategy. Burkina Faso has one of the highest

HIV/AIDS prevalence rate in west Africa after Côte d'Ivoire. Fighting the illness constitutes a major challenge.

The Gambia's full PRSP was completed in April 2002. The PRSP's main objectives are to create an enabling policy environment to promote economic growth and poverty reduction; enhance the productive capacity of the poor; improve the coverage of basic social services; build the capacity of local communities and civil society; and co-ordinate cross-cutting issues, such as food security, governance, and gender equality.

Ghana's GPRS is to ensure a sustainable and equitable growth, by notably investing in infrastructure, modernizing agriculture based on rural development, enhancing social services, and promoting good governance and private sector development. The strategy is aiming in the medium term to reduce the incidence of national poverty from 39 percent to 32 percent, extreme poverty from 27 percent to 21 percent and poverty among food crop farmers from 59 percent to 46 percent by 2004.

In keeping with *Guinea Vision 2010*, **Guinea**'s full PRSP, which was released in January 2002, establishes a poverty alleviation strategic framework that is based on the principle of decentralization. The government's program aims to boost economic growth (with a special emphasis on the private sector and rural development), improve basic services (education, health, electrification, social security), combat HIV/AIDS, promote gender equality and improve governance and administrative capacity. According to the PRSP estimates, 52 percent of the rural population and 25 percent of the urban population live below poverty in Guinea.

Two-third of the population in **Niger** lives in poverty. The PRSP, which was published in January 2002, focuses on creating a growth-conducive environment, promoting rural development, developing education, health, water and sanitation services; developing road transportation; promoting the private sector; and promoting good governance, capacity building and decentralization.

Senegal's final PRSP prioritizes the modernization of agriculture and rural development, the improvement of social services with particular emphasis on health and education, private-sector development, good governance and decentralization. Despite sustained economic growth since the mid-1990s, poverty in Senegal is high, touching 72-88 percent of the rural population and 44-59 percent of the urban population. Illiteracy rate is also high, at more than 60 percent.

Privatization

No major divestiture took place in West Africa in 2002. Privatization is at a more advanced stage in many West African countries, however, when compared to elsewhere in Africa.

Privatization in **Benin** has made little progress since a handful of small-to-medium state owned enterprises (SOEs), including SONACOP (fuel distribution), were sold in 1999. The government has reactivated its privatization program since late 2001 and preparations for the sale of SONAPRA (cotton) and the privatization and unbundling of SBEE (electricity and water), and OPT (post and telecommunication) are now under way. Other SOEs mooted for privatization include the Autonomous Port of Cotonou (PAC).

Trade union protests have hampered **Burkina Faso**'s privatization program since

the parliament ratified in July 2001 a government bill aiming to privatize 13 SOEs, including ONATEL (telecommunications), SONABEL (electricity), SONABHY (petroleum distributor), and ONEA (water). The last major privatization to take place in the country was that of Air Burkina in 2001. CIMAT (cement) whereas the Poura gold mine was liquidated in October 2002.

Cape Verde's public enterprise reform program has remained on track. SALMAR (cold storage) and CERIS (brewery) were sold in late 2001. In 2002, two loss-making SOEs, EMPA (food import and distribution) and TRANSCOR (urban transport) were liquidated. Other SOEs mooted for privatization include INTERBASE (cold storage), CABMAR/CABNAV (shipyards), and TACV (national airline).

The privatization program in **Côte d'Ivoire** produced limited results in 2001-02. Whereas Air France bought a majority share in Nouvel Air Ivoire in October 2001, the farmers organization which was to take over the textile firm CIDT Nouvelles, has proved unable to pay for its stake. New privately-owned institutions were meanwhile established to replace the cocoa parastatal, Nouvelle Caistab. In May 2002, the state sold half its share in the Banque international pour le commerce et l'industrie on the Bourse régionale des valeurs mobilières (BRVM). Most strategic utilities in Côte d'Ivoire, notably telecommunications and electricity, were sold in the later part of the 1990s; SIR (oil refinery) is still awaiting privatization.

The Gambia adopted a Privatization Act in June 2000, enabling the authorities to step up the privatization process. But progress has been hampered by lack of transparency and the SOEs' poor financial states. In 1999, the government seized the property of the Gambia Groundnut Corporation (GGC), owned by the Swiss company, Alimenta. The Alimenta dispute has now been settled, but the processing plants have yet to be returned to the private sector. Other enterprises long mooted for privatization include Nawec (water and electricity) and Gamtel (telecommunication).

Ghana's privatization program initially attracted international attention with major sales such as Ashanti Goldfields Corporation, Ghana Telecom, Social Security Bank and the Ghana Ports and Harbors Authority taking place in the 1990s. Allegations of corruption in earlier divestitures are being investigated. In 2001, the government re-structured the privatization agency and completed the audit of 11 major public enterprises; only one SOE– Mim Timber Company – was divested that year. Little progress was made in 2002, despite the announced "fast track" sale of 12 SOEs, including Electricity Company of Ghana and Ghana Telecom (Malaysia Telecom has agreed to relinquish its interest in Ghana Telecom, following the expiry of its contract in 2002); government's shares in Cocoa Processing Company were sold on the stock exchange market in 2002.

Guinea's difficult political situation and uncertain business environment has hindered the government's privatization program outside mining. Sotelgui (telecommunication) was sold to foreign interest in the mid-1990s, but Sogel (electricity) was re-nationalized in 2001. The assets of now dissolved Air Guinée were transferred to local interests in 2002.

Post-war reconstruction **Guinea-Bissau** launched a privatization program sponsored by the World Bank in 2001. The government is planning to privatize or liquidate 34 public companies by 2005. Three companies GuineNave, Ceramica Bafata, and GuineMetal, were sold in

2002, but public auction for the sale of three state-owned hotels failed to attract any buyers. The government in **Liberia** intends to privatize major public utility companies, including telecommunication, water, and electricity.

Following the sale of EDM (electricity) in 2001, attention in **Mali** has focused on preparation for the liberalization of the cotton sector by 2005. This involves opening the CMDT parastatal to private participation. The tendering process for the licensing of a private agro-industrial operator was launched in late 2002. Other enterprises mooted for privatization include Aéroports du Mali, RCFM (railway) and SOTELMA (telecommunication). A mobile and international phone license was awarded to France Telecom in 2002. Two major privatizations took place in **Niger** in 2001, with the sale of a majority share in SEEN (water) in April and that of SONITEL (telecommunication) in November. There are plans to privatize NIGELEC (electricity) and SONIDEP (petroleum distribution).

Nigeria's government has revived its privatization program since 1999. A first phase was completed at end-2000, involving the sale of 12 enterprises, among which, banks, petroleum distribution companies, cement and insurance companies. The second phase, initially due for completion in 2000, has been bogged down with problems. The privatization of Nigeria Telecom Limited was botched in 2002, after the selected bidder failed to come forward with the pledged US$1.4bn. In addition, the parliament has continued strongly to object to the sale of key public enterprises (notably the petroleum corporation and electricity and telecom parastatals). About 24 enterprises were due to be privatized in 2002, including steel and aluminum smelter companies.

The privatization program in **Senegal** encountered some difficulties in 2002. Negotiations with strategic investors to take over SENELEC (electricity, previously owned by Hydro-Quebec) have broken down. The government decided to disband Sonagraines (groundnut transport company) in September 2001, but the private sector failed to deliver satisfactory transportation services during the groundnut season in 2002. SONACOS (groundnut processing), Sodefitex (cotton) and the railway company have yet to be privatized. Strategic utilities already privatized include Sones (water, 1996), Sonatel (telecommunication, 1997) and Air Senegal (2000)

The government in **Sierra Leone** announced the privatization of some 24 SOEs in 2002, including strategic utilities in air transport, port, and electricity. **Togo**'s privatization program accelerated in 2001, when the management of country's main industrial complex, OTP (phosphate fertilizers) was handed over to private interests. OTP was formally dissolved in January 2002, while five-star Hotel 2 Février was sold to Libyan interests in May 2002. Progress has been slow elsewhere, with three banks, the water utility and Togo Telecom yet to be privatized.

Fiscal developments

The fiscal position in West Africa deteriorated during 2002, with the budget deficit widening to 5.2 percent of GDP from the yearly average of 3.7 percent during 1998-2001 (Table 2.15 and Figure 2.33). This mostly reflected Nigeria's expansionary stance and the impact of Côte d'Ivoire's crisis on the CFA zone's fiscal position. By virtue of their membership to the West African Economic and Monetary Union (WAEMU), CFA zone countries in West Africa

aim to harmonize their economic policy, by notably converging towards commonly agreed fiscal targets. These are: to keep the primary fiscal balance (outside grants, external debt payments, and donor-funded capital outlays) positive, no domestic and external payment arrears, a government debt not to exceed 70 percent of GDP, keeping the wage bill below 35 percent of fiscal receipts; financing at least 20 percent of capital outlays from domestic source; and maintaining fiscal receipts above 17 percent of GDP. These benchmarks, combined with the CFA zone rules on government borrowing, mean that CFA countries have overall maintained a sound fiscal stance over the years. The fiscal stance in non-CFA countries has been somewhat looser. Note, however, that all countries receiving HIPC debt relief in the region have sought gradually to increase their budget share for social spending (notably in education and health).

Strong donor support, continued tax efforts and prudent spending policy kept **Benin**'s average fiscal balance in surplus during 1998-2001. In 2002, the fiscal deficit widened to 2.2 percent of GDP, because the government decided to subsidy cotton producer prices in the context of falling international prices, and raise the civil servant wage bill in response to strikes during the first three months of the year. Measures to reinforce custom administration and curtail non-priority expenditures partly compensated for the spending overruns.

Momentum for tax reforms in **Burkina Faso** has increased since intra-UEMOA custom duties were lifted and the UEMOA common external tariff adopted in 2000. This has led to a marked decline in fiscal revenues as a percentage to GDP. Measures to broaden the tax base, fight tax evasion, and improve fiscal

Table 2.15: West Africa: Macroeconomic Management Indicators

Country	Inflation (%)		Fiscal Balance as % of GDP		Gross Domestic Investment as % of GDP		Gross National Savings	
	Average 1998-2001	2002[a]	Average 1998-2001	2002[a]	Average 1998-2001	2002[a]	Average 1998-2001	2002[a]
BENIN	3.5	1.6	0.2	-2.2	18.2	19.3	11.2	12.43
BURKINA FASO	2.1	1.1	-4.0	-5.9	31.6	32.1	19.3	23.28
CAPE VERDE	2.3	3.0	-9.2	0.2	21.6	21.2	8.4	11.74
COTE D'IVOIRE	3.1	3.6	-1.8	0.2	11.7	13.4	9.4	12.83
GAMBIA	2.5	5.5	-1.7	0.3	20.1	27.3	12.9	13.59
GHANA	21.3	14.5	-7.6	-7.0	22.5	22.9	15.2	18.26
GUINEA	6.5	6.0	-2.6	-2.5	21.8	26.0	15.0	19.26
GUINEA-BISSAU	4.9	4.0	-11.9	-14.6	15.8	7.8	1.9	-
LIBERIA	10.9	15.0	-	-	-	-	-	-
MALI	1.8	4.5	-4.4	-6.6	20.9	22.0	11.2	13.88
NIGER	2.3	3.0	-3.8	-4.9	11.0	13.3	4.6	5.89
NIGERIA	10.5	14.2	-4.1	-7.6	22.6	26.0	22.5	19.09
SENEGAL	1.5	3.0	-0.9	-0.4	18.0	18.8	12.5	12.81
SIERRA LEONE	17.9	1.0	-9.9	-18.1	5.4	17.2	-3.0	-3.28
TOGO	0.8	2.8	-4.2	-1.6	18.0	21.7	4.9	5.07
WEST AFRICA	**5.8**	**5.4**	**-3.6**	**-5.2**	**20.0**	**21.8**	**17.1**	**15.8**

Note: a/ Preliminary estimates
Sources: ADB Development Research and Statistics Divisions.

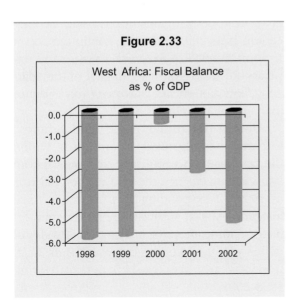

Figure 2.33

West Africa: Fiscal Balance as % of GDP

administration have been taken, but this did not prevent the central government deficit to rise in 2000 and 2001. Unbudgeted expenditures linked to election spending and rising subsidies contributed to a new widening in the fiscal deficit to 5.9 percent of GDP in 2002.

Cape Verde's fiscal position deteriorated sharply in 2000, as a result of overspending in the run-up to the presidential and legislative elections in 2001. The new government restored fiscal discipline under a standard monitored program in 2001, by notably collecting tax and non-tax payment arrears, reducing price subsidies, and tightening spending control. The country successfully negotiated a Poverty Reduction Growth facility with the

IMF in April 2002, the fiscal balance turning positive, at 0.2 percent of GDP in 2002. The government aims to introduce a value added tax and clear all domestic payment arrears by 2003, while accelerating its domestic debt reduction operation.

Budget performance in **Côte d'Ivoire** was satisfactory in the first three quarters that preceded the war, indicating economic recovery, reinforced tax collection, and resumed external assistance. Custom revenues had notably reached their annual target by September. President Laurent Gbagbo's administration had already made good progress in restoring fiscal discipline in 2001, owing notably to better public expenditure control and the introduction of a 20 percent value-added tax (VAT) in July 2001. The budget was estimated to have reached a small surplus equivalent to 0.2 percent of GDP in 2002. This may need to be revised, once military and other war-related spending and the fiscal and custom revenue shortfalls that took place in the fourth quarter of 2002 are taken in consideration. The stock of domestic payment arrears has meanwhile continued to rise, while capital outlays have been squeezed once again. This is the third year running that the government faces serious cash flow problems, owing to political instability.

The fiscal situation in **The Gambia** improved with the resumption of lending by multilateral donors and efforts to combat tax evasion and off budget spending during the 1998-2001 period. Fiscal slippages were noted in 2001, as a result of election outlays, unplanned expenditures in groundnut and electricity, a shortfall in custom revenues, tax arrears, and delays in grant disbursements. The government somewhat tightened its

fiscal stance in 2002 (also an election year), with the fiscal balance turning to a positive 0.3 percent of GDP.

In 2000, the government deficit in **Ghana** surged to 7.9 percent of GDP, owing to election spending. Ghana's fiscal position has strengthened since 2001, as a result of greater domestic tax efforts and tighter expenditure control. Even though the fiscal deficit stood at 7.0 percent of GDP in 2002 (notably reflecting a civil service wage increase), this compares favorably with the poor fiscal performance that characterized the second part of the 1990s. Revenue measures have been taken to broaden the tax base and strengthen revenue collection and administration. The government has also continued to strengthen its new expenditure commitment control system, which became operational in late 2001. Considerable amounts of arrears accumulated over the past years were cleared in 2002, which is in keeping with the gover-nment's policy to reduce domestic borrowing.

Guinea's fiscal deficit stood at 2.5 percent of GDP in 2002, against an average 2.6 percent in 1998-2001, reflecting continued donor support in spite of frequent revenue and expenditure slippage owing to lack of transparency, low tax efforts, and poor expenditure management control.

Guinea-Bissau has made little progress to curtail unauthorized expenditures, widen the tax base, and reinforce tax and custom administration since the end of the civil war in 1999. Overspending and tax fraud have instead resulted in a substantial accumulation of domestic payment arrears. The fiscal deficit rose to 14.6 percent of GDP in 2002, from a yearly average 11.9 percent during 1998-2001.

A series of external shocks has shaken **Mali**'s public finances since 2000. There were some exceptional outlays with the preparations of the 2002 presidential and legislative elections and with the hosting of the African football tournament in February 2002. The marked rise in transfers and subsidies meanwhile reflected the government's willingness to shelter consumers and farmers respectively from the hike in world energy prices in 2000 and from crumbling world cotton prices in 2001/02. Fiscal consolidation, with notably the introduction of a new petroleum tax structure and the intensified use of the unique tax payer identification numbering system, combined with the acceleration in earnings from the mining sector, has nevertheless helped to contain the fiscal deficit to 6.6 percent of GDP in 2002, which is still high when compared with the 1998-2001 average of 4.4 percent.

The **Niger** government heavily relies on foreign grants to finance its budget deficit, which averaged 3.8 percent of GDP in 1998-2001 and rose to 4.9 percent of GDP in 2002, as a result of a freeze in assistance from the European Community since June 2001. Measures to combat tax fraud have recently been taken, in an effort to boost domestic revenues, which rose just above 10 percent of GDP in 2002. The government remains committed to clear wage payment arrears and the land-for-salary scheme was pursued for the second consecutive year in 2002.

Nigeria's fiscal stance continued to be highly expansionary in 2002, based on an optimistic future direction of oil prices. The rise in oil revenue and higher receipts from import duties under the pre-shipment inspection scheme failed to compensate for spending overruns, and the fiscal balance, which had turned from a surplus of 2.4 percent of GDP in 2000 to a deficit of 2.2 percent of GDP in 2001, reached a negative 7.6 percent of GDP in 2002 as a result. The government's effort to contain expenditure is made difficult by Nigeria's fiscal federalism. In particular, lack of transparency and lack of fiscal accountability at the lower levels of government continued to lead to indiscipline in the management of resources.

Public finances in **Senegal** reaped the full benefits of the revenue enhancing reforms that were adopted in 2001 - notably the use of a single VAT, the re-introduction of an oil price pass through mechanism, and the creation of a single taxpayer identification number – in 2002, when the fiscal deficit declined to 0.4 percent of GDP, against a yearly average of 0.9 percent of GDP in 1998-2001. On the expenditure side, there was an increase in public sector salaries as part of the National Retirement Fund reforms and a drop in budgetary transfers (particularly high in 2001 owing to the government's decision to finance deficits in the electricity and groundnut parastatals), which freed up resources for public investment.

The completion of the disarmament exercise and the holding of general elections weighted on **Sierra Leone**'s fiscal position in 2002. Despite increased donor support, the fiscal deficit in 2002 surged to 18.1 percent of GDP, against an average 9.9 percent of GDP in 1998-2001. Fiscal discipline in **Togo** was loosened in 2002, reflecting the end of the staff monitored program with the IMF in September 2001 and the holding of legislative elections in November 2002. The fiscal deficit remains relatively modest, considering the freeze in foreign assistance, averaging 4.2 percent of GDP in 1998-2001 and 1.6 percent of GDP in 2002.

Monetary and exchange rate developments

West Africa witnessed an increase in money supply growth in 2002, averaging 9.6 percent against 5.1 percent in 2001 (Figure 2.32). All countries but Cape Verde and CFA countries had adopted a flexible exchange rate system, making price stability the main monetary target.

Monetary policy in the West African CFA Zone is conducted at a regional level by the Banque centrale des Etats de l'Afrique de l'ouest (BCEAO) in Dakar, Senegal. Like in the Central Africa CFA zone, two rules underpins the functioning of the zone, in exchange for which the French Public Treasury guarantees the convertibility of the CFA franc against the euro: the BCEAO is required to maintain 20 percent foreign exchange to cover its sight liabilities and governments are only allowed to draw a maximum of 20 percent of the previous year's budget receipts from the central bank. Direct advances by the central bank to governments have in fact been frozen since the late 1990s and gradually replaced by T-bills. Direct advances will no longer be permitted in 2003. The BCEAO has successfully switched to indirect instruments since the mid-1990s, with the central bank's discount rate, reserve requirements ratio and money market auctions being the main regulators of the zone's liquidity. The region's interest rates lack responsiveness to world interest rate fluctuations. The BCEAO last adjusted its discount rate in March 2001, when it was raised from 5.75 percent to 6.5 percent to rein in inflationary pressures. The CFA franc, which is pegged to the euro at a rate of CFA565:e1, recovered some of its external value against the US dollar in 2002, after three consecutive years of depreciation. The inflationary impact of CFA fluctuations against the world's main trading currencies outside the euro is limited, since the bulk of external trade takes place with the EU.

In April 2000, the leaders of six West African countries, namely Nigeria, Ghana, The Gambia, Guinea, Liberia and Sierra Leone, declared their intention to adopt a common currency by January 2003, as a first step toward a single monetary zone comprising all CFA and no CFA zone countries that belong to the Economic community of west African states (ECOWAS, see Recent Trends in Globalization). The ambitious project has made some headway in the past two years, with notably the establishment of a West African Monetary Institute and the adoption of a set of convergence criteria, including a restriction of the budget deficit/GDP ratio to 4 percent; a maximum 5 percent inflation rate; at least 6 months import cover; a ceiling on Central Bank financing of budget deficits limited to 10 percent of the previous year's fiscal revenues. In 2002, the date for the launching of the common currency, named ECO, was rescheduled for July 2005, after a report by the Convergence Council showed that none of the five countries had satisfied the four economic convergence criteria for the creation of the zone. It was meanwhile agreed that the member states' foreign exchange reserves will be pooled and managed by the proposed West African Central Bank.

The adoption of a new central bank law in **Cape Verde** indicates the authorities' commitment to tighten monetary policy and restrain the government's use of seignorage. The peg against the Portuguese escudo, which was introduced in July 1998, was left unchanged in 2002 as a result, at a rate of CVEsc0.55:Esc1.

Monetary policy in **The Gambia** has remained relatively prudent. In 2002, the central bank continued to mop up liquidity through sales of T-bills, although the rise in domestic credit, which was dominated by excess government borrowing in 2001, somewhat decelerated in 2002. The Central Bank also continued to intervene heavily in 2002 to support the currency, whose depreciation has accelerated since 2000. Tighter control has led to a shortage in foreign currencies. **Guinea**'s monetary policy has accommodated large fiscal deficit over the years, whereas the liberalization of foreign exchange has proved limited (the Guinean franc is not convertible).

Monetary policy in 2002 in **Ghana** focused on consolidating macroeconomic stabilization, after the turbulence in 2000, which saw inflation surged to 40.5 percent at end-December 2000 and the cedi depreciated by 49.5 percent, owing to external shocks and excess government borrowing. Tight monetary stance, coupled with greater fiscal discipline, has led to decelerating inflation since March 2001, permitting a continuous decline in nominal interest rates. The cedi depreciated by only 3.7 percent against the US dollar in 2001. In order to refocus the operations of the Bank of Ghana to ensure the maintenance of price stability, the formulation and implementation of monetary policy and support for the general economic policy of the government, Parliament passed a new Bank of Ghana law in December 2001. The law also commits the government to fiscal discipline by limiting the total government borrowing to an amount not exceeding 10 percent of previous year's total revenue.

Although the Central Bank of **Liberia** increased the reserve requirement ratios in 2001, excess government borrowing has continued to fuel monetary expansion, which has eroded price stability and given rise to a substantial depreciation of the Liberian dollar, which is officially at par with the US dollar.

The Central Bank of **Nigeria** has sought to compensate for the continued expansionary fiscal operations of the government, and the resulting large injections of liquidity into the economy, by adopting a tighter monetary policy since 2001. Reduced inflationary pressure in early 2002 permitted a reduction in the minimum rediscount rate in July by 2 percentage points to 18.5 percent. The naira depreciation meanwhile showed signs of slowing down, with the central bank starting up foreign exchange auctions in August in a move to establish a market determined exchange rate. Greater fiscal discipline in **Sierra Leone** has greatly reduced government's borrowing from the central bank since 2000. Broad money supply growth has decelerated sharply as a result, leading to a stabilization in inflation and the exchange rate.

Recent Trends in Globalization

Trade liberalization and regionalization

West Africa is relatively open by continental standards, with total trade averaging 71.6 percent of GDP in 2002 (Table 2.16 and Figure 2.34). Togo, Ghana, Côte d'Ivoire, and The Gambia are the most trade-orientated economies in the region with oil exporting Nigeria. This does not necessarily reflect successful export-orientated strategies, but rather the importance of transit activities in these countries, all main transit hubs in the region. All countries but Cape Verde are members of the World Trade Organization, and are thus

Table 2.16: West Africa: The External Sector

Country	Trade* Average 1998-2001	Trade* 2002[a]	Trade Balance as % of GDP Average 1998-2001	Trade Balance as % of GDP 2002[a]	Current Account Average 1998-2001	Current Account 2002[a]	Terms of Trade (%) Average 1998-2001	Terms of Trade (%) 2002[a]	Total External Debt as % of GDP Average 1998-2001	Total External Debt as % of GDP 2002[a]	Debt Service as % of Exports Average 1997-2000	Debt Service as % of Exports 2001
BENIN	44.0	41.0	-10.4	-10.4	-7.0	-8.0	1.8	-14.5	72.1	73.0	12.9	15.4
BURKINA FASO	41.9	36.1	-13.0	-12.2	-12.6	-14.2	-3.3	-1.3	65.2	67.5	22.7	26.0
CAPE VERDE	80.4	78.9	-36.0	-32.9	-13.2	-11.4	7.0	-0.4	52.6	60.3	25.7	33.6
COTE D'IVOIRE	72.4	73.5	13.8	18.5	-2.2	2.9	-0.9	9.1	104.9	103.9	21.6	25.3
GAMBIA	110.9	114.8	-17.0	-16.1	-4.7	-4.3	-4.9	0.0	119.6	125.2	11.3	13.6
GHANA	96.4	103.3	-14.5	-13.6	-7.2	-6.2	-5.0	6.8	107.9	121.6	22.0	12.0
GUINEA	51.4	60.0	3.1	3.8	-6.8	-7.0	-5.7	-0.1	101.7	100.6	20.3	12.5
GUINEA-BISSAU	73.3	81.0	-11.5	-15.9	-14.3	-19.4	3.7	3.3	394.1	379.9	11.3	1.0
LIBERIA	-	-	8.3	7.9	0.4	-	2.0	-	58.3	-	12.7	11.8
MALI	64.5	68.8	-0.7	2.0	-9.9	-9.2	-1.6	-10.2	107.1	96.1	14.1	12.1
NIGER	42.2	41.3	-2.8	-4.0	-6.4	-8.8	-3.0	1.4	85.7	91.2	9.4	12.5
NIGERIA	79.5	73.1	12.4	4.4	1.2	-5.4	13.1	-0.4	83.1	71.1	12.1	9.5
SENEGAL	68.1	67.2	-8.0	-8.3	-5.6	-5.9	-0.9	-0.5	72.0	63.8	16.3	11.4
SIERRA LEONE	42.8	57.6	-6.5	-17.2	-8.5	-17.0	-0.6	0.5	180.5	151.3	46.9	97.0
TOGO	80.4	83.0	-10.9	-12.0	-13.1	-16.9	-0.2	-11.9	91.6	85.5	15.7	16.1
WEST AFRICA	74.2	71.6	5.7	2.5	-2.1	-5.1	5.3	-1.4	87.9	81.4	15.4	13.3

Note: a/ Preliminary estimates
*: (Exports & Imports) of Goods and Non Factors Services at Market Prices
Sources: ADB Development Research and Statistics Divisions.

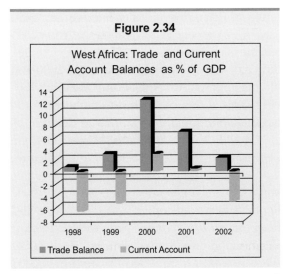

Figure 2.34

West Africa: Trade and Current Account Balances as % of GDP

■ Trade Balance   ■ Current Account

committed to according MFN treatment to all their trading partners.

All 15 West African countries form the regional organization, Economic community of west African states (ECOWAS). Founded in 1975, ECOWAS is the main vehicle for regional integration, a process that includes regional peace-keeping initiatives, enhanced regional trade and economic co-operation, free movement of persons, and the establishment of common institutions. Attention in recent years has focused on plans for ECOWAS's second monetary zone, next to the de facto West African Economic Monetary Union (WAEMU), which comprises 8 CFA franc countries. Mega-projects aimed at facilitating regional transportation and power distribution include the rail link Lagos-Accra-Abidjan-Dakar, the trans-coastal and trans-Sahelien highways, ECOAIR, ECOMARINE, the West African gas pipeline, the West Africa Power Pool and Intelcomm II.

One of the founding principles of ECOWAS is the suppression of customs duties and equivalent taxes and the establishment of a common external tariff. Progress under ECOWAS trade liberalization program has been slow, however. Some 1,925 products have been granted exemption from customs duties on an *ad hoc* basis under the trade liberalization scheme (TLS). While many tariff barriers have been lifted in respect of unprocessed products, Benin is the only country that applies lower tariffs on industrial goods originating from within the Community. In addition, there have been considerable delays in the adoption of ECOWAS common external tariff (5-20 percent) (now scheduled for 2005). In April 2002, the council of minister approved new decentralized procedures under the ECOWAS trade liberalization scheme, with national approval committees soon to be set up by member states. This is in keeping with the harmonization of the ECOWAS procedure with that of the WAEMU. ECOWAS and WAEMU tariff nomenclature are also being harmonized. In 2001, Nigeria and 6 other West African countries, Benin, Burkina Faso, Côte d'Ivoire, Ghana, Mali and Niger, formed a free trade area, as a first step towards wider regional integration. ECOWAS intra-regional trade constitutes 10.4 percent of the region's total exports and 12.3 percent of all imports.

WAEMU is by far the most integrated economic grouping in Africa. Beside having a common currency, the 8 member countries form a customs union since 2000, when all intra-regional tariffs were lifted and a common external tariff structure was adopted. There has also been considerable progress in harmonizing fiscal, economic, business and law procedures, with notably the adoption of an harmonized value-added tax, the creation of OHADA, and the formulation of a common mining code, and supra-national banking regulations. Most countries have made some progress in meeting the UEMOA convergence criteria. In 2002, work concentrated on a common policy for intra-regional air traffic and port transit activities, and the harmonization of national account statistics and budget nomenclature. Paradoxically, intra-regional trade is relatively small, (15.6 percent of all exports and 8.4 percent of all imports), reflecting the importance of informal trade, poor regional infrastructure and the lack of product diversification.

On an individual country basis, all CFA countries have adopted the WAEMU Common External Tariff since January 2000, with four rates running from 0 to 20 percent. A special tax may be imposed to protect goods in sensitive sectors for the first four years of the new regime. The average tariff rate is 12 percent. Some countries, notably Guinea-Bissau, have yet to achieve full compliance with the region's tariff rate structure and its common classification of goods, which was amended in November 2002 (and will take effect in 2003). Note that Benin was the only country to benefit from the adoption of the WAEMU Common External Tariff structure, its former trade regime being at large more liberal. Other WAEMZ countries have experienced significant custom revenue shortfalls, which were partly bankrolled by multilateral institutions that supported the trade liberalization scheme and with it, domestic tax reforms.

Cape Verde aims to lift custom exemptions and streamline its external tariff regime into seven tariff bands ranging from zero to fifty percent, with the average unweighted tariff rate lowered from 23½ percent to 12½ percent. The new tariff regime is to be introduced by January 2003. Progressive reductions in external trade

tariffs in Ghana have led to a maximum tariff rate of 22 percent in 2001, with the trade tariff regime simplified to four lines. The average tariff stood at 14.7 percent as of early 2000 and Ghana applies few formal non-trade tariffs barriers. This is one of the most liberalized trade regimes in the region, with that in Benin.

Of all ECOWAS countries, **Nigeria** has one of the most complex external tariff structure, with over 15 tariff bands, and custom duties varying from 0 percent to 100 percent. Trade liberalization is uncertain and inequitable and frequent *ad hoc* changes are made to the tariff and non-tariff nomenclatures. Peak tariffs were increased from 100 to 150 percent in 2002 (mostly affecting imported food items) and new products (mostly food and manufactured goods) were added to the import prohibitions list. The simple average tariff has increased to 34 percent as a result, against 24.4 percent in 1995.

Trade performance and export diversification

West Africa's external balance deteriorated in 2002, with the current account deficit rising to 5.1 percent of GDP from the annual average of 2.1 percent over 1998-2001 (Table 2.16 and Figure 2.34). Trade performance varied greatly on an individual country basis, however. The overall picture was greatly influenced by Nigeria, whose oil exports accounted for a large chunk of the region's exports in 2002. Other ECOWAS countries are net oil importers. The region's export base is poorly diversified and most countries rely on agricultural exports and/or non-oil mineral exports. Cross-border trade is often unrecorded and various minerals, notably diamonds, are smuggled from Liberia and Sierra Leone, despite international sanctions.

The region as a whole has failed to boost manufactured exports, although some progress has been made over the years in increasing the share of semi-processed primary products, notably phosphate fertilizers, canned fish, and cocoa paste and butter. Côte d'Ivoire is the only country that exports basic manufactured goods, including processed food, petroleum products, and textiles, mostly to the sub-region. Côte d'Ivoire, The Gambia, and Sierra Leone were declared eligible for trade preferences under AGOA II in 2002. All other west African countries, but Burkina Faso, Liberia and Togo, were already eligible for preferential treatment under AGOA I. The initiative is has spurred foreign interest in investing in the region's textile industry, like recently demonstrated in Senegal and Mali. All west African countries benefit from trade preferences under the EU Cotonou convention.

All countries but Nigeria experienced a sharp deterioration in their terms of trade in 2000, when world oil prices peaked from an average 17.9 US$/b in 1999 to 28.5 US$/b. The main gainers in 2002 were cocoa exporting countries. World cocoa prices, which fell sharply during 1999-2000 before rising slightly in 2001, peaked to 98.16 US cents/lb in September 2002, 112 percent up from the same month in 2001. By contrast, world cotton prices, which fell by about half in 2001, remained depressed through most of 2002, although there was some price recovery in the second part of the year.

Benin's trade balance deteriorated in 2002, as a result of a decline in cotton export earnings, the rise in cotton exports having failed to compensate for depressed world cotton prices. This, combined with higher service and income outflows and a fall in private transfers, led to a widening in the current account balance to 8.0 percent of GDP in 2002, against an average 7.0 percent of GDP in 1998-2001.

Burkina Faso's current account balance in 2002 was projected to improve, despite a rise in capital goods imports and falling world cotton prices, thanks to strong export performance and rising donor support (including debt relief). Côte d'Ivoire's crisis, however, had a negative impact on the country's livestock exports to the sub-region and workers remittances from Côte d'Ivoire (where up to 3 millions Burkinabès live) in the fourth quarter of the year, while border closures have greatly inflated freight costs. As a result, the current account deficit rose to 14.2 percent of GDP in 2002, against an average 12.6 percent in 1998-2001.

Cape Verde's external situation deteriorated in 2002, as a result of depressed tourism receipts following the September 11th event and lower workers remittances because of sluggish economic growth in the US and Portugal, where a large migrant community live. Rising donor support nevertheless helped to maintain the current account deficit at 11.4 percent of GDP in 2002, against an average 13.2 percent of GDP in 1998-2001.

Côte d'Ivoire's export performance was strong in the first three quarters of the year, mostly reflecting buoyant world cocoa prices and rising exports in petroleum products and cement. Fuelled by economic recovery, import growth nonetheless outpaced that of exports, suggesting a decline in the trade surplus. Both imports and exports contracted in the fourth quarter of the year, as a result of the crisis. This, coupled with delays in aid disbursements and falling tourism receipts, contributed to a lower-than-expected current account surplus of 2.9 percent of GDP in 2002, against an average deficit of 2.2 percent of GDP in 1998-2001.

The Gambia's current account deficit improved in 2002, to 4.3 percent of GDP, which is an improvement on 2001, when falling groundnut export earnings, depressed re-export activities and lower tourist arrivals, had led to a widening in the current account deficit to 6.2 percent of GDP.

Ghana's external performance improved in 2002, on the back of rising world prices and export volumes for cocoa and gold, the country's main foreign exchange earners, and limited import growth. Increased inflows of official capital and lower debt service payments also contributed to a decline in the current account deficit to 6.2 percent of GDP in 2002 from an average 7.2 percent of GDP in 1998-2001.

Guinea is the only country with Côte d'Ivoire and Nigeria to support a robust trade surplus. This reflects the country's rich mineral resources, notably bauxite, alumina, gold and diamonds, and a slowly rising demand for imported goods. The country's current account deficit nonetheless remained firmly in deficit in 2002, at 7.0 percent of GDP, owing to high freight costs and debt service payments.

Guinea-Bissau's current account deficit rose sharply in 2002 to 19.4 percent of GDP against an average 14.3 percent of GDP in 1998-2001, as a result of a 14 percent drop in the production of cashew nuts, which constitute the bulk of the country's exports, and a rising food import bill.

Bumper cotton harvests in 2001/02 and rising gold production and prices drove **Mali**'s external performance in 2002. Import growth meanwhile slowed compared to 2001, when imports were fuelled by investment in mining and construction works for the African football tournament. As a result, the current account deficit shrank to 9.2 percent of GDP in 2002,

despite falling world cotton prices, from an average 9.9 percent of GDP in 1998-2001.

Niger, whose main exports are uranium and livestock, experienced a slight deterioration in its external position in 2002, as a result of weaker export performance. The current account deficit rose to 8.8 percent of GDP in 2002, against an average 6.4 percent of GDP in 1998-2001.

Nigeria's current account balance is subject to large swings, reflecting changes in OPEC sales quota and fluctuations in world oil prices. The oil sector contributes 99 percent of the country's exports. The current account balance peaked with world oil prices to an all time high surplus equivalent to 11.9 percent of GDP in 2000, before declining to 6.0 percent of GDP in 2001 and falling into a deficit equivalent to 5.4 percent of GDP in 2002.

Senegal's current account deficit rose in 2002 to an equivalent 5.9 percent of GDP, against an average 5.6 percent of GDP in 1998-2001, as the strong performance of Industries chimiques de Sénégal, which almost doubled its exports of phosphoric acid and fertilizer in 2002, failed to compensate for the disastrous groundnut season and a sluggish tourist industry. The fisheries agreement signed with the EU in mid-2002 helped to meet the financing gap.

Post-war reconstruction efforts and a recovery in domestic consumption fuelled imports in **Sierra Leone** in 2002. Rising official transfers and external loans largely compensated for the widening trade deficit. The current account deficit reached 17.0 percent of GDP in 2002, against 8.5 percent of GDP in 1998-2001. Togo's trade position deteriorated in 2002. The current account deficit stood at 16.9 percent of GDP in 2002, against 13.1 percent in 1998-2001.

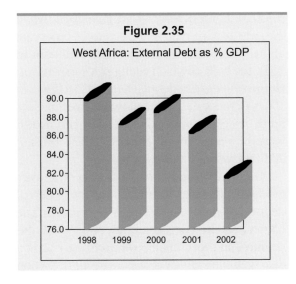

Figure 2.35

West Africa: External Debt as % GDP

(y-axis: 90.0, 88.0, 86.0, 84.0, 82.0, 80.0, 78.0, 76.0; x-axis: 1998, 1999, 2000, 2001, 2002)

External debt and other capital flows

West Africa has limited access to international capital markets. Most countries in the region have negotiated debt rescheduling deals with the London Club of commercial lenders and the Paris Club of sovereign lenders. In 1996, the Ivoirian government signed a debt reduction deal with the London Club of commercial lenders and bought back some of its debt via Brady Bonds. Ghana is soon to receive its first credit rating, which will help the country gain access to cheaper lending. West Africa's total debt stock, which is mostly made of concessional, long-term official loans, declined marginally in 2002 relative to 2001. All except Cape Verde, Liberia, Nigeria, and Togo, qualify for debt relief under the enhanced HIPC initiative. Burkina Faso is the only country in the region to have reached completion point under the enhanced initiative. West Africa's debt burden has eased since the beginning of the 1990s, with the debt/GDP ratio declining to 81.4 percent in 2002, against an average 87.9 percent in 1998-2001 (Figure 2.35).

Foreign participation on the Bourse régionale des valeurs mobilières (BRVM), the West African CFA stock exchange market, and on the Ghana and Nigeria Stock Exchanges has failed to pick up, although regulations concerning portfolio foreign investment have been relaxed in Nigeria and in Abidjan. Concerning non-debt creating capital flows, foreign direct investment in West Africa is driven by oil development in Nigeria. It remains erratic elsewhere, occasionally surging with privatization or large-scale operations in mining. FDI has declined in recent years, as a result of political instability in Côte d'Ivoire, the main host country for foreign investors after Nigeria. According to UNCTAD *World Investment Report 2002*, West Africa hosted US$ 933 million in FDI inflows in 2001.

Benin's debt burden declined for the third consecutive year in 2002, following a debt relief deal with the Paris Club in October 2000 and decision point in July 2001. With a debt-GDP ratio and debt service ratio standing at 73.0 percent in 2002 and 15.4 percent in 2001 respectively, Benin is moderately indebted by continental standards. **Burkina Faso** has strongly benefited from a series of debt reduction deals with multilateral institutions and the Paris Club, as it reached completion point under HIPC I in July 2000 and under HIPC II in April 2002. Despite this relief, the country's debt burden has not declined as fast as anticipated, because of exogenous factors to exports. In response, the IMF and World Bank have agreed to top-up the HIPC initiative, by bringing the total nominal debt service relief to US$900m. According to the IMF calculations, this should bring the debt service ratio down from 23 percent in 1999 to 6 percent in 2003. FDI inflows in Burkina Faso, which, according to UNCTAD World Investment Report 2002, amounted to US$26m in

2001, had mostly taken place in mining and construction.

The new administration in **Cape Verde** has pursued a prudent borrowing policy since 2001, by notably refraining from contracting non-concessional loans. Consequently, the rise in the country's nominal external debt decelerated in 2002, with the debt-GDP ratio nonetheless standing at 60.3 percent. The government has yet to clear the bulk of its outstanding stock of external arrears, which amounted to US$15.3 million at end-2001.

Côte d'Ivoire had made significant headways in restoring some creditworthiness in 2002, with notably the signing of a major debt rescheduling deal with the Paris Club in April. The country was expected to negotiate a similar deal with the London Club and reach decision point under the HIPC initiative before the end of the year. Multilateral and bilateral loan disbursements had meanwhile resumed following the signing of a new PRGF in March 2002. The subsequent rise in nominal debt, coupled with the economic decline, contributed to a heavier debt burden, with the debt-GDP ratio standing at 103.9 percent in end-2002. There was no accumulation in external payment arrears that year. FDI inflows in Côte d'Ivoire slumped from US$371 millions in 1999 to a yearly US$255-8 millions in 2000-2001, following the December 1999 coup and the period of violence that characterized the 2000 elections. After a short-lived hope for investment recovery in 2002, confidence in the economy has reached rock-bottom since September 19th, and it may now take years before foreign investors return.

The Gambia, which reached decision point in December 2000, paving the way for total nominal debt relief worth US$ 90 millions, has yet to negotiate a Paris Club Deal. External debt stood at 125.6 percent of GDP in 2002, while the debt service ratio increased to 13.6 percent in 2001. FDI inflows totaled US$35 millions in 2001, the bulk of which taking place in services. **Guinea**'s external debt-GDP ratio declined to 100.6 percent in 2002, following interim debt relief since decision point in 2000 and a deal with the Paris Club in May 2001. The bulk of FDI inflows take place in mining.

Guinea-Bissau is one of the most heavily indebted countries in Africa, with the external debt-GDP ratio exceeding 370 percent. The country reached decision point under the HIPC initiative in December 2000 and negotiated a deal with the Paris Club in January 2001, paving the way for some debt relief and slight improvement in the country's debt indicators in 2001 and 2002. Debt service (due) still exceeded total public revenues in 2002, however, with the government accumulating new external payment arrears that year.

Ghana's total external debt represented 121.6 percent of GDP in 2002. Ghana reached decision point under the Enhanced HIPC initiative in January 2002, paving the way for total debt relief from all of Ghana's creditors worth about $3.7 billion, which is equivalent to 56 percent of total debt outstanding. A debt relief deal was signed with the Paris Club of official, bilateral creditors as part of the initiative in May 2002. This will help to ease the country's heavy debt burden. The bulk of FDI in Ghana takes place in services. An Investors' Advisory Council, chaired by the President and which includes top-level executives from the Ghanaian business community, multinational companies investing in Ghana, and other major international companies was set up in April 2002 to advise the government on how to attract foreign investment to the country.

In September 2000, **Mali** reached the completion point under the original HIPC initiative and the decision point under the enhanced HIPC initiative, with debt relief amounting to $523 million. Consequently, its foreign debt to GDP ratio has come down significantly in recent years, reaching 96.1 percent in 2002. FDI inflows in Mali doubled in 2000-01, averaging US$ 100 m a year, reflecting bulky investment in the Morila gold mine and in telecommunication.

Niger reached decision point in December 2000, paving the way for a nominal debt relief worth US$ 850 million. External public debt as a share of GDP stood at 91.2 percent in 2002. FDI investment in Niger has been confined to French interests in the uranium industry, which partly reflects the country's political instability.

The external debt stock of **Nigeria** was 71.1 percent of GDP at the end of 2002. Nigeria has continued to pursue a Debt Conversion Program (DCP) as part of its debt management strategy. By the end of 2001, external debt worth $2.26 million was redeemed under the auction system, while $0.8 million was cancelled under the out-of-auction arrangement. In December 2000, Nigeria secured a debt rescheduling deal with the Paris Club of official bilateral creditors. But in August 2002, Nigeria admitted to a debt crisis and said it could no longer afford to service its external debt, because of plunging oil revenues. This was the first time that the country completely halted payments. The debt suspension was also in response to the sharp fall in Nigeria's external reserves. Foreign direct investment in Nigeria mostly consists of joint venture between the state and foreign oil giants. FDI inflows to Nigeria totaled US$1.1 billion in 2001, making it the third largest FDI destination in Sub-Saharan Africa after South Africa and Angola.

Senegal is moderately indebted by continental standards. The country, which reached decision point in June 2000, was to reach completion point in December 2002, paving the way for about US$800m in nominal debt relief. Debt relief schemes combined with the government's prudent borrowing policy permitted a decline in the country's debt burden, with the debt-GDP and debt service ratios respectively standing at 63.8 percent in 2002 and 11.4 percent in 2001. Many initiatives have been taken since 2000 to attract foreign investors, with notably the creation of the one-stop investment shop, APIX, the launch of mega-projects in infrastructure and energy, and the president's active participation in NE-PAD. Some major obstacles remain however, notably that concerning land ownership, and FDI inflows have yet to pick up.

Sierra Leone was the most recent county in west Africa to reach decision point under the HIPC initiative. The decision came 6 months after the signing of a PRGF with the IMF in September 2001. A deal with the Paris Club was subsequently signed as part of the initiative. The country's external debt declined to 151.3 percent as a ratio to GDP in 2002. Foreign investment in richly-endowed Sierra Leone is bound to rise as the post-war reconstruction program kicks off.

The **Togolese** government has pursued a prudent borrowing policy, despite having limited access to concessional lending, because of international sanction over human rights and election issues. The debt-GDP ratio has declined since the mid-1990s, to stand at 85.5 percent of GDP in 2002.

Outlook

Growth in West Africa is forecast to increase to 3.1 percent in 2003, over the 1.7 percent recorded in 2002. But the contrasting economic performances between the CFA zone and the non-CFA countries are set to deepen in 2003.

Burkina Faso's economy will continue directly to suffer from the political crisis in Côte d'Ivoire. The official growth projection of 6 percent for 2003 will need to be revised downwards, as a result. Agriculture will be the main source of growth, with cotton export earnings set to rise with the anticipated recovery in cotton world prices. Services and industry will be the sectors the most affected by the Ivorian crisis. Growth in **Cape Verde** is set to accelerate to about 5 percent in 2003, on accounts of growing tourism and strong donor support.

Côte d'Ivoire's economic situation will continue to deteriorate in 2003, with growth likely to be negative in all sectors. Even if a quick resolution to the conflict is found, confidence in the economy will be slow to return, as investors and the international community adopt a prudent wait-and-see approach. Tackling the humanitarian crisis and paying public servants on time will remain some of the government's immediate priorities. Post war reconstruction could lead to an acceleration in growth in the medium run.

Growth in **Ghana** will be strong in 2003, accelerating to around 5 percent, as traffic with Côte d'Ivoire's traditional trading partners (notably Burkina Faso, Niger, and Mali) increase, and export earnings receive a boost from a recovery in world cocoa and gold prices. Economic prospects in **Guinea-Bissau** could improve in the medium-term, assuming satisfactory weather conditions and an acceleration in the pace of reforms, starting with the settling of public payment arrears. Good cashew seasons, private sector led growth and infrastructure works will be essential to support the country's economic recovery.

The crisis in Côte d'Ivoire will continue to disrupt trade activity in **Mali**, as well as raising transport costs and consumer prices, and curtailing sources of public revenues. Satisfactory export and food crop harvests in 2002/03, the implementation of essential reforms and strong donor support (including debt relief) should nonetheless help to maintain economic growth above that of population in 2003.

OPEC's decision to increase production quotas from January 2003, and the rise in world oil prices stemming from oil supply disruption in Venezuela and tension in the Middle East, will boost **Nigeria**'s economy, with growth expected to turn positive again in 2003. Performance in the non-oil sector will very much depend on the government's efforts to push through already much delayed structural reforms. The 2003 legislative and presidential elections are likely to divert government attention away from the pressing issues of corruption, poverty and decaying infrastructure, however.

Growth in **Senegal** will decelerate, as a result of a 20 percent drop in agricultural production and continued marketing problems in the groundnut sector.

In **Sierra Leone**, growth prospects will hinge on continued momentum for post war reconstruction, including the resettlement of the population, and on strong external assistance. Peace consolidation will also be essential.

PART TWO

GLOBALIZATION AND AFRICA'S DEVELOPMENT

Overview

The theme of the 2003 ADR, *Globalization and Africa's Development*, is important because globalization is one of the titanic forces driving structural change in the world economies. Unleashed by the forces of technology, liberalization and instantaneous communications, globalization is redefining the bases of the competitiveness of nations and firms, and also throwing up new challenges for nations large and small. Globalization has, in its wake, amplified global market forces, making them increasingly important in the daily lives of virtually all the world's people. It has led to greater economic, political, and cultural interdependence among the nations of the world. It would indeed become difficult to find any corner of the world that is not affected in one way or other by this sweeping development. The phenomenon, which accelerated in the last decade of the 20th century — and which is likely to be a defining characteristic of the 21st century — is perhaps one of the most potent forces for change that mankind has witnessed.

Chapter 3 of the Report focuses on *The Process of Globalization*. It shows that economist see globalization as the growing interdependence and interconnectedness of the modern world, encapsulating the increasing ease of movement of goods, services, capital, people and information across national borders, which is rapidly creating a single global economy. Globalization is also reflected in the spread of global norms and values, including the worldwide acknowledgement of democracy as a political imperative and the proliferation of global agreements and treaties, including international environmental and human rights. The Chapter shows that globalization is multifaceted, having many important dimensions – economic, and social, political and environmental, cultural and religious – which affect everybody in some way. Globalization is a harbinger of both good and bad tidings. Whilst it can offer opportunities for developing nations to leapfrog across some of the ladders in the traditional development trajectory, it may also bring with it a deepening of external dependence and vulnerability. Historically, true globalization began in the nineteenth century with the unleashing of the economic forces of trade, mibration, and capital flows, with Britain's 19th century free trade leadership, as the critical impetus to the process. The literature generally distinguishes three waves of globalization: the first wave covering the period 1870 to 1914; the second wave covering the periof 1950 to 1980; and the thrid wave covering the period of 1980 to the present. The latest wave of globalization is remarkable because a large group of developing countrties – the new/post-1980 'globalizers' – broke into global markets. Other developing countries became increasingly marginalized in the world economy and suffered declining incomes and rising poverty. Furthermore, international migration and capital movements that declined during the second wave of globalization again became substantial. The most encouraging development in the third wave of globalization is that some developing countries, accounting for about three billion persons, have succeeded for the first time in harnessing their labor abundance to give them a competitive advantage in labor-intensive manufactures and services. In terms of broad measurement, globalization can be disaggregated into economic integration, political integration, and social integration. The main drivers of globalization today include rapid changes in communications and information technology, reduction in transportation costs, the growth of the neo-liberal economic management (especially economic liberalization), institutional architecture (especially through the works of multilateral institutions such as the UN, the World Bank, IMF, regional development banks, GATT/WTO which had given rise to economic reforms, Uruguay Round/Doha development agenda, etc), and the emergence of new regionalism across the globe.

Chapter 4 examines the issue of *Globalization and Africa's Development Experience*. In 1950, Africa delivered a tenth of world exports. Since then the share has declined to only 2.7 percent in 2000. The value of Africa's imports also declined from 2.8 percent of the world total in 1985 to a low of 1.8 percent in 1996, rising marginally to 2 percent in the year 2000. These figures greatly contrast with those posted by other regions. Asia and North America each accounted for nearly a fifth of world exports and imports over the period with Europe accounting for almost half of total world exports and imports. The loss of market shares by Africa for its major commodity exports over the last three decades is estimated to have caused annual revenue losses of about $11 billion in current (1996) prices. Also, Africa did not attract a large share of private capital during the 1990s, with an average 8 percent share of total private capital and only an average 3 percent share of FDI. Much of this investment is concentrated, geographically and sectorally, in a few countries and in extractive natural resources such as oil and solid minerals. External debt continues to be one of the major obstacles to the development efforts of the Africa. Africa's total debt as a share of the total debt of developing countries has seen a steady fall from a peak of about 16 percent in 1995 to about 12 percent in 2002. Yet, Africa, in spite Enhanced HIPC Initiative, remains the most indebted continent relative to its gross national income, and this undoubtedly makes policy making there more difficult. In addition, Africa, together with South Asia, is one of the least connected regions on the globe. Connectedness has the potential to make important contributions to improving economic growth performance in Africa, but that it is also, clearly, only one aspect of a much wider set of challenges to be addressed by the public authorities and the private sector.

Chapter 5 discusses *Towards Structural Transformation in Africa*. The Chapter emphasizes that Africa, more than any other region of the world, faces the danger of being left behind by the rapid changes being brought about by the forces of globalization. Developing Africa in the context of globalization, therefore, requires a coherent business plan. This should seek to minimize the risks of globalization while maximizing its benefits. To be effective, such a plan must be comprehensive and involve consistent and coherent strategies at three major levels: Domestic strategy, anchored on building the institutions and enabling environment for a private sector-led, competitive market economy. More fundamentally, such a domestic strategy must be guided by the ideology of aggressive outward or export-orientation, using open regionalism as a building block; Regional strategy, driven by the need to enlarge markets and to exploit complementarities, economies of scale and synergies in provision of regional public goods -- infrastructure, security/defense and collective regional institutions as agencies of restraint -- so that domestic reforms and policies can be locked in for credibility. Such a regional strategy must also involve defining and mainstreaming regional best practices in political and economic governance, and exert collective peer pressures on erring countries to conform to the regional 'convergence criteria'; and Global strategy, aimed at addressing many of the asymmetrical power relations and inequities in globalization, creating a level playing field, redesigning the global financial architecture, improving access to Africa's exports, removal of subsidies on agricultural products in industrial countries, increase concessional resources to African countries, provision of global public goods, and strengthening the programs and institutions for preferential and differential treatments to Africa.

Chapter 6 discusses *Africa's Responses to Globalization*. This Chapter examines the *collective* policy responses that African nations have taken to address the challenges posed by globalization. It also considers some of the initiatives that have been taken at the global level to help reverse Africa's downward spiral into global marginality. Africa's long-running development challenges and its marginalization in the world economy have not arisen for a lack of attempts or strategies to deal with the continent's crisis. The responses have been at various levels, including national policies, regional integration experiments (African Union and its precursors, including the African Economic Community, and NEPAD), and numerous bilateral and multilateral initiatives (including EU-ACP Agreement, AGOA, EBA, The Doha Round and its predecessor Uruguay Round, and the Enhanced HIPC Initiative). The Chapter also discusses the framework for a new African and global agenda to reverse Africa's marginalization. Finally, the role of the African Development Bank Group in financing and promoting external resource inflows is described, including the enhancement of development effectiveness, financing operations, debt relief, private sector development, promotion of capital inflows and other sources of capital mobilization for Africa's development and greater integration into the global economy.

CHAPTER 3
The Process of Globalization

Introduction

Globalization is a multifaceted process that so affects all countries and peoples of the world that it has become a concept of increasing significance in international debates. The dimensions of globalization are all-embracing and include human migration, trade in goods and services, movements of capital and integration of financial markets. It is a process that has been driven by the rapid development of communications, innovations in technology and industrial organization, as well as by major changes in public policy and economic management – factors which have helped to extend market forces beyond national borders. In this respect, globalization has increased the possibilities of human and economic interaction and, in theory at least, gives communities and countries greater access to more capital, technology, cheaper imports and larger export markets. Whatever the achievements and drawbacks, globalization is the culmination of international political and economic developments over the 19th and 20th centuries and has become the dominant framework within which the world faces the challenges of the 21st century.

Writing in the 1920s, John Maynard (later Lord) Keynes lamented the passing of the old European order at the outbreak of the Great War: "What an extraordinary episode in the progress of man that age which came to an end in August 1914... The inhabitant of London could order by telephone, sipping his

morning tea in bed, the various products of the whole earth.... he could at the same time and by the same means adventure his wealth in the natural resources and new enterprises of any quarter in the world" (1920, cited in Frankel, 2001). The great economist was merely expressing nostalgia at the passing of the first historic epoch of globalization, whose early landmarks date back to medieval Venice, the Ming Dynasty in China, the great trading states of the Western Sudan and the European Hanseatic League from the fourteenth to the nineteenth century. Today, we are witnessing a phenomenon similar to the great currents which swept away the old agrarian order of feudal Europe and which saw the birth of a new industrial age — a process which the economic historian Karl Polanyi (1944) depicted so well in his magisterial work, *The Great Transformation*.

To echo former US President William Jefferson Clinton, "globalization is the new reality of our times". During the last decade of the 20th century, globalization has been the name of the game throughout the world economy. Indeed, the metaphor of 'our common global neighborhood' rings far truer today than it ever did. What is unique about the new wave of globalization is the sheer extent of its reach — encompassing the entire planet, and touching nearly all cultures and communities across the world. Capital, information and knowledge now travel literally at the speed of light, creating new opportunities as well as risks for individuals, firms, civic communities and nation states. This remarkable process has accelerated over the last half century, driven by economic liberalization leading to the remarkable expansion of international trade and capital flows, as well as by the extraordinary advances in information and communications technologies. It has undoubtedly brought about several benefits in terms of worldwide economic and social development as reflected in unprecedented growth in global output and real per capita incomes and by improvements in human welfare worldwide. To all intents and purposes, we already live in a global economy where flows of trade, capital and knowledge across national borders are not only large, but are increasing. Countries that are unwilling to engage with other nations risk falling behind the rest of the world and becoming severely marginalized (Fischer, 2001).

Globalization has also become one of the controversial and emotive topics of our age. Technology, politics and markets are becoming increasingly intertwined, creating a new symmetry of linkages across nations and peoples, jangling in some cases cultural sensitivities and creating new forms of angst and alienation. Anti-globalization protesters from Seattle to London, from Rome to Barcelona, from Caracas to Durban, have pitched their tents with anarchists, human rights campaigners, ecologists and latter-day neo-Marxists in decrying globalization's allegedly negative impact on the environment, individual liberties and on the life-chances of the poorest of the world's poor. For many of them, globalization is synonymous with unleashing market forces, minimizing the role of the state, reinforcing enduring inequities and deepening global exploitation, poverty and inequality.

It is equally important to note that globalization has also spurred some inherently contradictory tendencies. On the one hand, liberalization and open markets are becoming the standard norms of public management and international economic relations. On the other hand, however, we are entering a period of competitive regionalism where new and powerful regional communities seek to preserve their economic domains from competition from developing countries, maintaining huge subsidies and building protectionist walls against human and material exports from the developing world.

Globalization may be inevitable but it is already clear that unbridled globalization can be good neither for Africa nor the world. Karl Polanyi understood the fact that the market is a human artefact, and as such, requires effective management and governance. The conclusions of this report are therefore premised on:

(i)   the need for an internationally managed globalization process based on the norms of guided markets;

(ii)   open regionalism and respect for the sovereignty and equality of nations;

(iii) the rights of countries both small and great to determine their own destinies in an atmosphere of freedom, justice and peace.

The emphasis is on how best to take advantage of the opportunities presented by the exponential growth and increased openness of the world economy and how to cope with the challenges that globalization may bring. The positive effects need to be harnessed. With reference to Africa, the challenge for policy makers and international institutions is to promote and support conditions for the kind of globalization that will accelerate growth and poverty reduction in Africa.

In assessing the implications for African development in a changing international economic order, the current chapter examines the concept and phenomenon of globalization and the forces underlying it. Chapter four examines African development in the context of globalization and the various African policy responses to globalization. The fifth and final chapter draws lessons and implications for African development and explores the policy options that would enable Africa reclaim its development in the emerging global economic order.

A Global Phenomenon

As a phenomenon, globalization has both simple and complex meanings. However, to be a useful concept for policy makers, globalization must mean more than just an increase in the value of trade, or in its share in output, or even a change in the structure of trade and other international flows. As a supplement to specific changes in economic variables, we can think of it as a change in attitude, a change in the way in which we approach and try to understand economic, political, and cultural influences. We now see global interaction, global opportunities, and global constraints as normal: they must always be considered as a possibility, even if in a particular instance action or policy remains national or local. There is now an awareness of international markets and suppliers, of the possibility that labor and capital can move, of the potential for cross border threats to the environment, to national or personal security, to health. There is also greater awareness of

differences: in incomes, in types of activity and in the nature of government strategies. The perceived range of both possible outcomes and possible policies has therefore increased.

Key Definitions

What is globalization? How is it to be distinguished from the more generalized secular process of internationalization and international economic integration? Is it inherently an economic process, or is fundamentally a technological process? Or indeed is it merely a phenomenon to be associated with cultural diffusion and the worldwide homogenization of consumer tastes as represented by the ubiquity of blue jeans, McDonalds and Coca Cola?

There are several definitions in the literature. Dollar (2001) defines globalization as the growing integration of economies and societies around the world as a result of flows of goods and services, capital, people and ideas. According to him, integration accelerates development, it reduces productivity gaps between workers in developing and advanced counties through trade in goods, foreign investment, international telecommunications and migration. For Ajayi (2001), globalization may be defined as the increasing interaction among, and integration of the activities, especially economic activities, of human societies around the world. It refers to the expansion of international flows of trade, finance, and information into an integrated global market. Daouas (2001) emphasizes the multidimensional aspects of the process, as it affects the economics, politics, culture and ecology. According to him, it is characterized by the intensification of cross-border trade and increased financial and foreign direct investment flows, which itself derives from rapid liberalization and advances in information technologies. Concentrating on the financial dimensions, Schmulker and Zoido-Lobaton (2001) define financial globalization as the integration of a country's local financial system with international financial markets and institutions. Integration takes place when liberalized economies experience an increase in cross-country capital movements, including an active participation by local borrowers and lenders in international markets and widespread use of international financial intermediaries. For Oyejide (1998), globalization refers to the increased integration across countries of markets for goods and services and capital, while according to O'Rourke (2001), it is a phenomenon encompassing declining barriers to trade, migration and capital flows, foreign direct investment and technological transfers. Milanovic (2002) gives the World Bank's definition of globalization as the "freedom and ability of individuals and firms to initiate voluntary economic transactions with residents of other countries".

As a concept, globalization began to be taken seriously in the 1980s, at the same time as technological advances began to make it easier and quicker to complete international transactions – both trade and financial flows. In essence, globalization refers to the extension beyond national borders of the same market forces that have operated for centuries at all levels of human activity – village markets, urban industries, or financial centers. Global markets offer greater opportunities to tap into larger markets around the world, giving people access to more capital flows, technology, cheaper imports, and larger export markets. In *The Challenge of Globalization for Africa,* Fischer (2001) made the following points:

- Globalization is multifaceted, it has many important dimensions – economic, and social, political and environmental, cultural and religious – which affect everybody in some way. Its implications range from trade and investment flows which interest economists, to the ease with which we talk to people all over the world, ease of travel, the ease with which we can see and hear hews and see events around the world, the Internet which gives us access to stores of knowledge, etc.

- Globalization is not new. Economic globalization is as old as history, a reflection of the human drive to seek new horizons. Globalization advanced during the 1930s, the pace picked up in recent decades as a result of three driving forces – improvements in technology, the lowering of barriers to trade, and capital flows. The most striking aspect of globalization has been the integration of financial markets made possible by modern electronic communications. We are indeed moving towards becoming one world, though we shall never get there, as all humans like to retain their individuality.

- The past century has witnessed not only intensified globalization, but also historically spectacular growth. The 20th century witnessed unparalleled economic growth, with global per capita GDP increasing almost five-fold (see Figure 3.1a and 3.1b). The greatest expansion came during the second half of the century. This was a period of rapid expansion in trade and, later, financial liberalization (IMF, 2000).

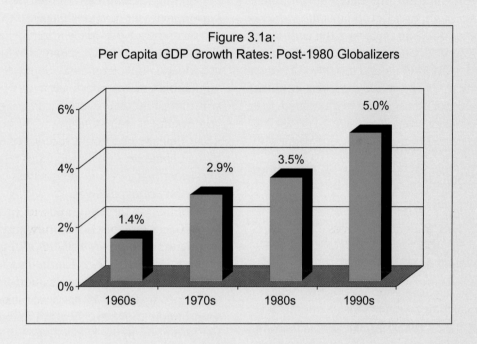

Figure 3.1a:
Per Capita GDP Growth Rates: Post-1980 Globalizers

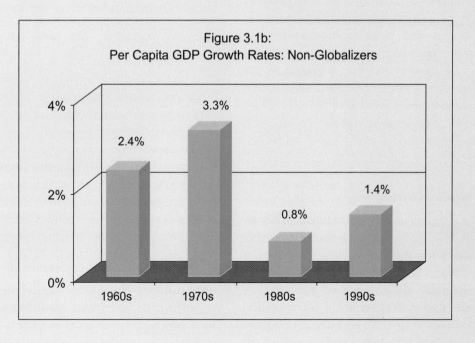

Figure 3.1b:
Per Capita GDP Growth Rates: Non-Globalizers

The relationship between globalization and growth validates the vision of the founding fathers of the post-World War II economic system built around the World Bank and the IMF. However, many of the world's poorest countries do not seem to have benefited from globalization.

From the several definitions above, it is clear that economists tend to place emphasis more on the economic aspects of globalization. From the viewpoint of the economist, globalization refers to the growing interdependence and interconnectedness of the modern world. It encapsulates the increasing ease of movement of goods, services, capital, people and information across national borders, which is rapidly creating a single global economy. It is a process that is driven by technological advance and reduction in the costs of international transactions, which encourage the diffusion of technology and ideas, raising the share of trade in world production, and increasing the mobility of capital. It is also reflected in the spread of global norms and values, including the worldwide acknowledgment of democracy as a political imperative and the proliferation of global agreements and treaties, including international environmental and human rights.

Universal Trends

The position taken in this report is that, however we look at it, globalization is the inescapable condition of our times. It is the culmination of the secular trends towards increasing integration unleashed by the forces of technology, structural change, economic liberalization and internationalization of production, markets and capital. As such, it is a harbinger of both good and bad tidings. Whilst it can offer opportunities for developing nations to leapfrog across some of the ladders in the traditional development trajectory, it may also bring with it a deepening of external dependence and vulnerability. How effectively we cope with it will ultimately determine our fate as nations, communities, individuals, and firms. At the same time, unlike some recent contributions to the debate on globalization, this report takes into account the historic uniqueness of Africa's development experience.

Defined as the integration of production, distribution, and use of goods and services among the economies of the world, globalization has been manifested at the factor level in the increasing flows of capital and labor, and at the product level in resounding growth in world trade above and beyond the growth of world output. In the last decade, international trade in goods and services has grown twice as fast as global output. In the same period, developing countries as a whole have increasingly assumed a larger role in world trade with their share climbing from 23 percent to almost 30 percent. Developing regions claimed 30 percent of global foreign direct investment (FDI) stock in 1997.

The relocation and integration of production processes across national borders have been reinforced by increasing flows of private capital, especially in the form of FDI and cross-border portfolio flows. Technological progress that reduces the cost of transportation, communications, and financial transactions, coupled with declining trade barriers, has enlarged opportunities for anyone searching for less costly production bases for exports and for spot production for local markets. From the point of view of the recipients, capital inflows enlarge import capacity above and beyond export earnings for a certain period. If inflows are used to increase domestic supply capacity and augment international competitiveness, countries are rewarded with higher productivity growth and export earnings, which preserves their import capacity in the longer run, thus creating a virtuous cycle of high growth and trade integration.

Increasingly mobile investment capital and the extension of global production networks by multinational enterprises (MNEs) have accentuated the economic effects of agglomeration. Given an establishment of economies of scale in a certain industry in a certain country, latecomers to the game are obviously placed at great disadvantage. Preserving the status quo can mean a gradual loss of global competitiveness. In this context, the failure in African economies to create an environment conducive to the private sector in general, and to the export sector and FDI capital in particular, throughout the 1980s when other regions of the developing world were working to establish a virtuous cycle of integration and growth, is an underlying reason for Africa's current state of marginalization in the global economy.

One of the main features of the recent wave of globalization is a visible involvement of MNEs in both trade and financial transactions. According to UN statistics, total sales of MNEs' overseas subsidiaries surpassed the value of world trade in goods and non-factor services by over 25 percent in 1993 (UN, 1996), and currently, more than two-thirds of world trade is carried out between MNEs and their overseas subsidiaries. About half of these trade transactions are intra-firm in nature. Another key feature of the current globalization is a rapid expansion in services trade. Due to the

revolution in information technology (IT) and declining transportation costs, services-supplying enterprises and services-demanding consumers engage more and more in cross-border transactions.

Another key feature of contemporary globalization is the deepening of international trade integration. Trade integration in this context is measured in terms of the ratio of trade (exports plus imports of goods and services) to output (GDP). Speed of integration, defined as the difference between the growth rates of trade and of GDP, is the first order approximation of the rate of change in the trade/output ratio, and is commonly used to measure the pace of trade integration. Available evidence shows that world aggregate trade/output ratio more than doubled in the past 35 years, from 20 percent in 1960 to 45 percent in 1996 (Figures 3.2a and 3.2b). During the same period, the ratio for developing countries increased from 31 percent in 1960 to 51 percent in 1996. The world speed of integration has not been constant during these years; there have been periods of rapid integration and stagnation. Yet overall, except for periods of macroeconomic instability, the world has kept a positive pace of integration since 1950; that is, international trade has grown faster than output. In this context, the recent wave of globalization may be seen as a mere evolution in the process of economic integration. Actually, for OECD economies, this recent upsurge in the speed of integration meant a revival in the trend of trade integration, which had been slowed by the macroeconomic instabilities and heightened non-tariff barriers in the 1970s and early 1980s. Figure 3.1 reveals that for developing countries, however, the rising trend in trade integration that started in the mid-1980s was

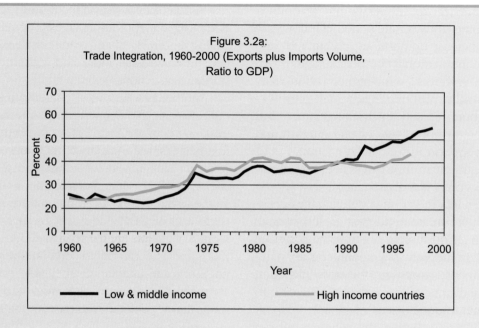

Figure 3.2a:
Trade Integration, 1960-2000 (Exports plus Imports Volume,
Ratio to GDP)

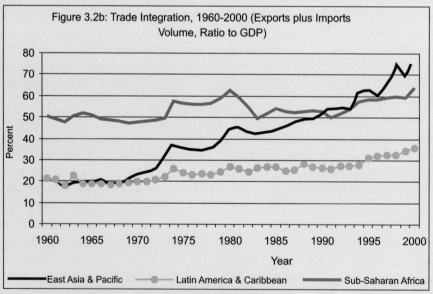

Figure 3.2b: Trade Integration, 1960-2000 (Exports plus Imports
Volume, Ratio to GDP)

Note: *Based on National Income Accounts. Trade in Goods and Services
Source: DEC Analytical Database, World Bank World Bank, World Development Indicators, 2002.

a rather new phenomenon. In fact, more than three-quarters of the 20 percent rise in developing countries' trade integration ratio (trade/GDP) since 1960 was observed only after the mid-1980s. A series of reform and liberalization efforts undertaken by developing countries in the past decade and a half represents an effective shift in development strategy from an inward-oriented, import-substituting, framework designed strategically to reduce dependence on the outer world, to an outward-oriented export-promoting framework designed to create a virtuous cycle of higher integration and faster growth with expanded opportunities. As far as developing countries are concerned, therefore, this upward kink in the integration trend is a revolution that signifies a shift in development strategy.

Together with the rapid spread of international production networks established via FDI from MNEs, a main feature of present-day trade integration is a rapid expansion in services trade. Thanks to innovations in IT and declining transportation costs, many professional services that were traditionally considered non-tradables have become tradable and are actively traded both through traditional international markets and through markets in cyberspace. Figure 3.3a illustrates the increasing shares of factor and non-factor services in the global transactions of goods and services (see also Figure 3.3b). The majority of factor receipts are the returns on investment other than FDI (i.e. such as portfolio investment). In fact, in the latter half of the 1990s, more than 80 percent of factor receipts are of this nature. Profits from FDI tend to be reinvested locally.

Table 3.1: Services Trade, 1975—1995

	(US$ billion)			Annual growth rate	
	1975 (% share)	1985 (% share)	1995 (% share)	1975-85 (%)	1985-95 (%)
Goods exports	841 (74%)	1,836 (69%)	5,066 (68%)	8.1	10.7
Non-factor services services exports	178 (16%)	410 (16%)	1,245 (18%)	8.7	11.8
Transport services	57 (32%)	114 (28%)	301 (24%)	7.1	10.2
Travel services	46 (25%)	122 (30%)	404 (32%)	10.6	12.8
Professional services	76 (43%)	177 (43%)	547 (44%)	8.7	12.0
Factor services exports	114 (10%)	400 (15%)	1,114 (15%)	13.4	10.8
Exports of goods, services and income	1,136 (100%)	2,647 (100%)	7,425 (100%)		

Note: Numbers may not add up to the total due to rounding. Growth rates are compound rates.
Source: World Bank, World Development Indicators, *1999.*

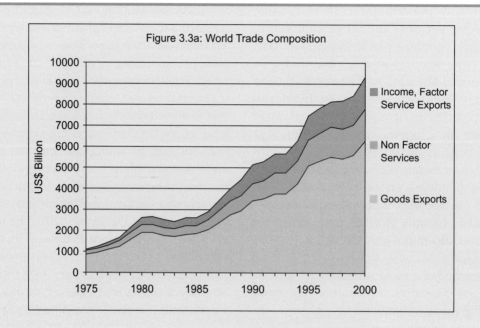

Figure 3.3a: World Trade Composition

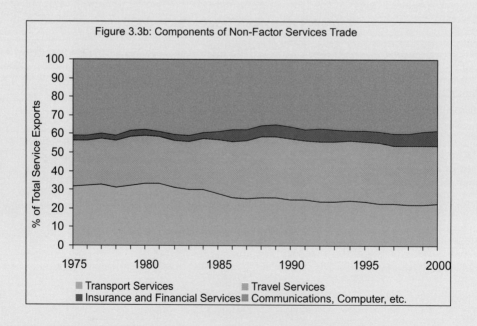

Figure 3.3b: Components of Non-Factor Services Trade

Table 3.1 shows that, during the period of 1985-95, the value of global trade in non-factor services expanded at an annual compound rate of 11.8 percent, faster than the rate of growth in goods trade (10.7 percent). During the same period, factor services exports expanded at a rate of 10.8 percent per annum, reflecting a surge in capital flows including FDI and their investment returns and dividends. By 1995, non-factor services already accounted for about 20 percent of global trade in goods and services. Among non-factor services, the value share of transport services has been declining, reflecting reduction in unit transportation costs. Value shares of insurance and financial services, and communications, computer, information, and other services, are rising (Figure 3.3). The latter category covers international telecommunications and postal and courier services; computer data; news-re-

lated services transactions between residents and nonresidents; construction services; royalties and license fees; miscellaneous business, professional, and technical services; personal, cultural, and recreational services.

Figure 3.4 shows an index of computing costs for the period of 1975-1994. The period starts with an IBM mainframe; after which subsequent developments including the advent of the IBM personal computer in 1981, and of Sun Microsystems 2 in 1984 contribute to cutting the cost of computation to one-hundredth of the original cost. In the following decade up through 1994 when Pentium chips were introduced, computing costs had again fallen to one-hundredth of the 1984 level. Showing similar drops in cost, Figure 3.5 illustrates the evolution of the cost of a 3-minute phone call between New York and London. It was about $245 in 1930, but by 1994, the same 3-minute

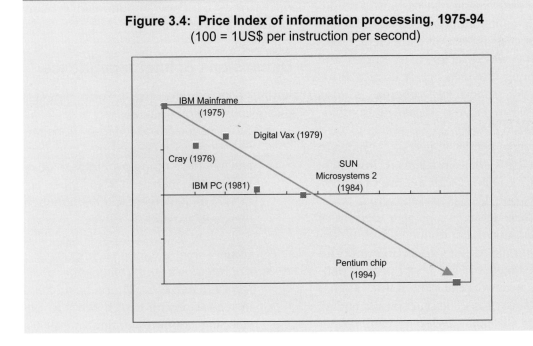

Figure 3.4: Price Index of information processing, 1975-94
(100 = 1US$ per instruction per second)

Figure 3.5: Cost of 3-Minute Telephone Call, New York to London
(1990 US$)

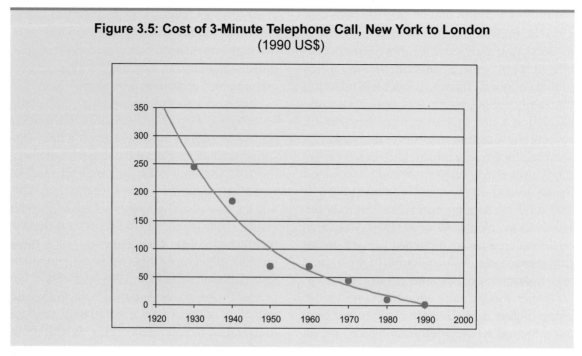

call cost only 3 dollars and 30 cents. This is indicative of declining cost barriers in the international communication network. Table 2 shows the gross income of bank credit clerks around the world in 1994. In Zurich and Tokyo, hiring one credit clerk costs $78,100 and $63,400 respectively, whereas it costs only $3,900 in Jakarta, $1,900 in Bombay, and $1,600 in Nairobi. There seems to be a huge potential for the industrial countries to outsource back-office functions to low-wage developing countries with the use of a computer network. Unlike manufacturing trade, services trade requires a smaller amount of initial fixed investment on the part of the entrepreneurs once the information infrastructure is provided by the public sector or by a public-private initiative. The same is true of other financial transactions, computer programming, accounting, designing and so on. With proper

training and investment in infrastructure, this opens the door for new opportunities in many developing countries.

Dimensions of Interdependence

Economists usually stress four aspects/dimensions of globalization:

- *Trade in goods and services:* Globalization leads to increased trade. In general, the developing countries' share of world trade increased from 19 percent in 1971 to 29 percent in 1999, although there are variations between regions. Africa has however fared poorly. The composition of exports is important.
- *Capital flows and integration of financial markets:* There have been increased private capital flows to developing countries during the 1990s.

Cross-border portfolio investments have become the most important category of private capital flows.

- *International migration:* There has been increased movement of workers between countries to find better employment opportunities. The flow of migrants from poor to rich countries is seen as a means through which global wages converge.

- *Spread of knowledge (and technology):* Information exchange is an integral part of globalization. Direct foreign investment involves not only expansion of capital stock, but also technical innovation. Furthermore, knowledge of production methods, management techniques, export markets and economic policies, is available at low cost.

Economic globalization includes a set of processes leading to the integration of economic activity in factor, intermediate, and final goods and services markets across geographical boundaries and the increased salience of cross-border value chains in international economic flows. This refers to the deepening of economic integration through increased trade, financial markets, and information technology, as well as the harmonization of (liberal) economic policies under the aegis of the global institutions. Following rapid technological changes, economic distances have shrunk considerably and coordination problems have diminished such that in several cases, it has become an efficient method of industrial organization for a firm to locate different phases of production in different areas of the world. Increasingly, the structure of foreign trade has become intra-industry and intrafirm, and foreign direct investment has become a major vehicle of global interdependence. Global interdependence now characterizes the spheres of technology transfers, modes of organization, marketing and product design as well as research and development (R&D) spillovers.

Also, new developments in biotechnology and materials science as well as high-speed, low-cost information processing and communications are transforming the business world. Biotechnology and materials sciences will produce an array of new products that could quickly make old processes and products obsolete. Competitive edge by firms increasingly depends on access to ideas and capacities Good market intelligence, flexible production structures, and the ability to respond quickly to new opportunities now define the boundaries for profitable operations. Beside these technological changes, the policy framework characterized by open, market-based economic systems promoted under the aegis of the Bretton Woods institutions (BWIs), the Organization for Economic Cooperation and Development (OECD), and the GATT (now WTO) framework of multilateral trade liberalization, have played critical roles in determining the course of globalization.

Historical Development

Looking back from the turn of the century, one can say that there was a marked acceleration in world integration through trade in the mid-1980s, as is highly visible in Figure 3.2a and 3.2b. As noted earlier, international trade in goods and services has grown more than twice as fast as global output on average since the mid-1980s. Similarly, we have observed a huge upsurge in cross-border capital flows from

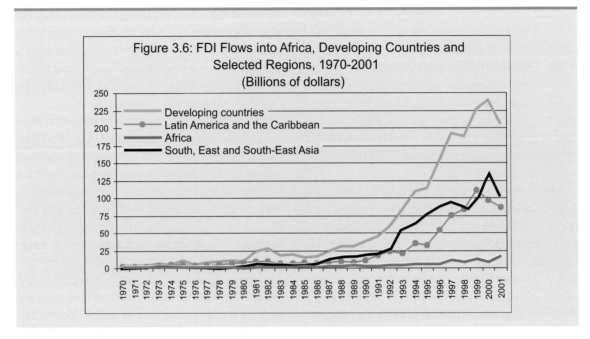

Figure 3.6: FDI Flows into Africa, Developing Countries and Selected Regions, 1970-2001 (Billions of dollars)

the developed into the developing countries since around 1990 (Figure 3.6). By centuries propelled first by the desire of the western European economies to open the commerce of the Levant in order to circumvent the dominance of merchants from Venice and Genoa in the Mediterranean Sea, and then by the rise in mercantilism that became prevalent toward the end of the 16th century and remained a dominant doctrine until the 18th century. In more recent history, one can recall the process of global integration from the late 19th century up through the 1914-1918 war, often associated with the second upsurge of colonialism in modern European history, characterized by the colonization of Africa, Asia and the Pacific by the Great Powers.

Where and how did globalization begin? This is still a subject of considerable debate. Some cite Marco Polo's travels seven centuries ago as the first step in the globalization pro-

cess; others cite the voyages of Christopher Columbus and Vasco da Gama as the true beginning of globalization. For Lindert and Williamson (2001), globalization has evolved in fits and starts since Columbus and Vasco da Gama sailed from Europe over 500 years ago. Since then, global economic integration through trade, factor movements, and communication of economically useful knowledge and technology has been on a generally rising trend. It has not always proceeded smoothly. For some observers, the late nineteenth century saw the apogee of historic globalization, culminating in a highly integrated world economy in 1914, which is very profound even by late 20th century standards (O'Rourke, 2001). Despite occasional interruptions such as in the interwar period in the last century, the degree of economic integration among different societies around the world has been rising. True globalization, according to Williamson (2002; IMF, 2002c), began in the nineteenth century with the unleashing of the economic forces of trade, migration, and capital flows, with Britain's 19th century free trade leadership, as the critical impetus to the process. The literature generally distinguishes three waves of globalization (see Box 3.1): the first wave covering the period 1870 to 1914; the second wave covering the period 1950 to 1980; and thee third wave covering the period from 1980 to the present.

The latest wave of globalization is remarkable because a large group of developing countries – the new/post-1980 'globalizers' – broke into global markets. Other developing countries became increasingly marginalized in the world economy and suffered declining incomes and rising poverty. Furthermore, international migration and capital movements that declined during the second wave of globalization again became substantial. According to the World Bank (2002), the most encouraging development in the third wave of globalization is that some developing countries, accounting for about three billion persons, have succeeded for the first time in harnessing their labor abundance to give them a competitive advantage in labor-intensive manufactures and services. In 1980, only 25 percent of exports of developing countries were manufactures, by 1998, this had increased to 80 percent. These countries included relatively low-income countries such as China, Bangladesh, and Sri Lanka. Others are India, Turkey, Morocco and Indonesia, Argentina, Hungary, Malaysia, the Philippines and Thailand.

Box 3.1 summarizes the three historical waves of globalization as documented in two World Bank reports (World Bank, 1996, 1999). Export volumes rose by 4.3 percent per year in real terms during 1900-13 for 32 countries representing some four-fifths of world output, population and exports (Maddison, 1989). Tariff levels were low, with many countries engaging in virtually free trade. The stock of foreign capital invested in developing countries (mostly in the form of FDI and public sector bonds) is estimated to have risen by 3.7 percent per year in real terms. Further, international migration was scarcely restricted and migration flows were substantial. However, unlike the present, most investment was concentrated on infrastructure projects such as railroads and on the primary sector, not manufacturing. In present-day trade integration, the shares of manufactures, intra-industry trade, and services trade are higher. Also in contrast with the earlier situation, today capital flows, specifically FDI, are channeled through MNEs. In addition, cross-border migration is much more restricted now.

Furthermore, the share of commercial services in exports of developing countries has increased from 9 percent in the early 1980s to nearly 17 percent. Factors responsible for this shift include (World Bank, 2002):

- Changing economic policy – this included continuous decline in tariffs on manufactured goods in developed countries and trade liberalization in developing countries;
- Liberalization of barriers to investment and improved investment climates in developing countries, the new globalizers cut import tariffs significantly, 34 points on average compared to 11 points for less globalized countries; and
- Continued technical progress in transport and communications. Containerization speeded up shipping and allowed countries to participate

Box 3.1: Three Waves of Globalization

The first wave: The first wave of globalization coincided with the emergence of the modern age, triggered off by declining transport costs in the 1870s. The switch from sail to steamships, reduction in tariff barriers and the introduction of railways created huge opportunities for land-intensive commodity exports which were exchanged for manufactures. Exports as a share of world income nearly doubled to about 8 percent. Primary production required labor, with some 60 million people migrating from Europe to North America and Australia to work on newly available land. Global capital markets became more integrated. Organized trade and international companies in Europe are normally dated to the emergence of first merchant alliances (the Hanseatic league from the 14th century), banking services, in the 14th and 15th centuries, and the emergence of trading companies like the English and Dutch East Indian companies from the 17th century. In other regions, for example in China or South America, common governance structures covered ever-widening expanses of territory. There is evidence of extensive intra-African trade, although less of formal institutions. The years 1914-45 marked an interregnum to this process. It witnessed also disequilibria occasioned by the collapse of the world order that was propped up by the classical balance of power and pre-eminence of Britain and of the Hapsburg and Ottoman Empires. Although technology continued to reduce transport costs during the period, trade policy went into reverse gear. The collapse of the gold standard increased monetary instability, leading to the Great Depression. Beggar-thy-neighbor tariff policies led to protectionism, as exemplified by the US Smoot-Hawley tariff of 1930. As a result, the world that emerged in 1945 was far more fragmented economically than the world that went to war in 1914.

The second wave: The disenchantment with the consequences of 'deglobalization' gave an impetus to a renewed internationalism in the immediate post-war era. The second wave of globalization is covered by the period 1945-1980. At the 1944 Bretton Woods Conference, a new architecture for global governance had emerged: the IMF and the World Bank, were created. In 1949 the General Agreement on Tariffs and Trade was created as a new framework for organizing freed trade and ensuring a multilaterally negotiated reduction in global tariffs. Efforts were made to reduce trade barriers, trade liberalization was however selective. Whilst some parts of Asia and most of Latin America took part in designing the international architecture, most African nations remained colonies. By 1980, the ICT revolution was beginning to be felt across the world, riding on the wave of the massive forces of economic liberalization that were being unleashed. Overall, trade doubled relative to world income, recovering the level reached during the first wave of globalization. Reduction of barriers enabled developing countries to expand their exports of manufactured goods. However, most other developing countries did not participate in the growth of global manufacturing and services trade. A combination of persistent trade barriers in developed countries, poor investment climates, and anti-trade policies in developing countries, confined them to dependence on primary exports.

The third wave: The latest wave of globalization is remarkable because a large group of developing countries broke into global markets whilst other developing countries became increasingly marginalized in the world economy and suffered declining incomes and rising poverty. Furthermore, international migration and capital movements that declined during the second wave of globalization again became substantial. The most encouraging development in the third wave of globalization is that some developing countries, accounting for about three billion persons, have succeeded for the first time in harnessing their labor abundance to give them a competitive advantage in labor intensive manufactures and services. These countries included relatively low-income countries such as China, Bangladesh, and Sri Lanka. Others are India, Turkey, Morocco and Indonesia, Argentina, Hungary, Malaysia, the Philippines and Thailand.

Source: World Bank, 2002.

in international production networks. New information and communications technologies made it easier to manage and control geographically dispersed supply chains.

Output and trade grew rapidly again in the quarter of a century after 1950, and this was geographically more widely spread, with African per capita income growing at almost 2 percent, This growth stalled in the 1980s and has been erratic in the last decade, but the assumption by most who discuss globalization is that these were merely temporary difficulties, and that the trend continues towards greater linkages.

One difference in flows between the last 50 years and the previous period of rapid globalization is the relatively limited role of migration: only about 2 percent of the world population is living outside their original country (World Bank, 2002). This suggests that the potential for globalization to distort relative incomes (by favoring capital) could be greater, but against this is an increase in the importance of labor-intensive production as a factor driving the direction of trade. Shifts in demand from goods to services and within goods from largely natural-resource-based to those where labor input is more important have increased the potential return to labor, and the globalization of production processes makes it easier to attain this potential. Developing country exports are now more manufacture-based than natural resources, and within this, more labor intensive. The size of international links (relative to domestic production), and therefore its potential impact on national economies and through that on national policies, is now at an unprecedented level, but the change from

minor to major linkages took place more than 100 years ago. The perception that external forces matter is not new, but has become increasingly global rather than regional or confined to particular types of activity or particular cultures or religions.

It must also be borne in mind that the 1980s, which is precisely the decade marking the latest wave of globalization, also coincided with what has been termed 'the lost decade' of African development. The oil crisis on the one hand, and the Sahelian drought on the other, began to take their toll on Africa's economic prospects. By 1980 famine in Ethiopia, combined with wars and conflicts all over the continent had created an unprecedented humanitarian catastrophe in Africa. The non-oil African countries had borrowed massively from international capital markets to finance petroleum imports. The prices of Africa's exports had collapsed in world commodity markets whilst the prices of manufactures from the developed countries had spiraled upwards. Meanwhile, the debt crisis was beginning to rear its head, necessitating the imposition of structural adjustment programs. Thus economic liberalization in Africa was born in a time of crisis; rarely was it accepted as an article of faith, and least of all by civic publics and organized interests such as farmers and workers.

Measuring Globalization

The different dimensions and epochs of globalization discussed in this chapter suggest that neither of the normal approaches to measuring globalization — whether looking at policy (trade or capital liberalization, domestic policy), or looking at outcomes (current levels of trade or investment, or, more fundamentally, evidence of convergence of prices or interest rates) — is sufficient. One is at best permissive while the other requires careful examination to determine the extent and nature of links, as well as their size. The first suffers, as well, from the well-known difficulties of measurement, of the coverage and level of tariff or non-tariff barriers, and of the impact of different types of capital controls. Both types of difficulty increase with large differences in the structure of economies, across income levels or through time. The second is probably the stronger base for analysis, but also presents both practical and conceptual difficulties: what is a high or increasing level of integration in different circumstances? We still lack sufficiently robust models of what determines trade, and the level will depend on the structure of production (varying across time and across different sectors) and of demand (not only tastes and needs, but level of income), location and size, and company organization and technology (shifts to and away from external processing). If we accept a definition in terms of deep integration attitudes and approaches, no quantitative measure will be unambiguous. Box 3.2 illustrates the key elements of one interesting approach to designing a Globalization Index.

Table 3.2 provides the ranking for the year 2000. Our concern here is mainly with the African countries, so we have included all of those that are included plus some other interesting emerging economies for comparison. The year 2000 was a year of high and increasing international economic interaction. This was followed by setbacks in 2001 such as the 11 September attack, the bursting of the IT-bubble and falling stock prices, economic slumps in major countries such as the US, financial crisis

Box 3.2: Constructing a Globalization Index

There exist different attempts at constructing a globalization index, that is, an index that weighs together different globalization dimensions. The indices try to measure the density of the cross-border web of relations in an increasingly border-less world. This methodology is so far very ad hoc, but it may still give an indication of global integration. One index that has been noted is A.T. Kearney/Foreign Policy Magazine Global-ization Index. This is an index that encompasses engagement in international relations and policy-making, trade and financial flows as well as the movement of people, ideas, and information across borders. The index is composed of the following sub-components:

A. Economic integration
　　1. Trade in goods and services
　　2. Foreign direct investment
　　3. Portfolio investment
　　4. Income payments and receipts

B. Personal contacts
　　1. International telephone traffic
　　2. International travel and tourism
　　3. Transfer payments and returns

C. Technology
　　1. Internet users
　　2. Internet hosts
　　3. Secure internet servers

D. Political engagement
　　1. Embassies in countries
　　2. Membership in international organiz-ations
　　3. Participation in UN Security Council Missions

For most of the variables inward and outward flows are aggregated, and for economic variables the sum is then divided by nominal output or in some cases population size. The resulting data for a given variable is normalized to be between

Box 3.2: (continued)

0 and 1. Then the various indicators are aggregated into one index. The values for foreign direct investment and portfolio investment are given double weight. The Internet and political variables are combined into one variable each, and the newly constructed Internet variable is given double weight. The international telephone traffic score is also given double weight. These weighting choices are based on a general notion of what globalization entails, and that those factors that are given high weight are particularly pertinent. It is not based on any systematic empirical analysis.

Though the Kearney/Foreign Policy Magazine Globalization index appears to be most widely cited, a more comprehensive index was recently developed by Dreher (2002), using a combination of three groups of sub-indices. The sub-indices relate to:

(a) Economic integration, composed of actual flows (trade-GDP ratio, FDI-GDP ratio, portfolio investment GDP ratio and income-GDP ratio) and restrictions (hidden import barriers, mean tariff rate, taxes on international trade);

(b) Political integration, composed of embassies in country, membership in international organizations, and participation in UN Security Council Missions; and

(c) Social integration, composed of personal contact (International telecommunications, transfers-GDP ratio), international tourism, telephone average costs of call to USA, and foreign population (as percent of total population), information flows (telephone mainlines (per 1000 people), Internet hosts (per capita), Internet Users (as a share of population), cable television (per 1000 people), Daily newspapers (per 1000 people, and radios (per 1000 people)), and cultural proximity (proxied by number of McDonald'restaurants) (per capita).

Source: Extracted from Foreign Policy (2002), and Dreher (2002).

Table 3.2: Globalization Index Ratings in the year 2000

Ranking number	Country
1	Ireland
2	Switzerland
3	Singapore
4	Netherlands
5	Sweden
6	Finland
7	Canada
8	Denmark
9	Austria
10	United Kingdom
11	Norway
12	United States
13	France
14	Germany
15	Portugal
16	Czech Republic
17	Spain
18	Israel
19	New Zeeland
20	Malaysia
29	Botswana
31	S Korea
32	Taiwan
33	Nigeria
34	Chile
35	Uganda
36	Tunisia
39	Russia
40	Senegal
45	Egypt
46	Morocco
47	Kenya
49	India
50	Mexico
51	Thailand
53	China
54	South Africa
58	Brazil
62	Iran

Source: Foreign Policy, Jan./Feb. 2002.

in Argentina, and the retreat of the Bush administration from the multilateralism of the Clinton era in areas such as arms and climate control. International trade was flat in 2001, and FDI dropped very significantly. Acts of terrorism such as the recent terrorist attack on tourists in Bali will have consequences for travel and if they continue the effects will be felt also in the general economy as investors withdraw and search for safe havens. Still, in spite of those setbacks the trend towards increasing global integration will probably continue, albeit somewhat more slowly than in the 1990s.

At the top of the globalization ranking (Table 3.2) we find small countries with high per capita incomes, which suggests that smallness and income levels do influence the degree of globalization as measured by this index. However, we also find some large countries relatively close to the top of the list of a total of 62 ranked countries, with the US at number 12. It has also been noted that the countries at the top of the table are also countries with a fairly equal income distribution. In those cases, at least, international economic integration is not correlated with high inequality.

The African countries as a group have seen their level of integration first fall, then rise and then fall again during the last six years covered by the survey. These swings largely reflect swings in commodity prices, which still are important for African economies. Many economists would like to measure globalization in terms of the extent of integration of international commodity markets. When a country is open in this sense, international forces rather than domestic conditions will determine prices. Transport costs and tariffs are factors that can isolate the domestic markets from the international ones, and create a wedge between domestic and foreign prices. Unfortunately, there exist little in terms of relevant price comparisons between Africa and the rest of the world.

In terms of the aggregate globalization measure provided here, the African countries do not stand out relative to emerging economies such as Taiwan, South Korea, Thailand, China and Brazil, which have done much better in terms of economic performance. The tentative conclusion that we can draw at this stage is either that a general measure of globalization is not sufficient to pick up the dimensions of globalization that are relevant to economic success, or alternatively and maybe more plausibly, that globalization by itself is not a sufficient condition for take-off. There may be other domestic or institutional conditions that must be in place before an economy can start to grow. There is on the other hand no evidence that a high degree of globalization is correlated with poor performance. The evidence rather points in the opposite direction, namely that there is a positive correlation between international integration and economic growth.

In a recent paper entitled "Does Globalization Affect Growth?", Axel Dreher (2002) of the University of Mannheim, Germany, developed a new index of globalization for five-year intervals between 1975 and 2000. An in-house study using STATA at the African Development Bank based on his data sets provides has extended the methodology for the measurement of globalization indices from comparative perspectives. The results (see Table 3.3) indicate that, in terms of the overall index of globalization, the SSA region ranks lowest, at 1.51 while the OECD ranks highest with 4.13.

Table 3.3: Comparative Mean Indices, 1980 – 2000

Region	Overall Index of Globalization	Index of Economic Integration	Index of Political Integration	Index of Social Integration
Global*	2.46	3.31	3.08	1.24
Africa**	1.58	2.25	2.35	0.41
SSA***	1.51	2.21	2.16	0.40
OECD	4.13	4.78	5.21	2.76
Latin America	2.36	3.24	3.36	0.82
East Asia	2.69	3.95	2.64	1.55

Note: * 123 countries included; ** 33 countries included, and *** 29 countries included.
Source: African Development Bank, January 2003 from data provided by Dreher (2002).

The Drivers of Globalization

While a steady fall in trade costs has certainly been the driving force for global integration throughout modern history, the roots of the change have differed somewhat over time. During the first wave of globalization (1870-1914), integration was driven mainly by changes in technology. During the modern post-World War II era, however, policy has been at least as important. Mussa (2000) identifies three fundamental factors that influence the process of globalization and are likely to continue driving it in future. He states that although these fundamental drivers exert independent influences on the pace and character of globalization, they also interact in important and complex ways. These are: technology, tastes and public policy. These drivers have influenced the pattern and pace of globalization in all its important dimensions — through trade in goods and services, capital movements, integration of financial markets, and through human migration.

Communications and Information

If the essence of globalization is in the awareness of global possibilities, changes in communications are likely to be among the most important influences. The new possibilities and low costs created by the revolution in communications of the last 20 years have transformed international interaction. The worldwide web increased its users from 0 in 1989 to 50 million in just three years in 1992, and the Internet traffic continues to double every 100 days (Yusuf, 2001). What is new is not the ability to transfer information or a request for a good or a service across borders, but that there is now no significant difference in cost or time between sending this across borders and doing it across the street. (Where there is still a difference is between doing it at any distance and communicating within a building or organization; we can still distinguish a border there). It is this that has made international transactions effectively the same as national (or indeed local) ones, except for artificial barriers like border controls, financial or currency differences, etc, and normal economic differences like the nature of the product or the cost of transport. It has also meant that it is no more difficult to know what possibilities exist, in income or production, but also in all aspects of culture and activity, across the world than to know about one's own country. This can lead to pressure to raise all types of standards. The change is particularly marked for those where trade had not previously given information about different national standards: ranging from those for the quality of services to those for labor or environmental practices.

The fact that direct forms of communication are now available to a wider number and at very low cost has also reduced the costs of entry into new markets, and therefore removed some relative disadvantages of small and medium firms. With some costs effectively externalized (the indexing by search engines can be a substitute for extensive or targeted advertising, for example), and without obvious signs that they are small in their web presence, such firms can compete effectively and internationally with large ones. Research and technology transfer are particularly assisted by better communications, so that the disadvantages of backwardness are reduced. Any form of national advantage over imports that depended on ignorance of possible alternatives disappears, whether in economic production, political systems, or culture. This increase in knowledge leads to some national characteristics disappearing because they are rejected as inferior, as competition from goods trade has always done for some goods.

The increase in awareness of what is happening, at both national and international level, has also itself contributed to acceptance that global flows are normal, reinforcing global-

ization as perception. This is reinforced by the increase in general levels of education: communication itself depends on ability to use both written and technical instruments (most direct communications, as opposed to broadcast, are still verbal, not pictorial): the shift to effectively universal literacy that took place in Europe and North America in the same 1870-1914 period of output and trade growth has now extended to most other areas of the world. Researchers and experts in particular subjects have traditionally been among the most globalized of communities: now these communities are strengthened and the numbers who can participate are greater. One particular type of education, in a global language, further eases communication (it is clear from several trade models that there is an association of common language and increased trade). Here also, there has been a clear increase in the numbers who can communicate with each other.

The arrival of the Internet has led to more radical ways of doing business by enabling a global protocol for connecting networks and facilitating the transfer of information around the world at nominal cost (UK DTI, 1998, cited in DFID, 2000). ICT is defined as the electronic means of capturing, processing, storing and disseminating information. It differs from the physical economy in terms of three key parameters – information, knowledge and speed. Information is a key input in the production process of most industries. ICT has enormous implications for international trade as international trade usually necessitates a lot of communication between actual and potential buyers and sellers and various middlemen. For a variety of services, communications make it possible and cost efficient to separate production and use in various ways that were not previously feasible.

Transportation

Transportation was almost certainly the great driver of the 19th century increase in trade linkage. Improvements in it have assisted the more recent growth, but this time is probably less important than the communications changes. In the period after 1870, freight rates fell in all parts of the world (O'Rourke and Williamson, 2000): new technology in shipping, new railroads for the first time reducing inland transport costs, innovations like the Suez Canal, all combined to reduce transport costs, in particular long-distance rates: across the Atlantic and between Asia and Europe, with falls of three quarters in freight rates between Europe and Burma or China. This permitted the shift of trade from non-competing to competing goods. In the period 1950-73 some transport costs fell (notably the long decline in the price of oil), but the changes were not as dramatic as in the 19th century, and oil prices have risen since then (O'Rourke and Williamson, 2000). There were, however, additional influences on the cost of transport such as the shift of trade from primary goods to manufactures, first among developed countries, then, in the last 25 years, from developing countries as well, reducing relative transport costs. Manufactures have a higher value/weight ratio, so even with no change in transport charges, the share of the price accounted for by freight has fallen. The shift to services further reduced the importance of freight charges in total trade. And while ocean freight charges were stagnant or rising, airfreight charges fell, and its share rose.

All these averages apply principally to inter-regional transport: within regions, it is the cost of national transport that matters more, and here the costs in some African countries remain exceptionally high. It is estimated that they can add as much as tariffs (so perhaps an average of 20 percent) to costs. In landlocked countries, the number of countries through which goods must pass multiplies these costs so that they gain little from the worldwide trends. Transportation is a still a force for globalization, but not as strong as communications or as it was in the past, and weaker for African countries than for others.

Technology and Industrial Organization

Some technology or organizational changes, in particular the greater use of subcontracting to external suppliers, increase the potential for trade. While the history of subcontracting goes back centuries for luxury goods, like porcelain and fabrics from Asia, the intensive use of it and the ability of companies to organize production across dispersed centers have greatly increased. The first large scale examples of sending inputs to be processed in Latin America and Asia and then returned to enter into developed country goods can be found in the late 1960s (the *maquiladora* arrangement with Mexico was signed in 1966). But if this is combined with 'just-in-time' production methods, the changes can increase the sensitivity of trade and production to transport costs, so that these have become more of a barrier than in the past. Clusters of industries, both to bind together suppliers and customers and to provide economies in the use of skilled labor, research, and other specialized services, have become perceived as increasingly important in industrial organization. It is not certain what their effect on trade or trade dependence might be. Some trade is diminished (if suppliers and purchasers are near), but if this means increasing specialization, inter-industry, as opposed to intra-industry, trade might increase. As some of the advantages of clusters can be met by improved communications this may not be a major force for or against increased global linkages. The increased awareness and concern about this, however, illustrate the global nature now of debate and policy on industrial organization.

Neo-liberal Economic Management

Several authors have identified the role of public policy in shaping the pace and dimensions of globalization and through liberalization of economic policies in several key areas. These include lowering of impediments to the flow of financial services, trade and capital movements. Anti-globalization policies were responsible for the collapse of trade in the period 1914-1950 already described earlier. Massive reductions in the artificial barriers to trade in the post-war era have contributed significantly to increasing global economic integration.

Policy reforms were important in the 19th century growth in trade. O'Rourke and Williamson (2000) identify the opening of Japan to free trade in 1858 as "the greatest 19th century 'globalization shock' in Asia." But there was also the switch by the major trader, the UK, from protection to free trade in agriculture in 1846 (the Repeal of the Corn Laws), and liberalization in the rest of Europe in the period after that, while China, Korea, and Siam all liberalized in the 1840s and 1850s. These produced an acceleration of growth in the mid-19th century in trade relative to pre-19th century performance, but it was not as great as the increase later in the century when the fall in transport costs also contributed. Capital flows were largely free in this period. The principal recent trade liberalization at global level was in the period 1950-73 when barriers in the major traders, Europe, North America and Japan, came down

to on average low levels, a fall from an average of 40 percent to around 6-7 percent (although peaks remained). In the subsequent 20 years, their barriers may have slightly risen (through greater skill in managing non-tariff controls and new barriers to trade such as anti-dumping). Developing country barriers did come down in the 1970s and 1980s, first in Asia, then Latin America, and then in the 1990s in Africa, but as these still have a much lower share of trade, the impact on world trade would be expected to be smaller, although the impact on the countries themselves was important.

For the developed countries, in both the 19th and the 20th century liberalizations, the removal of barriers to trade and capital was largely for national reasons: a combination of accepting the economic arguments for opening and growing awareness of external opportunities, partly because of previous liberalization, but also because of the revolutions in transportation (19th century) and communications (20th century). Liberalization in some developing countries, notably in South East Asia, was also autonomous; but in Latin America and Africa much of it was largely externally driven. (This is never completely true: it is open to governments to decide whether the benefits of external assistance and adjustment programs are greater or less than their costs, including the cost of having to adopt policies which they do not consider appropriate). For them, liberalization can therefore be considered as an independent driver of globalization, not an intermediate result of other forces. How important is it compared to these other changes? In some countries, there have been clear structural changes (reductions in manufacturing in some African countries following the adjustment programs of the late 1980s and early 1990s, for example), but, as always, there are many other forces, including deflationary policies and internal structural reforms. The question for the later parts of this report, on the African experience of globalization, is whether Africa's level of globalization has increased during the period of liberalization. The still high concentration of exports in some countries, low shares of world exports, low levels of investment, all suggest that the answer is by no means certain.

Economic Regulation and Governance

Increased contacts, whether through trade and capital or through softer means such as good communications and the formation of global communities of interest, lead to the same need for formal rules of practice and, therefore, for laws that prevail within countries. It is not true, as some theorists of globalization have argued, that a global market system produces a fundamental problem of governance. Effective markets require effective regulation; they are not antipathetic to it in principle. National market economies are not unregulated. One of the reasons that capital account liberalization has been problematic in some countries has been that a controlled system had required fewer regulations, and these needed to be introduced before an uncontrolled one could function. Particularly as the number of different types and direction of contact increases, and the number of ways in which the external world can have an impact on a country increases, the costs of the absence of a regulatory framework, and therefore of negotiating how these will be regulated in each case, become high. We have thus seen, in the same period since the mid-19th century in which most measures of economic

and other linkages have increased, an increase in the number of areas in which either bilateral or multilateral arrangements have emerged to supplement national laws.

The emergence in the 19th century of a plethora of bilateral trade treaties, by each offering a fairly standard package of arrangements, including Most Favored Nation (MFN) treatment, achieved some simplification and some certainty in trade arrangements. After these trade treaties broke down, the WTO, founded as GATT in 1947, was developed to replace them and to offer an even clearer and more standard set of rules. The rules for capital are subject to much more complex arrangements, partly under the international financial institutions, partly under the Bank for International Settlements and its 'voluntary' standards, partly governed by the bilateral investment treaties that have emerged as semi-standard arrangements in a way analogous to the MFN treaties of the 19th century, and partly, still, outside international control.

The emergence of regulations for trade arrangements of the 19th and 20th centuries thus does coincide with the observed growth in trade. The 19th century also saw the emergence of standards on copyright and patents, which were gradually adopted by countries. Early in the 20th century an international institution concerned with common labor standards, the ILO, was created, although with less legal force than the patent and copyright conventions. Regulations also began to cover other matters, including postal communications, telecommunications and transport.

There is a clear demand by both official and private decision-makers for predictable and (usually) non-discriminatory basic rules in international activities so that they can operate with some certainty. There are, of course, also advantages on both sides, in some circumstances, to not having rules: for governments to be able to act arbitrarily to promote particular policies, or for companies to be able to act in trade or investment towards foreign customers or suppliers in ways that would not be allowed by normal national laws. The question of which activities should be regulated, and of the form such regulation should take (multilateral or bilateral; by agreement or with sanctions), is not therefore one of fundamental principle, but of practical and policy advantage in particular cases. In many cases, where countries are at similar stages in the process, common needs can be reflected in common national regulation, rather than direct international intervention, or by the process of recognizing national standards, rather than harmonizing them. But where countries are at different stages in national development or have different development strategies, this may not be possible.

In negotiations on standards and intellectual property, the latest Trade Round (the Uruguay Round, ending in 1994) moved into new forms of international regulation. The increasing complexity of goods traded, and the increase in the share of manufactures, and also in the sophistication within manufactures, have been important forces for the imposition of minimum quality or other standards, reinforced by rising incomes, and therefore rising standards for health and safety. The WTO rules on areas like sanitary and phytosanitary standards for agricultural products specified general international standards that have to be used in most circumstances, except where a country can make a scientific case for its own rules. They also forbid discrimination between imports and domestic production. This goes beyond the traditional GATT rule of MFN (no discrimination by importers among suppliers) to National Treatment (no discrimination between imports and home production) and even further, with minimum standards, to international limits on national governments' behavior. This was, therefore a significant extension of international limits on national policy. Of course, the regulation of tariffs that is the oldest part of GATT could be considered an international standard, but extending rules to specifying national regulations greatly strengthened the WTO regime.

In the past, such restrictions would have conflicted with the use of interventionist policies on trade. But the newly-industrialized countries (NICs) have already passed the point of heavy dependence on trade controls, and many of the new generation of emerging countries have turned against these policies. In some cases, it is for the same reasons, whether of intellectual conviction or fashion, as the developed countries. Here, the only potential conflict would arise if a country should ever want to reverse a liberalized strategy or promote a sector. The new strictness and increased coverage of the international regulatory regime could limit the policy choices available to today's developing countries, but it does not do so entirely. However, for some countries, the change to less interventionist policies has been a direct result of external pressure, as a condition for receiving external assistance, sometimes giving rise to resistance by ruling cliques.

The requirements on intellectual property impose real costs, not only to users of the technology, but to national income, as many countries have adopted cheap or free transfer of technology as a tool for accelerating technical innovation. There is no direct compensation (although there may be technical assistance in implementing the rules), and only temporary exemption for least developed countries. This is an area where even countries with strict standards have had very different rules, in length of period of protection, in the nature of that protection and in provisions for new producers, so that the advantages of international standardization for efficiency are not clear-cut. Countries have lost not only a general tool of development, but also the ability to vary its application to suit their circumstances and policies. Proposed moves on environmental or labor standards could have similar effects.

Do developing countries at least have the advantages of certainty? In their actions on their own trade, the developed countries remain very sector-specific, with strongly differentiated tariffs; in particular peaks for clothing, some agriculture, and metal products, and non-tariff barriers and quota systems remain for clothing and agriculture. The preference schemes for developing countries are also very differentiated, and even the Generalized System of Preferences (GSP) can have different classes, according to degree of sensitivity, or according to recipient policy. In addition, both the EU and US have increasing numbers of special arrangements for various groups. Developed countries graduate countries that became competitive with developed countries (wholly or for particular products), or add new groups of countries, notably in the last decade South Africa and the former centrally-planned economies, and have introduced criteria based on environment, labor or human rights. The result is that developing countries face a trading environment which is highly policy-driven and differentiated, and which lacks any certainty

over time, in contrast to the implicit assumption in industrial countries and in international institutions that it is largely market-driven, with efficient price incentives.

Institutional Architecture

International institutions are sometimes seen as additional forces for globalization, separate from the interests of their members, and to the extent that any institution with a legal framework can develop a capacity to promote a consistent policy, even when its founders vary their own policies, this is a legitimate interpretation. The multilateral institutions, the UN, the IMF and the World Bank, and the GATT (WTO) all date from the 1940s when the economic disruption of the 1930s and World War II (1939-45) led countries to adopt global institutions and global regulation to prevent both economic and military wars. They are sometimes given a major share of the credit for the rapid growth of the quarter century after 1950. Although all these institutions respond to the changing policies of their members, the strategy that prevailed when they were founded remains a strong influence on the system and the way in which they administer it.

The bias against government intervention is muted. In spite of the change in fashion from such approaches within developed countries, planning and intervention remain the approach of the international agencies that influence the developing countries (although sometimes with different targets: stabilization rather than development), with both the World Bank and the IMF committed to strong fiscal and monetary measures to achieve clear objectives. And even the donors (in their prescriptions for others, if not in their internal policies) support stabilization and macroeconomic balance targets, and increasingly also specific poverty and administrative objectives. But while intervention can be consistent with the international constraints, one result of the change in national policies since the 1940s is that there is a bias now against sectoral targeting, as there is in the WTO against differential trade policies. Thus neither the emphasis on leading industries of the import substituting model nor the paths followed by the NICs (concentrating on particular export sectors) would be supported.

Khor (2000) suggests that "for them to maintain the choice of flexibility in policy options, developing countries have to collectively press their cases in international forums and institutions where decisions on the global economy are made", and South Africa's President Thabo Mbeki has called on Africa "to develop 'a sovereign continental capacity' to participate in processes that established the rules and institutions of global economic governance" (Laufer, 1999). But how far can developing countries use these institutions to guide the system in a direction favorable to them? Will African countries remain "generally...overwhelmed by the complexity of negotiations and the technical nature of many issues being discussed and/or negotiated" in the WTO (ADB, 2001)? Two pessimistic views argue that developing countries cannot gain from participating in negotiations. First, if the outcomes of negotiations depend on the balance of power, then no amount of negotiating will make a difference. But if countries have something that the more powerful countries want (for example, market access or compliance with international rules), then they do have some bargaining power. The second pessimistic argument is based on observation. It is argued

that developing countries have achieved little or even lost in trade negotiations and also climate change and other environmental negotiations. But in apparent contradiction to these views, developing countries themselves are putting more resources into participation in negotiations. And research on developing country participation in negotiations rejects this pessimistic standpoint (Page, 2002).

The Uruguay Round and the WTO

The successful completion of the GATT Uruguay Round underpins the heightened prospects for further integration by improving market access and securing a more conducive environment. The Uruguay Round achieved: a greater than one-third average reduction of tariffs on manufactures; a major scaling back of non-tariff barriers with the abolition of the Multi-Fiber Arrangement and voluntary export restraints; extension of multilateral discipline to trade in agriculture and services; stronger and clearer rules, standards, and dispute settlement procedures; and strengthening of the trading system through the creation of the WTO (World Bank, 1996). The WTO Millennium Round will cover trade in agricultural products and services among other things. These are the areas that could bring real opportunities to developing countries, including those in Africa. The Uruguay Round has given a boost to the process of trade integration. Reflecting the shift from the import-substituting to export-promoting strategies among many developing countries, a large number of developing countries participated and played an important role during this round for the first time in the history of GATT negotiations. A World Bank report summarizes the achievement and assesses the impacts of the GATT Uruguay Round (World Bank, 1996).

- Trade in manufactures will benefit from the substantial tariff reductions under the Uruguay Round and from the abolition of the Multi-Fiber Arrangement and voluntary export restraints (VERs). In industrial countries average tariffs will be reduced by 40 percent, and the coverage of non-tariff barriers against developing-country exports will decline from 18 percent to about 5 percent. In developing countries the agreed maximum tariffs will fall by 28 percent.
- Bringing agricultural trade under multilateral discipline and converting non-tariff barriers to tariffs are important accomplishments of the Round, but the actual liberalization achieved is limited and substantially less than earlier expectations.
- Gains from improved market access will be widespread but unevenly distributed across regions and countries. Countries' overall gains from liberalization will depend more on their own trade policy actions than on those of others.
- Gains from improved security of market access-increased coverage of binding, strengthened dispute settlement procedures under the new WTO, clearer rules and standards-are an important benefit of the Round.
- Two areas of major concern to least-developed countries during the negotiations-preference erosion and higher food import costs-are unlikely to cause significant adjustment strains.

Figures 3.7 and 3.8 illustrate the tariff reductions achieved in the Uruguay Round negotiations. In industrial countries the trade-weighted average tariff rate was lowered by 40 percent, from 6.2 to 3.7 percent. Average tariffs that developing countries levy on imported manufactures have also declined visibly except in Africa.

Established in 1995 as a successor for the GATT, the WTO will deal in its Millennium Round with new issues of relevance as well as the issues inherited from the Uruguay Round. Liberalization of agricultural trade that was brought up in the previous round and negotiations on services trade are the so-called built-in agenda for the Millennium Round. Other candidates for the new round can be categorized into two groups. One group relates to an enlargement of areas where the WTO's basic principles can be applied, such as trade barrier reductions on some mining and manufacturing products (in particular, textiles and clothing), and rule making for trade facilitation, electronic commerce (e-commerce), and for international investment. The other group of issues requires adjustments on the part of the WTO regime. These issues are an upsurge in antidumping practices permitted in GATT/WTO regimes, and a rise in new regionalism and the increasing numbers of regional integration arrangements that are again permitted under the auspices of the GATT Article XXIV. Apart from these issues that are naturally under the jurisdiction within the realm of the WTO, there are new challenges in the areas of trade and environment, and trade and labor standards that presumably have to be dealt with in coordination with other international organizations such as the ILO, the World Bank and UN organizations.

As noted before, two-thirds of world trade is now carried out though the global network of MNEs and their affiliates. The majority of FDI is undertaken in conjunction with this

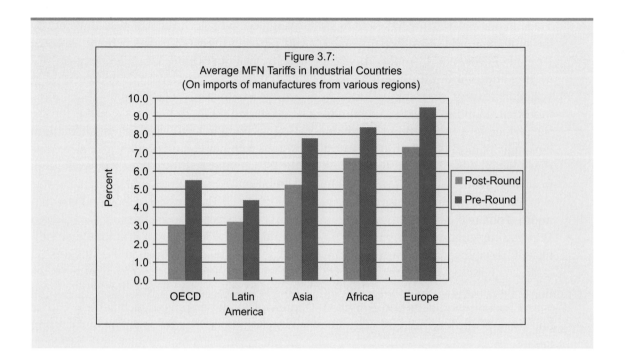

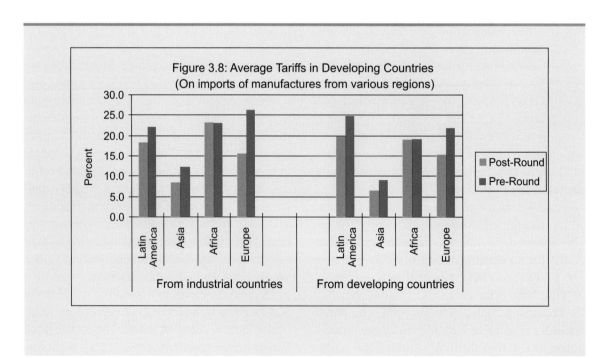

Table 3.4: Reported Antidumping Actions by Members of the GATT/WTO

	1987	1988	1989	1990	1991	1992	1993	1994	1995	1996	1997
New users	24	17	19	20	48	70	162	114	83	148	115
Traditional users	96	107	77	145	180	256	137	114	73	73	118

Note: Traditional users of antidumping laws are Australia, Canada, the European Community (and its successor, the European Union), New Zealand, and the United States. New users are Argentina, Brazil, India, the Republic of Korea, Mexico, and South Africa.

Source: Adopted from World Bank, World Development Report 1999/2000, Table 2.1.

Original source: Miranda, Torres, and Ruiz (1998).

Table 3.5: Number of Existing Regional Integration Schemes
(by their establishment year)

Regions	Prior to 1969	1970-79	1980-89	1990-	Total
Europe	1	2	0	36	39
Americas	2	1	15	22	40
Asia and Oceania	0	0	1	2	3
Middle East	0	0	3	1	4
Africa	2	2	0	4	8
Other (across multiple regions)	1	1	1	4	7
Total	6	6	20	69	101

Source: JETRO, White Paper on International Trade, 1996.

extension of the MNEs' global network. Rule making for and facilitation of these cross-border investment activities that benefit both FDI suppliers and recipients (including many developing country members) should be high on the WTO agenda. Although the recent Multilateral Agreement on Investment (MAI) hosted by the OECD has collapsed in its making, securing the MFN principle and non-discrimination in host markets for international investment including FDI would greatly enhance the prospects of further financial integration.

Table 3.4 replicates the increased incidence of antidumping measures reported in a recent World Bank report (World Bank, 1999). Whereas the number of antidumping measures applied by traditional users declined toward the completion of the Uruguay Round, those applied by new, developing country members skyrocketed in the 1990s. The abusive use of antidumping measures is clearly against the GATT/WTO principles and has to be curtailed and monitored. This probably requires adjustments on the part of the WTO. Table 3.5 shows the number of existing regional integration schemes by year of establishment. Of the 101 existing regional integration schemes counted, 69 were established in the 1990s. Motives for this recent upsurge should be carefully analyzed and the rules should be adjusted or re-established. The 1996 declaration from a WTO ministerial meeting held in Singapore indicated the generally positive attitude of the WTO regarding the new wave of regional trade arrangements (RTAs). The WTO should work to ensure that RTAs are complementary to the WTO's goal of global free trade. However, given the concurrent and heightened interest in the WTO process by developing countries manifested in the increasing number of memberships, many developing countries may regard regional integration schemes as a key to the global economy and to the negotiations at the global, multilateral level. If so, a careful, time-framed preferential treatment for the developing countries might be necessary for WTO-friendly regional integration initiatives.

This increase in interest began in the 1980s, when some of the major developing countries which had never joined GATT (e.g. Mexico and Venezuela) decided that the balance of advantage between freedom outside and trade privileges inside had changed. At the same time some of the countries which had always been members (India and Brazil for example) began to use their experience, plus the support from the growing number of other interested developing countries, to participate actively in the new, Uruguay, negotiating round.

Developing countries have lost ground when they have not realized that they had interests to defend (when their awareness of globalization was not sufficient), for example

the loss of preferences during the Uruguay Round. But they also proved in the Uruguay Round that they could modify the outcome, to gain access on textiles and clothing (India's objective) and on agriculture (Brazil joined with the Cairns group). Then at Seattle a much larger number of active developing countries (for the first time including the Africa Group) showed that they could block a settlement. Finally, at Doha, leaders, the continental groups, and new alliances all demonstrated that they could initiate their own issues: the inclusion of working groups on debt and on small economies. The countries that have succeeded have done so by gaining experience and by committing more resources to assessing national interests and preparing negotiating positions. This means that there has been an interaction with the growing awareness of globalization Both the actual effects of global flows and the perception of a threat from the agreements that were reached at the Uruguay Round impelled national decision makers, public and private, to participate more actively. Developing countries may, therefore be able to use the global regulatory institutions for their own advantages, and the institutions themselves are a semi-independent force.

The New Regionalism

One of the commonly supported hypotheses about world trade, often given without statistical validation, is that intra-regional trade has been growing faster than global trade. Some economists even express concern that the world will be trisected into three economic and trade zones: Europe, the Americas, and Asia. The former hypothesis has to be verified in light of available direction-of-trade statistics (Anderson and Norheim, 1993; Norheim, Finger, and Anderson, 1993; Braga, 1994). The latter hypothesis of a trisected world has been a controversial issue among world trade analysts and has been examined both qualitatively and quantitatively using theory-based computable models (Bhagwati, 1992; Krugman, 1992; Frankel, Stein, and Wei, 1993). In this subsection, the paper examines the trends in trade regionalization; and reviews cases of market-driven, geography-oriented integration versus policy-driven integration, often enacted within frameworks of RTAs. It also recognizes the failures of past inward-looking RTAs that were often formed without economic gravity, and discusses motives for new outward-oriented RTAs.

There are two ways to define trading regions. One method defines regions as natural geographical areas such as Asia and Latin America, and the other defines regions as countries and economies grouped through RTAs, which themselves range from loose cooperative bodies such as ASEAN before the enactment of the AFTA agreement, to freer trade and investment arrangements such as NAFTA, to common markets such as the EU. The two types of regions, geographical areas and RTAs, are highly correlated but not identical. Economic regionalism can be either market-driven or policy-driven (Hallett and Braga, 1993). Market-driven regionalism is the product of natural locational phenomena that promote stronger economic ties within a geographic area. This is regionalization formed around natural economic gravities such as market size (GDP and population), income levels (representing production and expenditure patterns), and distance (representing transportation costs). Whereas market-driven regionalism is a natural,

unlegislated phenomenon, policy-driven regionalism often results in RTAs. East Asia so far has been the only clear case of market-driven trade regionalization, whereas the EU has been the only case of policy-driven trade regionalization. The Canada-US Free Trade Area should be seen as more of a market-driven integration. One should also note that, even in the case of the EU, economic gravity between the member countries played an indisputable role in the success of this policy-driven integration. Conclusive evidence has not been observed yet for the cases of North-South RTAs such as NAFTA (and expanded NAFTA), APEC, and the expansion of the EU to Eastern Europe.

Globalization in Africa

It is evident that greater integration into the world economy through trade and capital flows enables countries to partake from the opportunities and benefits of globalization, to develop comparative advantages and gain access to newer and more appropriate technology. New trade theory leads one to expect that openness influences a country's rate of growth. A higher rate of interaction with the rest of the world speeds up the absorption of new technologies and global management best practices, spurs innovation and efficiency, and competes away monopoly. Rapid integration of financial markets is one of the more prominent features of contemporary globalization.

Recent innovations in communications and computer-mediated technologies have made available a vast array of new financial instruments and risk-management technologies. For developing countries, such technologies can easily be adaptable for use in micro financing for the poorest communities (see Box 3.3). The abandonment of fixed exchange rates in the early 1970s, in addition to deregulation of financial markets has led to a spectacular increase in cross-border capital flows. International capital flows have become the main catalyst for accelerating global economic integration. Important for developing countries is the fact that private capital is now the dominant resource flow. Foreign investment flows have also made a significant contribution to global economic integration in the sphere of production. Recent data show that inflows of FDI increased by 18 percent in 2000 to reach a level of $1,300 billion. An estimated 63,000 MNEs, with over 800,000 affiliates, drive FDI and increasingly shape trade patterns, account for about two-thirds of world trade. Foreign trade itself is increasingly becoming more and more intra-industry and intrafirm, especially for the advanced economies.

Another feature of globalization is greater access to technology and skill improvement. FDI allows the transfer of technology – particularly in the form of new varieties of capital inputs – that cannot be achieved through financial investments or trade in goods and services. It can also promote competition in the domestic input market. Recipients of FDI also gain employee training in the course of operating new businesses, which contributes to human capital development in the host country. Profits generated by FDI contribute to corporate tax revenues in host countries. In principle therefore, FDI can contribute to investment and growth in host countries. Empirical evidence also supports the view that FDI has a beneficial impact on developing host countries, although there are some potential risks which can be addressed by policy.

Growth and Inequality

A substantial proportion of the literature on globalization has addressed the relationships between globalization, growth and inequality. Several authors claim that globalization has been a force for growth and poverty reduction in a diverse group of countries. Advocates of globalization have often underlined the unparalleled rate of economic growth that has accompanied globalization. Dollar (2001) states that during the last 200 years, the various local economies around the world have become more integrated and the growth rate of the global economy has accelerated dramatically. He however asserts that it is impossible to prove causality. Adam Smith argued that a larger market permits a finer division of labor, which in turn facilitates innovation and learning by doing. Innovations involving transportation and communication technologies which lowered costs have fuelled integration which has resulted in accelerated growth of the global economy. The growth rate of the world economy accelerated from 1 percent per annum in the mid-19th century to 3.5 percent per annum in the final four decades of the 20th century. This higher growth rate has been sustained over several decades, making a difference in living standards. Furthermore, most of what we consume today did not exist 200 years ago, for example, air travel, automobiles, televisions, synthetic fibers, and various kinds of life-giving drugs. The productivity of man has increased tremendously (Dollar, 2001).

According to Krueger (2002), growth and globalization have gone hand-in-hand. Access to a buoyant international market has greatly facilitated faster growth. It has permitted a degree of reliance on comparative advantage and division of labor that was not possible in the nineteenth century. Not only has world trade grown rapidly, it has taken place in an environment where support facilities – communications, finance and insurance, wholesalers – are readily available from other nations. Furthermore, the experience of the post-World War II globalizers also suggests that integration into the world economy leads to faster growth of income. As these countries reformed and opened up their economies, they started to grow rapidly, accelerating from 2.9 percent in the 1970s to 5 percent during the 1990s. Whether there is a causal connection between openness and growth has been a subject of debate. However, opening up integrates an economy into the world market, and economists from Adam Smith on, suggest that the size of the market is important for growth (World Bank, 2002). Globalizers have reaped the benefits of late-comers which include ready access to all the blueprints developed over the past several hundred years in the more advanced countries, as well as benefits from large declines in the costs of transport and communications (Krueger, 2002).

Much of the literature has also focused on the interrelationships between globalization and inequality. With respect to world inequality, the weight of evidence suggests that world inequality has generally been increasing. The rise in global inequality has been driven by a rise in inequality between countries. The rich countries are able to pull ahead of developing countries that lack access to knowledge and the technological and institutional infrastructure to effectively deploy it. Between-country inequality rose continuously from 1870-1950, fell during the 1950s and 1970s, and rose again thereafter, confirming Pritchett's (1997) study that divergence, rather than convergence,

characterizes the long-run aggregate growth record (O'Rourke, 2001). In 1913, the difference in per capita income between rich countries and the poorest ones was roughly 16-fold. The rich countries have grown faster so that today, the gap is 64-fold (Dollar, 2001). However, some recent studies suggest some convergence starting from the 1980s, implying that world inequality is now declining. Dollar, Clark and Kraay calculated household income inequality for a large number of countries for the 1960-95 period, using cross-country differences in real per capita GNP adjusted for differences in purchasing power for over 100 countries. They found that worldwide inequality was rising from 1960 to 1975, and declined from 1975 to 1995 largely because of the acceleration of growth in China and India (Dollar, 2001).

Historical evidence suggests that when backward economies integrate with more advanced ones, their growth rates accelerate, and their income levels gradually converge on the leader. During the first wave of globalization, migration played a great role in convergence, while in the second wave, trade and investment played key roles in convergence (Dollar, 2001). Similarly, for the post-World War II wave of globalization among rich countries and a few open developing countries (new or post-1980 globalizers), Sachs and Warner (1995) provide evidence about how trade integration can spur convergence, they concluded that there has been a clear pattern of convergence among open economies. Ades and Glazer (1999) also found a similar result for the period 1960-1990 using as their measure of openness the ratio of trade to GDP. Closed economies tended to grow more slowly and to exhibit divergence rather than convergence. Lindert and Williamson's (2001) historical review of globalization and inequality concludes: "Globalization probably mitigated rising inequality between nations: the nations that gained most from globalization are those poor countries that changed their policies to exploit it."

Dollar (2001) asserts that the recent wave of globalization, starting around 1980 represents the first time in history that there has been a decline in the number of extreme poor in the world, that is, those living on less than one dollar a day at PPP. The number of the very poor increased since 1820; it increased sharply during the isolationist period of 1914-50. Since 1980, the number of the very poor has declined by about 200 million people. Chen and Ravallion (2001) estimated that the number of extreme poor declined by 120 million people in the post-1980 globalizers during the period 1993 and 1998, in the non-globalizing developing world, the number of the very poor increased by 20 million persons (Dollar, 2001). The decline in poverty is accounted for largely by China and India. In 1975, these two countries with about one-third of the world's population had more than 60 percent of the world's poor. Some of the new globalizers, namely, Uganda, India, Vietnam and China, have registered rapid growth rates and declining poverty. In Vietnam for instance, as per capita GDP increased, the level of absolute poverty declined from 75 percent of the population in 1988 to 37 percent in 1998, thus poverty was halved in ten years (Dollar, 2001). In Uganda, during the period 1992-1998, GDP grew at an average of 3.9 percent per annum while poverty declined by 5.9 percent per annum.

The factor proportions or Heckschler-Ohlin model suggests that greater openness will affect the distribution of income among factors of production. Thus if capital and labor are the two factors of production, open trade should lead to higher wages in labor-abundant countries and lower wages in labor scarce countries. Freeman, Oostendorp and Rama (2001) examined the effect of globalization on wages. They found that the growth rate of wages has been twice as rapid in globalizing developing countries than in non-globalizers, and faster than in the rich countries. Workers in general gain from openness, though there may be some losers, for example, workers in heavily protected sectors.

Conclusion

Clearly, globalization portends some risks. A major risk derives from financial globalization, that is, the integration of financial markets and institutions. The succession of financial crises and contagion in the 1990s – Mexico, Thailand, Indonesia, Korea, Russia, and Brazil – have suggested to some that financial volatility and crises are direct and inevitable results of globalization. Financial globalization tends to intensify a country's sensitivities to foreign shocks and can lead to financial crisis when it is not well managed. If the right financial infrastructure is not in place or put in place after integrating, liberalization followed by capital inflows can destabilize the system (Schmukler and Zoido-Lobaton, 2001). International market imperfections such as herding (sudden shifts of investor sentiment and the rapid movement of capital, especially short-term finance, into and out of countries), panics, boom-burst cycles and the fluctuating rates of capital flows can lead to financial crises and contagion in integrating markets.

Besides financial crises generated within a country, financial globalization can also lead to crisis through contagion, that is, shocks that are transmitted across countries. Contagion effects can be generated by fundamental linkages between economies or by herding behavior. Herding leads investors to panic and run away from countries, rapid capital outflows lead to financial crisis. Crises have resulted from the interaction of shortcomings in national policies and the international financial system. At the national level, several of the countries were not fully prepared for the potential shocks that could result from financial integration, while at the international level, some important lines of dense against crisis were breached.

Some anti-globalization advocates argue that increased integration, especially in the financial sphere, erodes national sovereignty by making it more difficult for governments to manage economic activity, for example by limiting government's choices of tax rates and tax expressed in systems, or their freedom of action on monetary or exchange policies. However, it has also been argued that globalization contributes to the attainment of the objectives of government which include sustainable growth, low inflation, and social progress. It promotes discipline, as countries will find it risky in a world of integrated financial markets to pursue policies that do not promote financial stability. That is, globalization encourages governments to pursue sound economic policies; it also creates incentives for the private sector to undertake careful analysis of risk.

There is also anxiety about globalization in advanced economies, where there is a perceived threat that competition from low wage economies displaces workers from high-wage jobs and decreases the demand for less skilled workers. There is a fear that developing-country growth led by expansion of manufactures exports will come at the expense of western expansion. This sentiment is expressed in a 1993 White Paper of the European Commission – *Growth, Competitiveness and Employment*. The Paper asserted that the rise of Third World manufacturing nations has already had serious adverse impacts. It claimed that the single most important reason for the secular upward trend in European unemployment rates was the rise of countries that "compete, even on our own markets, at cost levels that we simply cannot match" (Krugman and Venables, 1995). The answer, it is suggested, is that government should pursue globalization and put in place policies to help those adversely affected by resulting changes, for example, displacement of workers in declining industries (IMF, 2000).

Some critics, on the other hand, have argued that globalization is lop-sided and works largely to the benefit of the advanced countries. They argue that integration fosters inequality — that an integrated world economy spontaneously divides nations into a rich core and a poor periphery — and that the wealth of the core is at the expense of the periphery (Krugman and Venables, 1995). Furthermore, rich countries place barriers to trade, especially barriers to trade in agricultural products and textiles. This results from the unequal distribution of power in the world. Other concerns relate to the allegedly negative impact of globalization and rapid growth on the environment as well as its impact on national cultures. These have been subjects of anti-globalization demonstrations. This report takes the position that, on balance, the benefits of globalization outweigh the risks, and that what is needed are policies that can effectively address these concerns.

CHAPTER 4

Globalization and Africa's Development Experience

Introduction

Recent history has been characterized by increasing interdependence of national economies and by the international expansion of product markets, distribution systems, capital, labor and technology. This trend towards globalization has been manifested in the sustained growth of world trade, in flows of investment and technology, and in the convergence of national economic and social systems. The focus of this chapter is on the importance of this process of globalization for the development of Africa during the last half-century in the areas of international trade and finance in order to better appreciate Africa's place within the context of world development.

From the outset, one can say that in the all-important areas of international trade, financial integration and technology, much of Africa has so far remained beyond the reach of the dominant globalizing trends. In terms of standard measurements, most of sub-Saharan Africa has fallen, and has continued to fall, behind other regions of the world. In other words, much of the continent has become effectively marginalized. Contributory factors of this phenomenon can be said to include a wide range of inherent weaknesses, such as the uncertain political, social and economic endowment, inadequate commercial and financial organization, low levels of diversification and industrialization, the poor condition of economic and social infrastructure and the sometimes inappropriate formulation and application of policy. In many of Africa's fragmented or disjointed markets, it is clear that the key factors that have fostered globalization elsewhere have so far been largely absent, making it difficult to identify the routes by which Africa can, or will, begin to benefit from current worldwide economic trends.

By contrast, over the course of the last three decades some developing countries have been able to take advantage of the opportunities presented by increasing globalization to develop their comparative advantage and gain access to newer and more appropriate technology and international private capital, allowing them to achieve faster rates of growth. The expansion in output, trade and capital movements has been evident in South East Asia and some parts of Latin America. However, only very few African countries have been able to take advantage of these new opportunities. Instead, many have continued to stagnate and several have remained trapped in the vicious cycle of low export growth, low income and investment and increasing incidence of poverty.

In the year 2000, out of 34 countries classified by the World Bank as severely indebted countries, 28 were in Africa. Africa also performed poorly with respect to social indicators such as illiteracy, infant and maternal mortality. The performance of the agricultural and industrial sectors has been inadequate or insignificant. Agricultural output grew by less than

2 percent on average since the 1970s, with food production growing at less than the rate of population growth. Industrial growth has decelerated rapidly in the last two decades, leading to a trend of de-industrialization across the continent. Moreover, despite the significant progress in liberalizing their economies, especially as part of structural adjustment programs, African countries in general and sub-Saharan Africa (SSA) in particular, are yet to reap the benefits of globalization.

The share of Africa's GDP in global output is perhaps the best indicator of Africa's increased marginalization in the world economy. Until about the year 1000 world production was distributed more or less in line with world population (see Table 4.1). Per capita income in Africa was hardly different from that in Asia or Europe (Maddison, 2000). In subsequent years a clear gap has emerged as Africa's GDP share declined over time. By 1820, incomes in Africa were only a third of those in Western Europe, which means that the process of divergence had already started. The 19th century and the first half of the 20th century was then a period of increasing dominance by Western Europe and the US in the global economy, with a dramatically widening gap between them on the one hand and African and Asian countries on the other. During the second half of the 20th century there has been a dramatic revival in the fortunes of Asia, but not so for Africa (Melchior, Telle and Wiig, 2002.)

The following sections examine in detail Africa's performance and prospects in the context of international trade and global capital flows, with additional observations on the related issues of Africa's foreign indebtedness, labor migration and the information and communications technology revolution.

Africa's Share of International Trade

International trade is now widely accepted as one of the engines that propel rapid growth in poor low-income countries. Considering the historical experience of the 'Asian Tigers', outward-oriented development strategies based on increasingly diversified exports not only boost employment and income; they increase outward linkages which translate into higher inflows of capital and investment and increased skills and human capital formation. In 1950 Africa delivered a tenth of world exports (Table 4.2). Since then the share has declined to only 2.7 percent in 2000. At the same time the world as a whole saw a large increase in international economic interaction and integration. Exports as a share of world GDP rose from 5.5 percent in 1950 to 17.2 percent in 1998.

Sub-Saharan Africa's share in world exports was close to 4 percent in 1980, but this has declined significantly since then. SSA saw a continued decline in its share even during the 1990s, when its share in exports of goods and services fell from 1.9 percent to 1.4 percent of the total (Table 4.3). Africa's export structure has changed much less than that of other developing countries. Africa's exports are still dominated by minerals and agricultural goods.

Looking at the share of exports in GDP, Sub-Saharan African economies at independence in the early 1960s were more trade dependent than those of other regions, and have remained highly trade dependent even while they have become increasingly marginal (Table 4.4 and Figure 4.1). Although SSA export growth did pick up somewhat in the 1990s, it is still not at the levels required even to maintain its share of world exports (see Tables 4.5 and

Table 4.1: Regional Percentage Shares of World GDP, 1000-1998

	1000	1500	1820	1870	1913	1950	1973	1998
Western Europe	8.7	17.9	23.6	33.6	33.5	26.3	25.7	20.6
Western offshoots	0.7	0.5	1.9	10.2	21.7	30.6	25.3	25.1
Japan	2.7	3.3	3	2.3	2.6	3	7.7	7.7
Asia (excl. Japan)	67.6	62.1	56.2	36	21.9	15.5	16.4	29.5
Latin America	3.9	2.9	2	2.5	4.5	7.9	8.7	8.7
Eastern Europe & former USSR	4.6	5.9	8.8	11.7	13.1	13.1	12.9	5.3
Africa	11.8	7.4	4.5	3.7	2.7	3.6	3.3	3.1
World	100	100	100	100	100	100	100	100

Source: Maddison, 2001.

Table 4.2: Regional Percentage Shares of World Exports, 1870-1998

	1870	1913	1950	1973	1998
Western Europe	64.4	60.2	41.1	45.8	42.8
Western Offshoots	7.5	12.9	21.3	15	18.4
Asia	13.9	10.8	14.1	22	27.1
Latin America	5.4	5.1	8.5	3.9	4.9
Eastern Europe & former USSR	4.2	4.1	5	7.5	4.3
Africa	4.6	6.9	10	5.8	2.7
World	100	100	100	100	100

Source: Maddison, 2001.

Table 4.3: Regional Percentage Shares of World Exports, 1975-2000

	1980	1985	1990	1995	2000
High income	73.3	76.7	80.4	77.7	73.8
East Asia & Pacific		5.1	5.6	8.6	10.5
Europe & Central Asia	.	.	.	4.7	5
Latin America & Caribbean	4.9	5.2	4.0	4.3	5.3
Middle East & North Africa	8	4.3	3.1	2.3	2.7
South Asia	0.8	0.9	0.8	0.9	1.1
Sub-Saharan Africa	3.9	2.7	1.9	1.4	1.5
World	100	100	100	100	100

Note: Brunei, Japan and Singapore are included in the high-income category.
Source: WDI1 (2002).

Table 4.4: Regional Exports of Goods and Services as Percentage Shares of GDP, 1960-2000

	1960	1965	1970	1975	1985	1990	1995	1999	2000
High income	12.3	12.9	14.5	17.9	20.9	19.8	20.8	21.9	..
East Asia & Pacific	..	..	10.2	16.3	21.3	26	31.4	38	42.2
Europe & Central Asia	..	..	..	..	..	23	31.5	39.8	43.8
Latin America & Caribbean	10.3	9.9	9.5	10.4	15.6	14.1	15	16.5	17.4
Middle East & North Africa	..	..	..	46.6	25.6	33.1	31.8	30.3	38
South Asia	..	..	5.2	7.1	7	9	12.8	13.3	15.1
Sub-Saharan Africa	26	24.7	22.5	26	28.7	27.2	28.5	28.5	31.9
World	12.6	13.1	14	17.5	20.5	20	21.5	23.2	..

See note to Table 4.3
Source: WDI, 2002.

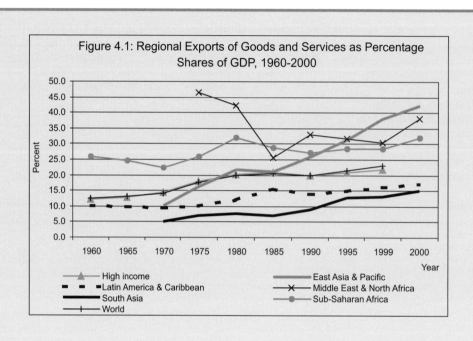

Figure 4.1: Regional Exports of Goods and Services as Percentage Shares of GDP, 1960-2000

Table 4.5: Regional Annual Percentage Export Growth, 1961-2000

	1961-1970	1971-1980	1981-1990	1991-2000
High income	8.3	6.3	5.0	5.1
East Asia & Pacific	6.7	13.0	9.1	12.3
Europe & Central Asia	.	.	.	1.6
Latin America & Caribbean	5.1	5.8	5.5	8.5
Middle East & North Africa	.	.	.	.
South Asia		4.7	6.7	9.6
Sub-Saharan Africa	5.6	2.6	1.6	4.0
World		7.8	5.1	5.2

See note to Table 4.3

Source: WDI (2002).

Table 4.6: African Trade by Type of Cargo (as a percentage share of world trade)

Year	Goods loaded				Goods unloaded			
	Oil Crude	Products	Dry cargo	Total all goods	Oil Crude	Products	Dry cargo	Total all goods
1970	25.5	2.4	9.1	15.2	1.7	4.7	3.6	2.9
1980	19	1.5	5.6	10.8	4	2	4.7	4.2
1990	24.1	7.6	4.3	11.2	5.6	2.3	4.3	4.5
1998	16.8	7.2	2.2	6.7	0.9	2.8	3.4	2.7
1999	16.2	7.3	2.2	6.5	1	3:4	3.6	2.9
2000	15.6	7.2	2.2	6.3	0.9	3.4	3.5	2.8

Source: UNCTAD (2001).

4.6). The picture is confirmed by transportation data (Table 4.6). The share of Africa in physical flows of world trade flows has fallen by more than half between 1970 and 2001.

Consonant with the long-term decline in the region's ability to compete internationally both in terms of price and non-price competition, Africa's trade performance has been poor. Export values declined by about 50 per cent over the period 1985-2000. The value of Africa's imports also declined from 2.8 percent of the world total in 1985 to a low of 1.8 percent in 1996, rising marginally to 2 percent in the year 2000. These figures greatly contrast with those posted by other regions. Asia and North America each accounted for nearly a fifth of world exports and imports over the period with Europe accounting for almost half of total world exports and imports. The loss of market shares by Africa for its major commodity exports over the last three decades is estimated to have caused annual revenue losses of about $11 billion in current (1996) prices (Ng and Yeats, 1996).

Inter-regional and intra-regional trade

The desire to link African countries through a series of regional integration and cooperation schemes has been and remains an enduring goal, in spite of the limited success of previous efforts. African regional integration arrangements have not succeeded in appreciably expanding intra-African trade, increasing Africa's total trade or enhancing the region's overall economic growth. Table 4.7 gives each African regional grouping's imports from itself and from other regions as a percentage of its trade with the world for the period 1996-2001.

Inter-regional trade has stagnated at around 10 percent of Africa's total trade. The lack of growth of this trade signals the urgent need for finding new approaches to trade policy in Africa, including a review and reformulation of African regionalism. It is argued that African countries need to cooperate to enable the region to participate more fully in the emerging new international relations that are increasingly structured along regional lines. However, no unanimity of view appears to have emerged

Table 4.7: African regions' Average Annual Imports
(as a percent of total imports, 1996-2001)

	AMU	CAEMC	COMESA	ECCAS	ECOWAS	Franc Zone	SADC	WAEMU	AFRICA	WORLD
AMU	3.07	0.17	0.58	0.17	0.8	0.6	0.27	0.43	4.86	100
CAEMC	0.91	3.43	0.55	3.65	8.37	6.22	1.94	2.79	14.44	100
COMESA	0.62	0.12	3.49	0.22	0.42	0.26	9.77	0.14	13.27	100
ECCAS	0.57	2.31	2.19	2.55	5.92	4.18	7.92	1.87	17.89	100
ECOWAS	0.81	0.27	0.2	0.28	10.19	4.9	1.31	4.63	12.5	100
Franc Zone	1.19	1.59	0.36	1.68	14.81	7.98	1.52	6.39	18.89	100
SADC	0.05	0.13	3.39	0.37	0.9	0.36	11	0.23	12.55	100
WAEMU	1.36	0.57	0.19	0.59	18.55	9.05	1.73	8.47	21.35	100
AFRICA	0.03	0.01	0.04	0.01	0.06	0.03	0.1	0.03	0.21	100

Source: Statistics Dept. African Development Bank, 2002.

regarding the specific form that this regionalism should take in Africa. New approaches to regionalism that spring from the guidelines of the Abuja Treaty must explicitly recognize the difficulties that frustrated previous attempts and thus reflect appropriate lessons drawn from past experience both in Africa and elsewhere.

One lesson is that no significant gains may be expected from essentially trade-focused regional preferential arrangements, given the structure of many African economies (ADR, 2000). For most African countries, only a very small share of regional import needs can be met from their export capacity. The non-complementarity of the region's exports and imports restricts the potential positive impact of trade-focused preferential trade arrangements among countries within the region. Such schemes could actually turn out to be counter-productive and thus retard Africa's industrialization and overall economic growth if they divert regional imports of intermediate inputs from lower (outside the region) to higher (within the region) cost sources.Another lesson of experience suggests that regional integration

schemes should constitute an extension of the domestic reforms of the member countries rather than act as a force to engineer them. In general, regional integration arrangements that specifically focus on trade expansion tend to perform poorly when they are used as a substitute for trade liberalization while they seem to work best when they build upon previous domestic trade reforms.

Regionalism should not necessarily be concerned primarily with preferential trade arrangements among groups of African countries, but more broadly with cooperation on a much wider range of economic issues. In particular, the new approach for regional integration and cooperation in Africa should directly target overall economic growth by focusing on the establishment and maintenance of macroeconomic stability, reduction of transaction costs, and rapid accumulation of human and physical capital. In the context of this approach, a stable macroeconomic environment whose credibility is sustained through the 'lock-in' mechanism of a regional integration arrangement will serve as a magnet for drawing in foreign direct investment. In addition, by encouraging stronger linkages among member countries it may encourage investments by firms interested in supplying the entire integrated region from a base in a single member country.

Is Africa's Declining Trade Share Atypical?

That Africa's share in world trade has declined is clear. The next question that one may pose is whether its current share is atypical relative to some benchmark. Researchers that have approached this issue have done so in somewhat different ways, but generally they have used gravity models. Foroutan and Pritchett (1993) compared Africa with other Third World Countries and concluded that the intra-Africa trade patterns are not atypical and that distances impose similar restrictions as in other similar regions. Coe and Hoffmaister (1999) investigated North-South trade and found that in 1970, Africa actually 'overtraded' with the North, while in the 1990s, its trade flows were not different from those of comparable non-African countries. Rodrik (1999) just looked at aggregate trade and found that Africa's total trade is not atypical after controlling for income, size, and distance to the world.

A recent study by Subramanian and Tamirisa (2001) investigates in greater detail whether Africa undertrades or overtrades and how the trading pattern has changed over time. The analysis shows that also relative to other developing countries, Africa has under-performed and became less integrated with the rest of the world, while the rest of the developing world has been rapidly integrating. Subramanian and Tamirisa show that distance imposes major costs on Africa's international trade. Distance as used

here is a proxy for transport and communications costs. But why is distance costly? Venables (2001) divides distance costs into four types: search costs or the cost of identifying a potential trading partner; direct shipping costs; control and management costs; and the cost of time involved in shipping in and communicating with distant locations. Costs are affected not only by geographical distance but they also depend on the quality of the infrastructure used for transportation as well as trade barriers in the form of tariffs and bureaucratic problems in crossing borders. Some forms of information are easy to transmit, but when it comes to monitoring, control, and information exchange of more complex character there is still a need for proximity and face-to-face contacts.

Non-price factors

Limao and Venables (2001) analyze the determinants of transport costs to see how they depend on geography and the quality of infrastructure respectively. The variables of the former type are the distance between countries, whether they share a common border, whether they are landlocked and whether they are islands. The infrastructure variables are the quality of transport and communications infrastructure. The study shows that infrastructure quality is a very important factor determining transport costs. Sharing a border substantially reduces transport costs, but overland transport is about seven times higher per distance than sea transport. Overman, Redding and Venables (2001) have surveyed the literature on the geography of trade and they find that there is a distance elasticity of transport costs with respect to distance in the range 0.2 to 0.3. Being landlocked increases transport costs by some 50 percent, which is an obvious problem in the case of many African countries. If those also have an unusually poor infrastructure, the cost disadvantage of the producers in those countries would be even greater. The elasticity of trade flows typically is estimated to be in the range –0.9 to –1.5. They look in particular on the implications of their findings for Africa. Their estimates show that several of the countries in the region have extremely high transport costs. A considerable part of Africa's poor trade performance may thus be explained by its poor infrastructure.

Hummels (2000) has furthermore investigated the time costs in shipping and finds that these are very significant, and also here Africa suffers from the slowness of the operations of for example its ports and airports. It is found that intra-SSA trade costs are substantially higher than those in non-SSA countries. Intra-SSA trade costs are 136 percent higher, and that trade flows are 6 percent lower than outside SSA. The key finding of the further analysis is that almost half of the trade cost penalty is due to poor infrastructure. They also find that African trade is concentrated on the sub-regional level, since longer distance transport costs within Africa are unusually high.

It has been argued in this regard that the sweeping price-oriented reforms implemented by the majority of African countries concentrated mainly on improving price competition through currency devaluation and demand management policies. But Africa's price competition was found to explain only a small proportion of the changes in its market shares. Non-price factors, on the other hand, were fund to be of much greater importance in determining the success, or otherwise, of a country in the international market (Hussain, 1998). Increased attention would, thus, need

to be devoted to improving aspects pertaining to non-price competition, particularly in the areas of marketing and product sophistication. These include: the improvement of packaging; communication and foreign contacts; export processing services, quality controls; transport and the speed of delivery of products; and the provision of export credit through financial reforms. Improving these non-price aspects will tend to increase the income elasticity of demand for Africa's exports.

Distribution of trade gains

It has generally been hard to establish a causal link from trade openness to growth (Greenaway, Morgan and Wright, 1998). In their review of the openness and growth literature, Rodriguez and Rodrik (2000) show that the main ingredients that did the trick in indices of openness used in studies from the 1990s are the black-market premium and the presence of state monopoly in exports, while the more traditional and direct measures of trade restrictiveness showed a smaller effect. The variables that work tend to be highly correlated with macroeconomic imbalances, and thus tend, to some extent, to be a proxy for other types of policy problems. It may also be that corruption, or bureaucracies and other institutional problems, cause a high black market, so maybe this is what the trade restrictiveness variable picks up in growth regressions.

Moreover, the black market premium is very sensitive to macroeconomic and political variables. Still, even if underlying social variables cause the black market, it does not mean that black market premia do not affect growth prospects. Rodriguez and Rodrik (2000) do not argue that trade liberalization on balance is not beneficial for growth, but that integration in the world economy cannot be a substitute for development strategy. Trade reform without accompanying domestic policy changes may not be sufficient. When exports grow, whether because of liberalization of trade or institutional reforms or whatever, there seems to be a beneficial effect on growth. A recent study by Irwin and Terviö (2002) found a significant effect of trade on growth. Greenaway, Morgan, and Wright (2002) also found robust results indicating that liberalization had a positive effect on growth with a lag. There was a J-curve, with an initial negative effect followed by a positive one.

There is nothing in the doctrine of free trade that guarantees an equal or equitable distribution of the gains from trade. Indeed, Africa's trade share continued to decline during the last two decades, which witnessed increasing liberalization African countries. In considering the distribution of the gains from trade the problem for many African countries is that the nature of the goods that they export have characteristics, which may cause both the terms of trade to deteriorate and resources to remain unemployment. Firstly, primary commodities have both a low price and income elasticity of demand, which means that when supply increases prices can drop dramatically, and demand grows only slowly with global income growth. Secondly, primary commodities are land-based activities and subject to diminishing returns, and there is a limit to employed in diminishing returns activities set by the point where the marginal product of labour falls to the minimum subsistence wage (Thirlwall 1999; ADR, 2000).

Africa's Trade in a Hostile Global Economic Environment

Will Africa be further marginalized given the so-called preference erosion under the GATT Uruguay Round? Will Africa have to fight its way to the global market in an increasingly hostile economic environment? It is expected that when the Uruguay Round agreements are fully implemented there will be a significant reduction trade barriers, and the resulting tariff reductions will, no doubt, erode the preferential tariff margins currently enjoyed by many African countries.

In the African context, possible erosions in the preference margins extended to Africa under the generalized system of preferences (GSP) and the Lomé Convention are of vital concern. GSP schemes impose tight rules of origin, exclude critical sectors such as foods and textiles from preferences, and constrain other sectors with quotas. Preferences are unilateral concessions and may be withdrawn at any time, particularly if the exporters fail the so-called 'competitive need' test. UNCTAD (1994) estimates that approximately 51.6 percent of developing countries' exports of products subject to OECD most favored nation (MFN) duties are afforded preferences under the GSP. However, only about 50 percent of GSP-eligible products actually receive this treatment for various reasons such as preference ceilings or rules of origin. This implies that only about one-quarter of developing countries' exports of goods subject to MFN duties actually enjoy preferential treatment under GSP schemes (Page and Davenport, 1994). The Lomé Convention provides by far the most favorable system of preferences for African (and other ACP) countries in terms of preference margins granted and scope of exports covered (Oyejide, 1998). They are contractual in the sense of being mutually agreed upon between the EU and its ACP partners, and they cannot be unilaterally modified or abrogated by the EU. Lomé trade preferences are meant to provide security of access for ACP exports to EU markets and thus reduce some of the inherent risks involved in investing in export-oriented activities in Sub-Saharan countries.

Yeats (1994) estimates that complete liberalization of MFN tariffs in the EU would generate total trade losses of over $250 million in Africa. For the 30 major SSA exporters, however, these losses would represent only as much as 2 percent of their current export revenues. Complete liberalization of MFN tariffs in the US and Japanese markets are estimated to be much less detrimental to SSA, with additional trade losses of only $14.3 million. Harrold (1995) states that the estimated negative effects on Africa should be much smaller. The trade in manufactures covered by the Round constitutes only a small proportion of Africa's exports, and preferential tariff margins on these products are already small. Harrold estimates a trade loss of $7.5 million in the OECD markets, with more than 70 percent of the loss incurred in the EU market, but a gain of $3.8 million in the US market due to wider access for textiles and clothing exports.

Using market-by-market estimates of the extent of GSP and Lomé preferences, similar conclusions are drawn by Lall (1994). He notes that since the least developed countries export mostly goods with relatively low MFN tariffs, preference margins offer at most a 3 to 4 percent price advantage relative to other suppliers. The least-developed countries in Africa as a whole turn out to be the loser again among the developing regions according to his computations. While the least-developed countries in Asia gain $38.4 million (with a gain of $36.4 in the US market, a gain of $2.8 million in Japan, and a loss of $0.8 million in the EU market), those in Africa are estimated to suffer a loss of

$7.7 million (with a loss of $5.5 million in the EU, a loss of $6.5 million in Japan, but a gain of $4.2 million in the US market). However, the estimated loss is again a small proportion, only 0.1 percent, of total exports.

Hertel et al. (1995), using the Global Trade Analysis Project (GTAP) applied general equilibrium multi-region multi-sector model, estimate the welfare impact of abolishing the Multi-Fiber Arrangement (MFA) in the year 2005. They state that about 20 percent of the total welfare gains from the Uruguay Round are accounted for by the phasing out of the MFA. According to their simulation results, the more efficient suppliers of textiles and clothing in ASEAN, South Asia, and China will gain, while less efficient suppliers in Africa and higher-cost suppliers in Latin America and among the NIEs will lose. Africa's MFA quotas actually restrict only three countries: Kenya, Egypt and Mauritius, although a threat of new restrictions for more African exporters remains as they become more 'competitive'. Given this structure of MFA quotas, exporters in Asia will naturally gain relative to those in Africa. Hertel, Masters and Elbehri (1998) simulate the welfare effects of the Uruguay Round, including the phase-out of the MFA, using the same GTAP model. Their results confirm that Africa is likely to be the only major region of the world to lose from the Uruguay Round implementation.

The World Bank asked several economic model builders (for the OECD, the World Bank, and GATT) to estimate the effects of the GATT Uruguay Round under various assumptions with regard to markets' competitive structure and economies of scale. According to the World Bank report, the model simulation analyses suggest, overall, substantial gains for developing countries as a whole and for the major developing-country regions. Only for Africa is there a divided assessment, with the RUNS (OECD/World Bank) model and the BANK (the World Bank) model suggesting small losses, and the GATT model suggesting a moderate gain (World Bank, 1995). The report argues that any losses are likely to be small and easily outweighed by improvements in domestic efficiency and gains from other aspects of the Round, such as improved security of market access.

AGOA and EBA Offer Some Hope

Given the right conditions, Africa can make a renewed trading presence on the international scene. In this regard the two new principal policy initiatives from the developed world that affect the continent's export prospects offer some hope. The first-ever US trade pact with Africa — the African Growth and Opportunity Act (AGOA) – was signed into law in May 2000. This program is based on an approach toward accelerated growth and development of Africa and the integration of the continent into the world economy and involves trade liberalization, enhanced market access, finance and investment. This approach is consistent with some of the basic elements of Africa's economic development strategy, in particular the New Partnership for Africa's Development (NEPAD), which, like AGOA, places a premium on good governance and transparency. The stated aim of AGOA is to help reforming African nations spur their export sectors through favorable trade benefits centered on duty-free and quota-free entry of products like textiles into the US market. In January 2003, the US announced that 38 SSA nations have qualified for preferential treatment under AGOA. This designation signifies that more African coun-

tries are making continued progress toward a market-based economy, the rule of law, free trade, economic policies that will reduce poverty, and protection of workers' rights in specific economic and social areas.

The performance under AGOA since its inception gives room for optimism. A good start appears to have been made towards a renewed African trading presence on the international scene. In 2001, the first full year of the program, although total US imports of goods from SSA declined, SSA producers sold $8.2 billion more in goods to America under AGOA, representing a 61.5 percent increase over the previous year. Also in 2001, US exports to SSA increased, rising by 17.5 percent, even as US exports elsewhere in the world fell by 6.3 percent. Currently, the US trades more with Africa than with the nations of the former Soviet Union and Eastern Europe combined. However, most of AGOA exports from Africa was accounted for by the energy sector, suggesting that there has not been much variety in US-Africa trade activity. Of the total $8.2 billion in exports of AGOA-qualifying goods in 2001, the energy-sector share was about 83 percent, accounted for largely by Nigerian crude oil. The non-energy-sector share of exports was only about 17 percent of the total. Non-energy-sector exports consisted of small quantities of textiles and apparel, minerals and metals, transportation equipment, agricultural products, and chemicals and related products.

The Everything But Arms (EBA) Initiative of the EU, which became applicable from 5 March 2001 extends duty and quota free access to all products originating in LDCs, except arms and ammunition. The EBA made the EU the world's first major trading power to commit itself to opening its market fully to the world's poorest countries. While this initiative may improve trading opportunities for LDCs significantly, concern still remain on its immediate impact. Although the duty and quota elimination for essentially all products took effect from 5 March 2001, the full liberalization of some major products of concern to Africa were phased in a transition period. For instance duties on fresh bananas will be reduced by 20 percent annually starting on 1 January 2002 and eliminated at the latest on 1 January 2006. Duties on sugar will be reduced by 20 percent on 1 July 2006, by 50 percent on 1 July 2007 and by 80 percent on 1 July 2008 and eliminated at the latest by 1 July 2009. These make the immediate impact of EBA limited.

With regard to both AGOA and the EBA, it is apparent that success to Africa would be enhanced if countries were offered assistance through transitional arrangements to diversify their economies and improve their competitiveness in this regard. This can be better ensured through negotiated bilateral trade pacts with individual African nations or trade blocs. In this regard, the current policy of the US, as exemplified by the Trade and Investment Framework Agreement with the Common Market of Eastern and Southern Africa in 2002, may be seen as in the right direction. African countries such as Botswana and Mauritius have made this transition.

Africa's Share of Global Capital Flows

Capital flows may be either in the form of transfers of real capital or of financial capital. The former are in a way a substitute for trade flows, and there is a broad consensus that they generally help increase the welfare of the recipient country. There is less agreement about the effects of flows of financial capital. The integration of a country's local financial system with international financial markets is referred to as financial globalization, by which a government liberalizes the domestic financial system as well as the capital account. Integration means that there is an increase in cross-border capital movement and that there is an active participation of local borrowers and lenders in the international capital markets and increased used of international financial intermediaries (Schmukler and Zoido-Lobaton, 2001). This section thus focuses on capital flow to Africa; its trends and distribution as well as the issues that have determined Africa's performance with regard to capital flows. Total capital flows to Africa are in the form of private capital flows and official development assistance (ODA). Private capital comprises foreign direct investment (FDI), portfolio investment and other investment flows, including official and private borrowings. ODA comprises grants and long-term concessional and non-concessional financing from bilateral and multilateral sources.

Private Capital

The 1990s witnessed a phenomenal increase in the levels of private capital flows from international capital markets to emerging market economies and a consequent shift in the composition of capital flows to these countries. Net private capital flows to emerging market economies reached the peak of $228.7 billion in 1996 and then followed a downward trend to $24.9 billion in 2001, although an upward turn was anticipated in 2002 (Table 4.8). The decline in private capital flows since 1996 was due to dramatic falls in private portfolio

Table 4.8: Emerging Market Economies' Net Capital Flows[a] (billion US$)

	1994	1995	1996	1997	1998	1999	2000	2001	2002[b]
Emerging Market Economies									
Total	155.2	237.9	226.4	170.5	131.9	97.1	29.6	40.3	83
Private capital flows, net	151.7	211.4	228.7	102	62	84.9	29.4	24.9	62.4
Private direct investment, net	80.6	98.2	114.4	141.7	153.6	164	158	172.1	151
Private portfolio investment, net	113	42.7	90.2	46.7	-0.1	34.3	-4.3	-42.6	-3
Other private capital flows, net	-41.9	70.5	24.1	-86.2	-91.5	-113	-124	-105	-85.9
Official flows, net	3.5	26.5	-2.3	68.3	69.9	12.2	0.2	15.4	20.6
Africa									
Total	17.6	16.8	8.3	11.4	14.9	15.7	7.8	8.2	9.8
Private capital flows, net	14.4	12.7	11.9	9.4	11.6	15	6.1	6.9	8.8
Private direct investment, net	3	1.9	3.6	7.8	6.4	9.3	7.7	22.3	11.8
Private portfolio investment, net	3.6	2.5	2.8	7	3.7	8.2	-2.2	-9	-1
Other private capital flows, net	7.8	8.3	5.5	-5.4	1.5	-2.5	0.6	-6.4	-2
Official flows, net	3.2	4.1	-3.6	2	3.3	0.7	1.7	1.3	1

Note: a/ Includes developing countries, countries in transition, as well as Korea, Singapore, Taiwan and Israel;
      b/ Estimates.
Source: IMF, World Economic Outlook (2002), September 2002.

investment and other private capital. FDI rose from below $100 billion in 1995 to $172.1 billion in 2001. Several factors accounted for the increase in FDI, among them policy liberalization, regional integration, and technological changes in transport and communication. A closer examination of the underlying trends in private capital flows to the emerging market economies indicates that the larger flows were concentrated in a few countries, namely in East Asia and Latin America. Similarly, although FDI flows have been more diversified in their country destination, they too have been highly concentrated in a few countries. Only ten middle-income countries accounted for about 70 percent of FDI flows, while middle-income countries as a group accounted for over 90 percent compared with 6-7 percent for low income countries.

Africa did not attract a large share of private capital during the 1990s, with an average 8 percent share of total private capital and only an average 3 percent share of FDI. Africa's share of global FDI, which halved between the 1970s and 1980s, again halved during the 1990s. Much of this investment is concentrated, geographically and sectorally, in a few African countries including Nigeria, South Africa, Angola, and Algeria, and in extractive natural resources such as oil and solid minerals (Figure 4.2). Generally, however, major recipients of FDI inflows in sub-Saharan Africa can be classified into three broad groups. The first group involves long-term recipients such as Botswana, Mauritius, Seychelles, Swaziland and Zambia. Given that these countries were early recipients, their net FDI flows have tended to plateau or even decline, as in Zambia and

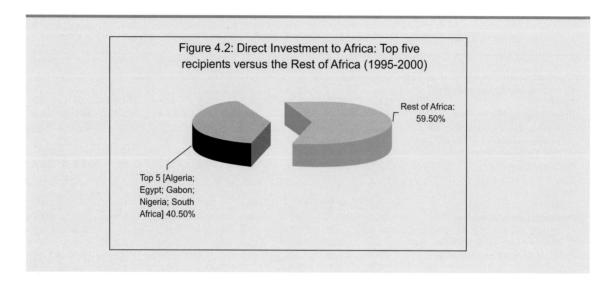

Figure 4.2: Direct Investment to Africa: Top five recipients versus the Rest of Africa (1995-2000)

Rest of Africa: 59.50%

Top 5 [Algeria; Egypt; Gabon; Nigeria; South Africa] 40.50%

Botswana. The second group is made up of countries, which recorded increases in FDI flows during the 1990s, including Nigeria, Angola, Cameroon, Gabon, Ghana, Guinea, Lesotho, Madagascar, Mozambique, Namibia, and Zimbabwe. A large proportion of inflows to these countries had gone to the oil and mining sectors. The third group attracted low FDI flows in the 1980s and early 1990s but witnessed an increase in the second half of the 1990s. The countries in this last category are Uganda, Mozambique, and Tanzania and their increased inflows are associated with improvements in the investment climate given their recent economic reforms.

Low levels of foreign investment have been attributable to armed conflicts, political and policy uncertainty and social problems that discourage foreign investment. Some African countries have also been adversely affected by a decrease in tourism activities after the events of 11 September 2001, and by low commodity prices that have resulted in reduced investment flows to those sectors. However, in 2001 Af-

rica received $22.3 billion in direct investment, representing about 12 percent of global FDI to developing countries.

Official Development Finance

Official development finance was the major source of finance throughout the 1970s and 1980s, when it constituted more than half the total capital flows to developing countries. Even at the start of the 1990s, net official flows made up a larger proportion of these resource flows. However, from a peak in 1998, when they reached about $69 billion, net official flows declined sharply to only $0.2 billion in 2000 before increasing to an estimated $20.6 billion in 2002. The prospects for sustaining the reversal of the declining trend in official flows since 2001, however, are at best mixed. Currently, official flows account for only 0.22 percent of the GNP of donor countries, with only four countries – Denmark, the Netherlands, Norway and Sweden – exceeding the UN target of 0.7 percent of GNP. Apart from the recent declines in the levels of official flows, there are other important trends that affect its role as a source of development finance. First the share of ODA directed to emergency and relief work has risen, as has the share going to the administration of aid programmes in donor countries themselves. According to recent estimates, at least 40 percent of ODA are being spent on providing global public goods rather than for development assistance in the narrower sense, especially over the last few years.

Official capital flows, which remain the most significant source of external finance for the vast majority of African countries, have declined over the last decade. Net official flows have fallen from about $4.1 billion in 1995 to only about $1.0 billion in 2002 (Figure 4.3). As part of the general cutback in ODA, even those countries that have undertaken domestic reforms have seen declines. On average, countries in SSA that have undertaken reforms have seen a 14 percent drop in ODA since the 1990s. It is rather ironic that official flows to Africa should be experiencing a steady decline

even as conditions are improving for its greater effectiveness.

Portfolio Capital

The phenomenal increase in the amount of portfolio investment capital going to developing countries during the 1990s has been reversed since the beginning of 2000. Net portfolio investment that rose to a peak $113 billion in 1994 fell gradually to $34 billion in 1999 and has since remained negative. Two factors were seen as driving foreign portfolio investment toward emerging markets during the early 1990s: investors' desire for diversification and higher profits, and macroeconomic and structural reforms in developing countries. However, the deterioration in confidence resulting from the East Asia crisis affected the supply of funds to emerging markets, and portfolio investments to developing countries have declined since. Africa's attraction for portfolio investment during the boom of the 1990s was driven largely by the continent's various

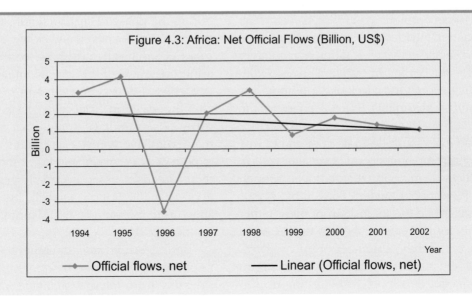

Figure 4.3: Africa: Net Official Flows (Billion, US$)

privatization programs. Consequently, only the few countries that started early privatization such as Egypt and South Africa attracted significant portfolio investment. For the majority of African countries, the key problem was in the financial sector, where poorly managed financial liberalization and distorted incentives contributed to low investor confidence. Financial sector weaknesses permitted a misallocation of investment in the economy and a buildup of non-performing loans that served as disincentive to portfolio flows. There was an overwhelming dominance of banks over financial intermediation, reflecting the underdevelopment of non-bank financial institutions (NBFIs) such as insurance companies, pension and provident funds, finance houses and stock exchanges.

Over the last decade, many African countries have implemented financial sector reform programs with varying degrees of comprehensiveness, but several have structural weaknesses that continue to deter portfolio investment. The weaknesses include the continual dominance of government- controlled banks, weak management, inadequate supervision, and the uncoordinated activities of different regulatory agencies for banks. In addition, poor settlement procedures and a lack of depositories are common shortcomings. In many countries the tax regime discriminates against bond issuance (income from bank deposits is often tax free while interest payments on bonds are taxed). Protection of minority shareholders through preemptive rights hinders convertible bonds issuance, while the imposition of merit rather than disclosure regulations discourages bond issuance. Recently, a number of governments have taken steps to reduce impediments to bond market development by setting up set-

tlement and clearance services, establishing market benchmarks to facilitate corporate bond issuance, and encouraging the development of pension and insurance companies that would increase the pool of domestic savers.

Financial globalization can bring benefits in the form of a more efficient financial system, but there are also risks in the form of crises and contagion. Since there will always be asymmetric information and imperfect contract enforcement this will be unavoidable and particularly so in the case of Africa (Obstfeld, 1998). There is not as yet general agreement about the balance of benefits versus costs, but the case for financial deregulation at least seems to be less clear-cut than the one for trade liberalization. The process towards increasing integration has accelerated since the 1970s, but so far the international financial system is far from perfectly integrated. It is mainly the rich countries and some of the most advanced emerging economies that are extensively involved. The process of capital accounts liberalization has accelerated in Africa during the phase of structural adjustment, but the rate is more uneven and slower than in the more economically advanced countries. The appropriateness of this type of integration has been discussed extensively, and in particular after the Asian financial crisis of the late 1990s many observers have argued that integration may even have gone too fast and too far. The experiences of Asian countries showed that there are risks associated with international economic integration as well, but it hardly suggests that countries should turn their backs on the world.

Before structural adjustment, domestic prices in African economies could differ considerably from international prices of similar goods (Bigsten and Durevall, 2002). This was due to trade controls and limited access to foreign currency. Interest parity did not hold because domestic interest rates were set administratively at low levels, the domestic currency was not convertible, and the authorities controlled capital flows in and out of the country. The subsequent liberalization of the African economies has increased the potential for international arbitrage considerably. Policymaking in a country that is becoming integrated in the global economy is thus very different from that in a controlled economy. Policymakers have to accept the discipline imposed by the new openness. If they do not, the negative consequences are will be more serious than before structural adjustment. The opening up could serve as a disciplining device and push governments to pursue more responsible macroeconomic policies. However, as the recent experiences of Zimbabwe shows, this is not always the case. The political economy may drive policy makers to pursue inappropriate policies, and the costs of such policies can be very high.

Premature financial liberalization has in several cases had a very negative effect. Collier and Gunning (1999) discuss the cases of Zambia and Zimbabwe, which both undertook adjustment measures, when a major fiscal stabilization effort was first required. The problem in Zimbabwe was that financial liberalization aggravated the fiscal crisis. If financial liberalization had been delayed the fiscal adjustment would not have had to deal with the extra problem of higher interest payments on the public debt. After fiscal adjustment had been achieved and the inflationary pressure reduced it would have been easier to undertake financial liberalization. In the case of Zambia

there was an early move to capital account convertibility and interest liberalization before stabilization had been achieved. Inflation shot up and tax receipts fell. The government then reduced government expenditures even more than planned beforehand. This had a negative effect on the poor.

One might think that the communications revolution has meant that distances matter less and less in financial transactions. This is probably true, but the distance frictions in financial transactions still remain high. For example, Portes and Rey (1999) have studied cross-border equity transactions using data for 14 major countries. They find the elasticity of transactions with regard to distance to be as high as –0.85 even when one controls for country characteristics. Di Mauro (2000) finds that the distance elasticity with regard to FDI flows is –0.42, which is also very high. There are general distance elasticities, and it seems plausible to argue that inefficiencies and anomalies in African financial system and economic environments may make the negative elasticities even larger.

Financial Openness

One approach that has been applied to try to measure actual openness is to apply the consumption-smoothing view to the external account. This means that one takes the permanent income theory of consumption and applies it to the nation. If cash flow is expected to increase over time, a country would by this argument tend to borrow. The approach provides a benchmark for judging what the capital flows ought to be, and this optimal path is then compared with the actual. This comparison then gives us an indication as to easily the country can use capital flows to smooth consumption. According to this approach a high-degree of capital mobility implies that agents are fully capable of smoothing consumption in the face of shocks. At the national level one investigates whether the current account acts as a buffer to smooth consumption when there is a shock to national cash flow.

It has been observed that even in countries which have extensive capital controls domestic interest rates tend to follow international rates adjusted for expected exchange rate changes. This suggests that the actual degree of capital mobility even in countries with high formal controls may be quite high. Ghosh and Ostry (1995) have applied the consumption-smoothing approach to a number of countries, and many African countries are in their sample. In only three of 13 African countries the null hypothesis of equal variance in the optimal and actual balances is rejected. This supports the notion that the ability to smooth is quite high. There thus seems to have been a fairly high degree in effective capital mobility in Africa even during the period with rather extensive capital controls, which ended in the early 1990s. African countries are, as we have already shown, quite open to trade, and by the large flows that actually occur it is probably possible to make sure that capital flows adjust.

The conclusion of this short discussion may be that African economies, after all, are relatively financially open, although many countries still have formal controls and interventions in the capital account. This notion is supported by the fact that the correlation between savings and investment is lower in Africa generally, than in some other poor regions such as Latin America and South Asia. There is thus probably no need to rush capital account liberalizations, although the situation varies across countries.

However, the system often needs to be both streamlined and transparent.

Sequencing Financial Liberalization

The globalization of financial markets caused portfolio equity flows to expand rapidly expanded by a factor of 17 in the last decade or so. However, with the advent of the Asian financial crisis and its contagion effects on Russia and Latin America, portfolio flows shrank quickly to a net -$42.6 billion in 2001. Given the highly volatile and destabilizing movements in short-term capital flows, developing countries were forced to ask themselves the question: Are the benefits of capital account liberalization worth the costs and risks?

There is strong evidence that financial liberalization if not properly sequenced can lead to financial crisis. The 1994 *African Development Report* foresaw the possibility of financial liberalization causing financial crisis and asserted that financial liberalization needs to be considered within the broader context of macroeconomic adjustment and other structural reforms. The Report raised the question of "the sequencing of financial liberalization, and how it interrelates with other aspects of liberalization, *particularly of the foreign sector*". (emphasis added). It concluded that financial liberalization against a background of large budget deficits, rising inflation and the abolition of capital controls may cause as many problems as it solves. The Report also stressed the importance of restructuring and strengthening financial institutions, relieving financial distress, and improving the regulation and supervision of the financial system before full financial liberalization. A World Bank study which focuses on the effect of the financial crisis in Asia reached similar conclusions (World

Bank, 1998). It asserted that financial crises are more likely in liberalized financial systems and that careful sequencing of domestic and external liberalization is needed. Restrictions on the capital account, especially on the more volatile capital flows, should be lifted only after the domestic financial sector has been strengthened with adequate regulatory and supervisory institutions. The Asian crisis has shown that reserves, even at very high levels, can be quickly depleted given the scale and volatility of short-term capital flows.

Exchange Rate Policy

The Asian crisis has demonstrated that sound macroeconomic policies should be accompanied by correct exchange rate policies. The crisis focused attention on the dilemma of exchange rate regimes in globalized capital and foreign exchange markets. While the fixed exchange rate regime adopted by the troubled Asian countries is held partly responsible for the crisis, past experience has shown that flexible exchange rate regimes encounter equally serious problems in the face of large capital inflows. In the case of fixed exchange rates large capital inflows would need to be sterilized to prevent capital inflows from expanding the domestic monetary base, which has destabilizing effects through increasing the fragility of the financial system. But sterilization might impose high fiscal costs and reduces the independence of monetary policy. The choice for policymakers lies in finding a balance between the consequence of not sterilizing and the cost of sterilization.

In the case of flexible exchange rate sterilization is optional, but if not adopted large capital inflows would cause exchange rate appreciation with adverse economic impacts,

such as a loss of international competitiveness. Again the policy choice lies, in the last analysis, in the balance between the consequence of not sterilizing and the cost of sterilization. Under both exchange rate regimes the surge of capital inflows complicates macroeconomic management and increases the risk of financial crisis (Hussain, Mlambo and Oshikoya, 1999). Financial crises are as likely to occur under flexible exchange rates as under fixed exchange rates. The policy implication for African countries where private capital inflow is assuming an increasing role is that constant monitoring of the dynamics between the exchange rate, domestic interest rates and capital inflows is paramount. This would need to be accompanied by fine-tuning based on early warning indicators. In this respect, an example is provided by Egypt which, having managed to keep the exchange rate virtually constant since the early 1990s in the face of large capital inflows, was recently forced to devalue its currency (see Table 4.9).

Africa and FDI

Another aspect of international economic integration is the increase in FDI flows. In the early 1990s, there was a surge of private capital flows to developing countries, motivated in part by successful policy reforms and export success. Net FDI inflows to developing countries increased from $24.5 billion in 1990 to $164 billion in 1999 and further to $172 billion in 2001. For the recipient countries, this meant much more financing for imports than they had access to previously. During the oil price hikes of 1973/74 and 1979/80, purchasing power was transferred to oil-exporting countries through changes in terms of trade, and eventually reached other developing regions,

Table 4.9: Operation Matrix of Exchange Rate Regimes Under Large Capital Inflows

Exchange Rate Regime	Advantages	Actions to be Taken in Case of Large Capital Inflows	Consequences of Taking the Action	Consequences if Action is not taken
Fixed Exchange Rate	•Avoids nominal appreciation of the exchange rate and maintains Export competitiveness •Helps domestic price stability •Reduces uncertainty of foreign investors by providing an anchor for risks •Exchange rate appreciation in response to capital inflows, reduces the burden of adjusting and allows a more independent monetary policy	•Increase foreign reserves to maintain exchange rate •Government must sterilise the effect of capital flows by buying foreign exchange and simultaneously selling domestic bonds or increasing reserve requirements	•Increases fiscal costs of paying interests on government bonds which reflects higher interest rate on bonds compared with what the central is getting on foreign deposits •Monetary policy becomes dependent •Sterilisation leads to higher domestic interest rates which attack further capital inflows	•Capital inflows will expand the domestic monetary base which will create a temporary lending boom and increase the financial fragility of the system. •Economic agents will eventually doubt the ability of the government to maintain the exchange rate which will cause an attack on currency
Flexible Exchange Rate	•Reduces incentives to over-borrow because agents are not sure about future value of exchange rate	•Sterilization might be adopted as an alternative option to suspend or modify the policy of flexible exchange rate	•Same as in fixed exchange rate	•Exchange and interests rates will become volatile •Large appreciation of the exchange rate will reduce export competitiveness, feed expectations of a lasting boom, reduce domestic interest rate, increase the demand for credit, raise the demand for domestic assets, thereby, encouraging more capital inflows. All these if not checked increase the likelihood of financial crisis

Source: African Development Review (1999), Vol. 11, No.2, December 1999.

notably Latin America, in the form of private capital flows. These transfers were translated into higher import demand by direct and indirect recipient regions. A surge in capital flows targeted to highly absorbent regions such as East Asia and Latin America created heightened import demand among recipients in a more direct manner, supporting the growth of world trade.

A recent study (Bekele, forthcoming) on the determinants of FDI in SSA attempted to quantify the pull-side determinants of FDI during the periods of economic crisis (1980-1984), economic reforms (1985-1989) and economic recovery (1995-1999). The study uses both descriptive and econometric analysis. In all three periods, the study found that natural resource endowment, infrastructure, market size, rate of inflation and exchange rate variability significantly determine FDI inflows. This implies that SSA countries which are endowed with large variety and abundant volume of natural resources, would need to formulate FDI policy that links natural resources with infrastructure. Helpful measures include preparing and making available detailed geological and physical resources profiles or information, linking the sites of the resources with sufficient infrastructure, and applying clear and transparent policies of natural resource utilization.

There are some factors that are found by the study to be important in certain periods. In the first period, for instance, the cost of labor, the degree of openness and the interest rate are found to significantly affect FDI inflows. In the second period, governance is found to be an important factor. In third period, the cost of labor, fiscal deficit, political instability and corruption are considered as important determinants. Strikingly, the results showed that the degree of openness was a negative determinant in the first period (1980-84) when most of African countries experienced economic decline, while it was a significantly positive determinant in the last period (1995-99), which witnessed economic recovery. The study found no sufficient evidence that foreign indebtedness, tax incentives, and availability of domestic credit were important in the determination of FDI inflows in any of the periods. African countries have abundant cheap labor. Literature suggests that labor legislation is an obstacle with regard to employing workers in SSA (Cockroft et al., 1991). Where there are severe restriction on hiring and firing of workers, the problem is serious because they are operational restrictions and require companies to deal with unfamiliar legislation, as they reduce flexibility when demand changes; but this increases risks. It is better if further efforts are made to establish a well functioning labour market.

Regarding corruption, the policy recommendation given by Tanzi (1998) is worth restating here: honest and visible commitment by the leadership against corruption, for which the leadership must show no tolerance; policy changes that reduce corruption by scaling down regulations and by making those that are retained as transparent and as non-distortionary as possible; and reducing the supply of corruption by making public sector wage incentives compatible with those of the private sector. These measures are relevant to SSA countries. Countries need to create institutions that solve internal and intra country political conflicts and develop democratic culture. Governments should create a conducive environment for political stability and good governance by preserving the rights of their citizens and by sustaining democracy.

FDI facilitates the transfer of real capital, technological, and managerial resources, and expands capital stock and productive capacity. It also triggers technological progress and productivity increases. If the recipient economy has a comparative advantage in relatively labor-intensive products, then the capital and technology go to these labor-intensive sectors. Domestic resources are also absorbed into these sectors as the rate of return to productive factors in these industries initially increases, resulting in increased production, exports, and imports of complementary capital-intensive goods. As such, trade-oriented FDI in developing countries should contribute to an increase in economic welfare and trade. Changes in the supplier country's employment situation should not be regarded as a consequence of FDI, as this is dominated by supply-side phenomena in the supplier's market. The employment situation in the recipient developing economies should improve as these economies still possess dualistic sectoral as well as labor-market structures, and FDI inflow creates new job opportunities. Macroeconomic balance will be altered in the long run as savings/investment behavior changes in response to the FDI in both the supplier and recipient economies.

Other Challenges of Globalization

Foreign Indebtedness

The accumulation of foreign debt in the case of many African countries is related, partly, to the structure of their economies and, partly, to the manner in which the borrowed funds are contracted and utilized (ADR, 2001). The production structure and pattern of trade in many African countries is such that these countries consistently import more than they export (invest more than they save), and hence borrow from abroad to bridge the gap. The persistence of this pattern led to accumulation of debt and to significant debt repayment problems. Such an outcome indicates that the borrowed funds to bridge the external financing gap were not used productively. They were either used to finance consumption, embezzled through corrupt deals, or invested in activities that did not alter the pattern of trade to generate sufficient foreign exchange earnings for debt repayment. While it is difficult to ascertain the magnitude of each of these contributory factors, the result is evidenced in the heavy debt burden shouldered by African countries. In essence, the reasons that cause Africa to be marginalized in terms of its share of international trade and private capital flows are also responsible for the country's heavy indebtedness. Africa's heavy debt burden is, thus, the mirror image of its marginalization in the global economy.

External debt has now become one of the major obstacles to the development efforts of the Africa. Africa's total debt as a share of the total debt of developing countries has seen a steady fall from a peak of about 16 percent in 1995 to about 12 percent in 2002. Yet, Africa remains the most indebted continent relative to its GNI (see Tables 4.10 and 4.11, Figure 4.4), and this undoubtedly makes policy making there more difficult. The Enhanced HIPC Initiative is at the moment the framework and the operational instrument for negotiations and for the provision of debt relief to developing countries. Currently, 22 African countries have qualified for assistance through the Enhanced HIPC initiative. This is starting to bring about a significant reduction in the debt stock and debt service obligations of these countries.

Table 4.10: Regional Total Debt Stocks (million, US$)

	1970	1975	1980	1985	1990	1995	1999	2000
East Asia & Pacific	1162	29019	94080	175068	273983	547489	673379	632953
Europe & Central Asia	5028	13825	75627	141940	219850	350925	496400	499344
Latin America & Caribbean	32548	82795	257197	408132	474720	649398	796192	774419
Middle East & North Africa	4822	27629	83832	135741	183471	214228	216166	203785
South Asia	12270	22953	37816	67569	129481	157289	167320	164375
Sub-Saharan Africa	6921	19633	60898	107104	176883	235256	216326	215794
All developing countries	72751	195854	609450	1035554	1458389	2154584	2565784	2490670

Note: Total debt stocks (EDT) consist of public and publicly guaranteed long-term debt, private non-guaranteed long-term debt (whether reported or estimated by the staff of the World Bank), the use of IMF credit, and estimated short-term debt.

Source: Global Development Finance (2002).

Table 4.11: Regional Total Debt as Percentage Shares of GNI

	1970	1975	1980	1985	1990	1995	1999	2000
East Asia & Pacific	8.4	11.0	21.1	29.1	29.8	31.0	36.3	31.2
Europe & Central Asia	.	.	.	.	17.8	36.2	58.1	53.9
Latin America & Caribbean	20.3	22.6	34.5	60.7	44.6	39.7	46.4	40.9
Middle East & North Africa	12.3	18.5	22.0	32.6	45.7	43.9	36.9	31.7
South Asia	14.9	17.0	16.2	23.1	32.4	33.3	28.8	27.0
Sub-Saharan Africa	11.4	15.3	23.5	56.4	63.0	77.7	71.6	71.3
All developing countries	10.9	13.3	21.0	34.0	34.1	38.3	43.7	39.1

Note: Total debt (EDT)/GNI (percent).
Source: Global Development Finance (2002).

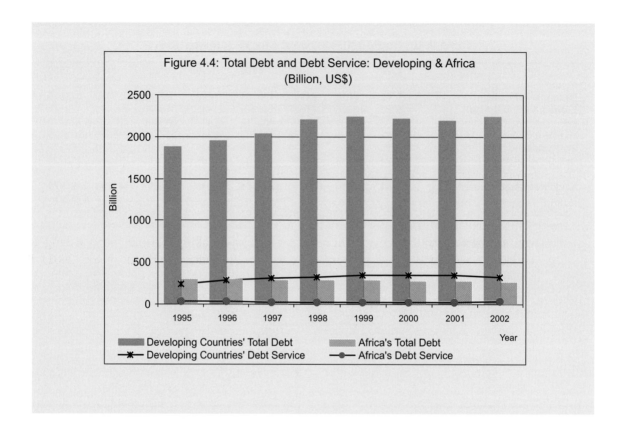

Figure 4.4: Total Debt and Debt Service: Developing & Africa (Billion, US$)

Largely as a result of the Enhanced HIPC Initiative, total debt service of Africa fell from about $32 billion in 1995 to about $26 billion in 2001. Nonetheless, it remains essential that the process is followed carefully to ensure that HIPC does indeed result in sustainable debt levels. This issue has become critical, as the recent slowdown in the global economy has resulted in the reduction of the export earnings of many African countries. Indeed, the international community has recently acknowledged that in view of these developments it may be necessary to augment the debt relief already offered to eligible countries. In addition, it is essential that the Enhanced HIPC Initiative be fully funded to ensure that the promised debt relief is fully delivered.

International Movement of Labor

During the previous globalization epoch, that is in the late 19th and early 20th centuries, there was extensive international migration of labor. For example, as many as 60 million Europeans moved to America. Basically the movement was from poor countries to rich countries, and there was a tendency towards factor prices equalization. Pass laws and immigration authorities did not restrict labor mobility. This situation has changed significantly today, at least in the industrialized countries. The ability of poor African people to enter industrialized countries, unless they have refugee status, is very limited. Among the mobile factors of production (capital and labor) the present phase of globalization restrict labor mobility. Thus, Africa cannot solve its problem of an abundance of labor in the same way as several European countries did at the time, that is by exporting labor (Williamson, 1998).

Although African migration out of Africa is limited, there are large flows across borders within Africa. In a few instances, border controls are non-existent. However, there have been recent clashes in some West African countries which have had their base in hostility of local-born people against foreign workers and families in some of the better-off countries, so labor transfers are not unproblematic, but they do probably contribute at least somewhat to a similar process of convergence as that previously observed between America and Europe.

One consequence of migration of labor is remittances back to the mother country. Here we see a dramatic difference for Africa vis a vis South Asia, where the latter reports much larger remittances. Much of these flows to South Asia come from workers in the Middle East, a region not penetrated by African workers to any significant degree. One special problem in the case of African migration is that the statistics are poor. Much of the remittances that actually occur come in the form of people carrying back money or purchased goods when they revisit their home-countries, such as various workers engaged in South African mines.

In the longer term we will probably see an increase in labor emigration out of Africa, but it seems more likely that those that manage to emigrate would be the better educated. This means that the pattern will be different from the one observed in Europe a century ago, and it is less certain that the effects of the exporting countries will be benevolent. There are, however, different possible interpretations of the effects of this brain drain. The straightforward interpretation would be that African countries will lose if some of its best people, and that this will be growth reducing. There is, however, a possible more positive interpretation of the exodus and it is that the possibility of moving to the wealthy West functions as an incentive mechanism making people more willing to invest in education (Stark and Wang, 2001). If this effect is strong, the brain drain may actually lead to increased human capital investment. This combined with the remittances from the émigrés and the potential for business relations built on the diaspora may in the end have a positive net effect on the labor exporting countries. This has not been empirically investigated as yet.

Observations from some North African countries complicate this argument and also add a gender dimension to it. For instance, realizing that an unskilled worker in the Gulf earns, by far, more than a university graduate in the home county, many males in some North African countries discontinued their education and migrated to the Gulf. Thus, the prospects of higher wages for unskilled labor in the Gulf acted as a disincentive for 'investing time' in education. It is also observed that girls, who are relatively immobile for cultural reasons, started to assume an important proportion in most university faculties. In Sudan, for instance, the proportion of females studying agricultural sciences (a field which has traditionally been dominated by males) increased to between 60 to 75 percent. The émigrés are mostly men and the social costs of leaving wives and children behind, and of disturbing the natural balance between males and females in a society, are not easily quantifiable. From this brief discussion it appears that arriving at quantifiable estimates of the net impact of exporting labor in the context of globalization is extremely difficult, as there are may other related elements that do not lend themselves to direct cost estimation. The net economic costs (benefits) that result from labor migration and its demographic and social impacts on Africa need to be the subject of a separate study.

The ICT Revolution

One of the factors that has driven the process of international economic integration has been the increasing ease of communication across the globe. The information and communications technology (ICT) revolution has had a large impact on how firms organize production. It is now much easier to divide up production process in different sub-processes, that is to outsource, while still keeping close control over the whole production chain. Some observers say that the manufacturing production process is disintegrating. With regard to the location of production this is undoubtedly the case, and this could potentially be an opportunity for African economies.

Remote management of production activities has generally become easier, and production networks have developed. The need to have close access to a pool of skilled labor is becoming more and more important, which may suggest that we will not see the death of distance. The information-based economy requires person-to-person contacts more than some thought. Cities thus play a major role in reducing the costs of distance. Agglomeration

forces will thus continue to be important, although they will be of another character than earlier. There has not been the same extent of agglomeration of economic activities in Africa as in Asia of certain types of production and production factors to certain locations. This means that one would expect the external agglomeration effects from learning and pooling to be smaller in Africa. However, it may well be that these new technologies do not imply the death of distance (Venables, 2001). First, new technologies will have mixed effects on different types of distance costs. Second, geography affects profitability not only via access to markets, but also via access to a whole cluster of related activities. The agglomeration forces are for example dense networks of local suppliers of specialized goods and services, the development of local labor markets with special skills, and there are also potential advantages of being close to research centers and to knowledge spillovers from other firms., It may be easier to manage and control production or production networks in a place where one has local knowledge and can benchmark the performance of the firm with other firms in the same location.

Agglomeration in Africa, or generally for that matter, has not been much studied empirically. What is clear from the accompanying (Tables 4.12-4.17 and Figures 4.5 - 4.8) is that Africa, together with South Asia, is one of the least connected regions on the globe. We can observe that connectedness has the potential to make important contributions to improving economic growth performance in Africa, but that it is also, clearly, only one aspect of a much wider set of challenges to be addressed by the public authorities and the private sector. Other factors weigh so heavily against investment

Table 4.12: Number of Internet Users (million)

	1995	1996	1997	1998	1999	2000
East Asia & Pacific	0.59	1.38	3.5	7.89	25.92	51.94
Europe & Central Asia	0.89	1.74	3.13	5.93	8.99	14.65
High income	31.57	52.47	84.38	131.87	190.26	269.82
Latin America & Caribbean	0.5	1.5	2.96	6.5	10.46	19.09
Middle East & North Africa	0.03	0.07	0.21	0.45	0.94	1.86
South Asia	0.25	0.47	0.77	1.54	3.03	5.41
Sub-Saharan Africa	0.46	0.65	0.89	1.47	2.37	3.69
World	34.3	58.27	95.84	155.65	241.96	366.47

Source: WDI, 2002.

Table 4.13: Mobile Phones per 1,000 People

	1990	1995	1996	1997	1998	1999	2000
East Asia & Pacific	0	5	8	15	25	42	70
Europe & Central Asia	0	2	5	11	23	47	92
High income	13	88	136	188	264	378	532
Latin America & Caribbean	0	8	13	25	42	79	123
Middle East & North Africa	0	1	2	5	8	12	30
South Asia	0	0	0	1	1	2	3
Sub-Saharan Africa	0	1	2	3	5	10	17
World	2	16	25	37	54	82	123

Source: WDI, 2002

Table 4.14: Personal Computers per 1,000 People

	1990	1995	1996	1997	1998	1999	2000
East Asia & Pacific	2	7	9	11	14	17	22
Europe & Central Asia	4	18	23	28	34	39	45
High income	115	204	233	268	306	347	393
Latin America & Caribbean	6	20	25	29	32	38	44
Middle East & North Africa	..	13	15	18	22	26	31
South Asia	0	2	2	2	3	3	4
Sub-Saharan Africa	..	..	..	8	7	8	9
World	25	42	48	54	61	68	78

Source: WDI, 2002

Table 4.15: Telephone Main Lines per 10,000 People

	1970	1975	1980	1985	1990	1995	1996	1997	1998	1999	2000
East Asia & Pacific	..	3	5	9	16	41	51	60	70	82	101
Europe & Central Asia	..	42	64	89	125	165	176	191	202	213	222
High income	201	263	333	400	465	528	542	558	573	585	604
Latin America & Caribbean	..	29	41	51	63	91	99	109	118	131	148
Middle East & North Africa	9	13	19	28	38	58	64	69	76	85	92
South Asia	2	2	3	4	6	12	14	17	20	23	27
Sub-Saharan Africa	6	7	8	8	10	11	12	12	13	14	14
World	..	62	78	86	100	122	129	137	144	152	163

Source: WDI, 2002

Table 4.16: Royalty and License Fees, Receipts (BoP, million current US$)

	1980	1985	1990	1995	1996	1997	1998	1999	2000
East Asia & Pacific	24	7	41	302	215	369	330	558	784
Europe & Central Asia	0	0	49	68	393	359	177	207	313
High income	10706	9888	26990	53112	57607	59460	63667	67105	70321
Latin America & Caribbean	50	56	195	308	438	524	587	502	501
Middle East & North Africa	1	7	5	51	61	59	73	63	106
South Asia	0	0	3	9	26	17	23	31	87
Sub-Saharan Africa	20	13	32	60	98	140	113	91	82
World	10801	9971	27315	53909	58838	60928	64969	68557	72194

Source: WDI (2002).

Table 4.17: Royalty and License Fees, Payments (million current US$)

	1980	1985	1990	1995	1996	1997	1998	1999	2000
East Asia & Pacific	208	386	1573	3114	3229	3919	3374	4147	5409
Europe & Central Asia	0	0	36	261	525	585	625	1069	1753
High income	8054	7030	21332	45002	49006	50637	57209	59869	62988
Latin America & Caribbean	407	709	976	1665	1977	2217	2433	2752	2666
Middle East & North Africa	37	13	62	224	176	491	567	532	614
South Asia	12	25	72	111	136	178	217	343	338
Sub-Saharan Africa	289	129	168	335	350	379	306	291	283
World	9008	8293	24219	50712	55400	58405	64730	69004	74051

Source: WDI (2002).

Box 4.1: Bridging Ghana's Digital Divide

In Ghana making a telephone call requires persistence. Roughly half of all calls do not connect because of system failures. The country has a mere 240,000 fixed phone lines—for a population of 20 million spread across an area the size of Britain. Moreover, telephone bills are inaccurate, overcharges common, and the installation of a new line can cost a business more than $1,000, the rough equivalent of the annual office rent. Lines are frequently stolen, sometimes with the connivance of employees of Ghana Telecom, the national carrier. The spread of mobile phones has only worsened telephone gridlock. There are more mobile phones in Ghana than wired ones—about 300,000, as of March 2002—but the network is clogged because of a shortage of cell stations. The situation limits the utility of the Internet and raises the costs of information services but defies straightforward conclusions. There is another side to the country's technological profile, a burgeoning homegrown technology culture that explodes assumptions about the inherent backwardness of Africa and the nature of the so-called digital divide.

The high-rise Pyramid building in Accra provides a look at one advanced-technology project that seems to be overcoming the barrier of faulty infrastructure. Behind glass walls, hundreds of men and women type at computer keyboards, reading American health insurance claims on their computer screens. Each claims form has been digitized in the US by Aetna, a large insurer, and sent over a computer network to Accra. Here a typist culls the name, address and other personal information from the form, entering it into a new electronic form, which is then sent back to the US. The key technology in this process is invisible: a satellite link that bypasses Accra's creaky phone system and enables data to be sent overseas instantaneously. All the workers at the data entry facility, from the site manager to the computer-networking technician to the typists, are natives of Ghana. American supervisors, located in Salt Lake City and Lexington, Kentucky, visit only occasionally; from their US bases they can view any form in Accra at any moment, peering electronically over the shoulder of any Ghanaian keypuncher, offering help and encouragement.

In March 2002, a second data entry company, Data Management International, opened shop in Accra. The privately held firm, based in Wilmington, Delaware, is handling government forms for one large US city at its Accra operation. The growth of data entry in Accra suggests that new information technologies can knit the world closer together by defeating distance and creating jobs. Yet despite working around Ghana's troublesome phone system, the Accra operation is hampered by other basic infrastructure problems that mock its high-tech sophistication. Frequent power cuts—sometimes three or four a day—disrupt work and add to the wear and tear on computers.

This constant struggle with the local infrastructure is also being waged in Accra's Internet cafés, whose numbers have expanded rapidly thanks to the ingenuity of their owners and employees. Two years ago, Accra lacked a single Internet café. Now the city boasts more than 600 of them, a consequence of plummeting prices for PCs and new ways of circumventing the phone system to reach Web servers. An hour online costs anywhere from 75 cents to $1.25. A few years ago, Web access was far more expensive, when users had to phone places like London or Paris in order to get connected. The rise of Web cafés, combined with free e-mail services such as Hotmail and Yahoo means that many Accra residents can receive personal electronic messages for the first time in their lives. This makes 'the IT deficit' probably smaller than most people think.

Source: Retrieved from MIT Technology Review, July/August 2002.

in Africa that connectedness is not enough. Thus Africa remains marginalized technologically (see for example, Box 4.1).

When one compares distance elasticity across types of transactions it seems as if technology flows are the most distance sensitive (Venables, 2001). Keller (2002) finds that the distance sensitivity is very high. Spillovers are found to be halved for about 1,200 kilometers. Africa is anyway definitely marginal in the international market for licenses as well as in the investment market. The transfer of technology needs to have a solid base in actual investments. Licensing and franchising cannot substitute for that. Also, African countries need to learn from the experiences of countries such as India, which has developed Bangalore into a major global computer center, and Malaysia, which is building a major Asia Pacific computer city.

Conclusion

It is clear that the benefits from globalization and liberalization would mostly go to those countries and regions that have well-developed manufacturing sectors and have sustained outwardly-oriented strategies in their trade and economic policies. By contrast, countries with weak performance in policy reforms and tenuous links to the global trading system have seen few gains. However, it is also true that the marginalization of the poorest nations has been exacerbated by protectionist policies in the advanced countries.

In the case of Africa, the structural rigidities of production, combined with pressures from the international economic environment, have not allowed the continent to optimize the advantages of globalization. First, there is the

significant shift in the composition of global exports away from basic commodities towards manufactures, clearly an area where Africa does not currently enjoy a comparative advantage. Secondly, there is the rapidly expanding phenomenon of intra-firm/intra-industry trade, which is an important indicator of globalization of production. Since Africa's share in global production has been declining, the region is unable to share in this fast growing aspect of global trade. Thirdly, there is a rising share of trade in services, which is expanding even faster than trade in physical goods. Fourthly, there is the fact of the balkanized structure of African markets, notwithstanding the emergence of several regional economic communities. As we have seen, the establishment of several regional economic groupings has not led to the emergence of effective trading blocs with effective sizeable markets sufficient enough to produce meaningful and competitive scale economies. Lastly, as we have also explained, even though the last decade has witnessed the expansion of worldwide flows of foreign direct investment, the share of Africa in these flows has been minuscule.

A basic conclusion of this chapter is that, if Africa is to end its global isolation and become an important beneficiary of the fast-expanding global trade which has spurred phenomenal growth in many parts of the world, African public authorities must implement appropriate economic and institutional reforms and create large and effective markets with links to the global economy and shift its production structure to value added products.

CHAPTER 5

Towards Structural Transformation in Africa

Introduction

The preceding chapters have shown that the majority of African countries have not succeeded in diversifying their production structures; nor have they been able to expand the range of their export products and external markets. Despite the macroeconomic reforms that have been implemented by several countries since the 1980s, and despite the large volume of foreign assistance that has been provided, most of Africa is yet to approach the threshold of self-sustaining growth, let alone graduate into the club of middle-income nations (see Box 5.1). Whilst a few countries such as Botswana, Mauritius, Tunisia and Morocco have shown that political stability and prudent economic management can boost growth and reduce poverty, the same cannot be said for the majority of African countries. Indeed, in our age of globalization, the life-chances of millions of Africans have worsened in recent decades. And judging by current trends, it would seem that the continent risks being 'ghettoized' under what the noted scholar, Professor Ali Mazrui (1995), has termed the 'new global Apartheid', a situation whereby a globalizing world generates new inequities through corporate exclusion, financial manipulation and commercial barriers by dominant interests in the richest countries. This, according to him, can lead to the incipient 'hierarchization' of nations, in which the rich few are able preserve their power and privileges whilst the impoverished majority are permanently condemned to a life of misery and destitution. Indeed, the recent proliferation of so-called 'failed states' in Africa — states in which the normal functioning of economy and polity has virtually collapsed — has further buttressed this viewpoint. If the survival of such states has to depend on coordinated economic and financial rescue efforts by the UN or a consortium of international donors, it would, in effect, subject the fate of Africa to a new form of transnational trusteeship – a scenario that is quite unprecedented in the history of world development. Even for those countries that do not fall into this category, economic liberalization and globalization have further weakened the instrumental capacity of the state to deliver in terms of both policy entrepreneurship and the provision of basic social services.

Structural Transformation is the New Goal

The New Partnership for Africa's Development (NEPAD) offers an opportunity for a fresh start in re-launching Africa's development based on partnership and shared responsibility with Africa's development stakeholders. The key proposition of this chapter is that what Africa needs is a bold new vision of autocentric development based on a paradigm of structural transformation. As understood here, structural transformation refers to an export-oriented strategy of development that ensures growth with poverty reduction and sustainability through balanced inter-industry linkages and export diversification, based on a mobilization of

Box 5.1: The Paradox of Africa

From the vantage point of all the accumulated wisdom of economic science, Africa's increasing impoverishment is a patently abnormal state of affairs. In terms of natural resources endowment, Africa ought to be the richest continent in the world. Some of the world's most rare and strategic minerals can be found only in Africa. Its enviably rich flora and fauna constitute a priceless heritage for humanity and for generations yet unborn. The inland waters of the Congo alone are said to be enough to generate hydro-electricity to feed the energy needs of the continent. Considering its abundant natural resources, its youthful and vigorous population and its variegated climatic conditions, Africa already has within itself all the ingredients that it requires for its own development.

It has to be remembered that the concept of a 'Third World' is a mere invention; and that there are no universal laws of historical motion that condemn Africa to economic servitude and global marginality. Africa has no reason to be permanently third rate in terms of world economics, government and public administration, technology and industrial organization. From the perspective of what French historian Férnand Braudel has termed the *long durée*, the Africa of classical antiquity – from the ancient Nile Valley to the great Cushitic kingdoms — was once the center of world gravity, the world leader in fields as diverse as mathematics, chemistry, astronomy and the moral sciences.

What is lacking in the Africa of today is good government, leadership and vision under conditions of just and peaceful development. Africans lack the kind of leaderships who can marshal a profound vision of Africa's transformation centered on the continent's unique vocation in a world rendered more cynical by greed and hubris. One of the greatest drawbacks of the neoliberal paradigm is the fact that it has virtually succeeded in removing the notion of self-responsibility out of Africa's development agenda. Thus development is being perceived not as what Africans can do for themselves, but what others can and must do for them. As a consequence, African leaderships seem to have lost the confidence to envision their own economic emancipation.

domestic savings as well as external resource flows that generate neither dependence nor international indebtedness. This paradigm does not negate orthodox reforms; rather, it insists that reforms must go beyond the familiar 'fundamentals', embracing the wholesale re-engineering of African economies and societies towards the path of autocentric development and self-directed growth within a framework of open regionalism. At present, African countries have similar export baskets and, hence, trade liberalization would not lead to the generation of substantial inter-African trade. The new approach is therefore premised on the need to revamp the structures of production, transform national economies and diversify export patterns within an ever-deepening framework of regional economic communities.

Towards a New Policy Agenda

All is not bad news for Africa. It is important to underscore that Africa's economic importance lies not so much in its present state and accomplishments but in its promise and potentials. Africa is endowed with abundant but largely untapped potentials of natural resources - fertile soils, water, oil, gas, minerals and metals — and a population that is full of energy, vigor and ingenuity. Significant socio-political changes have swept the continent in the last decade. Some 35 countries have been implementing structural adjustment programs while civil wars have ended in several others, with the prospects that the path towards peace and progress will be restored. A new wave of democratization has also swept through the continent, and the progress towards change, though slow and fragile, seems headed for the better. For the first time in two decades, aggregate growth in income per capita has been significantly positive since 1996, perhaps signaling an escape from an enduring trap. Some countries have indeed sustained almost 'miraculous' growth rates of 8 percent since 1992.

Furthermore, Africa has huge potentials for more diversified production and exports, including in agro processing, manufacturing, and services. Many better-managed economies are beginning to diversify and make themselves better business addresses for private enterprise to flourish. These economies are also seeing their non-traditional exports – including floriculture, other nontraditional agricultural goods, and nontraditional industrial products — growing by more than 30 percent per annum since the mid-1990s signaling that Africa is not destined to suffer marginalization in trade.

Having potentials is one thing, realizing them is another. In the context of the huge potentials, pro-active responses to globalization must be driven by a long-term vision (Box 5.2). Africa accounts for more than 10 per cent of the world's population. Its long-term development vision could be driven by the goal to account for at least 10 percent of world output and exports within the next 30 years. This is daunting but not impossible. But such a goal in the context of globalization requires a coherent strategy, or in other words a business plan. This should seek to minimize the risks of globalization while maximizing its benefits. To be effective, such a plan must be comprehensive and involve consistent and coherent actions/programs at three major levels:

- *Domestic strategy*, anchored on building the institutions and enabling environment for a private sector-led, competitive market economy. More fundamentally such a domestic strategy must be guided by the ideology of aggressive outward or export-orientation, using regionalism as a building block.

- *Regional strategy*, driven by the need to enlarge markets and to exploit complementarities, economies of scale and synergies in provision of regional public goods — infrastructure, security/defense and collective regional institutions as agencies of restraint — so that domestic reforms and policies can be locked in for credibility. Such a regional strategy must also involve defining and mainstreaming regional best practices in political and economic governance, and exert collective peer pressures on erring countries to conform to the regional 'convergence criteria'.

- *Global strategy*, aimed at addressing many of the asymmetrical power relations and inequities in globalization, creating a level playing field, redesigning the global financial architecture, provision of global public goods, and strengthening the programs and institutions for preferential and differential treatments to Africa.

The new strategies would require fundamental changes in the existing ways of doing business. It is axiomatic that growth in living standards results from the accumulation of physical capital (investment), human capital (labor), and through advances in technology. Experiences of countries that have increased output most rapidly demonstrate that it is necessary to create the conditions that are conducive to long-run per capita income growth (IMF, 2000). Economic stability, institution-building, and structural reforms are as important for long-term development as financial transfers. What matters is the whole

Box 5.2: Elements of a New Policy Agenda

During a high-level seminar on globalization and Africa held in Tunis on April 5-6, 2001, policy actions to be taken by African countries as well as by the international community were highlighted. In general, all speakers emphasized the need for more reforms by African countries.

The consensus was that African countries, to maximize growth and accelerate their integration into the global economy, should focus on:

- Promoting macroeconomic stability to create the right conditions for investment, savings and growth in the private sector,
- Reforming the financial sector and legal and regulatory framework to remove impediments to efficiency and competitiveness,
- Outward-oriented polices (trade liberalization) to promote efficiency through increased trade and investment,
- Structural reforms to encourage domestic competition,
- Strengthening public institutions, improve governance and root out corruption,
- Education, training, and research and development to promote productivity,
- External debt management to ensure adequate resources for sustainable development,
- Removing biases against agriculture and the diversification of exports to deepen integration into the world economy,
- Improving infrastructure,
- Promoting a sound banking system and financial development,
- Giving a boost to regional integration efforts, and
- Increasing the efficiency of public spending to free up resources for the poor, including cutting military outlays.

A liberal trade regime, it was argued, also enhances a country's ability to attract foreign investment. Amongst other things, African countries would need to do the following:

- Implement a sound macroeconomic policy framework that engenders an enabling environment for growth and sustainable development, in particular through investments by the private sector;
- Undertake large investments in trade-creating and trade-facilitating infrastructure, especially in such key sectors as telecommunications and transportation;
- Implement institutional reforms in trade-related public institutions, especially in customs and tax administration and export promotion and servicing organizations.

package of policies, financial and technical assistance as well as debt relief. Sub-Saharan African countries need to grow at 7 percent a year on average to reduce poverty by half by 2015. They have to be fuelled by much higher domestic savings, and by a flow of grants, loans and investment. Several suggestions have been made at different forums concerning what Africa should do to become integrated into the global economy.

It has been suggested that for a long time, most African countries resisted adopting the market-oriented policies and reforms needed to reap the benefits of globalization. The fundamental challenges facing Africa now are how to accelerate economic growth and poverty reduction. African countries should therefore strengthen their macroeconomic policies and structural reforms if they are to maximize the gains from globalization, accelerate growth and reduce poverty (Calamitsis, 2001). Priority should be given to consolidating macroeconomic stability and strengthening competitiveness through sound fiscal, monetary and exchange rate policies. Fiscal policy should focus on achieving faster growth and eradicating poverty, while monetary policy should try to contain the growth of money supply in order to reduce inflation.

It is also crucially important that African countries speed up the process of regional economic integration amongst themselves. Africa's economic and political geography presents challenging circumstances for economic development. Many countries are too small and balkanized to provide substantial economies of scale to support profitable investment (and some 15 countries are landlocked). This situation and the regional rather than global nature of much international interaction suggest that countries place a high priority on trying to generate sub-regional and regional dynamism. However, it is critical to underline the fact that regional integration can best work for Africa in the context of more open national economies.

The first step is to work towards trade and payments liberalization between neighboring countries in order to spur inter-country transactions. Liberalization has already led to increasing intra-regional trade within Africa. Another major step in this direction is to integrate national markets into sub-regional markets through building regional infrastructure networks, in roads and telecommunications, for example. Regional project aid could help here. Furthermore, while financial market development presents a potential channel for integration into the global economy, most economies in Africa are too small to justify the cost involved in setting up stock markets. One of the most viable ways to overcome this

problem is for governments to pool resources in developing regional institutions. These could include: regional securities and exchange commissions; regional self-regulatory organizations; regional committees to promote harmonization of legal and regulatory schemes; development of regional bond or debt markets; regional institutions for pooling information and research; credible regional credit rating agencies; and coordinated monetary arrangements.

Whether it is in the area of poverty alleviation programs, environmental and technological issues, macroeconomic adjustment and trade, resource mobilization and utilization, attraction of FDI, management of external debt and ODA, human capital development and utilization, solving ethnic conflicts and civil strife by enlarging the economic space and allowing migration, solving the infrastructural problems and achieving economic competitiveness, etc, the regional framework is the effective vehicle for delivery. It would require serious intellectual output to redefine the meaning of regionalism in Africa in the light of the emergency situation, and this would need Africans to face up to, and answer fundamental questions about, the concepts of sovereignty, definition and meaning of borders, etc.

Increasingly, African countries have risen up to the challenge of regional cooperation and coordination. The birth of the African Union, and the articulation of NEPAD signify Africa's commitment to a new kind of regionalism. Previous integration attempts, especially based on inward-looking schemes, failed to foster production diversification and in many cases even undermined trade and financial flows in the context of overvalued exchange rates and distortionary capital controls. In many parts of Africa, deeper integration among the sub-regional groupings is intensifying. In West Africa, the eight WAEMU countries have adopted a common external tariff regime and the rest of ECOWAS countries are under pressure to latch on to that. The proposed second monetary union in West Africa is scheduled for 2004. South Africa belongs to the Southern African Customs Union, but has successfully negotiated a free trade agreement with the EU. Some countries in North Africa (Tunisia and Algeria) are also negotiating such agreements with the EU. All these are positive developments and deepen the integration scheme.

Despite the progress made, there are several pressure points. For example, the many overlapping integration schemes need to be rationalized. The new AU and NEPAD initiative must take up this issue and resolve it as quickly as possible. There are also tensions, such as that between the political demands of sovereignty of nation states (even if they are not economically viable) on the one hand and the economic imperatives of more open borders within the region. Both forces pull in opposite directions and the extent to which countries are willing to give up much of their sovereignty will determine the extent of progress that can be made. Furthermore, it is important to root the integration process within the democratic processes in the countries. So far, integration is a top-down program in Africa. To cohere with the new democratic dispensation, citizens' involvement in key decisions needs to be mainstreamed, perhaps by holding country referenda on crucial issues.

The discussion on integration and trade has thus far been focused on economic issues and relationships. A necessary condition for regionalization is peace and security, or more generally speaking, stability. Political stability is an important imperative in a nation's ability to attract and keep investment. Regional stability is essential for trans-border investment in infrastructure and telecommunications which hold the key to industrialization in an era of linked borders and markets. For several years, if not decades, many Africa countries have faced internal conflicts and these have had severe cross-border spillovers. It is very unlikely that a region with so many conflicts will be able to attract FDI away from other more stable regions. Thus, if Africa is to stimulate trade and growth, stability must return.

Implementing NEPAD

While the regional mechanisms for implementing NEPAD are evolving, the core of the actions will be at the country level. Much of the expanded ODA provided through NEPAD will in fact be bilateral assistance at country level. Country level mechanisms would include the Poverty Reduction Strategy Papers (PRSPs), pooled budgetary support utilizing medium term expenditure frameworks, etc. NEPAD accommodates all these mechanisms but also includes the element of mutual accountability towards development outcomes. It is important that NEPAD recognizes the PRSP process as a core vehicle for building continent-wide priorities into national poverty reduction programs and coordinating international support. The PRSPs, with their emphasis on country ownership, broad participation, and dealing with economic and social fundamentals, represent a major paradigm shift and recognition of the imperatives of comprehensive planning. With a comprehensive action plan orchestrated through the PRSP process, the ownership of national stakeholders would be ensured, and hopefully the legitimacy and sustainability of the development agenda.

Box 5.3: The Primacy of Good Governance

Good governance and sound institutional development are critical to laying the foundations of a private sector-led economy. Although NEPAD is trying to mainstream best practices in good governance through the African Peer Review Mechanism, the African governments need to focus on the following governance priorities:

- Transparency of government — citizens must be kept informed of the decisions of the state and their justification;
- Simplicity of procedures — whether in fiscal matters, investment, or other areas, administrative procedures need to be as simple as possible, with the number of participants reduced to a minimum;
- Responsibility — public officials must be held accountable and, if necessary, penalized for offenses;
- Fight against corruption — eradication of this scourge is imperative for promoting healthy competition, eliminating surcharges, and strengthening the efficiency of economic management;
- Individual freedom and collective expression — a free and responsible press, in particular, is an important pillar of democracy and market economy;
- Independence of the legal system — the legal system must be free from pressure and intervention from political forces or any other organization, to ensure that its decisions are independent and impartial. This is central to enforcement of rule of law and protection of property rights — two pillars of a market economy;
- Competitive procurement systems — whose rules are clear and fair, and where efficiency and effectiveness are overriding considerations in award of contracts;
- Efficient public service delivery system — to ensure value-for-money;
- Efficiency in the delivery of public services.

Through effective governance and institutional reforms (see Box 5.3) citizens' participation in the articulation of the development agenda could be ensured. In turn, this could enable citizens to be aware of the threats and challenges posed by the new world order as well as it opportunities. Logically, the voices of the citizens should be heard in thinking through the strategy, if it is to be credible and sustainable.

Elements of the comprehensive development agenda must derive from the demands of the new world economic order, the imperatives of poverty reduction, and the resource endowments and prospective resource flows from the rest of the world. The agenda must focus on creating the environment for a private sector-led, competitive market economy for sustained poverty reduction. The guiding principle here is that it is impossible to be competitive globally if the domestic economy is uncompetitive. For a summary, the key elements must involve actions at several levels as follows.

Macroeconomic stability is not only good for the poor; it is a prerequisite for a sound business environment. High and variable inflation rates, unproductive spending, fiscal imbalances and large balance of payments deficits need to be contained. Reducing unproductive expenditures and eliminating waste would help to release resources for investment in infrastructure, health, education, electricity, etc. Expenditure reallocation to pro-poor programs is good for social cohesion. Such a reallocation should be accompanied by a strengthening of expenditure management systems, especially with a view to monitoring closely the delivery and impact of public services and social safety nets. To allow greater credit to the private sector, government borrowing from the banking system should be discouraged. As part of the program of downsizing bloated state bureaucracies and buoying up the private sector, African governments should aggressively privatize inefficient public enterprises. African countries should also strive to sustain competitive real exchange rates to facilitate their integration into the global economy, attract investment, and foster export diversification and growth.

Africa has acquired a reputation as a risky and expensive place to do business. Consequently, a key challenge is in building the necessary environment to convince, especially, domestic agents to invest their savings at home. This is required to reverse trends in capital flight. Given its serious under-capitalization and de-capitalization, Africa badly needs the return of capital. Everywhere in the world, domestic capital leads foreign capital. If Africans are not confident enough to invest in their economies it is futile trying to convince foreigners to do so. Creating such an environment is daunting. It requires heavy financial outlays in such areas as infrastructure development (roads, ports and airports, electricity, and water), institutional development to guarantee property rights and rule of law, efficient and stable financial system, and a change in mind-set that sees the private sector as partners rather than as competitors in development.

There are major resource reserves that are unexploited in Africa simply because of the policy environment. Such factors range from anachronistic property rights and foreign ownership laws, regulations that stifle savings and enterprise, and weak institutions for public service delivery. Self-inflicted high transaction costs often deter private investment, both domestic and foreign. For example, in many African countries, it takes several weeks for

firms to clear customs in order to have their imported inputs whereas it takes minutes/hours to do so in many of their competitor countries. Archaic regulations lead to poor and inefficient communications and transport infrastructure. Tourism remains underdeveloped in many countries because of absurdly complex visa requirements. The list is endless. Without addressing these transaction costs, it is difficult to see how Africa can diversify production, be internationally competitive or reverse the loss in global market shares. The point of emphasis is that countries need to do their utmost best to fully exploit their existing potentials in resource mobilization and utilization: there is little point in asking for millions of dollars in foreign aid whereas self-inflicted actions deter billions of dollars in domestic and foreign investment.

Building Capacity

African citizens need capacity to participate in the high technology and networked global environment. The high illiteracy level is a stumbling block. It is important to boost basic education programs to achieve universal primary education and eliminate gender disparities in both primary and secondary education. Beyond basic education, higher and vocational education would be required to help Africa bridge the digital divide, take full advantage of the vast knowledge available on the Internet, and improve their ability to compete on world markets. Heavy investment is also required in the area of health care, especially primary care, as well as heavy campaigns to redress the HIV/AIDS pandemic through comprehensive programs of prevention, care, and treatment.

There has to be a strategy of engagement with the global economy. The liberalization episodes of the 1980s and 1990s occurred without a coherent strategy. As is becoming clear, openness by itself would not guarantee prosperity. The past liberalizations have also been unilateral and not locked in within regional frameworks. African countries have always recognized (at least in rhetoric) the imperatives of regionalism as an important stepping-stone, but need to take this seriously as part of their domestic investment strategy to cope with globalization. Trade liberalization should be sequenced to follow diversification of the tax base and improved export performance. Governments should ensure that firms have access to imported inputs at world prices. Africa should recognize that the global governance structures are laden with politics. No one would come to develop Africa out of altruism, or grant concessions because they love Africa. African countries need to be more pro-active in shaping the global political struggles to reform the financial architecture. The Doha Development Round of trade negotiations under the WTO presents another opportunity to re-write the rules of the game and Africa must be prepared to play a decisive role.

Rapid Export Expansion

The export performance of a country is an important factor determining the limit to which its investments can be expanded and growth and poverty reduction can be accelerated without the country encountering balance of payments and debt repayment problems (see Box 5.4). Export proceeds are indispensable for a country to purchase the imports of capital goods required for investment, as well as the imports of consumer goods associated with the growth of income as the economy expands. Export proceeds are equally indispensable for improving a country's creditworthiness if it wants to borrow and for the repayments of external debt when

it falls due. The share of a country in international trade is an important determinant of its share in world income. Just as the income of an individual in a nation is determined by the capabilities of that individual, the share of a country in global income is determined by the capabilities of that country to compete in the international market and expand its exports.

The link between exports expansion and poverty reduction in the African context is quite a clear one. Accelerated growth is the first line of attack in the fight against poverty. Accelerated growth, however, requires large investments in capital goods, which are not produced by African countries and would need to be imported with foreign exchange. Also, as these investments start to raise the incomes of the people, the demand for consumer goods (including that for expensive durable goods like motor vehicles) will increase.

In the absence of domestic production to satisfy such an increase in demand, the excess demand will spill over into imports, generating additional needs for foreign exchange beyond the current foreign exchange earnings of the country. A country might be able to borrow commercially to satisfy the foreign exchange requirements of growth but borrowed funds have to be repaid, often with interest at market variable rates. Thus, if export expansion is not sufficient to meet the import demand associated with faster growth (in addition to servicing foreign debt) the sustainability of growth will be threatened, as the heavy burden of foreign indebtedness will eventually close in and capital inflows will eventually dry up. A country might obtain foreign aid to meet the foreign exchange requirements of growth, but in this case, the pace of growth will be limited by the amount of aid the country receives. Not only this, but

Box 5.4: Developing an International Market

A fundamental truth is that "the world market does not have an address" to which countries can ship manufactured exports at world market prices. Countries must search for, locate and contact potential foreign buyers. This requires strong government support. It is very difficult for individual private sector firms to invest in obtaining knowledge and information about foreign markets. Once such information is acquired, its 'consumption' cannot be privatized and private firms cannot capture the full return on their investment. Because of their public goods characteristics, knowledge and information about foreign markets might be provided by the public sector through the creation of public sector Trade Promotion Organizations (TPOs). Such TPOs are usually set up to support other export incentive measures.

Four successful exporter economies — Korea, Singapore, Hong Kong, and Taiwan — have all supported export marketing through the public sector. The experience of these countries, however, shows that the effectiveness of TPOs depends on the fulfillment of certain conditions. First, the overall economic environment should be outward looking and supportive of exports. Secondly, TPOs should be assigned one single objective. Multiple

objectives often make the achievement of any one objective difficult, if not impossible. For instance, regional dispersion and 'indigenization' of business are two objectives that can result in a TPO being ineffective at promoting exports (Hill, 1994). Thirdly, the regulations of TPOs should not hinder the private sector providing similar services in cases where it could do so more effectively. Fourthly, TPOs should have an independent administrative entity that can influence policymaking and claim resources from export proceeds (ADR, 1996).

Kenya provides a successful example of export promotion through marketing. The Horticultural Crops Development Authority (HCDA), created in 1967, helps smallholders market their crops by maintaining contacts with traders and exporters. It finances its activities by a direct tax on export produce and does not receive revenue from the government. It concentrates on smallholder development, extension services, and information on international prices. It also issues export certificates, which certify product quality and the reasonableness of prices, for a fee.

Source: Development Research Division, the African Development Bank, Abidjan, Côte d'Ivoire, 2003.

the country will forever be dependant on aid, unless it increases export earnings. This can hardly be achieved unless there is shift in Africa's pattern of trade towards the production and exportation of manufacturers. Sluggish growth, increasing poverty, heavy external indebtedness and aid dependency, which characterize Africa economies, can all be related to its poor export performance. As put more than a century ago by Alfred Marshall: "the causes which determine the economic progress of nations belong to the study of international trade" (Marshall, 1890).

It is mainly through the conduits of trade that the positive and negative economic forces of the global market are transmitted and the economic prospects of countries and continents are determined. While private flows such as FDI play a role in distributing the fortunes of globalization, export performance is the fundamental factor. The development effectiveness of FDI flows that do not contribute to the export performance of a country will be small and short-lived (ADR, 2002).

Beyond Primary Products

There is nothing in the doctrine of free trade or global liberalization that guarantees an equal or equitable distribution of the gains from trade. The distribution of the gains from trade will be determined by a country's international competitiveness in terms of both its price and income dimensions. As is well known, the demand for any commodity depends on its price relative to the price of competing products and on the income that might be devoted to the purchase of this commodity. This gives rise to the idea that competitiveness in the international market has two dimensions: price competitiveness and income competitiveness. Price competition has been the more talked-about measure of competitiveness: a country whose dollar export price is higher than that of competing countries selling the same product, is said to be uncom-petitive and will lose its market share. Among the interrelated factors contributing to a country's price competitiveness, are labor unit costs, wage/productivity relationship and the exchange rate.

More recently, the importance of non-price competition has become recognized. Most manufacturing industries have been characterized by highly oligopolistic market structures and aggressive price competition has been the exception and not the rule. Countries have increasingly been engaged in non-price competition which encompasses factors other than price that affect a country's market share. These factors are normally grouped into two broad aspects: the first is related to the act of selling or marketing; and the second is related to the characteristics of the product, including quality and level of product sophistication.

A demanding challenge facing African countries is in the domain of the income-di-mension of global competition. The majority of African countries are currently dependent on commodities which are becoming increasingly unattractive in the international market. The market for Africa's traditional exports is shrinking relative to the global export market. This implies that as world income grows, a smaller proportion of this income growth is devoted to the purchase of these commodities. In other words, the world's income elasticity of demand for Africa's traditional exports is less than unity. In addition, the majority of African countries are dependent on the importation of manufactured goods, which have income elasticities of demand grater than unity. Thus, the income dimension of global competition tends to work against African countries on account of both exports and imports.

Africa's weak income-competitiveness means that it has missed valuable opportunities emanating from the globalization of production and the liberalization of global trade. For instance, the net impact of the full implementation of Uruguay Round Agreement on the majority of African economies is more likely to be negative rather than positive because some crucial aspects of the Agreement will have direct adverse effects on the continent, but most importantly because the production structure of African economies is not poised to exploit the opportunities created by the Agreement. African primary-producing countries are, in fact, among the least to benefit form the expected trade expansion and global income growth, partly because of the low-income elasticities of demand for primary products which mean that the demand for such products will not increase appreciably as a result of the expected increase in global income, and partly because the trade barriers on some primary products are already low. The fastest growth of trade resultant from the Agreement is expected to be in manufacturing, in general, rather than in primary commodities. Hence, it can be assumed that most of the benefits of the new WTO trade regime are more likely to accrue to the more diversified economies of Asia and Latin America.

When considering the distribution of the gains from trade the problem for many African countries is that their export products, which are predominantly primary commodities have inherent tendencies for their terms of trade to deteriorate in relation to manufactured goods coming from the developed countries. Firstly, with the exception of petroleum, the global prices of most primary commodities have exhibited a secular tendency to decline over the years. Such products have not only low prices; they also have a low income elasticity of demand, which means that when supply increases prices can drop dramatically, and demand grows only slowly with global income growth. Secondly, primary commodities are land-based activities and subject to diminishing returns, and there is a limit to employment in diminishing returns activities set by the point where the marginal product of labor falls to the minimum subsistence wage (Thirlwall 1999; ADR, 2002). From the preceding account it is not difficult to argue that for African countries to accelerate their growth rate and reduce poverty major structural transformation towards the production of more attractive goods will be necessary.

A Vision of Industrial Development

Not all African countries can be expected to pursue the same policies in terms of industrial development and structural transformation. For some small, landlocked countries with low scale economies, their best hope lies in working within the framework of regional economic communities. Each country can select the relevant policy mix that will enable it to achieve a breakthrough in terms of structural transformation once the economic fundamentals are put in place, including macroeconomic stabilization and structural reforms, creation of stable exchange rates and viable payments systems, low inflation, an efficient bureaucracy and stable political conditions.

While it is true that no country can attain significant levels of development without industrialization, agriculture must be used as the take-off base for Africa. Box 5.5 documents the Malaysian strategy for inter-industry linkages as a long-term approach to development planning. Owing to its importance in the structure of African economies, the agricultural sector must play a crucial role in industrial development. The agricultural sector must provide in large measure not only the inputs for industry and food for the urban industrial population, but it must also generate demand for industrial goods and earn the foreign exchange to purchase the imports of capital goods and raw materials for industry. Increasing the productivity of agriculture is, therefore, an indispensable factor for any long-term industrial strategy.

One idea towards adopting an industrial strategy that might be suitable for African countries is the incremental or 'piecemeal' approach. In this, the aim is to attain the overarching objectives of sustained growth, poverty alleviation, and human capital development by promoting the sectoral division of labor according to factor endowments and end-uses. The general idea is to promote three sectors: the traditional sector, an intermediate sector and a modern export sector. The traditional sector, employing traditional technology and labor-intensive techniques, has to be promoted to meet, as much as possible,

Box 5.5: Linking Agriculture with Industry — The Experience of Malaysia

Malaysia is one of those Asian countries whose industrial development vision is worthy of emulation by African countries. In a matter of three decades, the country has made a major leap into the ranks of middle-income nations. Malaysia's Third National Agricultural Policy has sought to hinge the country's industrial advancement on strong inter-sectoral linkages with agriculture. For example, in the case of industrial crops, forestry and wood-based products, the aim is enhance and sustain their contribution to national income and earnings; ensure adequate supply of raw materials for the processing and industries in the production of high value-added products for export; within an overall national vision of strengthening Malaysia's position as a center of excellence for development, conserving, managing and utilizing natural resources on a sustainable basis. The policy directions to be pursued are as follows:

Improving productivity. The international competitiveness of this product group will be achieved through technology-driven improvements in productivity and efficiency. This will be mainly realized through increasing R&D efforts, enhancing technology capabilities and human resource development. To complement these efforts, restructuring of these resource-based industries through further integration of upstream and downstream activities as well as consolidation of the production units will be encouraged.

Enhancing value-added activities. To further enhance the development of the resource-based industries, the production of high-end products will be encouraged to capitalize on the increasing world demand for such products. This will require new product development and strengthening of support institutions and services.

Strengthening marketing capabilities. Malaysia will pursue a global orientated marketing strategy to become a world-scale and world-class manufacturer of high value resource-based products. This will require the development of global marketing capabilities to compete internationally. Efforts will be undertaken to intensify marketing research and intelligence, provide strong marketing information back-up, develop strategic networking and Malaysian brand products as well as expand and deepen markets. Additionally, institutional support will be strengthened to ensure and promote Malaysia as producer of high quality products globally.

Promoting agroforesty. To optimize land use and maximize return from investments, agroforestry, involving integration of forestry and agricultural activities, will be encouraged. This will require the establishment of an institutional framework to provide the supporting services including R&D, technology transfer, HRD and incentive packages and promote wide scale adoption of agroforestry system of planting.

Encouraging reverse investment. Malaysian companies will be encouraged to explore and expand their operations overseas through joint ventures and tripartite arrangements. This is to take advantage of lower cost of production and ready market in the host country and the surrounding region and to form strategic alliances to capitalize on Malaysian technologies and management expertise as well as financial strength of parties involved.

Ensuring sustainable development. Efforts will be undertaken to strengthen sustainable forest management and develop environmental friendly production processes and technologies. Sufficient area of land will be maintained under permanent forest cover to be managed sustainably for economic gain as well as environmental protection.

basic needs including food, clothing and shelter. The modern sector, which necessitates a shift to high knowledge-intensive production techniques, could be spearheaded by the export sector. The export sector is envisaged to take up the challenge of processing and manufacturing, aiming to advance certain manufacturers into a renowned market niche, encourage and host foreign investment, and act as the vehicle which pulls the overall economy to higher growth rates and as the window through which the country would acquire technological knowledge and managerial know-how.

Variants of this piecemeal approach have been successfully implemented by some developing countries. In Asia, for instance, the reforming economy of China moved to higher and sustained growth rates in the last decade through the promotion of the so-called 'Special Economic Zones' in which the country adopted an outward-oriented strategy similar to that of the NIEs and ASEAN economies, with heavy reliance on manufacturing exports and foreign investment. Between 1980-1990, these special areas recorded an average real growth rate of 15 per cent while the China's economy as a whole grew by an average real rate of 9 per cent.

In Africa, Mauritius engineered major impetus to growth, through the promotion of Export Processing Zones (EPZs) which relied heavily on manufacturing exports and foreign investment. The main objective of EPZs is to promote processing and manufacturing, aiming to advance certain manufacturers into an external market niche; encourage and host foreign investment; and act as the vehicle which pulls the overall economy to higher growth rates and as a window through which the country can acquire technological knowledge and managerial know-how (ADR, 1996).

There are two main justifications for adopting the piecemeal approach. First, that the process of transformation through industrialization requires huge investment in infrastructure and other production-servicing facilities that most African countries may not be able to provide countrywide. The available resources can be devoted to the provision of these facilities within a small confined area, the EPZ. Second, the effective application of countrywide export incentives, such as exemption or rebate systems, requires a high level of technical and administrative capacity. There is also the risk of abuse of these systems, with duty-free inputs not being used for export production and with exemptions and rebates provided to unqualified firms. An EPZ is meant to avoid these costs and risks, since the use of duty-free imports and the provision of other incentives are more easily monitored in a confined EPZ.

Experience has shown that greater and higher benefits accrue to those economies able to carve niches for themselves in the globalization process. It is not necessary for a country to develop an integrated national industry before competing with developed countries in manufactures. What is needed, is the vertical and horizontal linkages of the selected niche of industries with the local economy. It is possible for the country to specialize in exports of one or a few manufactured goods, and therefore secure a better export market prospect than from primary goods.

Information technology (IT) may offer attractive export niches for Africa's landlocked countries. The high cost of transportation costs is one of the major obstacles of export promotion in landlocked African countries. Software exports and cyber-related services such as outsourcing, which carry negligible transport costs,

Box 5.6: Software Outsourcing in India and Egypt

Outsourcing, particularly in ICT software, is increasingly becoming an avenue through which developing countries can reap maximum benefits from globalization. Global software outsourcing has had a positive impact on the economies of nations such as India and Israel, and is proving to be a lucrative industry in emerging economies like Egypt. In 2001, India for instance, exported $6.2 billion of IT software to the US and Western Europe. These exports are estimated to increase to $100 billion by 2010.

In the 1970s the Indian government created engineering and management institutes which are comparable in standards to any in Western Europe and North America. The availability of the large number of technically skilled English-speaking graduates, which these institutions turned out, prompted foreign companies to "test the Indian waters". The establishment of Agricultural research, which was a necessity for boosting India's food, supplies created further demand for high-tech solutions. Federal government support and guidance for private sector initiatives in the IT sector also provided further impetus. A very important aspect was the Computer Policy of 1984 which recommended the shipping of software exports via satellite-based data links, making for greater speed of delivery and eliminating transportation costs. The National Association of Software and Service Companies (NASSCOM) set the national agenda in the absence of a government ministry to cater to the IT industry. This association worked tirelessly to boost Indian software exports and fight software piracy. State governments lured private companies to set up software technology parks (STPs), which offered suitable infrastructure and attractive tax terms for export-oriented IT firms. Such parks provide an environment geared towards meeting the needs of non-Indian foreign markets.

Several other factors have contributed to India's success with technology outsourcing. Among them are its large domestic market, history of self-reliance, intense domestic rivalry which created efficient production mechanisms and cheaper production costs and the economic reforms of 1991 which created the right kind of climate for a vibrant software sector led by organizations like NASSCOM to flourish.

In Africa, Egypt is fast establishing itself as a regional hub and a software exporter to the developed world. A handful of the almost 150 software companies in the country have been focusing on exporting their products to Europe and the US. Offshore outsourcing revenues were estimated at $50 million in 2000, from $35 million in 1999. It is projected that the software outsourcing industry will rake in some $2.5 billion in the next five years. As in India, Egypt's success owes to the collaborative initiatives of government and the private sector. The government formed the Communications and Information Ministry in October 1999, which produced a national plan that sought to build an information society. The goals of the national plan in this respect are to: develop the IT industry; build an information society capable of absorbing and making use of the excessive flow of data; develop the communication and information infrastructure; increase the number of IT graduates. Incentives include: exempting computer and software importers and exporters alike from taxes for a period of ten years. In addition, the Ministry of Communications and Information since its inception has been improving communication and telephone networks, doubling the number of telephone lines and improving overall infrastructure services delivery.

Source: Development Research Division, the African Development Bank, Abidjan, Côte d'Ivoire, 2003.

offer great opportunities for African countries in general and landlocked countries in particular. This reduces the costs that can be incurred and increases the potential for higher benefits from the globalization process. With IT proving indispensable for the corporate world and its demand on the increase, it provides attractive opportunities Africa in general and landlocked African countries in particular (see Box 5.6).

IT outsourcing is fast becoming one of the most innovative global business processes. IT remains the largest sector in outsourcing constituting more than 20 percent of all outsourcing expenditure. A report by McKinsey, the global strategy consulting firm, estimates that the global IT software and services market is in the range of $400 billion–$500 billion and is steadily growing at 10-12 percent annually, with the software sector growing at 14 percent. It is predicted that multinational corporations of the developed economies will resort to outsourcing to shore up shareholders' value. Whilst growth in outsourcing in the US was 15 percent annually since 2000, there are major emerging offshore outsourcing markets in the Euro area, Australia and New Zealand. Besides, as offshore suppliers such as the big Indian services companies become more established and accepted such markets will experience both increased costs and prices. This presents excellent bargains for lesser-known markets of Eastern Europe and particularly landlocked African countries to derive some benefits from the globalization process. IT outsourcing, which is seen as an industry of the future, is not likely to decline soon. Latecomers in the globalization process, such as landlocked African countries, could capitalize by laying the foundation for this industry. The absence of transportation costs reduces the overheads in such an industry. However the

initial conditions that can provide the boost for take off – availability of technically competent graduates and an adequate infrastructure base – need to be put in place. Governments could also emulate the Indian and Egyptian models to provide the needed guidance and support. Tax incentives and the establishment of export processing zones to cater to the demands of foreign imports are essential. Establishment of government departments and ministries devoted to the communications and IT sector can provide a further boost.

The errors of the past must be avoided. In Africa, trade and industrial policies have long been characterized by high levels of protection and interventions in domestic resource allocation, a dominant role for public enterprises and a general distrust of the private sector. Small and fragmented local markets have led to the setting up of small-scale plants that could not compete internationally. Foreign direct investment has often been deterred by hostile and unstable policies, and by the small and stagnant domestic market, while export-oriented investments have gravitated to regions with better policies, skill bases and infrastructure. Indigenous industrial entrepreneurship has been weak, dominated by small and micro enterprises mainly concentrated in traditional low productivity activities serving very local markets. While these enterprises have multiplied in recent years, this has often been a survival strategy in the face of the adverse economic climate. African industrial policies will have to be reformed if industry is to survive and grow in the new environment of intensifying competition, increasing globalization and liberalizing trade and investment regimes.

The incentive structure that is relevant for industrial development refers to the competitive environment that firms face in allocating resources. These decisions include not just buying physical plant and facilities, but also obtaining technology and mastering and upgrading it. Industrial progress in developing countries depends essentially on how well firms invest in finding the right plant and technology, in developing the skills and technical knowledge to use that technology, in striking up the right supply and information linkages with other firms and with numerous institutions, and in finding and developing domestic and export markets.

However, such reform does not mean full exposure to international competition. There are different ways to expose industrial firms to a stimulating environment where they can build up healthy capabilities. In industries with difficult technologies and long, risky and costly learning process, there are market failures in the capability development process. The process of capability building may then be aborted by a premature exposure to free trade, where latecomers have to face firms that have already undergone the learning process and have a developed support structure of suppliers and institutions. Some infant industry protection is then essential for broad-based industrial development and diversification and for dynamizing comparative advantage.

As experience clearly shows, protection can be a dangerous tool. While providing a grace period and resources for learning, it can take away the incentive to invest in that learning. Efficient industrial policy thus requires that protection be limited in extent and duration, its deleterious effects be offset by measures to force firms to invest in developing their technological capabilities, and viable export activities are not handicapped by having to use expensive local inputs. The most effective way to do this is to combine domestic protection with strong export-orientation, and letting export activities operate in an effective free trade regime as far as their access to inputs is concerned.

The same reasoning applies to the process of reforming distorted incentive structures. Given the existence of learning processes, which are necessarily gradual and diffuse, rapid exposure to import competition can kill off industries that are potentially competitive but are not given the time or the resources to complete their learning process or to unlearn past distorted learning and become competitive. Adjusting industries to competition can be a slow and costly process, just like building up new industries and capabilities. Moreover, both need a range of supporting measures outside the firm itself, since learning within firms cannot substitute for deficiencies in the supply of essential inputs like education, training, technical information and supplier networks. The provision of these measures is a complex task, involving a great deal of government intervention and selectivity. However, to recommend a more gradual and nuanced strategy of liberalization is not to suggest that African countries simply slow down the adjustment process. What is needed is not to delay the adjustment, but to actively prepare for it in the grace period provided.

An important factor to take into account is that many African governments themselves do not at this time have the capabilities to mount effective support of industrialization. The levels of support they exercise must therefore be tailored to their relatively limited capacities to monitor and implement selective industrial promotion in accordance with the niche of exports they need to promote.

On other incentive measures, the liberalization of domestic competition is an important requirement of policy in Africa. This applies particularly to remaining biases against the entry of private enterprises of all kinds, local and foreign, in areas of activity reserved for public enterprises, though the situation today is quite liberal in many countries in the region. What is perhaps still not satisfactory is the bias in the incentive regime against smaller and micro enterprises and in favor of large firms. Smaller firms, while numerous, remain confined to low technology, low productivity activities and generally have tenuous relationships with the formal industrial sector. How they can be helped to upgrade and strike stronger supplier or subcontracting linkages with large firms is discussed below, with examples from Asia.

Facilitating access to importing foreign technology has to be a vital element of technology policy. Technology import can take several forms. At one end, it can be entirely internalized by the seller of technology, as with wholly foreign-owned direct investments. At the other, it can be fully externalized, with the buyer putting together its own package of equipment, know-how and other inputs, with no long-term contractual arrangement with a foreign supplier (an extreme example would be a firm buying machinery on open markets and 'reverse engineering' a product design with no explicit technology agreement). The choice of mode of technology import depends on various factors, including the capabilities of domestic firms and the level of technology aimed at. In general, the more capable the local firms, the easier it is for them to acquire externalized technology, since this is cheaper than getting the same technology through direct investment and may generate more local linkages and externalities. The more complex the technology and the more direct investment is important for obtaining access to export markets, the better it is to obtain internalized technology imports.

In Africa, there are strong arguments for seeking to increase internalized technology through FDI, because domestic industrial capabilities are generally low, even in relatively simple manufactured products like the ones that led the East Asian export drive. This does not mean that governments should not seek to develop the capabilities of indigenous enterprises. On the contrary, a strong local sector is needed to go into activities that foreign investors are unlikely to consider attractive, e.g. products geared to very localized markets and resources. It is also needed in sectors that complement foreign investments (as suppliers) and absorb the beneficial spillovers from their operations (as competitors). However, for the foreseeable future the main strategy in Africa should focus on attracting FDI, while supporting the technological development of local firms in all possible activities.

With reference to FDI, the Asian experience suggests that different approaches can be adopted depending on the development vision of the country. One is simply to adopt a laissez faire strategy and let market forces decide (the Hong Kong approach). This works well when there is a strong indigenous base of industrial skills, with dynamic local enterprises and a strong infrastructure of financial services, trade and communications. Even with these conditions the Hong Kong strategy runs the risk that letting market forces decide entirely the pattern of technology imports in a free trade setting will lead to a shallow industrial base that is unable to sustain growth and competitiveness with rising wages.

An alternative strategy, also in a free trade setting, is that of Singapore. This was intensely interventionist, with FDI being aggressively sought, targeted for particular activities, and induced to upgrade over time. With a much smaller economy than Hong Kong, Singapore has managed to deepen its industrial structure far more and to maintain high manufacturing growth and export rates. It intervened selectively to move its industry from labor-intensive to capital, skill and technology-intensive activities. The public sector often played an important role in leading particular activities that the government wanted to promote, acting as a catalyst to private investment. Singapore's technology acquisition policy was directed at acquiring, and subsequently upgrading, the most modern technologies in selected sectors. This allowed it to engage and specialize in the emerging global system of production under the aegis of MNEs, focusing of particular stages of production while drawing upon the continuing flow of innovation of the parent company. To attract foreign investment while inducing technological upgrading, Singapore invested massively in human capital and infrastructure, with these investments also highly targeted to the particular activities being promoted.

Yet another successful strategy from East Asia that is of relevance to Africa is that of Taiwan, a medium sized economy (population around 20 million) that started its industrialization with a strong base of human capital and a large population of small and medium sized enterprises (SMEs). It combined interventions in technology transfer with those in trade policy, aiming to provide strong support for technology acquisition and deepening by local enterprises. It drew upon the whole gamut of technology imports, changing the balance over time. In the 1950s it sought to attract FDI within a liberal policy regime, with no discrimination by origin, destination (only services were restricted for foreign entry) or degree of ownership. Over time, the regime be-

came more discriminatory, with the government exercising case-by-case approval to ensure that the technology was in line with national priorities (and new technologies were targeted), domestic technology benefited and certain performance requirements were met. Where domestic firms were strong, FDI was discouraged; where they were weak, foreign firms were made to transfer technology and contribute to the development of local capabilities. The government also sought to maximize benefits from FDI for local firms by promoting local sourcing and subcontracting — one of the most successful strategies for enhancing technological and skill linkages with foreign firms in recent times. This promotion was done by setting local content rules, insisting on foreign firms transferring skills and technology to subcontractors and raising the technological capabilities of local firms. The case of Singer in Taiwan is a well-known early example of successful subcontracting promotion of this sort. The local content policy was used extensively in Taiwan to promote technology upgrading among SMEs, which, unlike their counterparts in Japan (where long-term, stable relations with a few large buyers were the norm), competed aggressively for orders, switching customers, seeking out foreign joint venture partners and drawing on government assistance to upgrade their technologies.

The Taiwanese government also played a direct role in attracting advanced technologies by entering into joint ventures with technological leaders. For instance, when it found that Taiwan was lagging behind Korea in semiconductor production, and that local firms were too small to undertake the cost of setting up facilities, the Electronic Research and Service Organization (ERSO) started to import and develop process technologies for very large integrated circuits in the late 1970s. A decade later the government set up a joint venture for wafer fabrication, the Taiwan Semiconductor Manufacturing Company (TSMC), with Philips of the Netherlands and local private interests. Apart from manufacturing, TSMC orchestrated the design and manufacturing activities of numerous small electronics firms. Later private companies entered into production of semiconductors, microprocessors and related products.

Finally, the case of Korea represents the strongest selective strategy towards FDI. In accessing foreign technology, Korea preferred externalized technology imports to the maximum possible extent. FDI was permitted when it was the only way of obtaining the technology or gaining access to world markets; and even then the government encouraged local control by promoting majority Korean-owned or equal joint ventures. In some cases foreign investors were even induced to sell out after the technology had been absorbed locally (the most recent case is that of the Daewoo automobile company with respect to General Motors). In recent years, under pressure from its trading partners, the Korean government has liberalized its foreign investment law.

Upgrading SMEs

Perhaps the most important challenge to African policy makers in industrial development is the technological upgrading of the myriad medium, small and micro enterprises that form the backbone of industry and provide the bulk of employment. This sector includes large numbers of traditional enterprises that do not need technological improvement (in the modern sense) since they are based on very localized markets and simple technologies. However, it also comprises a number of enterprises that can enter the 'modern' industrial sector, linking up with larger enterprises

or being independent producers. This is the seedbed of modern industrial entrepreneurship in Africa, and could be the catalyst for the growth of new manufactured exports.

Available estimates suggest that SMEs account for roughly 60 percent of the workforce and 25 percent of industrial output in value terms in Africa. Compared to larger firms, they tend to use less capital per worker and have the capacity to use capital productively. For example, it has been found that in countries such as Colombia, Ghana, and Malaysia, small firms have significantly higher value-added to fixed assets ratios. Their choice of techniques is thus consistent with factor availability in African countries, which are labor-abundant economies. SME development in many African countries has been hindered by many economy-wide and sector-specific problems, including:

- Excessive state involvement in the economy which prevented indigenous entrepreneurs from gains managerial experience in dynamic medium and large-scale enterprises;

- Monopolies and subsidies given to public enterprises, and rules and regulations which stifled entrepreneurship;

- SMEs have been starved of capital and other inputs with credit directed to larger enterprises, even when practical experience has shown that it is possible to lend profitably and effectively to SMEs; and

- SMEs have scant access to foreign funds and foreign direct investment, reducing their ability to upgrade their technology and managerial know-how.

The process of increasing liberalization and globalization that is putting large industries as well as SMEs under increasing pressure has now compounded these problems. Large industries and SMEs are required to compete with the industrially advanced countries at a time when markets are more competitive and more volatile than ever before. A more open trading environment requires SMEs to compete with imports and increase their exports of industrial goods; but foreign producers are becoming more competitive and export markets are ever-more demanding in terms of quality, delivery and product features.

On their own, large as well as small firms will find it extremely hard to overcome these challenges. Whereas in the past it was conceivable for a single firm to meet all the input and technology requirements for its output, the degree of sophistication and expertise required to produce goods at internationally acceptable standards have made it necessary for firms to cooperate in their operations. As successful experiences have shown, for industries to succeed in the current economic environment, forming horizontal and vertical linkages is important. The factors that prompt industries to form networks and alliances to compete effectively in the current and rapidly changing global environment include:

- *The emergence of new exporting opportunities*. Existing and new markets are opening up as countries liberalize their trade under the auspices of the WTO and business becomes more globalized. While offering better exporting opportunities, these developments also pose considerable challenges. In order to access these markets or defend themselves against foreign competition in their own markets,

it is imperative that African SMEs adopt a global outlook and form strategic partnerships, both domestically and in foreign markets. For example, they could form strategic alliances with strong foreign distributors as a way of accessing new markets, while at the same time improving the quality of their products.

- *Non-price competition is becoming increasingly important*. The process of liberalization and globalization has made non-price competition increasingly important. These encompass all those factors, other than price, that affect market performance. African SMEs have traditionally tended to focus attention on production, sometimes at the expense of quality. SMEs will have to pay more attention to non-price elements such as packaging, quality, international standardization and timely delivery of products. Successful SMEs are going to be the ones that respond rapidly to changing customer needs. Strategic partnerships through industry linkages provide flexibility to allow SMEs meet such requirements.

- *Emergence of knowledge-based production structures*. Developments in information technology, transport, agriculture, manufacturing and finance are likely to erode further the competitiveness of African SMEs even in areas where Africa traditionally held a comparative advantage. If African firms are to respond effectively to changing customer needs and take advantage of changing production incentives, it will be imperative that they improve their technological capabilities. To keep up with these changes, African

SMEs will have to form strategic alliances with the providers of technology, giving them access to state-of-the art production techniques. African SMEs could also forge joint ventures with foreign firms. Forming joint ventures has a number of advantages to local firms. Involvement with a foreign company not only gives the domestic firm access to its partner's technology, but through learning-by-doing it may be able to adapt that technology to local conditions. Foreign firms can also supply technically skilled and managerial personnel.

The technological upgrading of SMEs is a very difficult task in all circumstances. The sheer number and dispersion of small enterprises makes any extension and support difficult to organize. Small size hampers the enterprises from undertaking the training, technical research and marketing investments needed for progress. In developing countries, many SMEs are unaware of their own technological problems, and are unable to articulate them sufficiently to take advantage of services on offer. They are unable or unwilling to pay the cost of many services, even if these may yield longer-term profits. Entrepreneurs from rural or traditional backgrounds, with low levels of education, are hostile to the use of modern technologies. Larger enterprises are reluctant to strike up supply or subcontracting linkages because of the costs inherent in bringing SMEs to requisite technical and reliability standards. These problems are not unique to Africa — they are prevalent in Asia, including the dynamic NIEs. However, the governments of the NIEs have been able to mount policies to overcome some of these handicaps and bring SMEs into modern industrial and export activity.

As industry liberalizes and restructures in Africa, the quality and spread of industry-support services has to improve, especially for firms to become exporters. For instance, the export of manufactured products to Europe increasingly requires adherence to strict quality standards, and the International Standards Organization's ISO 9000 series of quality management certificates is becoming a major asset in world markets. The technology infrastructure in most African countries is weak.

Although standards institutions exist in many countries and provide mandatory testing, calibration and certification services, they do not play an active role in disseminating and improving technology. Research institutions, where they exist, tend to be poorly staffed and funded, and do little work relevant to industrial needs. They do not provide information on the costs and characteristics of foreign technologies to African firms, and do not import and adapt them for local users. Their structures and incentive systems tend to be bureaucratic, with little motivation for going out to industry and meeting their needs. Universities and technical colleges have relatively little contact with industry, and industry in turn rarely goes to them for technical information and assistance.

Yet industry in the process of adjustment needs a strong and active technology infrastructure. The experience of the Asian NIEs (see Box 5.7.) again bears this out. All the NIEs invested heavily in such infrastructure. Take the case of quality standards: each Asian NIE made concerted efforts to promote the ISO 9000 standards. In late 1993, for instance, the number of ISO 9000 certified companies were: Hong Kong 10, Indonesia 8, Malaysia 224, Singapore 523, Taiwan 96, Korea 87 and Thailand 9. By late 1995, the numbers were much larger: Hong Kong around 200, Malaysia

Box 5.7: SME Development: Learning from the Asian Tigers

Singapore: In the 1970s the Small Industries Finance Scheme was set up to encourage technological upgrading in SMEs. Later, the Venture Capital Fund was set up to help SMEs acquire capital through low interest loans and equity. A Small Enterprises Bureau was established in 1986 to act as a one-stop consultancy agency – helping SMEs with management and training, finance and grants, and co-coordinating assistance from other agencies. In addition, the Singapore Institute of Standards and Industrial Research (SISIR) undertakes technology dissemination activities and helps exporters with information on foreign technical requirements. The National Productivity Board provides management advice and consultancy to SMEs. The Technology Development Center assists local firms identify their technology requirements and designs technology upgrading strategies. The Economic Development Board encourages subcontracting to local firms through its Local Industries Upgrading Program, under which MNEs are encouraged to source components locally by 'adopting' particular SMEs as subcontractors.

Taiwan: In 1981 the government set up the Medium and Small Business Administration to support SME development and co-ordinate the several agencies that provide financial, management, accounting, technological and marketing assistance to SMEs. The Taiwan Medium Business Bank, the Bank of Taiwan, the Small and Medium Business Credit Guarantee Fund, and the Small Business Integrated Assistance Center also provides financial assistance. The China Productivity Center, the Industrial Technology Research Institute (ITRI), has provided management and technology assistance. Government covers 50-70 percent of consultation fees for management and technical consultancy services for SMEs. The Satellite Factory Promotion Program of the Ministry of Economic Affairs integrates smaller factories around a principal one. By 1989 there were 60 networks with 1,186 satellite factories in operation, mainly in the electronics industry. In addition, the Program for the Promotion of Technology Transfer maintains close contact with foreign corporations that have developed leading-edge technologies in order to facilitate the transfer of those technologies to Taiwan. Closed links have been established between industry, universities and academic research institutes through the National Science Council's $200 million annual research grants.

South Korea: In the 1980s Korea took several initiatives to promote SME development: a host of tax incentives were provided; a credit guarantee scheme; a specialized bank to finance SMEs. A number of other institutions were set up, such as the Small and Medium Industry Promotion Corporation to provide financial, technical and training assistance and the Industrial Development Bank to provide finance. To promote subcontracting by the giant *Chaebols,* the government enacted a law designating parts and components that had to be procured through SMEs and not made in-house; by 1987 about 1,200 items were so designated, involving 337 principal firms and some 2,200 subcontractors, mainly in the machinery, electrical, electronic and ship-building fields. Generous financial and fiscal support was provided to subcontracting SMEs to assist in their operations and process and product development. In addition, subcontracting SMEs were exempted from stamp tax and were granted tax deductions for a certain percentage of their investments in laboratory and inspection equipment and for technical consultancy.

around 700, Singapore over 1,000, and Indonesia 60. The region is now the furthest advanced in the developing world in terms of ISO accreditation. Its standards bodies are playing aggressive roles in propagating the advanced quality management, and providing assistance and consultancy services. In 1994, the whole of sub-Saharan Africa, excluding South Africa, had less than 10 ISO 9000 certified manufacturing firms on the whole, and it appears that the numbers have risen only very gradually since.

Asian governments give strong financial and technical support to industrial firms seeking to improve quality and achieve ISO 9000 accreditation. In the process, the standards institutions have had to be restructured and upgraded. The case of the Standards and Industrial Research Institute of Malaysia (SIRIM) is of interest to Africa because it is a new institution, and combines the functions of a standards and metrology body with that of industrial research and extension. Its recent restructuring towards a market and private sector orientation has greatly increased its relevance to Malaysian industry. There are clear lessons for other countries in this.

The Korean government's support for the technology infrastructure is one of the most impressive in the developing world. In 1966 it set up KIST (Korea Institute of Science and Technology) to conduct applied research of various kinds for industry. In its early years, KIST focused on solving simple problems of technology transfer and absorption. In the 1970s, the government set up other specialized research institutes related to machinery, metals, electronics, nuclear energy, resources, chemicals, telecommunications, standards, shipbuilding, marine sciences, and so on. These were largely spun off from KIST, and by the end of the decade there were 16 public R&D

institutions. The government's strategic thrust in this sphere was mainly a series of national R&D projects launched in 1982. These were large-scale projects which were regarded as too risky for industry to tackle alone but which were selected as being in the country's industrial interest. National projects were conducted jointly by industry, public research institutes and the government, and covered activities like semiconductors, computers, fine chemicals, machinery, material science and plant system engineering. Centers of excellence were formed in these fields to boost Korea's long-term competitiveness. National Projects were a continuation of the strategy of interventions to identify and develop the country's dynamic comparative advantage, orchestrating the different actors involved, underwriting a part of the risks, providing large financial grants, and directly filling in gaps that the market could not remedy. Strategic technological activities are still targeted and promoted, and National Projects continue today.

Other policy measures to stimulate technological effort in Korea included the setting up of Science Research Centers and Engineering Research Centers at universities around the country to support R&D activities, the common utilization of advanced R&D facilities by smaller private firms, and the construction of science towns. Daeduk Science Town has been under construction since 1974, and a large number of research and educational institutions are already well established there. The construction of Kwangju Science Town has started; others are planned. Technology diffusion was advanced by the Korea Institute for Economics and Technology, which collected, processed and disseminated scientific and technical information to industry.

It is also worth looking at one aspect of the Indian technology infrastructure policies. This concerns the government's efforts to reform the public research institutes under the Council of Scientific and Industrial Research (CSIR). The role of these 34 large institutions in improving industrial technology was seriously questioned in the 1980s. They had turned out to be expensive, largely 'ivory tower' institutes, with little linkages to industry, producing technologies with little commercial application and doing research that industry had little use for — very much on the lines of the research institutes found in Africa, though on a much larger scale. The Indian government decided to reform the CSIR institutes to encourage greater co-operation with private industry. In 1991 a project was launched (with World Bank support) to promote industry-sponsored research at a number of public research institutes as well as universities and private research foundations. A Sponsored R&D (SPREAD) Program was initially allocated $15 million, and later another $10 million, to promote research awareness in industry, especially among SMEs, and reorienting the research culture of the research laboratories and higher education establishments to practical industrial needs.

The fund financed the contracting of research at subsidized interest rates, at 6 percent initially and 15 percent subsequently, or with a royalty option. The finance covered up to 50 percent of the cost of the research project contracted by industry, with the resources given as conditional loans (with eventual repayment at market rates if successful and written off if not). The projects covered prefeasibility studies, laboratory trials, prototype building and pilot plant operations for the development of new products and processes, significant improvements to existing products/processes and scaling up of a technology. The fund was administered by a leading private sector development finance company, whose technology unit appraised the projects put forward. By mid-1995, 53 firms had contracted 55 projects under the SPREAD program, with an average project size of $400,000 and a loan component of $170,000 (42.5 percent). So far, there have been no failures, but some 3-4 projects have been cancelled. Most of the companies using the program had never contracted research to a public research institute before. Their activities were spread over a range of industries: pharmaceuticals, electrical and electronics, chemicals, machinery, metallurgy, automotive, biotechnology, food processing, paper, rubber and polymers. Some 60 different technology institutes were involved, including 16 institutes of technology and science, 12 universities, four private research foundations, and 28 government laboratories. Broad ranges of new or improved technologies were developed, some fairly sophisticated. Overall, the project is highly successful, and the subsidy element was minimal.

This experience shows that existing research institutes can be reformed under the right set of signals and market incentives. It calls for appropriate financing measures and for a good intermediary that knows the industrial sector and has the technical capability to evaluate and monitor projects. Until this experiment was carried out, the potential demand for contract research in Indian industry was not known or appreciated.

In sum, a strong and pro-active technology infrastructure is necessary for the long-term upgrading of competitive capabilities of African industry. In a period of adjustment to market forces, all such services need to be strengthened. The main thrusts here should be to select industry clusters that are of greatest importance to each country and concentrate infrastructure resources on identifying their most pressing technological needs and meeting them. Research institutes should be made to earn a larger proportion of their keep (40 percent is the figure most countries aim at) from the sale of their services. At the same time, their equipment and skills should be improved, and industry should be offered financial incentives to subcontract research to the institutions. The promotion of quality awareness and adoption of international norms of quality management should be attempted by public campaigns backed by financial assistance for firms. The relevant standards institutions should be strengthened greatly and motivated to reach out to industry. The private sector should be encouraged to participate to the extent possible by setting up laboratories and consultancy services. There are considerable foreign resources available for quality and standards bodies, which Asian countries have been able to tap. African governments should explore these.

Promoting R&D by Industry

The level of R&D by industry in Africa is very low. Overall R&D shares in national income are low, and the great bulk of it is in agriculture and other activities rather than in industry. At the firm level, formal R&D is rare, and where firms claim to be doing it they generally mean production engineering and quality control/testing rather than technology development. For much of industry this does not matter for immediate purposes, since the main gap in Africa lies in the ability to master and adapt technology rather than to develop new technologies.

The line between mastering, adapting, im-

proving and adding to technologies is not a firm one, and as firms mature they move from one kind of technological activity into another. As the technologies used grow more complex, moreover, it becomes necessary for firms to set up formal R&D facilities in order to absorb and adapt technologies, even though they are not innovating in any real sense. Thus, the NIEs have increased their R&D investments significantly in recent years. Korea spends over 2 percent of GDP in R&D, Taiwan around 1.8 percent, and Singapore around 1 percent. Malaysia, Thailand and Indonesia spend much less (around 0.2 to 0.4 percent); but even this is far in advance of what takes place in African industry.

The Korean and Taiwanese experience may be instructive. Industrial R&D in Korea was promoted by a number of incentives and other forms of assistance. Incentive schemes included tax-exempt technology development reserve funds, tax credits for R&D expenditures as well as for upgrading human capital related to research and setting up industry research institutes, accelerated depreciation for investments in R&D facilities and a tax exemption for 10 percent of cost of relevant equipment, reduced import duties for imported research equipment, and a reduced excise tax for technology-intensive products. The Korea Technology Advancement Corporation helped firms to commercialize research results; a 6 percent tax credit or special accelerated depreciation provided further incentives. The main drive for rising R&D in Taiwan came, as in Korea, from the export-orientation of the economy, combined with measures to reduce dependence on technology imports. However, Taiwan's lighter industrial structure constrained the growth of private sector R&D in comparison to Korea's. However, the Taiwanese example is of greater relevance to African countries rather than Korea's. Not only do African countries have large numbers of SMEs, they also lack the political economy that is needed to create and discipline large private firms along Korean lines. The Taiwanese strategy involves less detailed direction of economic activity and resource allocation. The cost of this is that it entails much more pervasive and persistent support for research and development for small enterprises that are unable to undertake it themselves.

Summary and Conclusions

Globalization is one of the titanic forces driving structural change in world economics. Unleashed by the forces of technology, liberalization and instantaneous communications, globalization is redefining the bases of the competitiveness of nations and firms, and also throwing up new challenges for nations large and small. Globalization has, in its wake, amplified global market forces, making them increasingly important in the daily lives of virtually all the world's people. It has led to greater economic, political, and cultural interdependence among the nations of the world. It would indeed become difficult to find any corner of the world that is not affected in one way or other by this sweeping development. The phenomenon, which accelerated in the last decade of the 20th century — and which is likely to be a defining characteristic of the 21st century — is perhaps one of the most potent forces for change that mankind has witnessed.

While a number of developing countries benefited much from the changes brought about by globalization, we must also be aware of the continuing disparities between the developed and the developing world. The forces of globalization, relying on rapidly changing technologies and innovations, are still largely driven by developments and changing perceptions in the advanced countries. This has in turn introduced an element of volatility in global economic relations. The Asian financial crisis of 1997 was, for example, exacerbated by rapid and massive capital outflows. Similarly, the September 11 attacks in Washington and New York – which were themselves symbolic of the resentments and alienation fostered by globalization — have lead to a sharp decline in investment and capital outflows from the industrialized countries, with its attendant adverse impact on the economic well being of developing countries.

Despite occasional setbacks, there can be little doubt that globalization will continue and that it will profoundly affect the prospects of all developing countries. The leaders of the developing world therefore have a major task to formulate strategies that will allow their countries to share in the benefits and opportunities offered by globalization while at the same time seeking to reduce its possible adverse effects. The question is how best to harness the forces of globalization to improve economic performance and to help raise standards. In the paradigm of structural transformation proposed in this report, the roles of the state and the private sector are pivotal to poverty reduction (see Box 5.8).

This study shows that Africa, more than any other region of the world, faces the danger of being left behind by the rapid changes being brought about by the forces of globalization. African countries will need to build on the achievements of the recent past and deepen their economic reforms so as to make their economies more competitive and their countries more attractive for foreign investment. In this respect, it is important to distinguish between two groups of countries. The first is composed of African emerging markets – such as Morocco, Tunisia, Egypt in North Africa and Botswana, Mauritius

Box 5.8: PRSPs, the Private Sector and the State

The Poverty Reduction Strategy Paper (PRSP): The Poverty Reduction Strategy Paper is the country business plan for growth and poverty reduction. It integrates poverty reduction policies into a coherent macro-economic framework, and explicitly links the choice of public policies to their impact on poverty reduction and private sector growth. The country-owned PRSP now provides the basis for concessional assistance and guides the use of resources freed by debt relief under the enhanced HIPC initiative. The PRSP could also provide the framework for overcoming the weaknesses that thwart the development of the private sector. As can be learnt from East Asia, lasting development and poverty reduction require a true transformation of society driven by the countries themselves in close coordination with the civil society and the private sector.

The private sector as key: Poverty reduction efforts require more than an emphasis on implementing social programs; they also entail a greater focus on policies and investments to promote the productive sectors so as to create employment and enhance competitiveness. Improving access for African countries to world markets is also a key element of poverty reduction strategies. This implies the need to look more closely at the efficiency and equity impacts of tax and public expenditure policies. Under the framework for a private sector-led poverty reduction strategy, lie three well-established facts:

- Firstly, poverty is multi-faceted; hence, poverty is measured along several dimensions such as income, health, education, and social capitals such as skills and quality of labor;
- Secondly, in developing economies especially, it is predominantly the private sector which

creates and enhances value, hopefully with the public sector generally playing a supportive role in facilitating technology transfer and reducing private transaction costs; and

- Thirdly, with economic value created, the public sector generally takes the lead in redistribution. Redistribution not only provides a safety net but also has the potential for building up the asset base of households and thereby developing capabilities for participation in value-creating activities in the future.

Hence, poverty reduction entails increasing the rate of growth and enhancing fair redistribution of the gains from growth by way of public expenditure. Redistribution can be expedited to alleviate poverty through direct transfers of public resources to the poor, via public investments in social overhead capital, for example infrastructure, vocational training, etc.

The role of the state: For the poor to be better served, the state will continue to intervene in the social sectors and in up-front investments in infrastructure, and when possible in partnership with the private sector. This calls for quality in government and also for effectiveness in the delivery of services, financial accountability, transparent procurement, the establishment and maintenance of the rule of law, property rights and freedom of information. Successful policy making must reach out to all stakeholders; and it must also be seen as a joint responsibility. African governments must become more open to change and must be prepared to play a more creative and catalyzing role in boosting productive investment.

and South Africa in Southern Africa -- whose economies are quite diversified and which have made notable progress in strengthening their relations with the industrial countries. African emerging markets can therefore be expected to be in a position to increasingly take advantage of the possibilities offered by globalization. The second group of countries comprises the large number of low-income countries of the region. For this group, the Cotonou Agreement between the ACP countries and the EU and the Africa Growth and Opportunity Act of the US have opened up new possibilities for enhanced economic relations with the industrial world. Yet, there can be little doubt that globalization continues to pose major challenges. They will need to deepen and intensify their economic reform programs in order not to be left behind.

Most African economies will need to accelerate their economic growth rates by raising the levels and productivity of investment. Important measures in this regard include: continuing the gains made in creating macroeconomic stability; strengthening banking systems to enhance domestic resource mobilization; and developing capital markets by accelerating the pace of privatization and broadening the domestic investor base. Such measures will need to be complemented by efforts to attract larger volumes of foreign private capital inflows. These are essential for augmenting domestic savings and investment and to accelerate growth rates. In particular, efforts have to be invested in reforming and strengthening judicial and legal systems and putting in place effective and transparent regulatory frameworks. The experience of a number of African countries, such as Egypt, Morocco, Tunisia, Mauritius, Botswana, Uganda, and Mozambique have shown that it is indeed possible both to raise growth rates and attract large volumes of international capital once the appropriate policy framework is in place.

The need to enhance the competitiveness of Africa's traditional exports and to diversify them is absolutely vital for the long-term growth and sustainability of Africa's economies. In the course of the last decade, Africa has lost market share in some of its traditional exports. Clearly this trend has to be reversed by putting in place the necessary policy framework to assist producers enhance their competitiveness in the global market. In addition, there is a need to build market niches for products where world demand is high and technological progress rapid.

Africa needs no less than a new industrial vision. As the experience of successful developing countries has shown, foreign capital is essential in such an endeavor not only to provide the requisite resources but, as important, to introduce the modern technology so necessary to compete in the global marketplace. In addition, there is a need to strengthen R&D capacity, improve the framework for SMEs and build support services that enhance FDI and private sector development.

African countries will also need to increase their investments in the development of their human capital. Such investments are crucial for developing a labor force and managerial know-how, able to compete in today's global economy. And in this regard, as the HIV/AIDS pandemic and the resurgence of malaria now weigh heavily on Africa's human-capital development, it is essential that African countries take the necessary measures to arrest the spread of these diseases.

The prospects for Africa's economic growth, as well as its potential for an increased role in the global economy, would also be considerably enhanced if current regional integration and cooperation arrangements were to be strengthened. Indeed, such efforts must be seen as a necessary intermediate step to enable African countries to play a greater role in the global economy. But in seeking to strengthen regional economic ties, African countries need to promote such efforts within a framework of *open regionalism*. This would aim at putting in place the necessary protocols and arrangements to encourage the joint production of goods and infrastructural services within a larger economic space. Countries would then be able to take advantage of economies of scale allowing them in turn to compete more vigorously in the global market. Within such regional frameworks, tariff barriers should not be set at excessively high levels, as this would discourage the emergence of enterprises that could compete on the international level.

Critical to all this is the need for African countries collectively to coordinate the implementation of NEPAD, and in particular, ensure that they uphold the standards and norms of democratic governance and sound public management under the peer review mechanism. These commitments will need to be complemented by adequate international assistance, especially in three areas: the provision of concessional resources; debt relief; and improved access for African exports to the markets of the industrialized countries.

Concessional resources will continue to be needed to capitalize a large number of African economies, in view of the limits to effective domestic resource mobilization. These resources are important for sustaining economic reform and for helping countries develop the capacity to compete in the global market. They are also essential in creating the necessary social and physical infrastructure to attract private capital

flows. International development assistance to Africa has unfortunately declined in the last decade even as African countries implement far-reaching social and economic reforms. It is our hope that the donor community will, in the coming years, reverse this decline as it honors its commitment to the Millennium Development Goals, as well as its earlier pledge of committing 0.7 percent of GNP to ODA. It is also our hope that the recent events will not lead to either a decrease or a diversion of ODA flows from Africa.

Although Africa's debt burden has begun to decline, many African countries continue to have unsustainably high debt levels that hinder their development. Debt service obligations burden the budgets of governments, divert investment resources from key social and economic sectors, erode the confidence of the private sector, and weaken the prospects for sustainable growth and for reducing poverty. As debt relief accelerates under the HIPC initiative, we are optimistic that Africa's debt and debt-service will indeed decline significantly. Continued support of the international community will, however, be required if HIPC debt relief is to be implemented effectively. Moreover, as the expected slowdown of the global economy is likely to result in serious terms-of-trade shocks for many countries, it is essential for the international community to ascertain that the HIPC debt relief provided to poor countries will indeed lead to sustainable debt levels.

CHAPTER 6
Africa's Responses to Globalization

Introduction

The overriding message of the preceding chapters is that globalization constitutes both a challenge and an opportunity for Africa. In spite of various economic reform efforts, the majority of African countries have failed not only to diversify their production structures and their export baskets but also to diversify their external markets. It is also apparent that the success of regional integration schemes in Africa depends largely on the extent to which African countries succeed in transforming their economies and diversifying their export patterns. As has been argued previously, many African countries have very similar export baskets and, hence, trade liberalization would not in itself lead to the generation of substantial inter-African trade. To overcome these challenges, Africa needs a new vision of development, a vision that takes on board all the lessons of four decades of development, and which is anchored on the paradigm of structural transformation. The principal theme of this chapter is that structural transformation has to be pursued within the framework of *open regionalism* and in partnership with Africa's international development stakeholders.

Africa's long-running development challenges and its marginalization in the world economy have not arisen for a lack of attempts or strategies to deal with the continent's crisis. The responses have been at various levels, including national policies, regional integration experiments and numerous bilateral and multilateral initiatives. This chapter examines the *collective* policy responses that African nations have taken to address the challenges posed by globalization. It also considers some of the initiatives that have been taken at the global level to help reverse Africa's downward spiral into global marginality. It then discusses the framework for a new African and global agenda to reverse Africa's marginalization. Finally, the role of the African Development Bank Group in financing and promoting external resource inflows is described.

The African Union and its Precursors

Even before the establishment of the Organization for African Unity (OAU) in 1963, African leaders had realized that cooperation and integration among African states in the economic, social and cultural fields were essential for rapid transformation and sustained development of the African continent. This was concretized in the objectives of the OAU Charter, as well as at the OAU Summits of 1973 and 1976, and the Monrovia Declaration of 1980. In 1980, the OAU Extraordinary Summit adopted the Lagos Plan of Action as a major step towards achieving integration and African leaders stated their commitment to promote the economic integration of Africa, and to that end to establish national, regional and sub-regional institutions leading to a dynamic and interdependent economy, thereby paving the way for the establishment of the African Economic Community (AEC).

In June 1991, the Abuja Treaty establishing the AEC was signed by OAU Heads of State and Government. The AEC was launched in May 1994 as the OAU/AEC. The Abuja Treaty provided for the AEC to be set up by a gradual process (in six stages – see Box 6.1) that would be achieved through the coordination and progressive integration of the activities of existing and future regional economic communities (RECs) in Africa. The total transition period was expected to last 34 years. The RECs were regarded as the building blocks of the AEC.

In the Abuja Treaty, the concept of the Community, its eventual take-off and its progressive establishment were closely interrelated with the process of cooperation at the regional level. Accordingly, a protocol on relations between the AEC and RECs was concluded and signed in 1998. The protocol is the instrument and framework for close cooperation, program harmonization and integration among the RECs on the one hand, and between the AEC and the RECs on the other. However, the adoption of the Constitutive Act of the African Union during the 2000 OAU/AEC Summit in Lomé, Togo, necessitated a structural review of the Abuja Treaty.

At its final meeting in July 2001, the OAU announced its decision to transform into the African Union (AU) in the year 2002. The OAU had provided both practical resources and political backing for countries in their struggles against colonialism; it had also helped to mobilize the battle against the apartheid regime in South Africa. The OAU was however hindered in its activities by internal conflict and self-serving heads of state. Critics allege that the OAU protected the interests of the heads of state without addressing the real problems; it did little to address the problems plaguing the continent (Steinberg, 2001). The AU was proposed by Libyan leader Moam-

Box 6.1: The Six Stages for Implementation of the African Economic Community

I.   Strengthening existing RECs and creating new ones where needed (5 years).

II. Stabilization of tariffs and other barriers to regional trade and the strengthening of sectoral integration, particularly in the field of trade, agriculture, finance, transport and communication, industry and energy, as well as coordination and harmonization of the activities of RECs (8 years).

III. Establishment of a free trade area and a customs union at the level of each REC (10 years).

IV. Coordination and harmonization of tariff and non-tariff systems among RECs with a view to establishing a Continental Customs Union (2 years).

V.   Establishment of an African Common market and the adoption of common policies (4 years), and

VI. Integration of all sectors, establishment of an African Central Bank and a single African currency, setting up of an African Economic and Monetary Union and creating and electing the first Pan-African Parliament (5 years).

Source: OAU Department of Foreign Affairs; Abuja Treaty (Article 6).

mar Al Qaddafi as a more effective institution. At the Fourth Extraordinary Session of the OAU General Assembly at Sirte, Libya, in September 1999, Heads of State and Government met and "deliberated extensively on the ways and means of strengthening our continental Organization to make it more effective so as to keep pace with the political, economic and social developments taking place within and outside our continent". The Sirte Declaration – 'Towards a United Africa' – (see Box 6.2) spelled out the rationale for the transformation.

The Constitutive Act establishing the Union was adopted in Lomé, Togo in July 2000, and it recognized the need for Africa to face the challenges posed by globalization. Some of the objectives of the AU are shown in Box 6.3.

Box 6.2: Excerpts from the Sirte Declaration – Towards African Unity

"As we prepare to enter the twenty-first century, and cognizant of the challenges that will confront our continent and peoples, we emphasize the imperative need and a high sense of urgency to rekindle the aspirations of our peoples for stronger unity, solidarity and cohesion in a larger community of peoples transcending cultural, ideological, ethnic and national differences.

"In order to cope with these challenges and to effectively address the new social, political and economic realities in the world, we are determined to fulfill our people's aspirations for greater unity in conformity with the objectives of the OAU Charter and the Treaty establishing the African Economic Community (the Abuja Treaty).

"It is also our conviction that our continental Organization needs to be revitalized in order to be able to play a more active role and continue to be relevant to the needs of our peoples and responsive to the demands of the prevailing circumstances.

"We are also determined to eliminate the scourge of conflicts which constitutes a major impediment to the implementation of our development and integration agenda…"

Source: Sirte Declaration, September 2001.

The Constitutive Act adopted several elements of the Abuja Treaty such as the introduction of a Pan-African Parliament which is "to ensure the full participation of African peoples in the development and economic integration of the continent". Other elements of the Abuja Treaty (now signed and ratified by all 53 member states of the African Union) were the introduction of a Court of Justice of the Union as well as three financial institutions, namely, the African Central Bank, the African Monetary Fund, and the African Investment Bank. The AU intends to harmonize the economic and political policies of all African nations in order to improve pan-African welfare, and provide Africa with a strong voice in international affairs. This is in recognition of the fact that most regions of the world are forging bigger economic blocs and Africa does not want to be left behind. One of the aims is to reduce obstacles to trade among member states and the general idea is to first build regional blocs in West, East, Central, North and Southern Africa and ultimately merge them into one economy. A common currency is envisaged. In essence, Africa is hoping to follow the EU's example to achieve peace, unity and prosperity. It is hoped that the AU will have the authority to achieve economic and political integration among member states, as well as work towards a common defense, foreign and communications policy. Several issues, however, remain to be solved (Steinberg, 2001). These include:

- Economic disparities between member states;
- Historical perspectives, such as the existence of regional alliances;
- Political disparities, some countries are yet to embrace democratic principles;
- Threat of foreign interests that conflict with regional interests;

Box 6.3: Selected Objectives of the African Union

Determined to take up the multifaceted challenges that confront our continent and peoples in the light of the social, economic and political challenges taking place in the world; and convinced of the need to accelerate the process of implementing the Treaty establishing the African Economic Community in order to promote socio-economic development of Africa and to face more effectively the challenges posed by globalization.....have agreed that.... The African Union is hereby established in accordance with the provisions of this Act.

The objectives of this Union shall be to:

a) Achieve greater unity and solidarity between African countries and the peoples of Africa;
b) Accelerate the political and socio-economic integration of the continent;
c) Encourage international cooperation, taking due account of the Charter of the United Nations and the Universal Declaration of Human Rights;
d) Promote peace, security and stability on the continent;
e) Promote democratic principles and institutions, popular participation and good governance;
f) Promote sustainable development at the economic, social and cultural levels as well as the integration of African economies;
g) Promote cooperation in all fields of human activity to raise the living standards of African peoples;
h) Coordinate and harmonize the policies between existing and future Regional Economic Communities for the gradual achievements of the objectives of the Union....

Source: Constitutive Act of the African Union.

- The presence of multi-nation states (deriving from colonial history), which has contributed to the frequency of conflicts and wars in Africa; and
- Challenges posed by mass poverty, etc.

These issues have to be resolved if the AU is to be more successful than the OAU. The New Partnership for Africa's Development (NEPAD) is the instrument that the Union hopes to use to revive Africa's economy and promote its integration into the global economy.

The NEPAD Strategy

During 2001, African leaders took the initiative to draw up a new program for Africa's development. The program resulted from a merger of two initiatives — the Millennium African Renaissance Partnership Program (MAP) and the OMEGA Plan – variously led by the governments of Nigeria, South Africa, Algeria, and Senegal. The two documents were presented at an extraordinary meeting of the OAU in March 2001, which recommended their fusion. The two plans were initially merged into a single plan dubbed the New African Initiative that was adopted by OAU Heads of State in Lusaka, Zambia in July 2001. In October 2001, the Implementation Committee at a meeting in Abuja, Nigeria, renamed it as NEPAD.

NEPAD represents a pledge by African leaders, based on a common vision and a firm and shared conviction, that they have a duty to eradicate poverty and to place their countries on a path of sustainable growth and development. The program is anchored on the determination of Africans to extricate themselves and the continent from the malaise of underdevelopment and exclusion in a globalizing world (NEPAD, 2001). The ultimate goal is to bridge the gap between African and the developed countries "by bridging existing gaps in priority sectors to enable the continent catch up with developed parts of the world." NEPAD is envisaged as a long-term vision of an African-owned and African-led development program.

NEPAD is based on a double strategy – the use of the region as the basic operational space on the one hand, and the resort to substantial private investment on the other. As with the Abuja Treaty and the AU, NEPAD has opted for development based on the five regions and not on individual states, on the basis that the only way out of Africa's predicament is through a regional approach that offers larger markets to industries and more opportunities for foreign investments. Unlike in the past, where development was government-driven, NEPAD has decided to turn to the private sector as a key factor for growth and a source of capital needed for development in Africa. NEPAD is to encourage the development of an African private sector, including participation by African business people both within the continent and in the diaspora.

NEPAD emphasizes African ownership and a commitment on the part of leaders that the destiny of Africa lies in their hands. Sections 5 and 6 emphasize that "Africans are neither appealing for the further entrenchment of dependency through aid, nor for marginal concessions." Rather, Africa possesses in abundance or within its reach, the resources, including capital, technology and human skills, that are required to launch a global war on poverty and underdevelopment.

The long-term objectives of NEPAD (see Box 6.4) are to eradicate poverty in Africa and to place African countries, both individually and collectively, on a path of sustainable growth and development and thus halt the marginalization of Africa in the globalization process. NEPAD aims to achieve and sustain an average gross domestic product growth rate of above 7 percent per annum for the next 15 years, and to ensure that the continent achieves the agreed International Development Goals. The initiative is focused on four core elements (Kohler, 2001). These are:

- A clear awareness that peace, democracy, and good governance are preconditions for reducing poverty;
- Action plans to develop health care and education systems, infrastructure and agriculture;
- Reliance on the private sector and on economic integration at the regional and global levels; and
- More productive partnership between Africa and its bilateral, multilateral, and private sector development partners.

NEPAD and Globalization

NEPAD is essentially a response to Africa's exclusion from the globalization process. The document states:

"The poverty and backwardness of Africa stand in stark contrast to the prosperity of the developed world. The continued marginalization of Africa from the globalization process and the social exclusion of the vast majority of its peoples constitute a serious threat to global stability.... While globalization has increased the cost of Africa's ability to compete, we hold that the advantages of an effectively managed integration present the best prospects for future economic prosperity and poverty reduction".

NEPAD recognizes that while globalization is a product of scientific and technological advances, many of which are market-driven, governments, especially those in the advanced countries, have played an important role in shap-

Box 6.4: The New Partnership for Africa's Development - An African Framework for Faster Growth and Development

The New Partnership for Africa's Development (NEPAD) is a pledge by all of Africa's leaders to eradicate poverty and move towards sustainable growth and development. The partnership focuses on African ownership of the development process and seeks to reinvigorate the continent in all areas of human activity. Through the partnership, African leaders have agreed to:

- Strengthen mechanisms for conflict prevention, management, and resolution;
- Promote and protect democracy and human rights by developing standards for accountability, transparency, and participatory governance;
- Restore and maintain macroeconomic stability;
- Implement transparent legal and regulatory frameworks for financial markets;
- Revitalize and extend education, technical training and healthcare services;
- Promote women's role in social and economic development;
- Promote the development of infrastructure, agriculture, agro-processing, and manufacturing to meet the needs of export and domestic markets and local employment.

The NEPAD document draws Africa's attention to the seriousness of the continent's economic challenges, the potential for addressing them, and the challenges of mobilizing support for change. The main strategies proposed include:

- Fostering conditions for long-term peace, security, democracy, and good governance by, among other things, building capacity for early warning systems, addressing political

and social vulnerabilities, combating the illicit proliferation of small arms and light weapons, and implementing institutional reforms of public services;

- Promoting the provision of regional and sub-regional public goods such as water, transportation, energy, environmental management, and other infrastructure- notably telecommunications;
- Developing education and human resources at all levels, and in particular increasing the role of information and communication technology in education and training, inducing a "brain gain" for Africa, and eliminating gender disparities in education;
- Increasing domestic resource mobilization and accelerating foreign investment;
- Creating a more conducive environment for private sector activities, with an emphasis on domestic entrepreneurs;
- Promoting the inflow and effective use of official development assistance (to support the provision of international public goods in Africa) by reforming systems for delivering and evaluating aid;
- Pursuing gender equality in education, business, and public service;
- Supporting efforts by the Economic Commission for Africa to strengthen Poverty Reduction Strategy Paper Learning Groups.

Source: ECA, 2002, Economic Report for Africa 2002.

ing the form, content and course of globalization in partnership with the private sector. Experience of previously poor countries that have reaped the benefits of globalization show that globalization does not automatically reduce poverty. National authorities and private institutions have a role to play in guiding the globalization agenda along a sustainable path so that the benefits are evenly spread. It required the commitment on the part of governments, the private sector and other institutions of civil society, to the genuine integration of all nations into the global economy and body politic. NEPAD was of the view that it is within the capacity of the international community to create fair and just conditions in which Africa can participate effectively in the global economy and body politic (NEPAD, 2001).

NEPAD is primarily a new way of doing business. It is based on concepts of African ownership, good governance within Africa, mutual accountability of Africans and development partners towards development outcomes, and concrete steps to be taken to mainstream the private sector as the viable vehicle for Africa's long term development. Development of the African private sector partly depends on domestic investment climate but also depends on improved market access abroad. Three key functions of NEPAD germane to best practice performance for coping with globalization include: (i) the African Peer Review Mechanism (APRM) which is modeled after the OECD-DAC peer review mechanism although NEPAD includes political governance in addition to economic and corporate governance; the objective of the APRM is to identify strengths and weaknesses in government institutions and policies in order to recommend how weaknesses can be overcome; (ii) monitoring the Millennium Development Goals — which entails upgrading information gathering and analysis systems on the continent, and

finding ways of making the findings relevant to policymaking; (iii) the key feature of mutual accountability — all development partners should be accountable for outcomes, and all should have responsibility to promote best practices.

Support for NEPAD

The Heads of State and Government of the G8, the eight major industrialized democracies, and the representatives of the EU, meeting with African leaders at Kananaskis, Canada, in 2002, welcomed the NEPAD initiative, which they considered a bold and clear-sighted vision for Africa's development (see Box 6.5). They committed themselves to establishing enhanced partnerships with African countries that are committed to implementing NEPAD. They were determined to match Africa's commitments by their own efforts to find peace in Africa, to boost expertise and capacity, to encourage trade and direct growth-oriented investment, and to provide more effective official development assistance. The focus would be on countries that demonstrate a political and financial commitment to good governance and the rule of law, investing in their people, and pursuing policies that spur economic growth and alleviate poverty. The G8 Action Plan covers the following areas:

- Promoting peace and security;
- Strengthening institutions and governance;
- Fostering trade, investment, economic growth and sustainable development;
- Implementing debt relief;
- Expanding knowledge: improving and promoting education and expanding digital opportunities; and
- Improving health care and confronting HIV/AIDS.

Box 6.5: The G8 — Why We Support NEPAD

- Half of Africans live on less than -$1 per day, Africa is the only continent where poverty is on the rise,
- Africa is the only continent where the average life-span is becoming shorter, it is 16 years less than in the next lowest region, and has dropped 3 years in the last ten years,
- Africa is the only region where school enrolment is declining at all levels, and particularly among women and girls,
- While Africa accounts for 13 percent of the world's population, Africa's exports account for less than 1.6 percent of global trade, and that figure is falling,
- Africa currently attracts less than 1 percent of global investment, it is the only major region to see per capita investment and savings decline since 1970, as much as 40 percent of Africa's own savings are not invested within the continent,
- Total net Official Development Assistance (ODA) to Africa has fallen from previous levels of $17 billion to $12 billion today,
- African leaders have emphasized good governance and human rights as necessary preconditions for Africa's recovery,
- African leaders have formally undertaken to hold each other accountable for their individual and collective efforts to achieve NEPAD's economic, political and social objectives.

Source: G8 Africa Action Plan Highlights, Kananaskis Summit, Nova Scotia, Canada, 2002.

Dissenting voices

While the advanced countries generally welcomed the NEPAD initiative, there have been a number of dissenting voices from Africa (African Civil Society Declaration on NEPAD, 2002; CODESRIA, 2002; Bond, 2002). Critics argue that NEPAD sidelines past endeavors for the development of Africa by African themselves, such as the Lagos Plan of Action (1980), the Abuja Treaty (1991), etc. NEPAD, they argue, is only concerned with raising external financial resources, appealing to and relying on external governments and institutions. Past initiatives were undermined by policy frameworks developed from outside the continent and, crowding out Africa's own alternative thinking on development. NEPAD has also been criticized for being elitist and top-down in its approach, having been drawn up by a few Heads of State, and virtually excluding civil society in its preparation. Also, the neoliberal economic framework of the plan has been criticized as being a continuation of orthodox structural adjustment policies that have been increasingly discredited by the harsh realities of African economic experience over the last two decades. Other critics have argued that NEPAD will lead to further foreign exploitation and plunder of Africa's rich natural resources, rather than mobilizing them for the benefit of Africans and that continued engagement with institutions such as the IMF, World Bank, the WTO and developed countries will further lock African economies disadvantageously into this environment.

Other responses to the challenges of globalization have emerged from the civil society sections of African development stakeholders. Notable in this regard is the *Independent Commission on Africa and the Challenges of the 21ˢᵗ Century*, which is responsible for initiating ideas for the *African*.

Millennium Project (see Box 6.6). Professor Albert Trevoedjre, former Deputy Director General of the International Labor Office and former Beninois Minister of Planning, Economic Restructuring and Employment Promotion first mooted the idea, which later received the endorsement of UN Secretary-General Kofi Annan, and a proposal was subsequently developed by the UNDP, which also provided initial funding.

In spite of its critics, NEPAD holds out a promise to re-launch Africa's development based on shared interests and reciprocal obligations with Africa's international partners. However, it is yet to be seen whether the AU will be able to overcome many of the problems that hindered the erstwhile OAU in implementing past plans of action for the continent. Another problem is likely to be encountered in the area of financial resources, as it is expected that the continent would need to mobilize $65 billion for the implementation of NEPAD.

Africa has responded to the challenges of globalization by developing a vision statement to develop Africa and to ensure that Africa is integrated into the global economy. The question is whether NEPAD will be any more successful than past development programs. The answer to this see to lie in the domain of political and economic governance in Africa.

Initiatives To Promote African Trade

Africa needs better opportunities for trade if African countries are to integrate into the global economy. They need to be provided with freer access to the markets of industrial countries, especially those areas that are important to most poor countries such as agricultural products, textiles and clothing. Agricultural subsidies in

Box 6.6: The Millennium Project for Africa

The Millennium Project for Africa was established in 1999 as an independent commission to undertake reflection and analysis of Africa's prospects in the 21st century. The objectives of the African Millennium Project are to:

- Mobilize the entire political and economic leadership of Africa, opinion leaders, of the private sector and of civil society, by making them more aware of the new opportunities that the world can offer Africa at the dawn of the third millennium;

- Help African leaders formulate strategies and judicious measures to be taken with regard to Africa's entry into the 21st century;

- Indicate new cooperation measures that are more dynamic by incorporating the possibilities offered by the South-South dimension, of which a more active solidarity with the Arab world, a promising technological experience with Asia, and special opportunities brought in by the African diaspora;

- Specify the contribution of Africa to its own development and to the development of international solidarity.

The Independent Commission, the cornerstone of the project, comprises native Africans, as well as those from the diaspora, who are independent of any governmental or intergovernmental agency and who are known for their competence, integrity and commitment to the promotion of innovative approaches to development. The Commission's deliberations will evolve around the problems that undermine the continent's advancement. In addition, the Commission will identify challenges that must be taken up during the next century. The African Development Bank, the Global Coalition for Africa and the Intergovernmental Agency of *La*

Box 6.6: (continued)

Francophonie has been established to supervise the project and approve its program of work.

In June 2000, the members of the Commission noted the critical obstacles that must be overcome if Africa is to succeed in the 21st century: poor infrastructure; financial disadvantage; political instability; insecurity brought about by conditions of war, crime and other forms of destabilizing violence; and political, cultural and religious intolerance. These problems have "frequently lead the most skilled members of African society, those in whose development the continent has committed its most significant investment, to leave Africa altogether and seek to apply their skills elsewhere." It called on African leaderships and the international community to put in place policies that would help Africa overcome its dependence by revolutionizing its modes of agricultural production: "Without the means to feed its own workforce... Africa cannot achieve appropriate development of its infrastructure and industrial potential."

Source: The Independent Commission on Africa and the Challenges of the Millennium, Cotonou, 2002.

rich countries amount to almost $1 billion a day, roughly six times the level of aid to developing countries. According to Nicholas Stern, "It is hypocrisy to encourage poor countries to open up their markets while imposing protectionist measures that cater to powerful special interests in the rich countries" (IMF, 2002a). The average European cow receives about $2.50 a day in subsidy, while the Japanese cow receives $7.00 a day. In sub-Saharan Africa, 75 percent of the population live on less than $2 a day. Developing countries will therefore benefit from a lowering of industrial country tariffs. It is argued that substantial trade liberalization in the Doha Round of multilateral trade negotiations

was vital for global growth. The September 2002 communiqué of the International Monetary and Financial Committee also stressed that "urgent progress is essential in enlarging market access for developing countries and phasing out trade-distorting subsidies in developed countries. Developing countries should also further liberalize their trade regimes to maximize growth and development opportunities". Gains from eliminating tariff and quota restrictions on merchandise trade will far outweigh annual aid budgets.

Since the mid 1990s, out of concern for the continued marginalization of Africa, several initiatives, multilateral and bilateral have emerged, which if exploited could enhance the economic growth of the region and contribute to the reduction of its gaping poverty. Among these are the African Growth and Opportunity Act (AGOA), the Cotonou Partnership Agreement signed in June 2000 between the EU and 77 African Caribbean and Pacific (ACP) countries, and the EU's 'Everything but Arms' (EBA) initiative promulgated in February, 2001. Further trade preferences are also underway through the Doha Round that began in January 2002.

AGOA

In 2000, the US adopted AGOA to promote exports from some African countries (see Box 6.7). As part of US general policy to support the development of Africa and to end the marginalization of continent, the Act provides duty free access to the US markets of products originating from African countries. One of the premises of the Act is that it is more beneficial to developing and low-income countries, particularly African countries to have unrestricted export access to markets in developed countries than to be denied access and given aid.

AGOA-based eligibility to duty free access is, however, conditional on these countries demonstrating determination to have established, or to be making progress towards, the establishment of the following: market-based economies; the rule of law and political pluralism; elimination of barrier to US trade and investment; protection of intellectual property; efforts to combat corruption; policies to reduce poverty; increasing availability of healthcare and educational opportunities; protection of human rights and worker rights; and, elimination of certain child labor practices. As at January 2002, 34 African countries had been certified as meeting the criteria to export, quota free and duty, several items produced in Africa.

It is still too early to statistically measure the impact of AGOA on Africa's access to and participation in global trade. In general, a significant portion of African exports has traditionally gone to Europe with US, excluding petroleum imports, accounting for about 15 percent. All the same, some countries, such as Mauritius, could conceivable increase their export of textiles. There is an element of policy lock-in in AGOA since qualifying countries have measurable and enforceable policy commitments; any reversal from these policies could mean loss of access to US market.

The Cotonou Partnership Agreement

A successor to the Lomé Partnership Agreement between the African, Caribbean and Pacific (ACP) states and the EU was signed in Cotonou in 2000. The new Agreement covering 77 countries, of which 48 are in Africa, aims to promote economic, cultural and social development of the ACP states, with a view to enhancing peace and security and to promoting a stable and democratic political environment. The objec-

tive of the Agreement is the integration of ACP economies into the world economy, leading to the stimulation of growth and poverty reduction. The Agreement has four main components:

- Reinforcement of the political dimension of relations between ACP States and the EU;
- Poverty reduction within the context of the objectives and strategies agreed at international level;
- An innovative economic and trade cooperation framework; and
- Rationalization of financial instruments and a new system of 'rolling programming'.

The political dimension involves regular political dialogue to promote peace-building policies, conflict-prevention and resolution and good governance and the promotion of regional and sub-regional organizations. The economic and social dimensions include country ownership of development program, development of capacity in policy formulation and implementation, articulation of development strategies for poverty eradication investment promotion and private sector development and human capital development. Others are regional cooperation and integration, gender, environmental and natural resources development and institutional development and capacity building.

Unlike the Lomé Convention under which trade cooperation was based essentially on preferential tariffs, the new Agreement's main objective is to promote the progressive integration of the ACP countries into the global economy, by enhancing production and the capacity to attract investment, and ensuring conformity with WTO rules. The new approach emphasizes trade liberalization, including the adoption of

Box 6.7: The African Growth and Opportunity Act (AGOA)

In June 2000, the U.S. Congress passed the African Growth and Opportunity Act. Among other benefits, the Act eliminated US duties on textile imports from eligible sub-Saharan countries — a benefit not just for those countries but also for the international textiles industry, which is always seeking new low-wage countries with good access to industrial country markets.

The preferential tariffs provided by the Act have been an important boost to the textiles industry in Madagascar, one of the first countries to qualify for benefits. Textile exports surged in 2001, and in the first half of the year US imports from Madagascar totaled $133 million - a 115 percent jump from the first half of 2000. Among the most visible beneficiaries of the textiles boom are women who previously earned low, unpredictable incomes selling produce or working in rice fields. Moreover, the boom has spread to other industries such as construction and engineering. Formal employment has more than doubled boosting tax revenue. In addition, foreign investment has risen sharply in Madagascar and the 12 other sub-Saharan countries that have qualified for trade benefits under the US legislation. Lesotho has plans for more than $120 million in new investment. In Kenya the Act could create 50,000 jobs directly and another 150,000 indirectly.

Conditions to be fulfilled:

The US designated African countries eligible to benefit from AGOA subject to various conditions, including:
- Establishing a market economy,
- Developing political pluralism and the rule of law,
- Eliminating barriers to US goods and investment,
- Protecting intellectual property,
- Fighting corruption,
- Having policies to reduce poverty,
- Improving access to health care and education,
- Protecting human and worker rights, and
- Eliminating certain child labor practices.

The eligible countries:

Benin, Botswana, Cameroon, Cape Verde, Central African Republic, Chad, Congo, Djibouti, Eritrea, Ethiopia, Gabon, Ghana, Guinea, Guinea-Bissau, Kenya, Lesotho, Madagascar, Malawi, Mali, Mauritania, Mozambique, Namibia, Niger, Nigeria, Rwanda, Sao-Tome, and Principe, Senegal, the Seychelles, Sierra Leone, South Africa, Tanzania, Uganda, Zambia, and most recently Swaziland.

Source: OECD/ADB 2002: African Economic Outlook.

transparent competition policy, the protection of intellectual property rights, standardization and certification.

Financial cooperation, which is to be based on assessment of need and policy performance, will cover debt (support for debt relief) and structural adjustment support; support in cases of short-term fluctuations in export earnings; support for sectoral policies; and micro projects and decentralized cooperation. Over the 2000-2007 period, the EU has committed financial resources amounting to 25.1 billion to support development in the ACP States.

'Everything But Arms'

The EU has also demonstrated a very important gesture by proposing to grant the LDCs non-reciprocal, duty-free access to their markets under the Everything But Arms (EBA) initiative[1]. Effectively, 34 African countries would benefit but it would help if it were extended to all middle and low-income developing countries — and most African countries would then be eligible. For Europe, the potential short run negative impact of such a policy is negligible, compared to the potential medium to longer term gains – with more prosperous Africa providing larger markets for European goods, requiring less aid from Europe, and less migration pressure on Europe. Furthermore, by granting EBA status to almost all African countries, it would eliminate the potential complications of the rules of origin. Nevertheless, it is argued that if EBA is strictly enforced to benefit only the LDCs, it runs the risk of hindering the integration efforts of the African sub-regions.

There is a problem of capacity to exploit the benefits from these preferences (UK-DFID, 2000). Reducing policy barriers — in developing countries themselves, as well as in developed countries — is important, but not enough to guarantee expansion of trade. For example, under the Lomé Convention, the EU gave preferential market access to ACP countries, but exports from these countries to the EU fell from £16 billion in 1985 to £14 billion in 1994. Barriers that prevent poor people from engaging in trade, or from increasing production in response to new market opportunities, need to be removed. Transport costs are often a particular obstacle to trade. A halving of transport costs could double the volume of trade.

The Doha Round

The WTO was created in 1995 to oversee the GATT that had guided rules of international trade since 1947. The GATT role was to codify and record a series of tariff reductions and provide a structure to give credibility to those reductions. A key concept of GATT which underpins the present global trading system is non-discrimination between different sources of the same imported good which is achieved by required members to give each other most favored nation (MFN) treatment, except in specified circumstances. In addition to administering GATT rules, the WTO has far-reaching powers, requiring member countries to subscribe to virtually all its rules rather than treat some as optional. The Doha process, which seeks to integrate trade with the development agenda (see Box 6.8) is of particular importance for African countries.

The WTO can enhance the economic well-being of developing countries in four ways: (i) if sufficient members wish, it can organize periodic rounds (such as Seattle and Doha) of tariff negotiations that offer opportunities and incentives to members to reduce their barriers to trade; (ii) it provides for domestic policy, including providing informational support to members in debates shaping trading laws; (iii) it can protect the rights of members against certain rules violation by other members (court decisions and penalties); and (iv) it can provide a forum and mechanism for governments to manage the spillovers from members trade policies onto their partners. These four avenues provide the framework for assessing the WTO's current rules about regional integration arrangements. An enabling clause significantly relaxes the conditions for creating regional integration arrangements that include only developing countries.

Notwithstanding the good intentions of GATT/WTO rules, the application of the rules has not been evenhanded. Developed countries of the North and their regional trading arrangements, while giving notional support to open trade, continue to maintain restrictive policies that deny access to their markets of goods from developing countries.

Debt Relief, Poverty Reduction and Trade Diversification

For many years, the proposal to provide substantial debt relief to African and other developing countries was resisted by leading creditor nations, especially the US, Germany and Japan. Subsequently, traditional buyback methods were used to deal the Africa's commercial debts while the Paris Club provided mechanisms for rescheduling official bilateral debts. Until the early 1990s there was especially strong resistance to writing off debt owed to multilateral institutions because of fears that it might set a precedent and jeopardize the soundness of the multilaleral development banks.

The rising magnitude of the indebtedness and the potential consequences of the debt over-

Box 6.8: Trade and Development – The Doha Round

The new round of global trade negotiations, dubbed the Doha Development Round, began in January 2002. The negotiations are focused on agriculture and so are crucial to African prosperity. Member countries of the WTO have agreed to negotiate better access to their agricultural markets, reduce trade-distorting support for domestic agriculture, and eventually eliminate subsidies for agricultural exports. A level playing field would enable African farmers to compete more effectively in both domestic and export markets, and could generate an additional $400 million a year for Africa.

Africa's main goals during the negotiations are for WTO members to:

- Substantially reduce or eliminate all tariffs on agricultural products, including quota duties.
- Substantially reduce or eliminate all tariff escalation (that is, when a processed product has a higher tariff than an unprocessed product).
- Simplify complex tariffs - say, by converting all tariffs to an ad valorem or fixed percentage of a product's value.
- Substantially reduce or eliminate market-distorting export subsidies and domestic support.
- Recognize the special needs of the world's least developed countries.

Successful negotiations will require active participation by all of the WTO's 143 members. Africa's concern that it was poorly equipped to participate in the Doha Round was answered by pledges from the international community to help build capacity in complex trade negotiations. This is important, because Africa has committed to negotiating new issues such as investment, competition policy, and environmental concerns.

The Doha Round ministerial declaration confirms the right of developing countries to pro-

Box 6.8: (continued)

vide access to affordable versions of otherwise costly-patented drugs during public health emergencies. This is an important breakthrough for African countries, many of which are struggling with the ravages of HIV/AIDS.

Source: ECA, 2002, Economic Report on Africa 2002.

hang on the economic survival of developing countries, particularly those in Africa, ultimately led to the development of a mechanism, the Highly Indebted Poor Countries (HIPC) Initiative to deal with debt of the relevant countries on a case-by-case basis. Following the introduction of the HIPC initiative, Africa's debt stock has begun to decline, from $337.2 billion in 1999 to some $298 billion by end-2002. With GDP increasing while the debt stock fell, Africa's total debt to GDP ratio fell from 61.4 percent in 1999 to an estimated 54 percent in 2002. Despite this positive development the present value of debt as a proportion of exports of goods and services exceeds 200 percent in many countries.

The success of the HIPC initiative will depend on the international community fully funding the initiative and extending its coverage to other countries. The impact on debt reduction will meanwhile depend on eligible countries designing and implementing effective poverty reduction strategies that efficiently utilize the considerable budgetary resources that would now be available to them. The Enhanced HIPC introduced new features to facilitate quick delivery of resources. Although the initiative

has instituted an incentive-driven mechanism for providing debt reduction assistance, it is widely acknowledged that many African countries, including those that have actually received debt relief from the Initiative still face unsustainable debt service problems. Many African countries continue to suffer the effects of their marginalization and are unable to participate in expanding world trade and investment. More attention still needs to be devoted to factors that would enhance African participation in global trade, perhaps through regionally coordinated adjustment programs aimed at removing constraints to investment and trade promotion through appropriately designed and anchored regional integration arrangements.

With respect to international aid to Africa, there is a continuing debate about the purpose of external finance. Development thinking on the role of aid has gone full circle in the last 50 years, and has shifted almost decade by decade. However, the stated goal has always been to solve the problems of underdevelopment and reduce the incidence of poverty in poorer countries. In the 1950s and 1960s, aid was to finance the domestic savings gap and the balance of payments gap to promote growth. During the 1970s, it was thought that growth was not enough for poverty reduction, and aid served more of distributive purposes by helping to meet the basic needs of the poor in terms of basic education and health, rural roads, water, sanitation and shelter. The oil price and commodity price shocks of the 1970s led to the collapse of these economies thereby requiring fundamental adjustments. During the 1980s up to the mid-1990s, aid supported structural adjustment in the hope that it was paramount for growth, which in turn would reduce poverty. Aid in the 1990s also funded democratization and good governance, environmental issues, social justice and humanitarian relief. In 1999, both the World Bank and the IMF re-emphasized poverty reduction as the central mission. The World Bank launched its Comprehensive Development Framework (CDF) and the IMF renamed its Enhanced Structural Adjustment Facility (ESAF) as the Poverty Reduction and Growth Facility (PRGF) and replaced the contentious Policy Framework Paper (PFP) with the Poverty Reduction Strategy Paper (PRSP). This was, in part, a response to the international development goals to halve poverty by 2015. In the enhanced HIPC Initiative, debt relief is conditioned on measurable efforts to reduce poverty (largely through increased spending on the social sectors).

Elimination of poverty is the ultimate objective of development. However, analysts often disagree on how best to attain the objective. For some, in circumstances of pervasive poverty, policies to resume high growth are the surest bet. Such an approach might entail massive investment in infrastructure, effective governance institutions, developing export capacity and capability, skill acquisition and upgrading, etc. For others, an immediate impact can be experienced through increasing consumption and social services (health and education). These are also believed to be growth fundamentals. Others prefer programs that directly target the poor — including community development projects. Alternative spending plans would have different impacts depending on the rates of return on different sectors and their feedback effects on growth and poverty.

Determining which investments would have the highest payoffs would require country-specific analysis. Such country and regional needs-assessment approach would certainly be different from the swings of fads and fashions based on a one-size-shoe-fits-all approach. As part of the new aid regime, there is stress on 'ownership' by recipients of the development programming. Programs to be funded by aid are supposed to result from an orchestrated participatory process involving the major stakeholders, interest groups and NGOs in the recipient country. However, the reality is that donors prescribe the boundaries of their national programs by their emphasis on the social sectors and by requiring immediate impacts on poverty.

Cross-country growth regressions point to a laundry list of equally important growth determinants. But Africa faces binding resource constraints. Take the example of a country with a fixed annual aid receipt of $200 million. This amount is barely enough to finance either universal education up to the 9th grade, or universal access to quality health care, or repair and upgrading of basic infrastructure — roads, ports, electricity and water, etc. Assume that in this country also, the unemployment rate for primary and secondary school graduates is about 50 percent. Given the binding budget constraint, it is evident that spending the $200 million on education may not be the most immediate priority or the most efficient way to utilize it. On the other hand, a country could be one with a barely 20 percent adult literacy rate. In this case, education might have the highest immediate payoff.

The scenario above therefore calls for careful country analysis/planning involving proper prioritizing and sequencing of how to deploy external finance. Such an exercise should be guided by the considerations of the efficiency/productivity of alternative investment. More importantly, it should be guided by the potential of the particular spending to contribute to future growth and source of repayment of the capital. A major reason for past failures is insufficient attention to issues of priorities and sequencing or to the rates of return. Most analysis and projections regarding what aid should finance implicitly assume that aid is going to be available forever and in the quantity required. Unfortunately, that is not the case. With aid falling, spending tends to spread too thinly (and mostly for consumption purposes) to be effective for a sustainable exit strategy.

What should an exit strategy look like? We argue that such a strategy is one that addresses the fundamental traps of these economies—especially their structural vulnerability. Past aid programs (including the McNamara basic needs model) failed to address the issues of capacity and capability, especially the diversification of production structures and export competitiveness. As a consequence, once shocks emanating from these deficiencies hit the economies in the late 1970s, they literally wiped out all the gains made in the earlier decade, and two decades of adjustment have not returned the economies to their per capita income in the early 1970s.

UNCTAD has argued that "one of the biggest development challenges facing LDCs on the eve of the twenty-first century would appear to be how to establish the necessary export capacity to produce goods and services on a competitive basis" (UNCTAD, 1999). More broadly, it observed that "the most pressing development concern of LDCs on the eve of the twenty-first century could be encapsulated as how to address supply-side constraints to enable the countries to produce more competitively for domestic as well as international markets". If one is looking for a niche for aid, and one that would have the highest payoff in the medium and longer-runs, production diversification and competitiveness might be it.

In the context of small economies, export diversification is critical to Africa for several reasons. First, investment in these economies depends on imported capital goods and intermediate inputs. Domestic savings cannot readily be translated into investment without requirements for foreign exchange. Exports remain the only dependable and sustainable source of foreign exchange for these economies. Secondly, given the constraints of size, exporting is the surest guarantee for reaping the benefits of economies of scale (circumventing the problems of capacity utilization or absorptive capacity), learning by doing, etc. Thirdly, diversification of exports is the bulwark against the volatility in their terms of trade and vulnerability from excessive dependence on few primary commodities. Fourthly, exporting generates surpluses, which can be invested in other sectors. Fifthly, developing export capacity is an important signal to foreign direct investors that the economy is a profitable business address. Firms usually cluster in environments with a critical mass for networking. Thus, breaking into export markets can also unleash a momentum for an inflow of long-term capital. Finally, diversification of exports is the surest way to regain shares of global trade. Africa has been locked into sectors with low-income demand elasticity. Export diversification and capability thus appears to have multiple benefits in terms of sustainable long-term financing as well as feedback effects on the rest of the economy.

With falling aid, one area of spending in the transition period with potentially the greatest long-term payoff is diversifying the export base and building competitiveness. With the realized investible surplus from exporting, greater consumption as well as increased spending on the social sectors could be the second order priority. In this connection, the international community needs to re-visit the question of Africa's industrial development.

Since the 1980s, African countries have witnessed the phenomenon of de-industrialization. Much of traditional aid rhetoric focuses on poverty reduction and agriculture as the sole key to Africa's escape from economic backwardness. But such rhetoric has to face the fact that experience makes it abundantly clear that no nation can escape from destitution unless it ultimately embraces the imperative of industrialization. There is hardly a nation that escaped from the shackles of poverty without having in the long run developed a strong manufacturing base as a corollary to a productive agricultural sector. What it all boils down to is the fact that a rapidly urbanizing Africa, with its 800 million people, will simply be consigned to the status of a giant global ghetto of teeming unemployed youth, criminality and shantytowns, if it relies solely on agriculture and commodity exports and ignores the industrial sector, which in the long run, has to provide the bulk of employment for its burgeoning population as well as ensure relative self-sufficiency in the provision of basic consumer items.

Role of the African Development Bank Group

The African Development Bank (ADB) is Africa's premier financial development institution, dedicated to combating poverty and improving the lives of people of the continent and engaged in the task of mobilizing resources towards the economic and social progress of its regional member countries (RMCs). It is a multilateral development institution supported by 77 nations from Africa, North and South America, Europe and Asia. The Bank's mandate as stipulated in Article 1 of its founding Instrument is to "contribute to the economic development and social

progress of its regional members - individually and jointly." The Bank's mission, therefore, is to help African countries break the vicious cycle of poverty in which they are entrapped through mobilization of external and domestic resources — both public and private — for social and economic development.

The Bank's Vision focuses on promoting accelerated, sustainable economic growth with equity and poverty reduction as its central goal. The Bank believes that it can best implement it Vision through promotion of good governance, focusing on key sectors such as agriculture and rural development, regional integration, private sector development and programs that provide opportunities to the poor by improving their access to productive assets, technology, information and social services.

To fulfill its Vision the Bank is adopting a development assistance strategy that effectively promotes accelerated, sustainable economic growth with equity and poverty reduction as its central goal. This would be achieved through promotion of good governance as well as programs that provide opportunities to the poor by improving their access to productive assets, technology, information and social services. To bring the poor closer to the monetized economy, the provision of social services would be complemented by the provision of basic infrastructure. The ADB is one of several important players providing financial, policy and technical assistance to African countries. To maximize its development impact, the Bank must strive to ensure that its financial and staff resources are selectively targeted on projects, programs and advisory activities that represent priority elements in client countries poverty reduction strategies and are in line with the Bank's comparative advantages and division of responsibilities and partnership arrangements with other development partners.

Some recent developments afford important opportunities for accelerating progress on poverty reduction in Africa. A clear recognition has emerged among the OECD countries of the importance of paying increased attention to the problems of the low income countries, and in particular to the problems and challenges of African development, in the interests of global security, the control of communicable diseases and the promotion of global social equity. Accompanying this higher level of interest in Africa have been: (i) increased numbers of visits to Africa by top-level officials, including the US Treasury Secretary, that have helped focus media attention and increased public awareness on African issues; (ii) the decision that the G-8 Summit in June will place African development at the top of its agenda; (iii) the consensus reached at the Monterrey meetings on raising aid allocations, particularly for Africa; (iv) increased attention to low income developing country issues in the Doha global trade liberalization discussions; and (v) the consensus among donor countries to increase the proportion of IDA and ADF resources provided on grant terms.

The Bank has recently adopted a strategic plan for the 2003–2007 quinqennium, based on the following strategic priorities:

- Plan operational growth to utilize effectively available lending resources and the Bank's risk bearing capacity;
- Optimize resource application through greater selectivity in operations;
- Maximize the development effectiveness of country assistance interventions;
- Substantially strengthen the Bank's field presence by establishing a broader

network of field offices that are fully integrated into the Bank's management structure and work programs;
- Develop the Bank's human, institutional and knowledge management resources to enable the Bank to become the premier development institution for Africa;
- Enhance the Bank's organizational effectiveness by ensuring that all organizational units focus their activities in support of the Bank's strategic priorities;
- Maintain the Bank's financial soundness and operational efficiency.

Enhancing Development Effectiveness

The Strategic Plan places strong emphasis on enhancing the development impact of Bank Group operations, particularly in areas that contribute to attaining the Millennium Development Goals for poverty reduction. The Bank will give high priority to collaborating with the World Bank and other key multilaterals to develop quantifiable and measurable indicators for all sectors to monitor the expected development impact of Bank Group operations and progress towards achieving the desired outcomes. By 2003, all project documents will be required to contain clear and measurable indicators of expected development outcomes, and over the Plan period such indicators would continue to be refined. Achievement of intended development outcomes depends not only on the actions of the Bank, but also on the actions of client governments and their implementing agencies and of other development partners. Project documents will be required to spell out more fully the details of the country's development project or program that the Bank operation is intended to support, the actions to be taken by the various parties involved in implementation with the associated timetables and the expected development outcomes of the overall program. Project supervision will be carried out jointly, where feasible, with the other financing partners and will be required to monitor completion of expected actions by all parties involved in implementation, and to follow up where corrective actions are required.

Focusing Bank interventions at country level on fewer projects will permit greater Bank staff inputs into project preparation and appraisal. Field missions may be fewer in number but will comprise larger project teams that will seek to ensure that: (a) the underlying program that the project is intended to support is well designed, is a priority element in the country's poverty reduction strategy and has full government commitment; (b) expected development outcomes have been quantified and implementation benchmarks established; (c) key actions have been taken by government to set up the necessary policy framework and establish the required implementation arrangements ahead of loan approval; and (d) the Bank's role in the program is clearly identified, the expected impact of its contribution quantified and the implementation risks assessed. This should result in better quality at entry with shorter delays between loan approval, loan signing and first disbursement.

Expected development outcomes will only be achieved if the projects and the underlying programs they support are successfully implemented. Accordingly, the Plan aims to create a stronger implementation culture. Staff performance will be judged increasingly on the successful implementation of the projects for which they are responsible rather than the number of new projects they bring to the Board. With this in mind, supervision coefficients will be increased and supervision teams enlarged to allow thorough review of project and un-

derlying program progress and to ensure that implementation bottlenecks are addressed. The Annual Staff Performance Review format is being redesigned to give greater weight to supervision performance.

In line with the objectives of the recent Bank reorganization, project review and quality assurance procedures are being redesigned to more clearly assign responsibility for project quality and implementation success to Task Managers and their respective Division Managers. Project review procedures will focus on providing less frequent, but higher quality inputs at key points in the loan processing cycle, primarily at the project concept and post appraisal stages. Ex-post reviews will be undertaken periodically on a sample of recently approved projects to provide the Bank with a sounder basis for assessing progress in raising quality-at-entry standards. The Annual Project Performance Review (APPR) is being strengthened to more clearly identify projects at risk and to ensure that action programs to deal with problem projects are implemented vigorously. It will also focus more closely on progress in achieving expected development outcomes. Sector policies for almost all of the priority sectors have recently been revised. Emphasis during the next few years will be on disseminating these policies to staff and ensuring that they are fully reflected in operational designs and implementation follow-up.

The Bank will enhance the volume, quality and relevance of its knowledge-based support and analytical and advisory services. This will enable the Bank to better meet the special needs of individual client countries, including post-conflict countries and those for whom lending is not currently appropriate, as well as ADB countries whose demand for Bank assistance has been low. Complementing this will be: (a) implementation of a program of applied research on selected African development issues carried out in collaboration with international and regional research institutes; and (b) an expansion of workshops and seminars for RMC policy makers and senior officials provided through ADI/JAI to facilitate high level exchanges of views on vital development issues, including governance, communicable diseases and economic management.

An important additional step that will help raise the development effectiveness of the Bank's operations will be strengthening its field presence. In 1999 the Board approved a plan to reestablish a network of field offices in up to 25 countries as a key measure in improving dialogue with client countries, raising the Bank's profile at country level and enhancing implementation performance. Implementing this decision will be an important priority for the Strategic Plan. To date an initial set of four country offices have been opened. Based on the review of the operations of the existing field offices, the Bank has put forward proposals to open the next batch of four offices in 2003/4. It will aim to have a field presence established in 20-25 countries by 2006. The future models for field offices and their integration into the Bank's management structure are the subject of an ongoing. Based on cost considerations, staff availability and work program priorities, strengthening field presence in some countries may start with the appointment of a National Program Officer as an initial step towards eventually opening a full country office. In other cases, one Bank office may serve two or more countries. However, it is anticipated that the typical office would serve one country and have 8-10 staff, most of who would be recruited locally. Office staff would play a key role in strengthening country dialogue, and would have operational support, donor coordination and first level supervision responsibilities. Field offices would report to Country Directors and would be fully integrated into the Bank's work programs and management structure. The operational costs of field offices would be an integral part of the administrative budgets of the two Operations Complexes, which would carefully consider the costs and benefits, the potential for saving in HQ costs that would arise and the trade-offs with other operational priorities in deciding when to open and expand specific offices.

The Bank recognizes that the need to strengthen international economic cooperation and partnership has never been greater than today, and the stakes are high for Africa and the rest of the world. Recent events have provided strong signals that the international community shares this strategic approach broadly. Examples abound. At the Doha trade summit and the Monterrey meeting on Financing for Development, countries-developing and developed-signaled that they shared both this vision of development and views of the appropriate means of reaching shared goals. At the heart of this new paradigm is a transformed development partnership. African leadership and ownership of its policies and programs seeks a joint commitment to common agreed development goals, and mutual accountability in progress towards those goals. This represents an unbridled move from the past model of donor-imposed conditionalities towards self-monitoring and peer review among Africans. Another part of this new paradigm is having long-term predictable partnerships underpinned by guaranteed long-term resource flows to countries that have a clear commitment to these shared goals. This enhanced partnership entails supporting countries that will be the forerunners of Africa's transition from high aid dependency to a more robust development path led by the private sector.

The Bank seeks to seize this unique momentum through its 2003-2007 strategic plan, which contains specific, time-bound deliverables towards three desirables ends: achieving the International Development Goals, improving the results of development assistance, and fostering good governance and poverty reduction. In this context, the Bank will work to improve results by providing assistance in line with this strategic approach:

   (i) Selectivity across countries with enhanced performance-based allocations — ADF resources will go primarily to countries showing commitment to reform and good governance, and interventions will be tailored to country circumstances; and

   (ii) Selectivity within country — CSPs will be used to help focus Bank efforts and interventions. In close coordination with other partners, country-owned and country specific frameworks will guide the Bank's mechanisms for priority-setting and agreement on results, notably based on country's own PRSP.

The Bank will also aim to make appropriate use of all the instruments for assistance that are at its disposal: analysis and advice, programmatic approach, demonstration projects notably in SWAPS, and necessary steps that can support and signal a country's intention and commitment to reforms. The Bank has also continued to provide policy-based loans to support the creation of an enabling legal and regulatory environment for private sector activities. Direct support for private sector development has been

channeled through lines of credit and institutional support. Emphasis has been placed on providing assistance to small and medium scale enterprises through lines of credit to development finance institutions. Capacity building in regional member countries has been another major area of interest for the Bank. Technical assistance grants have been used for capacity building support, technical studies, and other components that support our regular projects and programs. In addition, the Bank has continued to provide training to officials of regional member countries in various disciplines. Further, the Joint Africa Institute, which was established in 1999 together with the IMF and the World Bank, had its first full year of operations and provided policy-related training to government officials and other participants.

Bank Group Financing Operations

Bank Group activities in 2002 totaled UA 2.04 billion, representing a slight decrease of 14 percent from the level attained in the previous year. The decrease was due in part to the delay in the finalization of the ADF-IX replenishment and also because of the difficult socio-political circumstances in the host country that impacted negatively on the Bank's operations. The Bank Group's activities comprised UA 1.07 million from the ADB window, UA 960.7 million from the ADF window, and the balance of UA 10.4 million from the Nigeria Trust Fund. Total approvals in 2002 covered 118 operations, including 50 project loans (5 to the private sector), 12 lines of credit (6 to the private sector); 7 structural adjustment loans; 1 sectoral adjustment loan; 30 technical assistance grants (8 for project cycle activities and 22 for institutional support); 1 project preparation facility (PPF) operation;

1 loan reallocation of unused loan balances, 2 operations under the supplementary financing mechanism, 8 HIPC debt relief operations in 5 countries (consisting of 2 ADB, 5 ADF and 1 NTF approvals) and 1 arrears clearance grant to assist in defraying arrears of the DRC to ADF. The Bank's Special Relief Fund provided grant resources for five emergency assistance operations to alleviate the effects of natural calamities that included a volcano eruption and the spread of the Ebola type hemorrhagic fever in Central Africa, severe flooding experienced in four RMCs and the drought in Southern Africa.

Bank Group operations in 2002 continued the trend of focusing more on critical sectors such as agriculture-rural development and the social sectors. Emphasis is placed on the two sectors, which accounted for over a quarter of the Bank Group's operations in 2002, because of their significant impact on efforts to alleviate poverty. The importance placed on agriculture and rural development and the social sectors was particularly pronounced in the case of ADF concessional resources that are specifically earmarked for financing poverty reduction activities in low-income countries. Altogether, the two sectors constituted close to 40 percent of ADF approvals in 2002. Particular emphasis was placed on fostering agricultural production, enhancing food security, and promoting income-generation activities, especially among the people living in rural areas. Social sector operations principally targeted support for education, health, and stand-alone poverty reduction projects aimed at improving the well being of the target population. Approvals to agriculture and rural development and the social sectors amounted to UA 491.1 million, or 30.1 percent of loans and grants approved

during the year. Lending to agriculture and rural development stood at UA 207.0 million for 24 operations, while approvals for 27 operations in the social sector accounted for UA 284.2 million. Approvals to the multisector category, consisting largely of economic reform programs and the promotion of good governance, amounted to UA 271.3 million (for 16 operations) or 17.1 percent of total Bank Group loan and grant approvals in 2002.

During the year, Bank Group support for infrastructure development included approvals for transportation, communication, water supply and sanitation projects, and increasing electricity generation in the power supply sector. Lending to these sectors amounted to UA 473.8 million (for 28 operations) or 29.9 percent of total Bank Group loans and grants. Approvals to the industry sector amounted to UA 15.5 million to renovate, refurbish and upgrade hotel facilities and for capacity building in mineral resource management. Lending to the finance sector accounted for UA 335.1 million (for 12 operations) or 21.1 percent of Bank Group approvals to finance small and medium scale enterprises. Approval to communication sector amounted to 90.4 (for one operation) or 5.7 percent of total Bank group loans and grants. Further details on Bank Group lending activities are provided in the respective sections on ADB, ADF, and NTF operations.

By end 2002, the Bank Group had cumulatively approved 2,643 loans and grants amounting to UA 31.45 billion since it opened its doors to business in 1967. ADB resources financed 60.6 percent of the total while ADF concessional resources accounted for 38.5 percent, with the remaining 0.9 percent coming from the NTF window. Fifty-two countries and several multinational institutions benefited from projects and programs in: agriculture and rural development (18.7 percent); transportation (16.0 percent); multisector (15.0 percent); finance (13.4 percent); social sectors (11.3 percent); power supply (9.5 percent); water supply and sanitation (7.0 percent); industry (6.0 percent); communications (2.9 percent); environment (0.05 percent); and urban development (0.01 percent). The regional distribution of cumulative approvals was as follows: 33.2 percent to member countries in the North Africa region; 24.6 percent to the West Africa region; 14.6 percent to East Africa; 13.7 percent to the Southern Africa region; and 12.2 percent to Central Africa countries. The remaining 1.8 percent went to multiregional operations to support regional cooperation activities.

Apart from its regular financing, ADF technical assistance operations through its Technical Assistance Fund (TAF) also continue to play a critical role in assisting RMCs in project-related activities such as feasibility studies, environmental impact assessments, sector and multisector studies, and detailed engineering studies, which enhance the capabilities of regional member countries to design, develop and implement development projects and programs. Such financing operations include activities aimed at building institutional capacity by strengthening national institutions and regional agencies that promote economic integration and cooperation among African countries. They serve further to bolster ownership and sustainability of programs. In 2002 the Board of Directors approved a total of 30 TAF operations for UA 46.6 million. Eight of these operations (UA 8.5 million) were allocated for project cycle activities and another 22 grants (UA 38.1 million) for institutional capacity building. Cumulatively, the Bank Group has approved 673 TAF operations amounting to UA 832.1 million. Project cycle activities account for

470 operations (UA 527.1 million), while institutional capacity building account for 203 operations (UA 305.0 million). The Project Preparation Facility (PPF) is an instrument by which the Bank assists RMCs to generate projects for the Bank's pipeline and also to ensure improvements in the quality of the projects at entry. In 2002, one PPF operation was approved for an amount of UA 0.4 million. Since the inception of the PPF facility in the year 2000, a total of 6 operations have been approved for a cumulative amount of UA 2.1 million.

The Bank Group's cofinancing activities are important in mobilizing resources for development in RMCs. Cofinancing activities involve a combination of Bank Group resources with those of other development partners — foreign and local official and private institutions — to finance projects and programs in specific sectors. During the period 1967-2002, the Bank Group approved a total of 755 cofinancing operations, valued at UA 72.74 billion with the Bank Group contributing UA 12.89 billion or 17.7 percent. Cofinancing in 2002 amounted to UA 4.11 billion for 31 projects and programs. Of this amount, the Bank Group contributed UA 678.19 million or 16.5 percent, local financiers and RMC governments contributed UA 1.26 billion (30.6 percent), and external cofinanciers contributed UA 2.17 billion (52.9 percent). In 2002, major multilateral cofinancing partners were the World Bank (UA 611.86 million), IMF (UA 198.36 million) and the EU (UA 203.70 million). The bulk of Bank Group contribution to cofinancing activities in 2002 went to the social sector, totaling UA 210.10 million. Projects in power supply received the second largest allocation (UA 182.22 million); multisector came third (UA 160.21 million), followed by agriculture and rural development (UA 76.34 million).

Debt Relief

The ADB has also been a major player in recent international debt relief efforts and has joint responsibility together with the World Bank for the management of the HIPC Trust Fund. Since the HIPC debt relief initiative was launched in 1996, the Bank Group has been an active participant, in collaboration with the Bretton Woods Institutions and other development partners. Under the original framework, the Bank Group provided debt relief to 4 countries, namely Burkina Faso, Mali, Mozambique, and Uganda. And under the enhanced initiative that came into force in 1999, it has provided interim relief to the 21 African countries that have so far reached their decision points, together with debt relief to Uganda, which reached its completion point at the start of the enhanced initiative. Among the 22 countries, the Bank Group has also concluded completion point agreements with 4 other countries – Burkina Faso, Mauritania, Mozambique, and Tanzania – that have since reached their completion points under the enhanced framework.

The Bank Group financed the debt relief to these countries from its own internal resources as well as from contributions made by bilateral donors through the HIPC Trust Fund. Under the agreement reached with ADF Deputies on June 30, 2000, the Bank Group agreed to provide US$ 370 million from its internal resources, with the balance to be financed from pledges by the bilateral donors. The ADF Deputies at their meeting on June 30, 2000 also endorsed management's proposed debt reduction modality. Following the Deputies meeting, the Boards of Directors of the Bank Group approved the participation of the Bank Group in the enhanced HIPC Initiative on July 6, 2000. The Boards also approved the proposed debt relief modality.

The Bank Group debt relief modality mandates it to deliver debt relief through annual debt service reductions, and to release up to 80 percent of annual debt service obligations as they come due until the total debt relief is provided. In addition, interim financing – between the decision and completion points – of up to 40 percent of total debt relief is provided, whenever possible, within a 15-year timeframe. This is to assist countries attain the internationally agreed MDGs for the year 2015.

With 22 African countries having reached their decision or completion points, and estimates having been revised for 7 other eligible countries, the Bank Group's costs for its participation in the HIPC Initiative has been accordingly adjusted. The total estimate for the 29 countries now stands at US$ 3.07 billion. This includes US$ 906.3 million for the DRC, which under the special arrears clearance scheme approved by ADF Deputies and the ADB Board is expected to be financed as follows: ADF contribution at US$ 43 million; donor contribution to ADB for partial payment at US$ 76 million; ADB contribution at US$ 615.2 million; HIPC Trust Fund contribution at US$ 172 million.

The Bank Group has to date approved debt relief to 22 African countries. Of these, 17 countries are decision point approvals, while for 5 countries (Burkina Faso, Mauritania, Mozambique, Tanzania, and Uganda) an irrevocable commitment of debt relief has been made, as these countries reached their completion points. Total approvals for these 22 countries currently stand at US$ 1.6 billion (in relevant NPV terms). This total could be subject to upward revisions if more countries qualify for topping-up operations as they reach their completion points. Seven other countries are expected to qualify for debt relief in 2003.

The 2 most significant in terms of size of operations were Côte d'Ivoire and Democratic Republic of Congo. The share for the Bank Group of the debt relief for these 2 countries was estimated at US$ 1.2 billion. However, the operation for Côte d'Ivoire was aborted due to the sociopolitical instability that beset the country. The preliminary figure for the other 5 countries stands at US$ 269.4 million. As these countries have significant arrears to the Bank Group, schemes for arrears clearance will need to be worked out with the assistance of donors, to enable them to qualify for HIPC debt relief.

Private Sector Development

In the long-term, private sector development will gain increasing prominence, as it is one of the priority areas of the Bank, as outlined in its Vision Statement. The Bank has accordingly put great emphasis on formulating a strategy and appropriate instruments to promote private sector initiatives in its regional member countries. The Bank supports the private sector through both its public and private sector windows. Public sector loans and technical assistance grants are provided to help countries reform their governance structures, including regulatory, legal and judicial systems. Through its private sector window, the Bank provides financial assistance to entrepreneurs as well as advisory services. The Bank now provides financial assistance to private enterprises as well as advisory services, using a wide array of instruments. These include term loans to private enterprises without requiring government guarantees; equity participation; quasi-equity investments; guarantees; syndication and underwriting. The Bank also extends lines of credit to private financial institutions for onlending to small and medium size enterprises

(SMEs). A total of $1.2 billion has been provided in this form to major national and sub-regional development banks.

In the coming years the Bank will continue to sharpen and expand its private sector operations. While it will continue to be involved in direct financing of projects in traditional sectors, it will expand its intervention in a number of strategic areas such as private financing of infrastructure and financial services and capital markets. Priority will also be accorded to activities that support privatization, foreign direct investment, entrepreneurship development, capacity building, as well as regulatory and legal reforms. In addition, special attention will continue to be given to the development and strengthening of small and medium enterprises.

Promoting Capital Flows

The African Development Bank is currently rated triple-A and double A-plus on its senior and subordinated debt respectively, with a stable outlook, by the rating agencies, Moody's, Fitch and the Japanese Credit Rating agency. Their rating reflects: (i) the Bank's solid capital structure and membership support; (ii) its preferred creditor status; (iii) its long track record of consistent income generation; and (iv) its conservative financial policies. Standard & Poors' current long-term issuer ratings of the African Development is double A + for the senior debt and double A- for the subordinated debt, with a stable outlook. This rating is based upon: (i) the Bank's conservative leverage policies; (ii) the improving shareholder base; and (iii) the close cooperation with the Bretton Woods Institutions.

Like other multilateral development banks, the ADB limits risk to creditors by limiting leverage. Our capitalization ratios are governed by three limits set by statute and management policies. Management policy calls for senior debt not to exceed 80 percent of callable capital of non-borrowing –member countries (versus our statutory limit of 100 percent). Similarly, total debt is not to exceed usable capital (defined as paid-in capital, reserves, and callable capital of 'AA' and 'AAA' rated shareholders), nor 80 percent of callable capital of all shareholders. According to the Bank's statutes, callable capital may be used only to meet the bank's debt obligations. In relation to its borrowing activities, the Bank is guided by the need to conform to its own assets and liability management goals, its risk management policies and its overall prudential objectives. The Bank therefore strives to raise funds at the lowest possible cost in the capital markets. In order to support its borrowing activities, the Bank has available for its use, an array of instruments to access the international capital markets. These include, a Global Debt Issuance Facility, as well as a Euro Commercial Paper Program. These programs are flexible documentation facilities allowing continuous issuance under standard documentation. They also allow for convenient and flexible borrowing and give access to a larger investor base, and capital markets.

The optimization of the Bank's funding activities on the financial markets requires a balanced management of assets and liabilities in order effectively to manage the associated market risks. The Bank uses derivatives such as currency swaps and interest rate swaps to mitigate both its foreign exchange and interest rate risks. Furthermore, the Bank, through its debt allocation process, assigns each borrowing transaction to a corresponding asset class, so as to achieve an optimal match in terms of size, currency and interest profile. This matched funding policy protects the Bank against market

risks. The Bank has put into place strict credit standards to reduce its credit risks. For example, the Bank may not enter into a swap transaction with a counterpart that is not rated at least AA. To further mitigate its credit risk, the Bank has implemented a credit limit system whereby approved counterparts are allocated a credit limit reflecting both their size and their rating. Those limits are monitored daily.

Over the years, the Bank has undertaken several co-financing operations with other sister international development finance institutions. There has also been collaboration with the International Finance Corporation, the UNDP and the World Bank in providing a range of specialized facilities that support the quality and efficacy of investment in the region. The African Project Development Facility (APDF) was established in 1986 to assist African entrepreneurs in preparing project documentation, identifying of technical and financial partners and mobilizing debt and equity financing. The African Management Services Company (AMSCO) was established in 1989 to providing management services to African companies by sourcing and supplying competent management staff and technical personnel internationally. The agency also has a training component which aims to upgrade the skills of local management so that they could function effectively when the foreign management leaves. The African Enterprise Fund (AEF) was established in 1988 to provide debt/equity financing for African companies. Up to 40 percent of project costs could be funded from this facility. Enterprise Support Services for Africa (ESSA) was established in 1997 to provide post-funding support to African firms through a range of consultancy services to enhance prospects for long-term success. These include management information services, production efficiency and marketing.

One of the ways by which the Bank mobilizes foreign capital is through guarantees, easily one of the best instruments so far in modern finance for channeling private funds to perceived risky environments. In offering guarantees, multilateral development banks such as the ADB seek to leverage their preferred creditor status to assist eligible borrowers to obtain financing from the private sector, including through the international capital markets. The Bank's guarantee can attract new sources of financing, reduce financing costs and extend maturities. Principally, the Bank's objective is to cover risks that it is uniquely positioned to, bear given its international financial standing, credit experience with African countries and special relationship with governments.

Ninth Replenishment of the ADF

Crucial to the Bank's role in external resource mobilization is the triennial replenishment of the African Development Fund window. During the first quarter of last year the Bank commenced discussions with our external partners on the replenishment of the ADF window. Deputies representing state participants met in Valencia, Spain, from May 31–June 1, 2001, for the first consultations, with subsequent meeting taking place in Yamoussoukro, Côte d'Ivoire and in Maputo, Mozambique. The fourth meeting was held in Stockholm, Sweden, in December 2001. The consultations focused on the need to strengthen the overall development effectiveness of ADF activities. Although many deputies expressed a willingness to consider an increase of grant resources under ADF-IX operations, management deemed it necessary to reiterate the rationale for such an increase, given the disparate views voiced by deputies on the issue. Such a rationale includes the intervention of the

Fund in post-conflict assistance, the fight against communicable diseases, particularly HIV/AIDS, certain aspects of governance reforms, and the provision of basic social services. The resource implications of the Fund's involvement in NEPAD also need to be taken into account, particularly in view of the lead role assigned to the Bank Group in banking and financial standards and in infrastructure development. Towards the end of 2002, the sum of UA 3.5 billion was approved for the ADF-IX cycle, a figure that exceeds in real terms the amount that was provided under the preceding cycle.

Summary and Conclusions

What this report has shown is that, in a rapidly globalizing world, Africa risks being consigned to the margins of world development. Despite the efforts that several countries have made in terms of economic reforms, the challenges of overcoming poverty and achieving sustainable growth remain daunting. In recent years, there has been a palpable spirit of goodwill from the international community, as exemplified by a number of new initiatives that have been taken in the areas of trade, debt relief and development financing. Through the new NEPAD initiative, African leaders have recommitted themselves to the pursuit of good governance, responsible leadership and sound economic management within the framework of just and peaceful development. For a comprehensive attack on poverty, a global action plan is required. No doubt, there has been no shortage of global agenda, and in particular, there have been more than a dozen special international initiatives on Africa since 1980. So far, they have not worked well. Poverty and inequality continue to rise. And there is a broad consensus that a global response is required, although there is hardly agreement on how to do so. Our argument here is that the world is in need of a fundamental rethinking of the governance structure in the light of the increasing economic interdependence.

Given the strong influence of the international environment on Africa, the international community has an important role to play in ensuring Africa's integration into the globalization process. The need for the support of the international community in ensuring that the benefits of globalization are equitably distributed has been recognized. In an address to the World Economic Forum in Davos (IMF, 2001), the UN Secretary-General Kofi Annan stated that policy-makers must ensure that globalization works for all. He emphasized that "if we cannot make globalization work for all, in the end it will work for none." Similarly, at the Monterrey Conference on Financing for Development, it was noted that while globalization offers opportunities and challenges, the developing countries and countries with transition economies face special difficulties in responding to those challenges and opportunities. To be sustainable, globalization has to be inclusive and equitable. There is therefore a strong need for policies and measures at the national and international levels, formulated and implemented with the full and effective participation of developing countries to help them respond to those challenges and opportunities. The international community has a responsibility to provide an external environment that will allow Africa to fulfill its potential. The industrialized countries have particular responsibility in the following areas:

- Guaranteeing African exporters unfettered and tariff-free access to their markets, especially for agricultural products;
- Supporting countries that are trying to boost growth and tackle poverty by increasing aid flows and guaranteeing them over long periods;
- Doing more to help Africa bring peace to its war-torn regions. In addition to direct efforts to resolve and prevent conflicts, this means restraining arms sales and countering the smuggling of raw materials and natural resources to finance wars;
- Boost aid flows from their current low levels and make medium term commitments to aid provision;
- Channel help to countries pursuing the right policies, and assist with debt relief; and
- Helping Africa fight the spread of the HIV/AIDS pandemic.

A New Global Action Agenda

Crucial to all this is the need for a new global governance structure and action agenda to provide global public goods and ensure poverty reduction for the poorest countries in the developing world. The World Development Report 2000 argues that a global action agenda is required both to ensure that the opportunities from global integration and technological advance benefit poor people and to manage the risks of insecurity and exclusion that may result from global change. Consequently, the Report recommends five key actions: (a) promoting global financial stability and opening the markets of rich countries to the agricultural goods, manufactures, and services of poor countries; (b) bridging the digital and knowledge divides, thus bringing technology and information to people throughout the world; (c) providing financial and non-financial resources for international public goods, especially medical and agricultural research; (d) increasing aid and debt relief to help countries take actions to end poverty, within a comprehensive framework that puts countries themselves—not external aid agencies—at the center of the design of development strategy; and (e) giving a voice to poor countries and poor people in global forums, including through international links with organizations of poor people. We summarize other aspects of the international response needed to ensure Africa's effective integration into the global economy and poverty reduction.

Two other elements of the global response are needed. First, there is need to evolve a new international legal regime that makes stolen money unsafe anywhere in the world. It is estimated that Africa's stolen wealth stashed away in Western commercial banks are far in excess of $300 billion. African leaders such as President Olusegun Obasanjo have been calling precisely for this kind of legal regime. The wealth stolen by succeeding generations of Nigeria's military rulers, for example, has been estimated at over $120 billion. So far, the global system functions in a hypocritical manner with regards to the fight against this kind of corruption. A caricature of the prevailing rule, especially as practised by the industrial countries reads like this: "Corruption is bad at the national level, but if you manage to loot and bring it to our economies, we will help you to keep it safe." Indeed, if a global transparency and fight against corruption leads to the repatriation of looted wealth back to their owners — citizens of the poorest countries — many of these countries could write a check and repay their debt in one day, and still have surpluses for other development programs. Without an effective international response against the massive pillage of African treasuries, the extent of poverty and risks in

these countries would guarantee that capital (including aid money) would continue to flee them into the richer economies.

The second element is trade. First, the subsidies to agriculture in the West (which is about the size of sub-Saharan Africa's GDP) need fundamental reforms. Secondly, the industrial countries can aid the transition from aid dependency to sustainable development by opening their markets unconditionally to all exports of the poor countries (except arms). This should be a major plank of an international strategy for poverty eradication. Sachs (1996) adds his voice in proposing a simple but effective solution: "The biggest source of support from donor nations would also be the cheapest. America, Europe and Japan should launch a 'New Compact for Africa', guaranteeing open markets for African exports and committing themselves to help reintegrate Africa into the world economy. The commitment should help prove to both sides that the long period of economic marginalization is over, and would energize both African nations and the West to overcome the practical obstacles to a new dawn of rapid growth throughout Africa." This way, the LDC African farmers, producers and the poor could then be empowered through higher returns from trade to take effective charge of their destiny. This would be the most effective contribution of donors to poverty reduction in Africa thereby enabling the region to outgrow aid. This agenda is the litmus test that should demonstrate whether development finance has evolved to the point of financing development or perpetuating dependency.

Greater Equity in Global Governance

One final element that needs to be addressed is the need for equity in global decision-making. It is often forgotten that African nations were not represented at the 1944 Bretton Woods Conference that set up the postwar international architecture. Till today, the continent remains a minor player in global economic decision-making structures. With the developed countries having overwhelming control of the Bretton Woods Institutions as well as the WTO, and with their membership of an entire array of exclusive clubs such as G8, the OECD and the Trilateral Commission, among others, Africa's nearly one billion people have no effective voice in international decision-making. At the same time, they have been at the receiving end of policy prescriptions that in some cases would seem to amount to undue pressure on the authorities of those countries.

A major agenda for global reform therefore has to include the encouragement of African participation in international decision-making. And this must be based on respect for African sovereignty and equality. The erosion of legitimate authority can only sow the seeds of socio-economic chaos and political tragedy. What Africa needs are not weakened states, but strong states which, divested of the unnecessary encumbrances of bloated bureaucracies and unproductive parastatals, can become effective driving forces for structural transformation. Such states would then be effective global partners for building a just and peaceful world. The African Development Bank Group, in partnership with its sister multilateral finance institutions, is fully committed to realizing this vision in all its operational activities in its 52 regional member countries. The emerging generation of new leaders in Africa therefore have to take hold of the future with renewed courage and determination, building on the lessons of the past and seeking to build no less than a new civilization based on African values of humaneness, freedom and justice.

In conclusion, we have to acknowledge that the forces of globalization, despite occasional setbacks, are likely to continue apace, profoundly affecting the development prospects of all countries. African nations have therefore little option but to rise to the challenge and work within the broad framework of closer integration into the world economy. Deepening their regional economic communities based on the principle of *open regionalism* is a critical imperative for survival in the coming years. Preparing to take advantage of the opportunities of globalization while minimizing the attendant risks is therefore one of the most important policy challenges facing the leaders of the developing world. Africa, more than any other region of the world, faces the greatest challenge. But humanity itself faces the enduring challenge of instituting a more efficient and equitable architecture of global governance, in particular, ensuring that globalization does not lead to the breakdown of the international equilibrium; and that the needs of the poorest are not ignored – that the world is not rendered more inhospitable by alienation, resentment and the economic insecurity of nations. In the words of former IMF Managing Director Michel Camdessus (2000): "Let us all join hands in a new partnership – a partnership in which Africa itself will have to play the pivotal role – so that history records the dawn of the new millennium as ushering in an African renaissance."

BIBLIOGRAPHICAL NOTE

Introduction

The background papers prepared specifically for the Report are listed below, along with the selected bibliography used in the Report. These papers synthesize relevant ligerature. The Report has drawn on a wide range of African Development Bank reports, including ongoing research as well as countries' economic, sector and project work. It has also drawn on outside sources, including published and the unpublished works of institutions such as the IMF, the World Bank, IFC, the United Nations and its agencies such the ECA, FAO, ILO, IFAD, UNAIDS, UNCTAD, UNIDO, UNDP, WHO, WTO and OECD. Other sources include publications from various national economic and statistics agencies, African Economic Digest, Africa Financing Review, Africa Research Bulletin; Business Africa, The Economist, Economist Intelligence Unit, Financial Times; Intenational Capital Markets; Middle East Economic Digest; and Southern Africa Monitor.

Background papers

(ii)   Bigsten Arne (2002), "African Development Experience and Globalization".

(iv)   Hassan Kabir (2002), "A Framework for Integrating Africa into Global Economy for Economic Development".

(iii) Okojie Christiana (2002), "Globalization and Development in Africa".

iii)   Page Sheila (2002a), "Globalization Process".

(iv)   _____ (2002b) , "Forces Driving Globalization".

(i)   Soludo Charles (2002), "Africa: Strategies for Adapting to Globalization".

Sources for Boxes

1.1   UNIDO (2002)

1.2   World Bank (2000); Report of the UN Financing for Development; CBN, Quarterly Bulletin of International Economic Developments, Jan 2003, the Global Poverty Report (2002)

1.3   Report of the UN-Secretary-General to the Security Council (1998); Achodo (2000)

1.4   Odd-Helge Fjeldstad (1998)

1.5   Gray C.W. and D. Kaufman (2002)

1.6   UNIDO (2002), *Industrial Development Report 2002/2003*

3.1   World Bank (2002)

4.1   MIT Technology Review (2002)

5.4   ADB (2003)

5.5   Third National Agricultural Policy, Ministry of Agriculture, Kuala Lumpur, 2000.

5.6   ADB (2002)

5.7   ADB (2003)

6.1   OAU Department of Foreign Affairs; Abuja Treaty (Article 6).

6.2   Sirte Declaration (2001).

6.3   Constitutive Act of the African Union.

6.4   ECA (2002)

6.5   G8 Africa Action Plan Highlights (2002)

Selected Bibliography

Achodo C. C (2000), "Conflict and Post Conflict Patterns, Issues, Impact on Economic Development and Poverty Cycle in Countries in Africa", Paper presented at Africa Forum on Poverty Reduction Strategies, June 5- 9, Yamoussoukro, Côte d'Ivoire.

Ades A. and E Glaser (1999), "Evidence on Growth, Increasing Returns, and the Extent of the Market", *Quarterly Journal of Economics,* Vol. 114, No. 3, pp.1025-1046.

African Development Bank (1994-2002), *African Development Report.* Abidjan, Côte d'Ivoire.

_____ **and Organisation for Economic Cooperation and Development (2002),** *African Economic Outlook.* Abidjan, Côte d'Ivoire.

Ajayi S. I. (2001), "What Africa Needs to do to Benefit from Globalization", *Finance and Development,* Volume 38, No. 4, December, pp.6-8.

Alfred Marshall (1890), "Principles of Economics. Book Four: The Agents of Production: Land, Labour, and Capital and Organization".

Anyanwu, John C. (2002), Economic and Political Causes of Civil Wars in Africa: Some Econometric Results, *Economic Research Papers,* No. 73, December, African Development Bank, Abidjan.

Bigsten Arne and Durevall Dick (2002), *Is Globalisation Good for Africa?,* Göteborg, Department of Economics, University of Göteborg.

Calamitsis Evangelos A. (2001), "The Need for Stronger Domestic Policies and International Support", *Finances & Development (IMF),* Volume 38 - n° 4 - December 2001, pp. 10-13 .

CBN (2003), *Quarterly Bulletin of International Economic Developments,* Jan 2003

Chen S. and Ravallion M. (2001), "How did the World's Poor fare in the 1990s?", Mimeo, May, Development Research Group, the World Bank.

Cockroft Laurence and Riddell Roger (1991), "Foreign Direct Investment in Sub-Saharan". Africa", Overseas Development Institute, London.

Coe David T. and Hoffmaister A. W. (1999), "North-South Trade: Is Africa Unusual?" *Journal of African Economies,* Vol. 8, No. 2, pp. 228-256.

Collier P. and Gunning J. (1999), "Explaining African Economic Performance", *Journal of Economic Literature,* vol. 37.

Daouas M. (2001), "Africa Faces Challenge of Globalization", *Finance and Development,* Volume 38, No. 4, December, pp.4-5.

Di Mauro, F. (2000), 'The impact of Economic Integration on FDI and Exports; a Gravity

Approach', CEPS Working Document No. 156, Brussels.

Dollar D. (2001), "Globalization, Inequality, and Poverty since 1980", Background Paper for the World Bank Policy Research Report, *Globalization, Growth and Poverty,* November.

Dollar D. and Kraay A. (2001a), "Growth is Good for the Poor", Policy Research Working Paper No.2587.

_____ **(2001b)**, "Trade, Growth and Poverty", *Finance and Development,* Vol. 38, No. 3, September, pp.16-19.

Dreher, Axel (2002), *Does Globalization Affect Growth?*, University of Mannheim, Mannheim, Germany.

ECA (Economic Commission for Africa) (2002), *Economic Report on Africa 2002*: Tracking Performance and Progress. Economic Commission for Africa

FAO (Food and Agriculture Organization (2002), "Food Outlook", Global information and early warning systems on food and agriculture, FAO, Rome. No. 5 December 2002.

Fjeldstad Odd-Helge (1998), " Corruption", CMI Working Paper 8.

Foroutan Faezeh and Pritchett L. (1993), "Intra-Sub-Saharan African Trade: Is It Too Little?" *Journal of African Economies*, Vol. 3, pp.74-105.

Frankel J. A. (2000), "Globalization of the Economy", Working Paper 7858, National Bureau of Economic Research, August.

Freeman R., R. Oostendorp and Rama M. (2000), "Globalization and Wages". World Bank, Washington DC, Processed.

GDF (Global Development Finance) (2002), "Financing the Poorest Countries", The World Bank

GEP (Global Economic Prospects) (2002), Global Economic Prospects and the Developing Countries 2002. World Bank.

Ghosh A. and Ostry J. (1995), "The Current Account in Developing Countries: a Perspective from the Consumption-Smoothing Approach". *The World Bank Economic Review*. (9). 305-333.

Global Poverty Report (2002), "Achieving the Millennium Development Goals in Africa Progress, Prospects, and Policy Implications", African Development Bank in collaboration with the World Bank with contributions from the Asian Development Bank the European Bank for Reconstruction and Development International Monetary Fund and the Inter-American Development Bank.

Gray C.W. and Kaufman D. (2002), "Corruption and Development", in Finance and Development, IMF.

Greenaway D., Morgan C.W and Wright P.W. (1998), "Trade Reform, Adjustment and Growth: What Does the Evidence Tell Us?", Economic Journal, 108.

_____(2002), "Trade Liberalisation and Growth in Developing Countries", *Journal of Development Economics*, Vol. 67 (2002)

Harrold Peter (1995), "The Impacts of the Uruguay Round on Africa" Africa Technical Department Discussion Paper Series 311. World Bank, Washington, D.C.

Hertel Thomas W., Will Martin, Koji Yanagishima and Betina Dimaranan (1995), "Liberalizing Manufactures Trade in a Changing World Economy." In *The Uruguay Round and the Developing Economies*, edited by Will Martin and L. Alan Winters. World Bank Discussion Papers 307. pp.73-96.

Hertel Thomas W., William A. Masters and Aziz Elbehri (1998), "The Uruguay Round and Africa: A Global, General Equilibrium Analysis", *Journal of African Economies*, Vol. 7, No. 2, pp. 208-234.

Hummels D. (2000), "Time as a trade barrier", mimeo Purdue University.

Hussain M. N., Kupukile Mlambo and Temitope Oshikoya (1999), "Global Financial Crisis: An African Perspective", *African Development Review, vol. 11, No. 2*. African Development Bank, Abidjan.

Hussain M. N. (2000), "Linkages between SMEs and Large Industries for Increased Markets and Trade: An African Perspective", *Economic Research Papers, No. 53*, African Development Bank, Abidjan.

ILO (International Labour Organization), various years, World Employment Report. Geneva, Switzerland: United Nations.

IMF (International Monetary Fund) (2000a), *"Globalization: Threat or Opportunity"*, IMF Staff, April 12, 2000

_____ (2000b), "Globalization: Threat or Opportunity?", IMF Staff April 12, 2000.

_____ (2001), "The Challenge of Globalization for Africa", Stanley Fischer's Address at the France-Africa Summit Yaoundé, Cameroon January 19, 2001

_____ (2002a), "Charting the Future from the Past", IMF Survey, Vol.31, No. 17, September 16, 2002, IMF, Washington DC.

_____ (2002c), " ABCDE 2002 – Trade, Investment and Productivity have key Roles in Development", IMF Survey, Vol. 31, No.9, May 13, 2002.

Irwin Douglas A. and Marko Terviö (2002), "Does Trade Raise Income? Evidence from the Twentieth Century." Journal of International Economics 58(1):1-18.

ITU (International Telecommunications Union) (2002)

Keynes John Maynard (1920), "The Economic Consequences of the Peace", London: Macmillan.

Khor Martin (2000), "Globalisation and the South: Some Critical Issues", Third World Network.

Krueger A. (2002), "Supporting Globalization", Remarks at the 2002 Eisenhower National Security conference on 'National Security for the 21ˢᵗ Century: Anticipating Challenges, Seizing Opportunities, Building Capabilities', September 26, IMF, Washington DC.

Krugman P. and enables A. (1995), "Globalization and the Inequality of Nations". Working Paper No. 5098, National Bureau of Economic Research, April.

Lall A. (1994), "Impact of Uruguay Round Agreements on Least Developed Countries' Exports: An Initial Assessment", International Economics Department, World Bank, Washington, D.C. Processed.

Laufer Stephan (1999), "Africa must embrace Globalisation", President Thabo Mbeki At the OAU summit on globalization, *Business Day*, Johannesburg, 14 July 1999.

Lindert P. H. and Williamson J. G. (2001), "Globalization and Inequality: A Long History", Invited Address at the World Bank *Annual Bank Conference on Development Economics – Europe*, Barcelona, June 25-27.

Maddison A. (1995), "Monitoring the World Economy, 1820-1992", Development Centre Studies, Organization for Economic Cooperation and Development, Paris.

Melchior Arne, Kjetil Telle and Henrik Wiig (2000), "Globalisation and Inequality: world income distribution and living standards, 1960-98." (6B):1–42.

Milanovic B. (2002), "Can We Discern the Effect of Globalization on Income Distribution?

Evidence for Household Budget Surveys". World Bank Policy Research Working Paper 2876, April.

Mussa Michael (2000), "Factors Driving Global Economic Integration" Presented in Jackson Hole, Wyoming at a symposium sponsored by the Federal Reserve Bank of Kansas City on "Global Opportunities and Challenges", August 25, 2000

NEA (Economic Agenda for the New Millennium), (2000), World Bank Group Countries, Mauritius

Ng Francis and Alexander Yeats (1996), "Open Economies Work Better! Did Africa's Protectionist Policies Cause Its Marginalization in World Trade?" Policy Research Working Paper 1636. World Bank, Washington, D.C.

Obstfeld Maurice (1998), "The Global Capital Market: Benefactor or Menace?," NBER Working Papers 6559, National Bureau of Economic Research, Inc.

Ohiorhenuan J. F. E. (1998), "The South in an Era of Globalization", *Cooperation South*, Number Two, pp.6-15, UNDP.

OPEC (Organization of Petroleum Exporting Countries) (2002), Petroleum Economist, *The International Energy Journal*, December 2002

_____ (2003), Petroleum Economist, *The International Energy Journal*,

O'Rourke K. H. and Williamson J. G. (2000), "When Did Globalization Begin?" Working Paper 632, National Bureau of Economic Research, April.

O'Rourke K. H. (2001), "Globalization and Inequality: Historical Trends", Working Paper 8339, National Bureau of Economic Research, June.

Overman H. G., S. Redding and Venables A. J. (2001), 'Trade and Geography: A Survey of Empirics', Department of Economics, London School of Economics and CEPR.

Oyejide T. A. (1998), "African Trade Prospects in A Globalizing Era", *Cooperation South,* Number Two, pp.107-117, UNDP.

Oyejide Ademola (1998), "Trade Policy and Regional Integration in the Development Context: Emerging Patterns, Issues, and Lessons for Sub-Saharan Africa." *Journal of African Economies*, Vol. 7., Sup. 1, pp. 108-145.

Page Sheila and Michael Davenport (1994), "World Trade Reform: Do Developing Countries Gain or Lose?" London: Overseas Development Institute.

Polanyi Karl (1994), "The Great Transformation. The Political and Economic Origins of Our Time", Boston: The Beacon Press, 1944. Ch. 6, The Self-Regulating Market and the Fictitious Commodities: Labor, Land and Money, pp. 68-76. Karl Polanyi (Beacon Hill 1944)

Portes Richard and Rey Helene (1999), "The Determinants of Cross- Border Equity Flows", NBER Working Papers 7336, National Bureau of Economic Research, Inc

Rodriguez F. and Rodrik D. (2000), "Trade Policy and Economic Growth: A Skeptic's Guide to Cross-National Evidence", University of Maryland and Harvard University, Cambridge, Massachusetts. Processed.

Rodrik D. (1999), "Making Openness Work", Overseas Development Institute, London.

Sachs J. D. and A. Warner (1995), "Economic Integration and the Process of Global Integration", *Brookings Papers on Economic Activity,* (1), pp.1-118.

Sachs J. (1996), "Growth In Africa: It Can Be Done", *The Economist*, June 29th; pp. 19-21.

Schmukler S. L. and P. Zoido-Lobaton (2001), "Financial Globalization: Opportunities and Challenges for Developing Countries: Draft Background Paper", World Bank, May.

Stark Oded and Yong Wang (2001), "Inducing Human Capital Formation: Migration as a Substitute for Subsidies", April 2001.

Subramanian A. and Tamirisa N. (2001), "Africa's Trade Revisited", IMF Working Paper WP/01/33, Washington DC.

Tanzi Vito (1998), "Corruption Around the World: Causes, Consequences, Scope, and Cures", IMF Staff Papers, Vol. 45 (4) pp. 1.

The Ministry of Agriculture Malaysia (2000), Third National Agricultural Policy, Ministry of Agriculture, Kuala Lumpur, 2000.

Thirlwall Anthony (1999), "Trade, Trade Liberalization and Economic Growth: Theory and Evidence"

UNCTAD (United Nations Conference on Trade and Development) (1994), *Review of the Implementation, Maintenance, Improvement and Utilization of the Generalized System of Preferences.* TD/B/SCP/6. Geneva.

_____ **(1999)**, The *Least Developed Countries 1999 Report*, Geneva: United Nations.

_____ **(2001)**, *World Investment Report.* UNCTAD, Geneva.

_____ **(2002)**, *World Investment Report.* UNCTAD, Geneva.

UNDP (United Nations Development Programme) (2002), "Creating a Development Dynamic: Final Report Of The Digital Opportunity Initiative", July 2002

UNIDO (United Nations Industrial Development Organization) (2002a), *Industrial Development Report 2002/2003*, Competing Through Innovation and Learning, UNIDO.

_____ **(2002b)**, "Foreign Direct Investor Perceptions in Sub-Saharan Africa", Vienna, UNIDO

UNIDO (2002c) Database.

United Nations (1998), *Report of the UN-Secretary-General to the Security Council on the Causes of Conflict and the promotion of Durable Peace and Sustainable Development in Africa*, April 1998.

_____ **(2000)**, "The United Nations Millennium Declaration", General Assembly, 18 September 2000, Fifty-fifth session

Venables A. J. (2001), "Geography and International Inequalities: The Impact of New Technologies", Paper prepared for World Bank Annual Bank Conference on Development Economics, Washington

Williamson Jeffrey G. (1998), "Globalization, Labor Markets and Policy Backlash in the Past", *Journal of Economic Perspectives.* Vol. 12, Number 4, pp. 51-72.

_____ **(2002)**, "Winners and Losers Over Two Centuries of Globalization", NBER Working Paper No. w9161. Issued in September 2002

World Bank (1995), *World Development Report 1995*: Workers in an Integrating World New York: Oxford University Press.

_____ **(1998)**, "Global Development Finance", Washington D.C.

_____ **(2000)**, *World Development Report 2000/2001*: Attacking Poverty New York: Oxford University Press.

_____ **(2001)**, "Globalization, Growth, and Poverty", Policy Research Report. Washington DC: The World Bank.

_____ **(2002a)**, Millennium Development Goals, - From the World Development Indicators, The World Bank, Washington DC.

_____ **(2002b)**, *Globalization, Growth and Poverty: Building and Inclusive World Economy,* A World Bank Policy Research Report, World Bank and the Oxford University Press.

_____ **(2002c)**, World Development Indicators 2002, CD-ROM. World Bank Group

WTO (World Trade Organization) (2001) "International Trade Statistics 2001", WTO.

_____ *Annual Report*, various issues. Geneva.

Yeats Alexander J. (1994), "What Are OECD Trade Preferences Worth to Sub-Saharan Africa?" Policy Research Working Paper 1254. World Bank, Washington, D.C.

Yusuf Shahid (2001), "Globalization and the Challenge for Developing Countries", World Bank, DECRG, June 2001.

Electronic Sources

African Civil Society Declaration on NEPAD, CODESRIA, Bond (2002)
http://www.red.org.za/index.php?meta=capitalist%20 globalisation&all=yes

Annan Kofi (2001), "Address of Secretary-General Annan to the World Economic Forum in Davos, Switzerland", January 31, UN Press Release SG/SM/6881 http://132.230.108.107/studying/2-3_Int_Institutions.htm

A.T. Kearney/Foreign Policy Magazine (2002), Globalization Index
http://www.foreignpolicy.com.

Dreher Axel (2002), "Does Globalization Affect Growth?"
http://www.axel-dreher.de/globalization.pdf

Jensen Mike (2002), "The African Internet - A Status Report", Updated: July 2002
http://www3.wn.apc.org/africa/afstat.htm

Keynes John Maynard, 1920s
http://www.omhros.gr/Kat/History/Eco/KeynesJM.htm

Kohl Richard and O'Rourke Kevin (2000), "What's New About Globalisation: Implications for Income Inequality in Developing Countries", OEDC
http://www.oecd.org/pdf/M00020000/M00020968.pdf

Maddison (2001) http://www.ekh.lu.se/lektionsplaner forelasningar/EKH401D4F3.pdf

Mazrui Ali (1995), The Cold War: Globalizing or Marginalizing? From Slave Ship To Space Ship: Africa Between Marginalization And Globalization.
http://web.africa.ufl.edu/asq/v2/v2i4a2.htm

MIT Technology Review (2002), July/August 2002
http://www.technologyreview.com/articles/zachary0702.asp

NEPAD (The New Partnership For Africa's Development) (2001) http://www.acdi-cida.gc.ca/INET/IMAGES.NSF/vLUImages/G8-2/$file/NEPAD_ang.pdf

OAU Department of Foreign Affairs; Abuja http://www.dfa.gov.za/for-relations/multilateral/treaties/aec.htm

Sirte Declaration (2001), September 2001. http://www.au2002.gov.za/docs/key_oau/sirte.pdf

The Independent Commission on Africa and the Challenges of the Millennium, Cotonou, 2002. http://www.parlanepad.org/docs/an_decfinal.doc

The United Nations Conference on Financing for Development (2002), Monterrey, Mexico, March 2002: http://www.un.org/esa/ffd/sideeventsmarch21.htm

World Bank (2003), Development Economics Prospects: Commodity Price Data (Pink Sheets) (2003), January: http://www.worldbank.org/prospects/pinksheets/Pink0103.pdf

WTO (World Tourism Organization) (2003), January http://www.world-tourism.org/newsroom/Releases/2003/jan/numbers2002.htm

PART THREE

ECONOMIC AND SOCIAL STATISTICS ON AFRICA

Contents

Preface

The main purpose of this part of the Report is to present basic data that enable the monitoring of economic and social progress in regional member countries of the African Development Bank (ADB), and provide benchmark data for analysts of African development. The data cover the Bank's 53 regional member countries, with statistics on Basic Indicators, National Accounts, External Sector, Money Supply and Exchange Rates, Government Finance, External Debt and Financial Flows, Labor Force, and Social Indicators.

Throughout this part of the Report, statistical tables are arranged in sections and according to indicators. The tables contain historical data from 1980 to 2002. Period averages are provided for 1980-1990, and 1991-2002.

The data are obtained from various international sources and supplemented, to the extent possible, with data directly obtained from ADB regional member countries, and estimates by the ADB Statistics Division. Statistical practices vary from one regional member country to another with regard to data coverage, concepts, definitions, and classifications used. Although considerable efforts have been made to standardize the data, full comparability cannot be assured. Care should be exercised in their interpretation. They provide only indications on trend or structure that allow for the identification of significant differences between countries.

Technical information on these data is provided in the explanatory notes to facilitate appropriate interpretation. However, users are advised to refer to technical notes of the specialized publications of the main sources for more details.

The designations employed and the presentation of data therein do not imply any opinions whatsoever on the part of the African Development Bank concerning the legal status of any country or of its authorities. They were adopted solely for convenience of statistical presentation.

Symbols used

...   not available

0   zero or insignificant value

| break in the comparability of Data

TABLE 1.1
BASIC INDICATORS

COUNTRY	AREA ('000 Sq. Km)	POPULATION (Millions) 2002	GNI PER CAPITA (US $) 2001	CONSUMER PRICE INFLATION (%) 2002	LIFE EXPECTANCY AT BIRTH (Years) 2002	INFANT MORTALITY RATE (per 1000) 2002	ADULT ILLITERACY RATE (%) 2001
ALGERIA	2,382	31,403	1,630	3.0	70	43	31
ANGOLA	1,247	13,936	500	109.0	46	118	...
BENIN	113	6,629	380	1.6	54	81	58
BOTSWANA	600	1,564	3,630	5.6	36	67	22
BURKINA FASO	274	12,207	210	1.1	48	87	75
BURUNDI	28	6,688	100	-2.7	45	111	51
CAMEROON	475	15,535	570	4.0	50	79	23
CAPE VERDE	4	446	1,310	3.0	71	50	25
CENT. AFR. REP	623	3,844	270	3.0	44	93	52
CHAD	1,284	8,390	200	6.0	46	116	56
COMOROS	2	749	380	3.0	61	67	40
CONGO	342	3,206	700	7.6	52	66	18
CONGO DEM. REP	2,345	54,275	...	25.0	52	77	37
COTE D'IVOIRE	322	16,691	630	3.6	48	81	52
DJIBOUTI	23	652	890	2.0	41	117	35
EGYPT	1,001	70,278	1,530	2.8	68	40	44
EQUAT. GUINEA	28	483	700	6.0	52	99	16
ERITREA	118	3,993	190	...	52	82	43
ETHIOPIA	1,104	66,040	100	-7.0	43	106	60
GABON	268	1,293	3,160	2.3	53	80	...
GAMBIA	11	1,371	330	5.5	47	115	62
GHANA	239	20,176	290	14.5	57	62	27
GUINEA	246	8,381	400	6.0	49	114	...
GUINEA BISSAU	36	1,257	160	4.0	45	121	60
KENYA	580	31,904	340	1.8	49	59	17
LESOTHO	30	2,076	550	10.0	40	111	16
LIBERIA	111	3,298	...	...	56	79	45
LIBYA	1,760	5,529	...	1.0	71	25	19
MADAGASCAR	587	16,913	260	15.0	54	91	33
MALAWI	118	11,828	170	16.7	39	130	39
MALI	1,240	12,019	210	4.5	52	120	57
MAURITANIA	1,026	2,830	350	3.0	53	97	57
MAURITIUS	2	1,180	3,830	6.4	72	16	15
MOROCCO	447	30,988	1,180	3.0	69	42	50
MOZAMBIQUE	802	18,986	210	9.5	38	128	55
NAMIBIA	824	1,819	1,960	11.3	35	65	17
NIGER	1,267	11,641	170	3.0	46	126	84
NIGERIA	924	120,047	290	14.2	52	79	35
RWANDA	26	8,148	220	3.5	41	119	32
SAO T. & PRINC.	1	143	280	9.0	...	...	...
SENEGAL	197	9,908	480	3.0	54	57	62
SEYCHELLES	0.5	83	6,530	...	...	...	...
SIERRA LEONE	72	4,814	140	1.0	41	146	...
SOMALIA	638	9,557	...	20.0	49	113	...
SOUTH AFRICA	1,221	44,203	2,900	5.9	47	59	14
SUDAN	2,506	32,559	330	8.5	57	78	41
SWAZILAND	17	948	1,300	11.8	38	92	20
TANZANIA	945	36,820	270	4.6	51	73	23
TOGO	57	4,779	270	2.8	52	75	42
TUNISIA	164	9,670	2,070	2.8	71	26	28
UGANDA	241	24,780	280	-2.2	46	94	32
ZAMBIA	753	10,872	320	...	42	80	21
ZIMBABWE	391	13,076	480	98.0	43	55	11
AFRICA	**30,061**	**830,902**	**671**	**9.8**	**53**	**78**	**38**

TABLE 2.1
GROSS DOMESTIC PRODUCT, REAL
(MILLIONS US DOLLARS, CONSTANT 1995 PRICES)

COUNTRY	1980	1990	2000	2001	2002	Av. Ann. Real Growth Rate (%) 1981-1990	Av. Ann. Real Growth Rate (%) 1991-2002
ALGERIA	31,386	41,236	48,681	49,703	50,921	2.6	1.8
ANGOLA	5,076	6,368	6,874	7,088	8,115	1.3	2.6
BENIN	1,310	1,705	2,595	2,725	2,870	3.1	4.4
BOTSWANA	1,272	3,574	6,001	6,550	6,884	11.2	5.6
BURKINA FASO	1,258	1,743	2,749	2,903	3,034	3.1	4.7
BURUNDI	728	1,126	946	966	995	4.2	-0.9
CAMEROON	6,310	8,752	10,040	10,572	11,038	3.1	2.0
CAPE VERDE	171	381	670	689	710	11.3	5.4
CENT. AFR. REP.	964	1,069	1,258	1,240	1,289	0.6	1.7
CHAD	788	1,311	1,710	1,855	2,057	4.5	4.1
COMOROS	167	223	243	248	255	3.6	1.2
CONGO	1,281	2,050	2,388	2,457	2,553	6.4	1.9
CONGO DEM. REP.	7,509	8,186	4,647	4,443	4,576	1.1	-4.6
COTE D'IVOIRE	9,550	10,254	13,186	13,199	13,199	-0.4	2.2
DJIBOUTI	507	544	495	504	517	1.2	-0.4
EGYPT	29,899	50,921	77,868	80,438	82,207	5.9	4.1
EQUAT. GUINEA	94	117	731	1,063	1,386	1.2	24.3
ERITREA	...	...	558	612	666	...	16.7
ETHIOPIA	4,541	5,137	7,430	8,002	8,402	2.0	4.3
GABON	3,633	4,345	5,025	5,145	5,197	2.1	1.6
GAMBIA	243	347	494	524	555	2.4	4.0
GHANA	4,231	5,236	7,978	8,313	8,679	2.1	4.3
GUINEA	2,265	3,075	4,479	4,640	4,835	3.3	3.9
GUINEA BISSAU	134	217	233	233	234	2.9	1.1
KENYA	5,612	8,360	9,875	9,994	10,153	4.2	1.6
LESOTHO	500	768	1,076	1,112	1,157	3.8	3.5
LIBERIA	...	...	...	...	...	...	...
LIBYA	40,160	27,268	34,001	34,188	33,983	-3.1	1.9
MADAGASCAR	3,048	3,212	3,814	4,043	3,562	0.6	1.0
MALAWI	992	1,234	1,739	1,714	1,744	2.0	3.2
MALI	1,986	2,108	3,075	3,121	3,283	0.2	3.8
MAURITANIA	753	887	1,318	1,379	1,449	1.9	4.2
MAURITIUS	1,875	3,127	5,261	5,567	5,789	3.9	5.3
MOROCCO	21,590	31,506	39,317	41,859	43,617	4.4	2.9
MOZAMBIQUE	1,938	1,967	3,382	3,852	4,198	-1.8	6.7
NAMIBIA	2,434	2,751	4,156	4,257	4,389	0.8	4.0
NIGER	1,833	1,813	2,164	2,328	2,391	0.6	2.4
NIGERIA	22,357	24,864	33,015	33,973	33,667	1.6	2.6
RWANDA	1,658	2,027	2,061	2,199	2,342	2.7	3.5
SAO T. & PRINC.	48	42	50	52	55	0.2	2.3
SENEGAL	3,057	4,150	5,806	6,131	6,432	2.7	3.7
SEYCHELLES	315	441	533	490	478	2.9	0.8
SIERRA LEONE	1,123	1,227	769	811	864	1.4	-2.5
SOMALIA	...	...	...	...	...	...	...
SOUTH AFRICA	127,410	144,763	172,144	177,012	182,323	1.9	2.0
SUDAN	4,399	4,906	10,056	10,589	11,118	1.2	7.2
SWAZILAND	640	1,187	1,604	1,633	1,659	6.5	2.8
TANZANIA	3,474	4,808	6,407	6,768	7,167	3.4	3.4
TOGO	1,175	1,304	1,461	1,500	1,545	2.4	1.7
TUNISIA	10,509	14,915	23,693	24,920	25,419	4.0	4.6
UGANDA	2,799	4,102	7,771	8,207	8,674	3.3	6.5
ZAMBIA	3,351	3,716	3,971	4,177	4,294	1.3	1.3
ZIMBABWE	4,356	6,703	7,818	7,239	6,414	5.4	-0.2
AFRICA	385,155	464,066	596,178	615,896	632,125	2.4	2.8

TABLE 2.2
GROSS DOMESTIC PRODUCT, NOMINAL
(MILLIONS OF US DOLLARS AT CURRENT MARKET PRICES)

COUNTRY	1980	1990	2000	2001	2002	Av. Ann. Nominal Change (%) 1980-1990	Av. Ann. Nominal Change (%) 1991-2002
ALGERIA	42,318	62,031	54,195	54,678	55,017	6.2	-0.4
ANGOLA	5,400	10,260	8,859	8,982	10,143	9.3	4.0
BENIN	1,405	1,845	2,248	2,363	2,687	4.9	4.5
BOTSWANA	1,057	3,516	4,971	5,025	5,155	15.1	3.4
BURKINA FASO	1,709	2,765	2,312	2,329	2,543	6.1	0.3
BURUNDI	920	1,132	694	652	646	3.7	-4.3
CAMEROON	6,741	11,152	8,185	8,622	9,426	6.6	-0.5
CAPE VERDE	107	339	558	557	613	17.4	5.3
CENT. AFR. REP.	797	1,488	953	946	1,046	8.1	-1.8
CHAD	1,033	1,739	1,407	1,603	1,925	5.7	1.9
COMOROS	124	263	202	220	251	9.0	0.7
CONGO	1,706	2,799	3,220	2,751	3,024	9.0	2.5
CONGO DEM. REP.	14,391	9,348	4,851	4,480	4,646	-3.3	-4.3
COTE D'IVOIRE	10,175	11,893	10,599	10,735	11,562	3.3	0.7
DJIBOUTI	296	418	553	575	601	3.5	3.1
EGYPT	22,913	43,094	99,377	96,256	87,310	8.6	6.5
EQUAT. GUINEA	61	132	1,341	1,846	2,154	5.8	30.8
ERITREA	...	...	614	578	669	...	4.9
ETHIOPIA	5,024	6,842	6,312	6,144	5,773	3.7	-0.7
GABON	4,279	5,952	5,065	4,748	5,074	7.7	-0.6
GAMBIA	241	317	421	390	335	5.0	0.7
GHANA	4,445	5,886	5,102	5,437	6,546	4.0	2.0
GUINEA	6,684	2,818	3,063	2,985	3,128	5.3	1.1
GUINEA BISSAU	139	262	215	199	217	7.8	-0.1
KENYA	7,265	8,531	10,449	11,396	11,876	3.2	3.9
LESOTHO	431	615	862	752	671	6.7	1.2
LIBERIA	...	...	...	...	...	...	...
LIBYA	36,273	28,905	34,912	28,605	23,180	1.9	-1.2
MADAGASCAR	4,042	3,081	3,875	4,604	4,502	-0.2	3.9
MALAWI	1,238	1,881	1,707	1,749	1,813	5.7	3.3
MALI	1,787	2,473	2,446	2,629	2,970	4.9	2.7
MAURITANIA	709	1,020	977	962	969	4.5	-0.1
MAURITIUS	913	2,642	4,554	4,526	4,780	11.1	5.2
MOROCCO	18,805	25,821	33,322	33,876	36,948	5.4	3.3
MOZAMBIQUE	3,526	2,463	3,813	3,583	4,618	-0.3	6.3
NAMIBIA	2,166	2,350	3,458	3,163	2,858	5.5	1.9
NIGER	2,509	2,481	1,798	1,954	2,177	2.6	-0.2
NIGERIA	64,202	28,472	42,076	42,677	42,569	-2.5	4.8
RWANDA	1,163	2,584	1,811	1,703	1,752	8.7	1.9
SAO T. & PRINC.	47	58	46	47	51	4.8	-0.7
SENEGAL	2,987	5,699	4,371	4,620	5,242	8.1	0.3
SEYCHELLES	147	368	595	570	612	10.5	4.5
SIERRA LEONE	1,100	650	636	749	810	-0.9	2.9
SOMALIA	...	...	...	...	...	...	...
SOUTH AFRICA	80,423	112,014	127,965	114,174	104,050	8.0	-0.4
SUDAN	7,617	13,167	11,014	12,099	13,239	6.0	2.1
SWAZILAND	544	882	1,394	1,238	1,179	8.7	2.8
TANZANIA	4,771	4,259	9,079	9,341	9,293	2.9	7.1
TOGO	1,136	1,628	1,221	1,259	1,385	6.9	-0.2
TUNISIA	8,743	12,314	19,469	20,073	21,224	5.3	4.9
UGANDA	1,245	4,304	5,414	5,699	6,030	7.3	4.2
ZAMBIA	3,878	3,288	3,239	3,612	3,694	2.7	1.4
ZIMBABWE	6,679	8,773	7,077	4,771	5,332	5.8	-2.4
AFRICA	398,030	468,314	565,026	545,638	536,425	3.8	1.2

TABLE 2.3
GROSS NATIONAL SAVINGS
(PERCENTAGE OF GDP)

COUNTRY	1980	1990	2000	2001	2002	Annual Average 1980-1990	Annual Average 1991-2002
ALGERIA	30.4	31.6	41.1	39.6	35.5	26.9	30.9
ANGOLA	20.8	1.7	45.4	32.0	33.0	12.1	21.8
BENIN	29.1	12.0	10.9	12.5	12.4	9.8	11.5
BOTSWANA	30.7	37.8	33.8	34.6	32.7	31.5	30.1
BURKINA FASO	13.3	16.4	20.2	20.7	23.3	16.6	18.3
BURUNDI	4.8	3.5	1.4	3.0	3.7	7.0	5.4
CAMEROON	20.4	16.2	14.7	15.6	12.6	20.0	13.7
CAPE VERDE	-108.0	19.0	6.1	11.3	11.7	13.0	18.6
CENT. AFR. REP.	-2.8	8.8	7.4	2.7	4.3	4.5	5.4
CHAD	11.3	0.4	3.3	4.8	5.3	2.6	4.0
COMOROS	14.7	18.3	10.5	8.5	7.8	17.1	10.2
CONGO	36.2	8.2	27.2	30.3	28.9	26.6	11.5
CONGO DEM. REP.	6.4	5.2	0.4	2.4	4.5	6.2	7.9
COTE D'IVOIRE	22.1	-2.1	7.7	7.4	12.8	10.3	7.7
DJIBOUTI	25.3	11.8	5.1	4.8	4.8	8.1	7.0
EGYPT	16.5	19.1	22.6	22.2	22.3	16.0	22.5
EQUAT. GUINEA	-29.4	-9.0	2.3	15.8	18.1	-12.3	8.0
ERITREA	...	...	...	...	...	...	...
ETHIOPIA	7.3	10.5	10.0	13.7	11.4	9.8	12.7
GABON	54.5	24.2	25.1	22.6	14.2	37.5	23.9
GAMBIA	-1.1	17.8	12.7	10.9	13.6	16.3	13.9
GHANA	4.9	10.7	15.6	17.3	18.3	8.1	14.7
GUINEA	9.0	2.7	14.7	18.4	19.3	7.1	14.2
GUINEA BISSAU	9.5	14.2	2.8	...	...	9.3	5.5
KENYA	7.5	19.9	12.7	11.5	10.2	18.1	15.4
LESOTHO	43.1	46.4	21.1	29.1	31.5	31.9	24.3
LIBERIA	...	...	...	...	...	...	...
LIBYA	...	...	...	...	...	...	...
MADAGASCAR	1.2	4.1	9.4	12.7	13.0	3.2	6.6
MALAWI	8.1	12.1	7.3	3.6	-2.5	11.2	5.6
MALI	7.0	14.9	11.1	9.1	13.9	9.7	13.8
MAURITANIA	14.2	6.4	31.1	21.2	17.7	11.4	16.4
MAURITIUS	14.9	25.9	24.2	26.7	27.4	20.5	26.5
MOROCCO	16.5	22.9	21.7	28.2	28.3	19.3	21.8
MOZAMBIQUE	1.3	-8.7	17.3	18.9	19.3	0.5	7.1
NAMIBIA	19.1	32.3	29.1	28.9	31.6	18.3	26.0
NIGER	17.1	7.4	5.0	5.8	5.9	10.0	4.8
NIGERIA	23.3	28.0	27.8	24.7	19.1	15.2	19.8
RWANDA	8.8	3.6	13.4	13.1	12.8	8.8	7.4
SAO T. & PRINC.	-10.4	-9.3	23.0	38.7	25.4	-6.2	15.4
SENEGAL	-1.8	10.4	11.6	12.0	12.8	4.4	11.2
SEYCHELLES	11.5	20.0	23.7	11.6	10.7	16.6	18.2
SIERRA LEONE	3.6	-1.5	-1.8	-6.5	-3.3	3.2	-3.9
SOMALIA	...	...	...	...	...	...	...
SOUTH AFRICA	33.9	19.1	15.5	15.2	15.7	23.9	16.1
SUDAN	-68.7	9.1	...	...	...	14.2	...
SWAZILAND	16.7	24.9	16.8	17.5	20.0	21.2	18.8
TANZANIA	20.7	20.9	15.8	14.1	10.7	16.7	11.9
TOGO	18.3	20.4	3.9	4.8	5.1	13.8	6.7
TUNISIA	24.6	21.6	23.1	23.3	21.8	22.6	22.2
UGANDA	42.4	5.9	12.0	13.1	10.5	16.6	11.8
ZAMBIA	11.8	14.8	-0.2	-0.2	-1.8	8.9	6.1
ZIMBABWE	14.5	15.6	1.6	1.6	1.4	14.7	10.4
AFRICA	21.6	18.5	20.1	19.9	19.4	18.3	17.6

TABLE 2.4
GROSS CAPITAL FORMATION
(PERCENTAGE OF GDP)

COUNTRY	1980	1990	2000	2001	2002	Annual Average 1980-1990	Annual Average 1991-2002
ALGERIA	39.1	28.9	24.2	27.2	28.2	33.7	27.7
ANGOLA	20.4	2.2	26.5	34.0	29.0	16.7	29.4
BENIN	35.5	14.2	18.9	19.2	19.3	19.7	17.2
BOTSWANA	40.4	37.8	18.5	13.7	14.0	32.4	25.9
BURKINA FASO	14.6	19.9	33.9	32.8	32.1	18.9	27.0
BURUNDI	13.9	14.5	8.4	8.2	12.0	16.4	10.9
CAMEROON	21.0	17.8	16.4	17.8	18.6	23.3	16.4
CAPE VERDE	38.7	24.4	21.7	21.8	21.2	43.7	27.6
CENT. AFR. REP.	15.7	9.1	9.6	8.4	10.0	12.7	9.0
CHAD	11.2	11.5	13.5	41.7	58.8	10.9	21.6
COMOROS	20.5	19.7	10.3	9.3	12.5	17.7	14.9
CONGO	12.4	15.9	21.0	27.2	29.3	17.4	29.3
CONGO DEM. REP.	9.2	12.8	4.4	4.8	10.7	11.6	10.8
COTE D'IVOIRE	22.8	6.7	10.6	9.8	13.4	15.0	11.6
DJIBOUTI	13.1	17.4	15.3	12.0	17.1	16.1	13.2
EGYPT	35.7	29.4	23.7	22.3	22.3	30.5	21.6
EQUAT. GUINEA	35.7	17.4	40.7	64.8	18.9	23.9	57.1
ERITREA	...	...	28.7	32.7	34.1	...	24.5
ETHIOPIA	12.6	12.0	15.3	18.0	20.2	13.9	15.5
GABON	32.9	21.7	21.9	18.2	22.7	36.8	24.5
GAMBIA	28.9	20.4	17.3	27.1	27.3	21.4	19.8
GHANA	5.6	14.4	24.0	21.3	22.9	9.2	21.1
GUINEA	13.4	12.7	22.1	22.1	26.0	14.3	20.9
GUINEA BISSAU	53.4	27.9	16.0	18.9	7.8	36.3	22.5
KENYA	22.8	24.2	15.4	14.5	13.9	22.8	17.7
LESOTHO	35.2	50.9	38.3	38.8	36.4	37.5	49.0
LIBERIA	...	...	...	...	...	...	...
LIBYA	24.3	16.6	12.8	12.9	13.0	22.7	14.7
MADAGASCAR	15.0	14.8	15.0	18.3	22.4	11.0	13.9
MALAWI	24.7	20.6	12.5	10.9	11.1	18.8	15.7
MALI	14.8	20.7	21.5	21.1	22.0	17.1	21.3
MAURITANIA	36.1	18.8	30.3	26.8	24.7	28.6	20.8
MAURITIUS	24.8	31.2	25.8	24.9	25.9	24.4	27.7
MOROCCO	24.2	25.3	23.2	23.4	24.4	24.4	22.2
MOZAMBIQUE	12.2	22.5	35.2	36.6	53.3	15.0	28.4
NAMIBIA	20.0	33.3	24.0	24.5	26.9	17.8	22.5
NIGER	28.1	11.0	10.8	11.5	13.3	14.9	9.7
NIGERIA	18.5	21.5	18.7	20.7	26.0	18.9	20.9
RWANDA	12.4	11.7	17.5	18.4	18.8	15.1	15.1
SAO T. & PRINC.	16.8	29.5	43.5	50.0	44.8	18.5	45.0
SENEGAL	10.9	13.8	18.4	16.8	18.8	11.7	16.9
SEYCHELLES	38.3	24.6	30.6	37.2	20.3	26.2	29.3
SIERRA LEONE	17.7	9.4	8.0	7.9	17.2	11.7	6.0
SOMALIA	...	...	...	...	...	...	...
SOUTH AFRICA	29.9	17.2	15.6	15.1	14.9	23.1	16.1
SUDAN	-3.6	7.3	18.1	18.3	18.2	3.5	19.2
SWAZILAND	40.7	19.1	19.8	19.7	19.1	27.1	20.9
TANZANIA	37.8	26.1	17.6	15.8	16.9	28.8	19.8
TOGO	28.7	26.6	18.0	20.7	21.7	21.0	16.4
TUNISIA	29.4	27.1	27.3	27.5	27.1	28.6	26.7
UGANDA	4.8	11.9	19.9	20.4	19.9	6.9	17.4
ZAMBIA	27.0	17.3	18.6	20.0	18.4	19.6	15.3
ZIMBABWE	18.8	17.4	3.5	0.4	0.3	18.2	15.4
AFRICA	24.9	20.4	19.3	19.9	20.8	22.3	19.7

TABLE 2.5
TERMS OF TRADE
(1995 = 100)

COUNTRY	1980	1991	1997	2001	2002	Average Annual Growth (%) 1981-1991	Average Annual Growth (%) 1992-2002
ALGERIA	171.0	136.3	125.1	141.3	130.9	-0.4	1.7
ANGOLA	268.8	122.9	138.1	164.4	158.7	-4.6	5.5
BENIN	39.9	83.9	89.7	86.6	74.1	11.0	-0.3
BOTSWANA	26.9	110.9	110.8	110.2	112.0	24.4	0.3
BURKINA FASO	61.0	86.8	92.2	79.2	78.2	3.9	-0.7
BURUNDI	100.1	75.3	69.5	51.1	50.9	-0.5	-1.7
CAMEROON	206.2	112.8	96.9	114.3	103.1	-4.7	0.2
CAPE VERDE	467.4	117.9	92.8	90.7	90.4	-5.1	-2.0
CENTRAL AFRICAN REP	115.9	87.5	89.4	78.8	75.1	-1.2	-1.1
CHAD	48.3	75.9	95.7	100.6	88.9	6.0	2.2
COMOROS	285.1	190.1	65.0	394.6	293.2	-3.7	13.0
CONGO	214.2	117.4	112.8	143.7	125.0	-5.6	2.9
CONGO, DEM. REP.	61.8	70.6	93.1	120.5	109.1	2.4	4.8
COTE D'IVOIRE	88.2	67.4	93.3	74.3	81.1	-1.5	2.4
DJIBOUTI	411.4	137.3	96.6	92.5	93.6	-9.0	-3.3
EGYPT	138.2	111.8	110.8	118.6	112.5	-1.1	0.3
EQUAT. GUINEA	101.2	123.2	65.8	91.7	118.7	2.6	4.4
ERITREA							
ETHIOPIA	130.8	95.8	83.9	51.5	48.1	0.5	-3.8
GABON	88.7	114.4	112.5	132.6	122.5	3.4	4.9
GAMBIA	84.6	108.8	94.1	94.1	94.1	3.1	-1.2
GHANA	84.3	88.0	99.7	86.5	92.3	2.2	0.8
GUINEA	88.3	158.5	115.1	113.8	113.7	7.2	-2.6
GUINEA BISSAU	171.9	120.3	104.7	81.5	84.2	-2.5	-2.4
KENYA	117.5	76.2	100.4	89.0	89.2	-3.4	1.6
LESOTHO	113.3	95.3	101.9	120.7	117.0	-1.4	1.9
LIBERIA	124.2	99.4	104.1	112.8	...	-1.8	...
LIBYA							
MADAGASCAR	150.2	97.7	84.1	92.1	91.3	-1.4	0.8
MALAWI	108.9	117.3	110.0	96.0	101.8	2.0	-0.8
MALI	94.3	85.3	118.1	110.8	99.5	-0.4	2.3
MAURITANIA	58.6	75.1	105.2	101.3	94.1	3.7	3.5
MAURITIUS	63.6	100.1	101.3	109.6	106.8	4.8	0.7
MOROCCO	133.0	93.0	102.1	99.3	102.5	-3.1	1.1
MOZAMBIQUE	84.0	100.0	100.0	100.0	103.5	2.8	0.3
NAMIBIA	135.9	104.0	85.6	88.1	88.9	-0.6	-1.2
NIGER	134.9	126.8	82.5	82.7	83.9	-0.0	-3.1
NIGERIA	161.9	121.0	119.8	165.6	164.9	0.9	5.3
RWANDA	151.9	86.4	124.2	96.0	90.7	-3.3	2.5
SAO T. & PRINC.	167.1	104.5	105.1	107.3	101.7	1.5	0.3
SENEGAL	101.1	101.9	102.3	100.4	99.9	0.4	-0.1
SEYCHELLES	20.3	138.5	81.3	65.3	63.3	29.9	-5.6
SIERRA LEONE	76.9	69.2	94.6	92.6	93.1	-1.0	3.3
SOMALIA	105.9	101.6	99.8	99.4	...	-0.4	...
SOUTH AFRICA	105.1	101.0	97.9	94.3	96.8	-0.3	-0.4
SOUDAN	64.6	...	...	...	...	...	...
SWAZILAND	93.4	97.4	98.8	91.8	93.1	0.4	-0.4
TANZANIA	178.0	95.6	77.4	103.6	102.8	-5.9	2.3
TOGO	207.0	145.0	79.2	88.6	78.1	-3.1	-3.4
TUNISIA	133.9	101.5	99.5	94.8	94.3	-2.6	-0.6
UGANDA	84.2	106.8	76.9	45.3	44.3	6.8	-5.7
ZAMBIA	136.7	101.1	84.3	75.8	74.0	-0.8	-2.5
ZIMBABWE	68.7	103.3	110.9	94.0	92.7	4.6	-0.8
AFRICA	**140.9**	**108.5**	**105.6**	**114.3**	**112.7**	**-2.3**	**0.6**

TABLE 2.6
CURRENT ACCOUNT
(AS PERCENTAGE OF GDP)

COUNTRY	1981	1991	1997	2001	2002	Annual Average 1981-1991	Average 1992-2002
ALGERIA	-0.5	5.1	2.7	12.4	8.1	-0.1	3.6
ANGOLA	-3.6	-1.1	-4.4	-2.0	5.1	-4.0	-8.9
BENIN	-24.4	-2.8	-4.2	-6.7	-8.0	-9.8	-6.0
BOTSWANA	-31.0	7.7	10.3	7.4	6.2	0.2	8.2
BURKINA FASO	-1.7	-6.4	-9.8	-12.4	-13.9	-3.1	-9.3
BURUNDI	-6.9	-8.2	-9.9	-13.3	-19.9	-9.4	-10.2
CAMEROON	-6.8	-2.2	-4.1	-2.2	-3.8	-1.3	-3.1
CAPE VERDE	-16.9	-5.3	-6.8	-10.5	-11.4	-5.5	-10.5
CENT. AFR. REP	-6.9	-3.0	-3.3	-5.6	-5.8	-6.5	-3.9
CHAD	1.3	-8.9	-8.3	-36.3	-56.9	-8.4	-17.3
COMOROS	1.3	-9.3	-12.7	-3.3	-8.4	-13.9	-11.4
CONGO	21.3	-18.5	-34.0	3.8	5.2	4.6	-16.0
CONGO, DEM. REP.	-3.9	-10.4	-0.6	-2.8	-4.3	-5.9	-4.2
COTE D'IVOIRE	-10.9	-11.5	-1.7	-2.3	2.9	-6.5	-3.4
DJIBOUTI	-3.7	-3.8	-3.3	-4.3	-8.2	-10.7	-5.5
EGYPT	-4.6	3.6	-0.3	-0.0	-0.2	-3.4	0.7
EQUAT. GUINEA	-98.9	-52.3	-104.4	-49.0	2.6	-35.0	-48.5
ERITREA	...	...	...	...	...	...	...
ETHIOPIA	-4.5	-5.1	-3.0	-4.2	-7.0	-3.5	-3.8
GABON	16.6	1.7	10.6	-2.2	-3.9	2.7	-1.0
GAMBIA	-12.7	-0.1	-13.1	-6.2	-4.3	-2.4	-4.7
GHANA	-1.6	-3.6	-3.1	-4.0	-6.2	-1.9	-6.8
GUINEA	-4.3	-2.9	-8.5	-3.7	-7.0	-5.5	-7.1
GUINEA BISSAU	-21.7	-24.3	-16.5	-18.9	-19.4	-25.2	-17.3
KENYA	-9.7	-1.8	-2.1	-3.0	-4.6	-4.2	-2.5
LESOTHO	-12.3	-45.8	-30.3	-9.8	-10.7	-16.6	-24.1
LIBERIA	7.1	0.5	0.2	0.5	...	1.5	0.4
LIBYA	...	...	...	...	...	...	...
MADAGASCAR	-10.1	-9.4	-5.0	-5.6	-3.6	-7.4	-6.6
MALAWI	-7.0	-7.0	-7.1	-7.3	-11.2	-5.1	-9.8
MALI	-6.7	-2.4	-10.2	-11.7	-9.1	-6.9	-8.3
MAURITANIA	-21.3	-7.4	-1.6	-5.7	3.8	-15.3	-3.2
MAURITIUS	-15.1	-1.5	-0.6	1.8	1.3	-3.1	-1.2
MOROCCO	-7.4	-2.2	0.1	4.9	1.3	-5.6	-0.6
MOZAMBIQUE	-11.2	-18.0	-17.7	-17.7	-35.9	-13.8	-20.7
NAMIBIA	2.0	3.9	4.8	4.4	3.3	2.2	3.6
NIGER	-8.9	-1.1	-5.5	-5.7	-8.8	-4.1	-5.8
NIGERIA	-9.9	-1.3	6.8	6.0	-5.4	-5.7	-1.4
RWANDA	-4.9	-9.4	-6.7	-6.5	-11.5	-6.9	-8.0
SAO T. & PRINC.	-40.0	-60.1	-53.3	-39.4	-29.5	-40.4	-46.2
SENEGAL	-18.2	-8.2	-4.3	-4.8	-5.9	-10.1	-5.8
SEYCHELLES	-14.2	0.6	-13.2	-25.5	-23.1	-11.1	-12.5
SIERRA LEONE	-14.3	-10.9	-10.8	-14.5	-17.0	-8.2	-9.6
SOMALIA	-3.1	-13.3	-7.4	-3.4	-3.4	-7.4	-7.0
SOUTH AFRICA	-5.8	1.9	-1.3	-0.1	0.8	0.6	-0.3
SOUDAN	-19.3	-9.3	-18.8	-10.2	-9.9	-13.6	-19.3
SWAZILAND	-14.2	5.2	-3.9	-2.2	-3.5	-3.3	-3.1
TANZANIA	-6.8	-5.0	-13.8	-1.6	-4.9	-4.3	-7.8
TOGO	-9.7	-3.7	-7.4	-15.9	-16.9	-6.5	-10.3
TUNISIA	-9.7	-4.4	-2.4	-4.2	-4.6	-6.5	-4.5
UGANDA	-1.5	-9.9	-5.6	-11.3	-12.4	-2.4	-7.5
ZAMBIA	-21.6	0.3	-3.7	-20.2	-17.5	-9.3	-9.8
ZIMBABWE	-9.1	-5.2	-1.1	-1.8	-3.8	-3.1	-3.1
AFRICA	**-6.1**	**-1.1**	**-1.3**	**0.2**	**-1.4**	**-3.1**	**-1.8**

TABLE 2.7
BROAD MONEY SUPPLY (M2)
(PERCENTAGE ANNUAL CHANGE)

COUNTRY	1980	1990	2000	2001	2002	Annual Average 1980-1990	Annual Average 1991-2002
ALGERIA	17.4	11.4	13.2	48.9	-10.3	14.4	17.5
ANGOLA	...	...	...	...	...	...	...
BENIN	48.9	28.6	26.0	12.2	-9.3	12.7	12.5
BOTSWANA	19.0	-14.0	1.4	31.2	4.4	22.6	18.0
BURKINA FASO	15.1	-0.5	6.2	1.6	1.5	11.8	8.7
BURUNDI	1.4	9.6	4.3	15.7	9.8	11.6	13.5
CAMEROON	21.4	-1.7	19.1	15.1	-0.3	11.1	4.5
CAPE VERDE	30.6	14.6	13.7	9.9	5.9	18.7	11.7
CENT. AFR. REP.	35.0	-3.7	2.4	-1.1	2.8	8.4	7.0
CHAD	-15.3	-2.4	18.5	22.0	22.1	8.4	10.4
COMOROS	...	3.9	14.5	46.7	8.1	12.7	7.7
CONGO	36.6	18.5	58.5	-22.8	1.0	14.0	6.0
CONGO DEM. REP.	...	...	...	...	...	...	...
COTE D'IVOIRE	2.8	-2.6	-1.9	12.0	5.0	4.0	7.8
DJIBOUTI	...	3.6	1.1	7.5	3.2	7.6	0.0
EGYPT	51.4	28.7	11.6	13.2	0.5	25.7	11.4
EQUAT. GUINEA	...	-52.0	36.2	35.1	35.7	-9.0	35.4
ERITREA	...	...	...	...	...	...	...
ETHIOPIA	4.2	18.5	14.2	9.8	8.0	11.9	11.3
GABON	24.6	3.3	18.3	7.5	6.3	8.6	7.2
GAMBIA	10.4	8.4	34.8	19.4	3.2	18.8	14.3
GHANA	33.8	13.3	38.4	...	...	42.2	35.1
GUINEA	...	...	...	12.9	3.0	...	10.9
GUINEA BISSAU	...	574.6	60.8	7.3	17.9	...	36.6
KENYA	0.8	20.1	4.5	2.5	2.9	12.7	17.1
LESOTHO	...	8.4	1.4	17.2	9.4	18.0	11.6
LIBERIA	...	...	...	...	...	...	...
LIBYA	26.6	19.0	3.1	4.3	-2.8	7.2	4.8
MADAGASCAR	20.6	4.5	17.2	23.8	1.0	16.9	20.9
MALAWI	12.6	11.1	41.4	14.4	8.3	17.6	30.5
MALI	4.5	-4.9	12.2	19.6	15.6	8.1	13.1
MAURITANIA	12.5	11.5	16.1	17.3	2.3	13.0	4.7
MAURITIUS	23.2	21.2	9.2	10.9	4.9	21.0	13.4
MOROCCO	10.8	21.5	8.4	14.1	1.1	14.1	9.5
MOZAMBIQUE	...	37.2	38.4	28.2	-5.4	39.5	36.2
NAMIBIA	...	...	13.0	4.5	8.7	...	18.4
NIGER	20.8	-4.1	12.4	31.4	-2.4	7.5	0.9
NIGERIA	46.1	32.7	48.1	27.0	14.8	18.1	32.2
RWANDA	8.1	5.6	15.6	11.0	...	7.8	14.7
SAO T. & PRINC.	...	...	24.9	40.1	11.9	...	41.2
SENEGAL	10.3	-4.8	10.7	13.6	6.3	7.6	9.2
SEYCHELLES	33.2	14.5	9.1	12.0	6.1	11.7	15.2
SIERRA LEONE	21.6	74.0	12.1	33.7	4.6	51.8	28.0
SOMALIA	...	...	...	...	...	...	...
SOUTH AFRICA	22.8	11.4	7.2	16.7	8.3	17.2	13.0
SUDAN	29.4	48.8	36.9	24.7	15.5	38.0	55.8
SWAZILAND	13.7	0.6	-6.6	10.7	8.0	17.1	12.2
TANZANIA	26.9	41.9	14.8	17.1	11.5	25.7	22.7
TOGO	9.1	9.5	15.2	-2.6	5.8	9.0	5.1
TUNISIA	18.5	7.6	14.1	10.7	0.3	14.9	9.5
UGANDA	34.8	...	18.1	9.2	8.4	83.6	21.8
ZAMBIA	9.0	47.9	73.8	13.6	9.5	38.6	42.2
ZIMBABWE	29.6	15.1	68.9	128.5	32.3	16.8	41.5
AFRICA	23.2	19.9	17.3	20.2	13.8	11.2	21.9

TABLE 2.8
REAL EXCHANGE RATES INDICES (PERIOD AVERAGE)
(NATIONAL CURRENCY PER US $, 1995 = 100)

COUNTRY	CURRENCY	1980	1990	1999	2000	2001*	Annual Average Growth (%) 1980-1990	1991-2001
ALGERIA	DINAR	37.5	54.9	113.2	131.6	133.2	4.4	10.2
ANGOLA	NEW KWANZA	...	23,875.0	113.4	...	...	...	...
BENIN	CFA FRANC	...	78.2	117.0	134.4	136.9	...	6.3
BOTSWANA	PULA	75.0	104.2	133.2	139.7	154.4	3.5	3.8
BURKINA FASO	CFA FRANC	44.4	63.5	116.9	143.2	144.6	-1.5	9.1
BURUNDI	FRANC	112.2	163.5	213.3	136.0	147.5	4.6	4.4
CAMEROON	CFA FRANC	74.4	69.7	121.4	139.1	142.4	0.9	8.2
CAPE VERDE	ESCUDO		104.7	116.3	139.3	147.9	-2.6	3.5
CENT. AFR. REP.	CFA FRANC	42.9	65.1	130.4	151.9	155.4	5.5	9.8
CHAD	CFA FRANC	...	67.2	117.0	125.2	125.0	-2.4	6.9
COMOROS	FRANC	...	87.4	115.9	136.9	140.1	...	5.0
CONGO	CFA FRANC	86.5	96.6	111.2	124.3	132.2	-2.7	4.7
CONGO DEM.REP.	FRANC	...	...	...	33.7		...	-13.1
COTE D'IVOIRE	CFA FRANC	59.0	73.0	117.3	139.9	141.8	3.1	7.7
DJIBOUTI	FRANC	...	110.8	97.0	98.5	99.9	...	-0.9
EGYPT	POUND	101.6	96.6	91.2	93.5	107.5	-1.6	5.3
EQUAT. GUINEA	CFA FRANC	...	72.9	110.7	134.6	131.0	...	6.9
ERITREA	NAKFA	...	...	...	...	...	...	...
ETHIOPIA	BIRR	51.5	53.0	131.0	143.7	165.5	1.3	13.0
GABON	CFA FRANC	55.1	63.9	121.0	150.7	156.3	3.6	9.5
GAMBIA	DALASI	66.2	97.6	119.6	137.6	166.4	3.9	5.2
GHANA	CEDI	15.6	82.4	99.8	169.8	172.7	25.4	9.7
GUINEA	FRANC	...	93.7	128.1	161.2	168.9	...	5.7
GUINEA BISSAU	CFA FRANC	...	310.0	55.9	112.1	113.0	6.4	4.8
KENYA	SHILLING	70.3	112.5	112.9	119.4	119.8	4.3	1.4
LESOTHO	MALOTI	75.2	112.9	136.2	150.6	179.7	4.1	4.6
LIBERIA	DOLLAR	163.6	131.5	3,116.5	...	...	...	...
LIBYA	DINAR	...	267.5	33.0	58.3	62.1	...	-7.9
MADAGASCAR	FRANC	38.5	85.1	110.2	109.5	101.1	8.0	2.3
MALAWI	KWACHA	51.7	61.9	111.6	120.4	118.1	1.9	7.9
MALI	CFA FRANC	...	62.2	120.6	148.4	149.3	...	9.8
MAURITANIA	OUGUIYA	...	75.2	143.4	163.6	169.1	5.8	8.0
MAURITIUS	RUPEE	74.2	103.2	121.8	125.9	136.4	3.2	2.7
MOROCCO	DIRHAM	67.4	110.9	116.5	128.2	139.3	5.7	2.3
MOZAMBIQUE	METICAL	...	61.2	96.5	105.7	119.5	...	6.8
NAMIBIA	DOLLAR	68.2	106.6	135.9	145.9	170.0	5.8	4.6
NIGER	CFA FRANC	37.0	61.2	119.2	141.5	143.7	5.6	9.1
NIGERIA	NAIRA	66.3	219.4	280.0	298.2	283.8	16.9	19.8
RWANDA	FRANC	85.8	79.2	111.6	129.6	143.3	-2.9	12.6
SAO T. & PRINC.	DOBRA	...	34.0	146.4	152.3	158.6	...	16.0
SENEGAL	CFA FRANC	56.2	65.1	123.7	150.3	154.4	2.7	9.2
SEYCHELLES	RUPEE	106.1	104.2	116.9	118.4	117.9	0.1	1.2
SIERRA LEONE	LEONE	80.4	110.3	101.5	122.7	116.3	5.7	1.0
SOMALIA	SHILLING	27.5	161.9	97.8	...	...	...	...
SOUTH AFRICA	RAND	77.7	104.4	140.5	156.4	188.7	3.2	5.8
SUDAN	POUND	447.4	236.1	102.4	...	...	-2.8	38.4
SWAZILAND	EMALANGENI	75.3	112.5	141.0	147.2	174.7	3.4	4.5
TANZANIA	SHILLING	39.8	103.6	87.0	86.9	93.5	9.9	0.0
TOGO	CFA FRANC	52.4	74.5	115.4	138.3	145.8	4.1	7.3
TUNISIA	DINAR	67.0	105.5	120.4	139.0	148.0	0.6	3.4
UGANDA	SHILLING	...	93.8	134.6	153.0	162.4	19.7	6.2
ZAMBIA	KWACHA	69.1	101.0	110.4	114.9	113.0	-0.9	2.1
ZIMBABWE	DOLLAR	49.5	81.3	160.8	123.3	91.4	5.1	3.0

* estimates

TABLE 2.9
INTERNATIONAL RESERVES
(MILLIONS OF US DOLLARS)

COUNTRY	1980	1990	2000	2001	2002	Average Annual Growth (%) 1980-1990	1991-2002
ALGERIA	3,772.6	724.8	12,023.9	18,081.4	21,899.0	-4.3	45.8
ANGOLA	...	...	1,198.2	731.9	843.9	...	...
BENIN	8.1	64.9	458.1	578.0	564.3	116.0	27.4
BOTSWANA	334.0	3,331.5	6,318.2	5,897.3	5,751.3	29.2	4.8
BURKINA FASO	68.2	300.5	243.6	260.5	287.7	17.8	1.7
BURUNDI	94.5	105.0	32.9	17.7	25.1	8.4	-6.5
CAMEROON	188.9	25.5	212.0	331.8	558.8	12.7	...
CAPE VERDE	42.4	77.0	28.2	45.5	63.0	6.8	26.1
CENT. AFR. REP.	55.0	118.6	133.3	118.8	135.8	10.3	3.9
CHAD	5.1	127.8	110.7	122.4	182.7	33.5	11.2
COMOROS	6.4	29.7	43.2	62.3	75.4	...	9.6
CONGO	85.9	5.9	222.0	68.9	85.0	-0.4	...
CONGO DEM. REP.	204.1	219.1	...	...	...	1.2	...
COTE D'IVOIRE	19.7	4.0	667.8	1,018.9	1,428.9	1.2	...
DJIBOUTI	...	93.6	67.8	70.3	64.5	...	-2.8
EGYPT	1,046.0	2,683.6	13,117.6	12,925.8	13,553.0	19.5	19.3
EQUAT. GUINEA	...	0.7	23.0	70.9	72.0	...	343.9
ERITREA	...	...	...	...	...	...	...
ETHIOPIA	80.1	20.2	306.3	427.6	725.0	6.6	57.1
GABON	107.5	273.8	190.1	9.9	70.8	107.4	...
GAMBIA	5.7	55.4	109.4	...	93.3	98.9	...
GHANA	180.4	218.8	232.1	...	365.0	6.0	...
GUINEA	...	...	147.9	...	194.2	...	...
GUINEA BISSAU	...	18.2	66.7	69.5	105.6	...	26.7
KENYA	491.7	205.4	897.7	1,064.9	1,119.9	-4.9	60.3
LESOTHO	50.3	72.4	417.9	386.5	392.9	...	18.0
LIBERIA	5.5	...	0.3	0.5	0.6	...	...
LIBYA	13,090.5	5,839.2	12,460.8	14,800.5	14,799.0	5.9	...
MADAGASCAR	9.1	92.1	285.2	...	324.7	49.4	...
MALAWI	68.4	137.2	246.9	206.7	200.2	33.8	19.0
MALI	14.5	190.5	381.2	348.8	515.0	47.4	12.2
MAURITANIA	139.9	54.1	...	...	...	-2.3	...
MAURITIUS	90.7	737.6	897.4	835.6	1,130.0	62.4	5.3
MOROCCO	398.6	2,066.5	4,823.2	8,473.9	9,829.0	39.5	16.3
MOZAMBIQUE	...	...	725.1	715.6	711.4	...	...
NAMIBIA	...	...	260.0	234.2	265.0	...	...
NIGER	125.9	222.2	80.3	106.9	105.9	13.8	-0.7
NIGERIA	10,234.8	3,864.3	...	...	...	18.4	...
RWANDA	186.6	44.3	190.6	212.1	193.5	-7.5	21.5
SAO T. & PRINC.	...	...	...	15.5	19.6	...	...
SENEGAL	8.1	11.0	383.5	446.2	531.1	9.7	...
SEYCHELLES	18.4	16.6	43.8	37.1	72.0	10.7	17.9
SIERRA LEONE	30.6	5.4	50.9	51.6	58.3	-5.8	26.8
SOMALIA	...	...	...	...	...	...	...
SOUTH AFRICA	725.8	1,008.3	6,082.8	6,045.3	7,601.0	-1.2	44.6
SUDAN	48.7	11.4	247.3	...	224.0	17.2	...
SWAZILAND	158.7	216.5	351.8	271.8	276.9	8.9	4.8
TANZANIA	20.3	192.8	974.2	1,156.6	1,336.5	68.4	21.9
TOGO	77.6	353.2	152.3	126.1	193.0	20.4	-0.1
TUNISIA	590.1	794.8	1,811.1	1,989.2	2,226.1	8.2	10.7
UGANDA	3.0	44.0	808.0	983.4	867.3	103.5	31.8
ZAMBIA	78.2	193.1	244.8	183.4	364.7	...	...
ZIMBABWE	213.5	149.2	193.1	64.7	84.3	-0.9	11.1
AFRICA	40,646.7	27,609.5	72,207.8	84,669.0	103,296.1	4.3	12.0

TABLE 2.10
CONSUMER PRICE INDICES (GENERAL)
(1995 = 100)

COUNTRY	1980	1990	2000	2001	2002*	Average Annual Change (%) 1990-1999	Average Annual Change (%) 2000-2002
ALGERIA	11.6	29.3	135.6	141.4	145.6	9.7	2.5
ANGOLA	...	0.0	415,684.0	1,049,855.0	2,194,562.5	-9.5	195.5
BENIN	...	59.8	120.0	124.7	126.7	3.0	3.2
BOTSWANA	20.2	55.2	148.9	158.6	167.6	10.9	6.8
BURKINA FASO	51.6	73.6	112.5	118.0	119.3	4.5	1.9
BURUNDI	29.0	60.0	239.7	261.9	254.8	7.2	10.3
CAMEROON	30.8	67.1	115.8	119.8	124.6	8.4	2.9
CAPE VERDE	...	74.6	122.3	126.0	129.7	10.0	1.2
CENT. AFR. REP.	53.3	71.9	106.1	109.8	113.1	3.3	3.2
CHAD	...	69.6	128.8	136.5	144.7	3.9	5.3
COMOROS	...	71.4	117.7	121.8	125.5	6.1	3.7
CONGO	26.5	48.4	129.7	129.0	138.8	7.9	2.1
CONGO, DEM. REP.	0.0	0.0	104,674.8	479,410.8	599,263.5	59.2	312.2
COTE D'IVOIRE	38.8	64.1	115.2	120.3	124.6	6.1	3.5
DJIBOUTI	...	77.4	114.7	116.3	118.7	5.3	1.9
EGYPT	11.0	52.4	123.7	126.6	130.1	17.3	2.6
EQUAT. GUINEA	...	64.1	119.7	130.2	138.1	17.0	6.5
ERITREA	...	...	158.5	187.2	...	...	19.0
ETHIOPIA	35.3	54.4	104.9	96.4	89.7	4.6	-4.4
GABON	41.6	73.2	107.0	109.2	111.7	6.6	1.6
GAMBIA	14.7	72.6	110.0	114.7	121.0	17.0	3.5
GHANA	0.8	28.3	302.3	401.8	460.1	47.3	24.2
GUINEA	...	61.0	123.5	135.4	143.5	31.2	7.5
GUINEA BISSAU	...	15.1	258.2	271.1	282.0	45.8	5.9
KENYA	11.1	34.0	140.1	148.1	150.8	12.1	4.5
LESOTHO	15.4	54.2	143.5	153.4	168.7	13.7	7.7
LIBERIA	33.1	65.2	...	...	...	7.9	12.4
LIBYA	...	42.0	282.5	320.9	324.1	4.5	9.7
MADAGASCAR	7.0	35.3	163.7	177.6	204.2	17.9	11.8
MALAWI	5.6	24.7	365.6	465.1	542.7	16.3	24.5
MALI	...	75.2	108.6	114.3	119.4	3.4	3.0
MAURITANIA	...	70.8	127.1	135.2	139.2	13.3	4.2
MAURITIUS	32.2	71.0	135.4	142.8	151.9	11.4	5.3
MOROCCO	37.0	74.6	109.7	110.3	113.7	7.5	1.8
MOZAMBIQUE	...	14.4	179.4	218.7	239.5	52.3	14.4
NAMIBIA	17.0	57.4	148.1	162.1	180.5	12.9	10.0
NIGER	62.0	76.4	113.9	118.7	122.3	3.2	3.4
NIGERIA	2.0	14.3	176.0	208.0	237.5	21.6	13.1
RWANDA	22.3	34.1	129.6	137.0	141.8	4.7	4.4
SAO T. & PRINC	...	25.4	416.8	456.0	497.0	17.4	7.8
SENEGAL	40.7	71.8	107.2	110.6	113.9	6.3	2.3
SEYCHELLES	68.5	92.3	114.5	121.4	...	4.0	5.7
SIERRA LEONE	0.1	15.6	255.1	262.7	265.3	67.3	1.1
SOMALIA	0.2	27.5	193.2	215.4	258.5	62.5	14.3
SOUTH AFRICA	14.9	58.6	138.2	146.1	154.7	14.6	5.7
SUDAN	0.1	2.8	510.2	507.1	550.2	38.6	6.0
SWAZILAND	15.4	54.3	146.7	157.7	176.3	14.9	10.5
TANZANIA	2.0	29.5	181.1	189.6	198.3	30.6	5.1
TOGO	43.7	62.8	116.5	117.1	120.3	4.7	1.7
TUNISIA	34.6	75.5	117.2	119.0	122.4	8.3	2.4
UGANDA	...	40.5	125.4	129.6	126.8	102.8	1.3
ZAMBIA	0.1	3.0	354.0	429.8	...	46.9	23.7
ZIMBABWE	8.1	29.8	469.6	807.2	1,598.2	13.2	75.2
AFRICA	5.9	26.4	204.9	230.9	253.5	14.6	12.1

* : estimates

TABLE 2.11
OVERALL GOVERNMENT DEFICIT(-) / SURPLUS(+) AS A PERCENTAGE OF GDP AT CURRENT PRICES
(PERCENTAGE)

COUNTRY	1980	1990	2000	2001	2002	Annual Average 1980-1990	Annual Average 1991-2002
ALGERIA	9.9	3.6	9.8	3.4	1.7	1.3	0.2
ANGOLA	-9.9	-23.7	-1.7	-1.8	9.8	-10.2	-17.0
BENIN	-4.2	-4.1	-1.8	-1.5	-2.2	-4.7	-1.4
BOTSWANA	31.0	10.4	4.4	-0.9	-2.9	16.0	3.8
BURKINA FASO	-7.6	-4.5	-4.3	-4.8	-5.9	-4.9	-3.6
BURUNDI	-6.2	-2.7	-1.9	-5.2	-5.3	-7.6	-4.5
CAMEROON	0.3	-7.6	1.4	2.4	1.7	-2.7	-2.8
CAPE VERDE	-8.0	-3.3	-18.9	-2.9	0.2	-8.7	-9.3
CENT. AFR. REP.	-8.5	-7.0	-1.8	-0.9	-1.3	-2.8	-3.6
CHAD	6.4	-5.9	-6.8	-5.1	-12.7	-0.5	-6.2
COMOROS	-16.0	-1.7	-1.9	-3.2	-3.9	-8.4	-3.4
CONGO	-0.9	-6.6	1.2	1.0	0.8	1.3	-8.7
CONGO DEM. REP.	-0.4	-10.9	-5.3	-1.3	-3.2	-6.3	-9.0
COTE D'IVOIRE	-12.8	-19.3	-1.3	-1.0	0.2	-7.7	-4.5
DJIBOUTI	6.3	-7.3	-1.8	-0.7	-2.3	-4.4	-5.1
EGYPT	-9.6	-12.6	-3.9	-5.5	-5.8	-16.5	-4.4
EQUAT. GUINEA	-16.3	-5.3	7.6	15.1	22.4	-10.5	-0.0
ERITREA	...	...	-47.8	-32.3	-57.1	...	-27.1
ETHIOPIA	-3.6	-9.7	-11.5	-5.7	-9.9	-6.0	-6.8
GABON	7.4	-4.1	11.7	4.8	4.8	-2.7	0.1
GAMBIA	-23.0	-1.7	-1.4	0.5	0.3	-7.4	-1.7
GHANA	-11.7	-2.2	-7.9	-6.4	-7.0	-4.2	-7.7
GUINEA	-0.5	-5.5	-3.2	-3.5	-2.5	-2.8	-3.1
GUINEA BISSAU	12.2	-5.9	-10.8	-10.8	-14.6	-5.3	-11.9
KENYA	-7.8	-6.8	-0.7	-2.5	-5.3	-5.8	-2.9
LESOTHO	-10.1	-0.9	-2.3	1.9	-1.6	-9.7	-0.3
LIBERIA	...	...	...	...	...	...	...
LIBYA	...	...	...	...	...	...	...
MADAGASCAR	-14.2	-0.6	-2.6	-4.7	-6.0	-6.1	-5.2
MALAWI	-11.6	-2.8	-4.9	-7.3	-5.2	-7.1	-6.6
MALI	-4.2	-2.7	-3.9	-7.4	-6.6	-5.2	-3.9
MAURITANIA	-13.7	-5.2	-3.2	-4.0	8.9	-7.2	0.4
MAURITIUS	-10.6	-2.1	-3.8	-5.7	-6.5	-6.3	-4.2
MOROCCO	-11.2	-0.6	-6.4	-5.6	-6.3	-7.8	-3.8
MOZAMBIQUE	-2.0	-5.9	-4.1	-5.3	-6.7	-7.7	-3.6
NAMIBIA	...	0.4	-4.9	-4.9	-5.5	-0.1	-3.8
NIGER	-1.0	-7.0	-3.5	-3.8	-4.9	-3.7	-3.9
NIGERIA	-3.4	3.1	2.4	-2.2	-7.6	-5.2	-2.2
RWANDA	-3.3	-7.2	0.1	-1.1	-0.6	-4.2	-4.8
SAO T. & PRINC.	-27.7	-42.2	-16.5	-17.7	-6.3	-26.7	-29.2
SENEGAL	-8.2	-0.5	0.1	-2.0	-0.4	-4.2	-0.9
SEYCHELLES	-6.6	5.6	-15.2	-10.8	-10.4	-7.0	-7.7
SIERRA LEONE	-12.1	-8.8	-9.3	-10.5	-18.1	-9.1	-8.2
SOMALIA	...	...	...	...	...	...	...
SOUTH AFRICA	-0.9	-3.1	-2.1	-1.5	-2.1	-3.9	-4.3
SUDAN	-8.9	-14.9	-0.8	-0.6	-1.0	-11.1	-5.6
SWAZILAND	...	6.5	-1.5	-3.3	-5.1	-0.7	-1.2
TANZANIA	-5.7	-3.2	-1.7	-3.1	-4.3	-5.8	-2.3
TOGO	-5.7	-2.8	-5.4	-2.0	-1.6	-3.9	-5.5
TUNISIA	-2.8	-5.4	-3.3	-2.6	-2.1	-4.9	-3.4
UGANDA	-4.7	-4.1	-8.1	-0.9	-4.1	-5.7	-3.0
ZAMBIA	-18.5	-8.3	-5.7	-7.0	-6.2	-13.2	-4.3
ZIMBABWE	-9.6	-6.2	-21.7	-12.0	-14.7	-7.8	-9.2
AFRICA	**-3.6**	**-4.6**	**-1.4**	**-2.1**	**-2.9**	**-6.3**	**-3.7**

TABLE 2.12
TOTAL EXTERNAL DEBT
(MILLIONS OF US DOLLARS)

COUNTRY	1981	1991	1997	2001	2002	Average Annual Growth (%) 1981-1991	1992-2002
ALGERIA	17,806.8	28,204.0	33,428.0	22,571.0	23,451.4	4.2	-1.4
ANGOLA	9,389.8	11,587.0	9,195.3	8,773.6	8,069.9	2.3	-2.7
BENIN	144.6	1,009.3	1,556.1	1,800.1	1,718.7	43.2	5.0
BOTSWANA	178.3	769.0	923.2	1,190.2	1,279.6	16.1	4.8
BURKINA FASO	419.9	762.8	1,281.1	1,655.5	1,552.7	15.0	6.8
BURUNDI	177.4	940.0	1,207.8	1,186.1	1,317.5	18.2	3.3
CAMEROON	1,209.5	7,209.8	8,661.6	7,086.4	6,629.2	19.2	-0.2
CAPE VERDE	...	137.2	201.8	345.7	331.3	10.6	8.9
CENTR. AFR. REP.	226.2	748.3	879.8	823.4	709.2	15.4	-0.2
CHAD	...	575.0	930.9	1,226.1	1,158.2	20.5	7.0
COMOROS	49.2	180.2	200.3	227.7	214.5	20.1	1.9
CONGO	...	3,754.3	5,391.1	5,387.9	5,272.3	-3.5	3.4
CONGO, DEM. REP	4,425.6	11,165.6	12,168.1	12,736.8	9,642.1	9.1	-0.8
COTE D'IVOIRE	5,642.3	16,326.8	16,169.9	12,760.3	10,780.1	12.6	-3.1
DJIBOUTI	30.0	196.6	301.3	393.6	401.6	24.3	6.9
EGYPT	30,100.0	35,473.0	31,043.0	26,559.7	29,441.5	2.1	-1.5
EQUAT. GUINEA	57.2	225.5	254.4	288.2	261.9	16.8	1.6
ERITREA	...	...	...	...	...	...	...
ETHIOPIA	1,091.3	8,778.8	9,870.8	5,614.0	5,999.4	28.1	-1.8
GABON	1,208.2	3,259.4	4,028.3	2,690.3	2,678.3	11.1	-1.3
GAMBIA	287.0	263.3	436.2	559.1	504.3	3.7	6.4
GHANA	1,645.6	3,282.2	5,581.8	7,028.2	6,362.5	12.5	7.5
GUINEA	1,243.2	2,385.1	3,143.9	3,198.9	2,966.1	10.1	2.2
GUINEA BISSAU	469.6	788.0	866.5	818.4	751.0	5.3	-0.2
KENYA	4,513.3	6,488.1	6,082.4	4,715.7	4,556.8	4.0	-3.1
LESOTHO	93.8	334.8	573.1	538.4	508.3	15.1	4.4
LIBERIA	714.2	2,096.6	2,117.0	2,047.6	2,047.6	11.8	-0.2
LIBYA	...	...	...	...	...	...	...
MADAGASCAR	1,474.5	3,422.5	4,476.4	3,181.0	3,785.3	12.3	1.4
MALAWI	829.6	1,817.5	2,156.1	2,847.8	2,589.8	8.2	3.5
MALI	796.5	2,117.0	2,916.4	2,730.6	2,494.1	10.5	1.7
MAURITANIA	951.9	2,245.5	2,411.5	1,708.8	1,905.0	10.1	-1.1
MAURITIUS	452.2	841.6	1,322.5	928.6	980.1	9.2	2.0
MOROCCO	10,118.4	21,273.0	21,727.4	15,676.8	15,281.7	7.7	-2.8
MOZAMBIQUE	1,300.1	4,698.2	5,912.9	3,258.7	1,799.5	16.8	-6.5
NAMIBIA	...	313.9	356.5	76.0	81.3	0.7	-4.9
NIGER	604.9	1,388.6	1,522.5	1,323.8	1,759.2	12.3	3.1
NIGERIA	10,505.0	33,815.0	31,453.3	29,650.5	29,391.8	17.8	-1.1
RWANDA	190.6	718.7	1,116.5	1,303.5	1,247.1	14.1	5.3
SAO T. & PRINC.	20.3	191.6	267.7	303.0	296.1	23.6	4.1
SENEGAL	1,374.8	2,939.3	3,715.4	3,216.4	2,901.1	9.4	0.3
SEYCHELLES	28.8	230.0	346.0	293.0	352.0	26.5	4.5
SIERRA LEONE	469.2	1,594.0	1,960.4	1,814.6	1,068.1	12.6	•2.4
SOMALIA	898.1	2,109.3	2,790.0	3,006.3	3,439.8	9.4	4.7
SOUTH AFRICA	18,889.0	24,889.0	34,540.0	35,854.9	31,493.0	5.0	2.5
SUDAN	6,190.0	...	...	...	21,556.0	10.6	...
SWAZILAND	...	212.9	245.7	381.9	419.6	5.5	6.8
TANZANIA	3,044.6	6,362.2	7,538.8	6,574.6	7,468.4	8.2	1.7
TOGO	...	1,241.6	1,416.5	962.0	1,062.5	6.1	-1.1
TUNISIA	3,643.0	8,555.5	11,429.7	9,697.4	11,356.9	8.5	3.0
UGANDA	...	2,591.6	3,516.6	3,824.7	3,563.1	14.6	3.1
ZAMBIA	3,257.0	6,971.3	7,289.6	4,148.0	5,076.1	7.9	-2.0
ZIMBABWE	1,410.9	3,136.0	5,434.6	4,676.0	6,002.5	8.8	6.8
AFRICA	**148,163.7**	**294,546.3**	**331,004.0**	**292,164.2**	**297,648.0**	**7.4**	**0.2**

TABLE 2.13
TOTAL DEBT SERVICE
(MILLIONS OF US DOLLARS)

COUNTRY	1981	1991	1996	2000	2001	Average Annual Growth (%) 1981-1991	1992-2001
ALGERIA	4320.0	9510.0	7464.6	4593.1	4888.9	8.5	-6.0
ANGOLA	228.4	1748.5	1566.4	2104.5	2432.7	29.6	9.4
BENIN	...	17.6	66.7	52.5	73.6	-22.0	19.2
BOTSWANA	9.5	141.0	135.5	208.5	266.1	37.1	7.6
BURKINA FASO	17.1	28.9	66.1	103.7	93.5	42.2	22.2
BURUNDI	9.9	37.7	...	55.2	83.5	16.4	-11.0
CAMEROON	...	240.4	509.5	340.7	294.3	11.7	29.1
CAPE VERDE	...	8.6	0.9	23.9	47.1	27.8	783.2
CENTRAL AFRICAN REP.	...	2.6	6.3	8.1	12.6	-9.7	59.5
CHAD	...	...	...	45.0	61.4	...	36.6
COMOROS	...	...	1.3	2.0	6.1	...	27.9
CONGO	...	...	680.6	231.1	227.0	...	7.9
CONGO, DEM. REP.	865.8	1329.9	625.3	927.4	1032.5	21.5	5.1
COTE D'IVOIRE	1062.4	1279.5	877.3	1383.7	1332.4	5.6	1.7
DJIBOUTI	4.5	9.8	...	20.3	14.0	12.5	-12.2
EGYPT	2998.6	5083.1	1973.0	1837.4	1839.7	6.0	-7.3
EQUAT. GUINEA	...	...	53.7	141.9	198.8	...	34.0
ERITREA	...	...	...	...	...	...	...
ETHIOPIA	...	219.9	134.1	158.6	216.0	...	8.5
GABON	873.6	598.1	779.4	778.3	823.3	1.7	15.2
GAMBIA	11.5	23.7	27.5	31.6	41.8	23.1	7.7
GHANA	...	265.3	670.3	557.2	339.0	12.7	6.1
GUINEA	104.7	157.1	174.8	208.0	113.1	6.7	33.1
GUINEA BISSAU	0.4	3.8	7.2	8.3	0.9	28.8	13.2
KENYA	238.1	484.8	769.5	585.7	470.5	15.5	5.8
LESOTHO	...	20.3	28.4	54.4	21.9	0.5	5.7
LIBERIA	45.1	96.0	116.8	130.6	134.4	35.5	3.4
LIBYA	...	...	...	...	...	...	...
MADAGASCAR	258.1	206.3	85.9	77.5	56.6	-55.8	-1.2
MALAWI	...	...	...	92.9	91.6	...	-1.5
MALI	20.8	45.3	113.2	90.7	84.3	11.7	8.9
MAURITANIA	2.1	98.0	114.0	74.2	75.0	993.9	-1.4
MAURITIUS	94.3	178.4	229.4	215.1	254.2	8.9	5.6
MOROCCO	1320.0	1726.0	3278.6	2638.4	2308.2	5.0	5.3
MOZAMBIQUE	345.1	19.4	106.0	69.9	112.3	...	36.1
NAMIBIA	...	14.2	6.7	20.9	25.7	-29.4	21.8
NIGER	...	...	2.2	22.4	44.5	...	253.3
NIGERIA	1645.5	2378.8	2298.5	1981.7	1823.7	16.3	1.5
RWANDA	...	...	13.7	9.8	9.8	...	3.3
SAO T. & PRINC.	...	0.4	2.8	5.8	7.4	177.8	85.1
SENEGAL	189.1	387.8	248.4	186.1	160.6	8.6	-4.9
SEYCHELLES	0.6	37.5	45.7	40.7	108.8	137.8	23.3
SIERRA LEONE	4.1	83.5	62.9	53.2	118.9	282.1	10.6
SOMALIA	3.0	155.2	189.9	212.1	218.7	...	3.5
SOUDAN	203.1	...	...	...	...	1.8	...
SOUTH AFRICA	2745.4	4225.2	6990.9	5959.9	5127.4	6.8	3.0
SWAZILAND	...	...	...	...	...	...	...
TANZANIA	178.8	206.7	457.7	395.1	460.2	2.5	12.6
TOGO	...	68.7	65.5	115.3	79.4	3.9	7.2
TUNISIA	1095.6	1379.3	1741.8	2097.2	1611.7	5.4	2.5
UGANDA	...	190.7	142.8	141.5	124.8	...	-1.3
ZAMBIA	532.0	583.1	328.2	178.0	237.1	54.8	19.4
ZIMBABWE	194.1	448.0	475.9	287.5	87.3	9.6	-9.9
AFRICA	20136.4	33243.4	34213.7	29606.9	28645.9	5.5	-1.2

TABLE 3.1
LABOR FORCE BY SECTOR
(PERCENT IN)

COUNTRY	AGRICULTURE				INDUSTRY				SERVICES			
	1980	1985	1990	1996	1980	1985	1990	1996	1980	1985	1990	1996
ALGERIA	31	25	19	14	27	29	32	35	42	46	49	51
ANGOLA	74	72	70	68	10	10	11	11	17	18	19	21
BENIN	70	65	59	54	7	7	8	10	23	28	32	36
BOTSWANA	70	61	52	42	13	19	28	41	17	20	20	17
BURKINA FASO	87	86	85	84	4	5	5	5	9	10	10	11
BURUNDI	93	92	92	91	2	3	3	3	5	5	5	6
CAMEROON	70	63	56	49	8	10	13	15	22	27	32	36
CAPE VERDE	52	46	40	35	23	27	31	36	26	27	29	29
CENT. AFR. REP.	72	67	61	56	6	8	10	12	21	25	29	32
CHAD	83	80	76	72	5	5	6	7	12	15	18	21
COMOROS	83	81	79	77	6	6	7	8	11	12	14	15
CONGO	62	61	60	58	12	12	12	13	26	27	28	29
CONGO DEM. REP.	71	68	64	60	13	14	16	17	16	18	20	23
COTE D'IVOIRE	65	60	54	49	8	10	12	14	27	30	34	37
DJIBOUTI	...	...	...	...	...	...	...	...	...	...	...	...
EGYPT	46	42	39	36	20	22	24	27	34	35	36	37
EQUAT. GUINEA	66	61	57	52	11	13	15	18	23	26	28	30
ERITREA	...	...	...	...	...	...	...	...	...	...	...	...
ETHIOPIA	80	77	74	72	8	9	10	12	12	14	15	16
GABON	75	73	71	69	11	12	12	13	14	15	16	18
GAMBIA	84	83	82	80	7	7	8	9	9	10	11	11
GHANA	56	54	53	52	18	18	19	19	26	27	28	29
GUINEA	81	78	76	74	9	10	11	13	10	11	12	13
GUINEA BISSAU	82	81	80	79	4	4	4	5	14	15	15	16
KENYA	81	79	77	75	7	7	8	9	12	13	14	16
LESOTHO	86	84	82	81	4	5	5	6	10	11	12	13
LIBERIA	74	73	71	70	9	9	9	9	16	18	20	21
LIBYA	18	14	11	8	29	30	32	34	53	55	57	58
MADAGASCAR	81	79	78	76	6	7	7	8	13	14	15	16
MALAWI	83	78	75	70	7	10	13	17	9	11	12	13
MALI	86	84	82	80	2	2	3	3	12	14	16	17
MAURITANIA	69	61	53	45	9	12	16	21	22	27	31	34
MAURITIUS	28	25	23	20	24	24	23	23	48	51	54	57
MOROCCO	46	40	35	30	25	29	35	40	29	31	31	30
MOZAMBIQUE	84	83	82	81	7	8	9	10	8	8	9	9
NAMIBIA	43	44	43	40	22	20	27	37	36	6	31	23
NIGER	91	89	88	86	2	2	2	2	7	9	10	12
NIGERIA	68	67	65	64	12	12	13	13	20	21	22	23
RWANDA	93	92	92	92	3	3	3	3	4	5	5	5
SAO T. & PRINC.	...	...	...	...	...	...	...	...	...	...	...	...
SENEGAL	81	79	78	77	6	7	7	7	13	14	15	16
SEYCHELLES	...	...	...	...	...	...	...	...	...	...	...	...
SIERRA LEONE	70	67	64	61	14	15	16	17	16	18	20	22
SOMALIA	76	74	72	70	8	9	10	11	16	17	18	19
SOUTH AFRICA	17	...	14	...	35	...	32	...	48	...	54	...
SUDAN	71	68	65	62	7	8	9	11	21	23	25	27
SWAZILAND	74	71	67	64	9	10	12	13	17	19	21	23
TANZANIA	86	84	81	79	5	5	6	7	10	11	12	14
TOGO	73	71	69	67	10	10	11	12	17	18	20	21
TUNISIA	35	31	28	25	36	43	49	56	29	26	23	19
UGANDA	86	84	82	81	4	5	6	6	10	11	12	13
ZAMBIA	73	71	70	68	10	11	11	12	17	18	19	20
ZIMBABWE	73	70	68	66	10	12	13	14	17	18	19	20
AFRICA	70	67	65	62	11	12	13	15	19	21	22	23

TABLE 3.2
LABOR FORCE PARTICIPATION RATE
(Percentage of population of all ages in labor force)

COUNTRY	TOTAL			FEMALE			MALE		
	1980	1995	2001	1980	1995	2001	1980	1995	2001
ALGERIA	26.0	31.1	35.2	11.0	15.2	20.1	41.1	46.5	49.9
ANGOLA	49.4	46.0	45.1	45.7	42.2	41.2	53.3	50.0	49.1
BENIN	47.9	45.2	45.3	44.5	42.9	43.0	51.5	47.5	47.7
BOTSWANA	43.6	43.0	43.8	41.8	39.0	39.0	45.5	47.3	48.7
BURKINA FASo	53.6	49.1	47.3	51.5	46.6	45.0	55.9	51.8	49.8
BURUNDI	54.9	53.4	52.8	53.2	51.1	50.5	56.9	55.7	55.2
CAMEROON	41.9	40.5	41.2	30.5	30.1	31.2	53.7	51.0	51.3
CAPE VERDE	32.5	38.9	41.0	20.4	28.8	31.0	46.7	50.6	52.9
CENT. AFR. REP.	52.5	47.9	47.1	48.7	43.5	42.6	56.6	52.5	51.8
CHAD	48.0	46.4	45.8	41.1	40.8	40.7	55.2	52.2	51.0
COMOROS	45.2	46.0	46.9	39.5	39.7	40.5	50.9	51.9	53.5
CONGO	42.1	41.4	40.8	34.8	35.1	34.7	49.8	47.9	47.1
CONGO DEM. REP.	44.5	41.6	40.5	38.8	35.8	34.8	50.4	47.4	46.3
COTE D'IVOI	40.7	39.8	40.9	26.6	26.2	27.5	54.0	52.7	53.6
DJIBOUTI	...	49.9	48.9	...	47.4	46.4	...	52.7	51.8
EGYPT	35.0	36.4	38.5	18.9	21.3	24.1	50.7	51.0	52.5
EQUAT. GUIN	44.7	41.8	41.3	30.7	29.1	29.0	58.3	54.9	53.9
ERITREA	...	50.1	49.9	...	47.2	47.0	...	53.1	52.9
ETHIOPIA	49.5	44.6	44.1	41.6	37.1	36.6	57.5	52.3	51.6
GABON	52.5	46.8	44.9	46.3	41.0	39.6	58.8	52.8	50.3
GAMBIA	51.5	51.1	51.4	45.6	45.2	45.7	57.6	57.0	57.1
GHANA	46.6	47.9	49.5	47.2	48.3	49.6	46.1	47.6	49.5
GUINEA	51.8	49.8	49.6	48.8	47.3	47.1	54.8	52.2	52.1
GUINEA BISS	48.6	46.4	45.6	38.1	36.9	36.5	59.5	56.2	55.0
KENYA	47.2	49.5	51.7	43.5	45.7	48.0	50.9	53.3	55.5
LESOTHO	42.5	42.0	42.5	31.1	30.2	30.8	54.5	54.2	54.3
LIBERIA	42.1	38.3	39.8	32.6	30.5	31.7	51.5	46.0	47.8
LIBYA	31.0	31.7	34.1	12.2	13.7	16.8	47.7	48.1	50.3
MADAGASCAR	49.6	48.2	47.8	44.2	42.9	42.5	55.2	53.6	53.2
MALAWI	50.3	48.7	48.1	49.3	47.1	46.3	51.4	50.3	49.9
MALI	51.5	49.9	48.8	47.0	45.4	44.1	56.2	54.6	53.5
MAURITANIA	48.1	44.5	44.2	42.8	38.8	38.3	53.5	50.4	50.2
MAURITIUS	35.5	42.3	43.8	18.0	26.5	28.8	53.5	58.1	59.0
MOROCCO	35.9	38.2	39.7	24.1	26.5	27.7	47.7	49.9	51.7
MOZAMBIQUE	54.6	52.9	52.4	52.7	50.5	50.0	56.6	55.3	54.8
NAMIBIA	41.4	40.1	39.6	33.1	32.9	32.4	50.1	47.8	46.9
NIGER	48.1	46.6	46.0	42.2	40.6	40.2	54.0	52.6	51.8
NIGERIA	41.2	39.6	39.7	29.3	27.9	28.5	53.1	51.1	50.8
RWANDA	51.1	53.4	54.4	49.6	51.5	52.1	52.6	55.4	56.6
SAO T.& PRI	...	42.9	42.1	...	...	...	...	...	...
SENEGAL	45.9	44.5	44.4	38.7	37.9	38.1	53.1	51.1	50.8
SEYCHELLES	...	47.8	47.9	...	...	...	...	...	...
SIERRA LEON	38.6	37.3	37.0	26.9	26.4	26.8	50.8	48.5	47.5
SOMALIA	45.2	43.2	42.7	38.8	37.1	36.7	51.8	49.4	48.7
SOUTH AFRIC	36.8	40.3	41.7	25.8	30.2	31.5	48.0	50.7	52.2
SUDAN	37.0	38.5	39.5	20.0	21.8	23.6	54.0	54.9	55.2
SWAZILAND	35.7	36.2	37.0	23.5	24.8	25.9	48.0	47.9	48.4
TANZANIA	51.2	51.4	51.6	50.2	50.3	50.3	52.2	52.6	52.9
TOGO	42.8	42.1	42.3	33.2	33.3	33.5	52.6	51.1	51.3
TUNISIA	34.3	37.6	40.9	20.1	23.2	26.6	48.0	51.8	55.0
UGANDA	51.7	49.9	48.8	48.9	47.2	46.0	54.5	52.7	51.6
ZAMBIA	43.1	42.7	42.2	37.7	37.0	36.4	48.6	48.4	48.0
ZIMBABWE	44.4	44.9	44.7	39.1	39.4	39.2	49.8	50.5	50.3
AFRICA	42.7	42.7	43.3	34.1	34.3	35.1	51.7	51.2	51.5

TABLE 3.3
COMPONENTS OF POPULATION CHANGE

COUNTRY	TOTAL FERTILITY RATE (PER WOMAN)			CRUDE BIRTH RATE (PER 1000 POPULATION			CRUDE DEATH RATE (PER 1000 POPULATION)			RATE OF NATURAL INCREASE (PERCENT)		
	1980	1990	2002	1980	1990	2002	1980	1990	2002	1980	1990	2002
ALGERIA	6.7	4.4	2.8	42.4	30.9	23.5	11.6	7.1	5.3	3.1	2.4	1.8
ANGOLA	6.9	7.2	7.2	50.7	51.2	51.3	23.5	20.6	19.0	2.7	3.1	3.2
BENIN	7.1	6.6	5.7	51.5	47.0	41.1	19.2	15.2	12.3	3.2	3.2	2.9
BOTSWANA	6.1	5.1	3.9	44.7	38.2	30.6	10.2	8.2	24.5	3.5	3.0	0.6
BURKINA FASO	7.8	7.3	6.8	49.8	47.5	46.8	19.4	17.9	15.9	3.0	3.0	3.1
BURUNDI	6.8	6.8	6.8	45.8	46.3	43.5	18.3	20.4	20.8	2.8	2.6	2.3
CAMEROON	6.4	5.9	4.7	45.1	41.7	36.3	16.6	14.2	14.6	2.9	2.7	2.2
CAPE VERDE	6.5	4.2	3.2	37.2	34.7	29.1	10.4	8.2	5.6	2.7	2.6	2.4
CENT. AFR. REP.	5.8	5.6	4.9	43.2	41.5	37.5	19.4	18.0	18.6	2.4	2.3	1.9
CHAD	6.7	6.7	6.7	48.1	48.5	48.5	22.9	20.5	18.6	2.5	2.8	3.0
COMOROS	7.0	6.1	5.0	48.6	40.6	37.7	14.4	10.9	8.5	3.4	3.0	2.9
CONGO	6.3	6.3	6.3	44.7	44.5	44.2	16.3	14.9	14.0	2.8	3.0	3.0
CONGO DEM. REP.	6.6	6.7	6.7	48.0	48.0	47.2	16.8	15.0	13.6	3.1	3.3	3.4
COTE D'IVOIRE	7.4	6.2	4.6	50.8	41.4	35.3	16.4	14.6	15.3	3.4	2.7	2.0
DJIBOUTI	6.6	6.3	5.8	52.8	45.5	38.0	20.8	17.6	20.8	3.2	2.8	1.7
EGYPT	5.1	4.1	2.9	38.8	31.3	23.3	13.3	8.6	6.1	2.6	2.3	1.7
EQUAT. GUINEA	5.7	5.9	5.9	43.1	43.6	43.2	21.7	18.6	15.1	2.1	2.5	2.8
ERITREA	6.4	6.2	5.3	45.2	43.9	38.5	19.6	16.0	13.3	2.6	2.8	2.5
ETHIOPIA	6.8	6.9	6.8	46.3	46.2	43.8	20.9	18.8	19.4	2.5	2.7	2.4
GABON	4.5	5.1	5.4	33.0	36.4	37.6	18.5	16.6	15.2	1.4	2.0	2.2
GAMBIA	6.5	5.8	4.8	48.3	44.5	37.2	23.9	20.5	17.0	2.4	2.4	2.0
GHANA	6.8	5.6	4.2	45.9	38.9	32.6	13.8	11.5	10.4	3.2	2.7	2.2
GUINEA	7.0	6.5	5.8	51.5	45.1	43.4	24.5	19.9	16.8	2.7	2.5	2.7
GUINEA BISSAU	6.0	6.0	6.0	45.0	45.1	44.6	25.4	22.2	19.3	2.0	2.3	2.5
KENYA	7.7	5.9	4.2	50.8	41.3	34.1	13.3	10.7	13.7	3.7	3.1	2.0
LESOTHO	5.6	5.1	4.5	40.9	37.4	32.5	14.7	11.9	21.9	2.6	2.5	1.1
LIBERIA	6.8	6.8	6.8	47.2	42.0	55.5	16.8	19.7	12.2	3.0	2.2	4.3
LIBYA	7.3	4.7	3.3	46.3	27.6	26.8	11.6	4.9	4.8	3.5	2.3	2.2
MADAGASCAR	6.4	6.2	5.7	45.6	44.7	41.5	17.6	16.4	13.2	2.8	2.8	2.8
MALAWI	7.6	7.3	6.3	55.0	50.9	44.9	22.5	20.9	22.6	3.2	3.0	2.2
MALI	7.0	7.0	7.0	50.4	50.1	49.6	21.9	19.3	17.3	2.9	3.1	3.2
MAURITANIA	6.4	6.1	6.0	43.3	44.1	43.7	19.1	16.5	14.2	2.4	2.8	3.0
MAURITIUS	2.7	2.2	1.9	23.9	20.2	15.7	6.4	6.5	6.7	1.7	1.4	0.9
MOROCCO	5.6	4.2	3.0	38.0	30.6	24.8	12.0	8.1	6.0	2.6	2.2	1.9
MOZAMBIQUE	6.6	6.4	5.9	46.0	45.2	41.7	20.9	20.4	23.9	2.5	2.5	1.8
NAMIBIA	6.5	6.0	4.9	42.2	41.6	34.5	13.9	12.7	17.8	2.8	2.9	1.7
NIGER	8.2	8.0	8.0	56.7	55.5	55.2	24.6	22.6	19.1	3.2	3.3	3.6
NIGERIA	6.9	6.5	5.4	47.6	44.8	39.5	18.0	15.4	13.3	3.0	2.9	2.6
RWANDA	8.3	6.8	5.8	51.4	43.5	42.1	19.5	34.4	20.6	3.2	0.9	2.2
SAO T. & PRINC.	...	...	...	...	...	...	...	...	...	...	...	...
SENEGAL	6.8	6.2	5.1	48.0	43.0	37.6	20.4	16.0	11.6	2.8	2.7	2.6
SEYCHELLES	...	...	...	...	...	...	...	...	...	...	...	...
SIERRA LEONE	6.5	6.5	6.5	48.9	49.3	49.1	28.8	28.8	23.3	2.0	2.0	2.6
SOMALIA	7.3	7.3	7.3	51.8	51.9	51.8	22.4	23.2	17.0	2.9	2.9	3.5
SOUTH AFRICA	4.7	3.5	2.9	34.3	28.3	24.6	11.2	9.1	17.1	2.3	1.9	0.8
SUDAN	6.1	5.4	4.5	42.4	38.3	33.6	16.7	13.9	11.1	2.6	2.4	2.3
SWAZILAND	6.2	5.5	4.4	43.1	39.4	33.4	14.7	11.6	23.0	2.8	2.8	1.0
TANZANIA	6.7	6.1	5.0	46.6	43.5	37.9	15.2	12.9	13.1	3.1	3.1	2.5
TOGO	6.9	6.3	5.4	46.1	42.9	38.7	16.5	14.2	13.2	3.0	2.9	2.5
TUNISIA	5.2	3.5	2.1	35.2	27.4	18.6	9.0	6.7	6.4	2.6	2.1	1.2
UGANDA	7.1	7.1	7.1	50.4	50.5	50.6	18.3	20.7	17.2	3.2	3.0	3.3
ZAMBIA	7.0	6.3	5.0	46.3	44.8	41.5	15.4	16.5	18.8	3.1	2.8	2.3
ZIMBABWE	6.7	5.7	4.5	44.5	41.4	35.1	10.5	13.0	17.8	3.4	2.8	1.7
AFRICA	6.5	5.8	5.1	43.8	41.0	37.6	16.6	14.5	13.9	2.8	2.7	2.37

TABLE 3.4
MORTALITY INDICATORS

| COUNTRY | INFANT MORTALITY RATE (PER 1000) | | | LIFE EXPECTANCY AT BIRTH (YEARS) | | | | | |
| | 1980 | 1990 | 2002 | 1980 | | 1990 | | 2002 | |
				M	F	M	F	M	F
ALGERIA	98	64	43	59	61	61	67	69	72
ANGOLA	153	131	118	40	43	43	46	45	47
BENIN	115	99	81	46	48	50	50	53	52
BOTSWANA	71	59	67	56	60	59	63	37	36
BURKINA FASO	125	110	87	45	51	46	54	47	56
BURUNDI	122	129	111	45	49	42	45	40	41
CAMEROON	108	90	79	48	51	51	54	49	51
CAPE VERDE	85	68	50	59	63	62	68	67	73
CENT. AFR. REP.	117	104	93	43	48	45	49	43	46
CHAD	148	131	116	40	44	43	46	45	48
COMOROS	110	88	67	50	54	54	58	59	62
CONGO	88	80	66	47	53	49	54	50	54
CONGO, DEM. REP	112	96	77	47	51	50	53	51	53
COTE D'IVOIRE	112	97	81	48	51	49	52	48	48
DJIBOUTI	136	121	117	43	46	46	49	39	42
EGYPT	121	68	40	54	57	61	64	67	70
EQUAT. GUINEA	142	121	99	42	45	46	49	50	54
ERITREA	128	107	82	43	46	47	51	51	54
ETHIOPIA	142	125	106	42	45	44	47	43	44
GABON	114	97	80	47	50	50	53	52	54
GAMBIA	159	138	115	39	42	42	45	46	49
GHANA	94	79	62	52	55	54	57	56	59
GUINEA	161	139	114	39	40	43	44	48	49
GUINEA BISSAU	169	145	121	37	40	41	44	44	47
KENYA	87	71	59	53	57	55	59	49	50
LESOTHO	121	103	111	51	55	56	58	41	40
LIBERIA	138	143	79	49	52	43	45	55	57
LIBYA	53	33	25	59	62	67	70	69	73
MADAGASCAR	119	111	91	47	49	48	50	53	55
MALAWI	167	153	130	44	45	44	45	40	39
MALI	162	139	120	45	47	48	50	51	53
MAURITANIA	120	112	97	45	48	48	51	51	54
MAURITIUS	32	22	16	63	69	66	73	68	76
MOROCCO	102	68	42	56	59	62	65	67	71
MOZAMBIQUE	140	135	128	42	45	42	45	37	39
NAMIBIA	91	81	65	52	55	54	56	44	44
NIGER	158	148	126	40	41	42	42	46	47
NIGERIA	120	101	79	47	48	50	51	52	52
RWANDA	131	131	119	44	47	31	32	40	42
SAO T. & PRINC.	...	...	...	...	...	...	...	...	...
SENEGAL	91	71	57	43	48	48	52	53	56
SEYCHELLES	...	...	...	...	...	...	...	...	...
SIERRA LEONE	190	190	146	34	37	34	37	39	42
SOMALIA	145	152	113	41	44	40	43	47	51
SOUTH AFRICA	70	57	59	53	60	56	64	47	48
SUDAN	117	98	78	47	50	51	54	56	58
SWAZILAND	100	82	92	49	54	54	58	38	38
TANZANIA	105	89	73	49	52	51	54	50	52
TOGO	110	93	75	48	49	50	52	51	52
TUNISIA	78	41	26	61	62	66	68	70	72
UGANDA	121	121	94	45	49	42	44	45	47
ZAMBIA	104	99	80	49	52	47	48	43	42
ZIMBABWE	69	69	55	57	61	52	53	43	4
AFRICA	**115**	**95**	**78**	**48**	**51**	**51**	**54**	**52**	**54**

Note : M and F refer to Male and Female respectively

TABLE 3.5
POPULATION WITH ACCESS TO SOCIAL INFRASTRUCTURES
(PERCENT OF POPULATION)

COUNTRY	SANITATION			SAFE WATER			HEALTH SERVICES		
	1985	1990-93	2000	1985	1990-93	2000	1985	1991	1992-99
ALGERIA	59	90	73	69	90	94	...	...	98
ANGOLA	18	31	44	28	31	38	70	24	...
BENIN	10	70	23	14	70	63	...	42	18
BOTSWANA	36	70	...	77	70	...	...	86	...
BURKINA FASO	9	42	29	35	42	...	70	...	90
BURUNDI	52	58	...	23	58	...	45	80	80
CAMEROON	36	41	92	36	41	62	20	15	80
CAPE VERDE	10	67	71	31	67	74	...	...	...
CENT. AFR. REP.	19	18	31	24	18	60	..	13	52
CHAD	14	33	29	31	33	27	30	26	30
COMOROS	...	48	98	63	48	96	82	...	...
CONGO	40	27	...	20	27	51	...	...	83
CONGO DEM. REP.	23	60	20	33	60	45	33	59	26
COTE D'IVOIRE	50	82	...	17	82	77	...	60	...
DJIBOUTI	37	24	91	43	24	100	...	...	...
EGYPT	80	64	94	75	64	95	99	99	99
EQUAT. GUINEA	...	95	53	...	95	43	...	...	...
ERITREA	...	68	13	...	68	46	...	...	...
ETHIOPIA	19	27	15	16	27	24	44	55	46
GABON	50	67	21	50	67	70	80	87	...
GAMBIA	...	76	37	45	76	62	90	...	93
GHANA	26	57	63	56	57	64	64	76	...
GUINEA	21	55	58	20	55	48	13	45	80
GUINEA BISSAU	25	27	47	31	27	49	64	...	40
KENYA	44	49	86	27	49	49	...	...	77
LESOTHO	22	62	92	36	62	91	50	80	80
LIBERIA	21		...	37	...	...	35	..	39
LIBYA	91	97	97	90	97	72	100	100	95
MADAGASCAR	3	16	42	31	16	47	65	65	38
MALAWI	60	77	77	32	77	57	54	80	35
MALI	21	49	69	17	49	65	35	...	40
MAURITANIA	...	72	33	37	72	37	30	...	63
MAURITIUS	97	100	99	99	100	100	100	99	100
MOROCCO	46	58	75	57	58	82	70	62	70
MOZAMBIQUE	20	24	43	15	24	60	40	30	39
NAMIBIA	14	60	41	52	60	77	72	...	59
NIGER	9	52	20	37	52	59	48	30	99
NIGERIA	35	40	63	36	40	57	66	67	51
RWANDA	58	79	8	49	79	41	80	...	80
SAO T. & PRINC.	15	70	...	42	70	...	...	...	...
SENEGAL	55	50	70	44	50	78	40	40	90
SEYCHELLES	99	97	...	95	97	...	99	99	...
SIERRA LEONE	21	34	28	24	34	28	36	...	38
SOMALIA	15	37	...	31	37	...	20	...	...
SOUTH AFRICA	...	87	86	...	87	...	...	...	...
SUDAN	5	77	62	40	77	75	70	70	70
SWAZILAND	...	60	...	54	60	...	...	55	...
TANZANIA	64	49	90	52	49	54	73	93	42
TOGO	14	63	34	35	63	54	61	...	...
TUNISIA	52	99	...	89	99	...	91	100	...
UGANDA	13	42	75	16	42	50	42	71	49
ZAMBIA	47	59	78	48	59	64	70	75	...
ZIMBABWE	26	74	68	52	74	85	71	...	85
AFRICA	**35**	**55**	**60**	**42**	**55**	**60**	**61**	**66**	**62**

TABLE 3.6
SCHOOL ENROLMENT RATIO (GROSS)

	PRIMARY						SECONDARY					
	1975		1990		1996-99		1975		1990		1996-99	
COUNTRY	Total	Ratio F/M	Total	Ratio F/M	Total	Ratio F/M	Total	Ratio F/M	Total	Ratio F/M	Total	Ratio F/M
ALGERIA	93	0.69	100	0.84	108	0.90	20	0.53	61	0.80	63	0.95
ALGERIA	93	0.69	100	0.84	114	0.90	20	0.53	61	0.80	63	0.95
ANGOLA	130	0.60	92	0.92	64	0.92	9	0.40	12	0.66	12	0.66
BENIN	50	0.45	58	0.50	86	0.58	9	0.34	12	0.41	18	0.44
BOTSWANA	71	1.23	113	1.07	108	1.01	15	1.06	43	1.12	65	1.10
BURKINA FASO	14	0.56	33	0.63	43	0.65	2	0.46	7	0.53	9	0.55
BURUNDI	21	0.63	73	0.83	62	0.83	2	0.43	6	0.57	8	0.61
CAMEROON	95	0.80	101	0.86	91	0.90	13	0.50	28	0.70	25	0.68
CAPE VERDE	127	0.90	121	0.96	144	1.00	7	0.86	21	0.95	...	0.94
CENT. AFR. REP.	73	0.53	65	0.64	56	0.65	8	0.23	12	0.41	10	0.42
CHAD	35	0.35	54	0.45	70	0.52	3	0.20	8	0.23	10	0.25
COMOROS	64	0.43	75	0.73	84	0.86	13	0.39	18	0.68	24	0.81
CONGO	136	0.75	133	0.88	84	0.91	48	0.54	53	0.69	52	0.72
CONGO DEM. REP.	93	0.67	70	0.62	47	0.69	17	0.36	22	0.48	30	0.62
COTE D'IVOIRE	61	0.57	67	0.71	77	0.87	12	0.39	22	0.47	24	0.48
DJIBOUTI	30	0.54	38	0.71	37	0.73	7	0.36	12	0.65	14	0.70
EGYPT	70	0.67	94	0.85	100	0.88	40	0.56	76	0.81	75	0.88
EQUAT. GUINEA	140	...	...	...	125	...	14	0.25	...	...	...	...
ERITREA	...	...	23	0.96	61	0.82	...	...	15	0.93	20	0.71
ETHIOPIA	21	0.49	33	0.67	71	0.55	6	0.38	14	0.77	12	0.79
GABON	178	1.65	163	...	151	...	30	0.55	...	...	...	...
GAMBIA	33	0.49	64	0.68	75	0.77	9	0.36	19	0.43	26	0.56
GHANA	72	0.77	75	0.83	78	0.85	36	0.61	36	0.64	31	0.63
GUINEA	31	0.52	37	0.47	63	0.58	14	0.35	10	0.34	13	0.35
GUINEA BISSAU	65	0.45	56	0.58	83	0.58	4	0.40	9	0.45	11	0.48
KENYA	104	0.86	95	0.96	91	1.00	13	0.55	24	0.73	24	0.85
LESOTHO	106	1.42	112	1.23	104	1.12	13	1.17	25	1.48	31	1.46
LIBERIA	40	0.52	30	0.69	118	0.69	17	0.32	14	0.40	14	0.40
LIBYA	137	0.82	105	0.94	117	1.00	55	0.54	86	1.03	100	0.94
MADAGASCAR	92	0.72	103	1.00	102	0.97	13	0.71	18	0.97	16	0.99
MALAWI	56	0.62	68	0.84	158	0.91	4	0.34	8	0.29	...	0.55
MALI	25	0.56	27	0.57	55	0.65	7	0.35	7	0.48	12	0.51
MAURITANIA	20	0.56	49	0.74	84	0.89	4	0.12	14	0.48	16	0.51
MAURITIUS	105	0.98	109	1.00	108	0.99	38	0.83	53	1.00	65	1.04
MOROCCO	62	0.58	67	0.69	90	0.76	17	0.57	35	0.74	39	0.76
MOZAMBIQUE	83	0.55	67	0.75	85	0.72	3	0.50	8	0.62	7	0.63
NAMIBIA	...	...	129	1.10	113	1.01	...	...	44	1.27	61	1.18
NIGER	19	0.54	29	0.56	32	0.62	2	0.37	7	0.43	7	0.54
NIGERIA	50	0.64	91	0.76	82	0.79	8	0.53	25	0.73	34	0.84
RWANDA	55	0.84	70	0.98	122	0.97	4	1.23	8	0.78	13	0.77
SAO T. & PRINC.	...	...	...	...	...	...	...	...	...	...	...	...
SENEGAL	40	0.73	59	0.74	73	0.81	11	0.40	16	0.52	16	0.60
SEYCHELLES	...	...	96	...	...	...	...	...	...	...	...	...
SIERRA LEONE	39	0.64	50	0.69	65	0.69	12	0.46	17	0.57	17	0.58
SOMALIA	42	0.71	10	0.52	8	0.52	4	0.30	6	0.53	5	0.53
SOUTH AFRICA	104	1.02	122	0.98	119	0.98	27	1.00	74	1.16	84	1.19
SUDAN	47	0.57	53	0.75	55	0.84	14	0.44	24	0.80	21	0.90
SWAZILAND	97	0.94	111	0.96	125	0.87	32	0.83	44	0.99	54	0.99
TANZANIA	53	0.71	70	0.98	63	0.98	3	0.55	5	0.71	5	0.88
TOGO	98	0.53	109	0.65	124	0.71	19	0.31	24	0.34	27	0.36
TUNISIA	97	0.67	113	0.89	118	0.94	21	0.55	45	0.80	65	0.97
UGANDA	44	0.66	71	0.80	141	0.84	4	0.33	13	0.54	14	0.59
ZAMBIA	97	0.84	99	0.93	79	0.94	15	0.52	24	0.61	29	0.63
ZIMBABWE	70	0.84	116	0.98	97	0.97	8	0.70	50	0.87	49	0.85
AFRICA	71	0.68	78	0.85	88	0.81	14	0.54	25	0.77	29	0.81

Explanatory Notes

The main objective of the notes below is to facilitate interpretation of the statistical data presented in Part III of the Report. Data shown for all African countries are annual totals or five year averages. Period average growth rates are calculated as the arithmetic average of annual growth rates over the period. These statistics are not shown in the tables when they are not significant or not comparable over years.

Section 1: Basic Indicators

This section contains one table (Table 1.1) which presents some basic indicators as background to the tables in this part of the Report. The table provides cross-country comparisons for area, population, GNI per capita, Consumer Price Inflation, life expectancy, infant mortality and adult illiteracy rates. The main sources of data in this table are the United Nations Organizations, the World Bank, Country reports and ADB Statistics Division's estimates.

Area refers to the total surface area of a country, comprising land area and inland waters. The data is obtained from the Food and Agriculture Organization (FAO). The population figures are mid-year estimates obtained from the United Nations Population Division.

GNI per capita figures are obtained by dividing GNI in current US dollars by the corresponding mid-year population. GNI measures the total domestic and foreign value added claimed by residents. It comprises GDP plus net factor income from abroad, which is the income residents receive from abroad for factor services less similar payments made to nonresidents who contribute to the domestic economy. The data are obtained from the World Bank Atlas.

Life expectancy at birth is the number of years a new born infant would live, if patterns of mortality prevailing at the time of birth in the countries were to remain unchanged throughout his/her life. The infant mortality rate is the annual number of deaths of infants under one year of age per thousand live births. Adult illiteracy rate is the percentage of people aged 15 and above who cannot, with understanding, both read and write a short simple statement on their everyday life. The data are obtained from UNESCO.

Section 2: Macroeconomic Indicators

Table 2.1. Gross Domestic Product, real

National accounts estimates are obtained from regional member countries data, the World Bank, the IMF and the United Nations Statistical Division. In several instances, data are adjusted or supplemented with estimates made by the ADB Statistics Division. The concepts and definitions used for national accounts data are those of the United Nations 1993 System of National Accounts (SNA). Many countries continue to compile their national accounts in accordance with the 1968 SNA, but more and more are adopting the 1993 SNA.

Gross Domestic Product (GDP) measures the total final output of goods and services produced by a national economy, excluding provisions for depreciation. GDP figures are shown at constant 1995 market prices, and have been converted to US dollars using constant 1995 exchange rates provided by the IMF and the World Bank. For a few countries where the official exchange rate does not reflect effectively the rate applied to actual foreign exchange transactions, an alternative currency conversion factor has been used.

Aggregate growth rates for Africa are calculated as weighted averages of individual country growth rates using the share of the country's GDP in aggregate GDP based on the purchasing power parties (PPP) valuation of country GDPs.

Table 2.2. Gross Domestic Product, nominal

Data shown in this table are given at current market prices and are obtained by converting national currency series in current prices to US dollars at official exchange rates. Annual changes in GDP are presented in nominal terms.

Table 2.3. Gross National Savings

Gross National Savings (GNS) is calculated by deducting total consumption from GNI at current prices and adding net private transfers from abroad.

Table 2.4. Gross Capital Formation

Gross Capital Formation consists of gross domestic fixed capital formation plus net changes in the level of inventories.

Table 2.5. Terms of Trade

Terms of trade estimates are obtained from the IMF and supplemented by ADB Statistics Division estimates. These are obtained by dividing unit value indices of exports by unit value indices of imports. The terms of trade indices for the entire set of regional member countries are also ratios of the unit value of exports and the unit value of imports.

Table 2.6. Current Account Balance

Data in this table are obtained from the IMF, and based on the methodology of the fifth edition of the Balance of Payments Manual. The current account includes the trade balance valued f.o.b., net services and net factor income, and current transfer payments. The data is given as percentage of GDP.

Table 2.7 Broad Money Supply

Broad Money supply (M2) comprises currency outside banks, private sector demand deposits, (and, where applicable, post office and treasury checking deposits) and quasi-money.

Tables 2.8 Real Exchange Rate Index

The real exchange rate index is defined broadly as the nominal exchange rate index adjusted for relative movements in national price or cost indicators of the home country and the United States of America.

Table 2.9. International Reserves

International Reserves consist of country's holdings of monetary gold, Special Drawing Rights (SDRs) and foreign exchange, as well as its reserve position in the International Monetary Fund (IMF).

Table 2.10. Consumer Price Index

Consumer price index shows changes in the cost of acquisition of a basket of goods and services purchased by the average consumer. Weights for the computation of the index numbers are obtained from household budget surveys.

Table 2.11. Overall Fiscal Deficit or surplus

The overall surplus/deficit is defined as current and capital revenue and official grants received, less total expenditure and lending minus repayments. The data is given as a percentage of GDP.

Tables 2.12-.2.13 Total External Debt; Debt Service.

The main source of external debt data is the IMF. Total external debt covers outstanding and disbursed long-term debt, use of IMF credit, and short-term debt. Debt service is the sum of actual repayments of principal and actual payments of interest made in foreign exchange, goods, or services, on external public and publicly guaranteed debt.

Section 3: Labor Force and Social Indicators

This section presents data on labor force by sector (agriculture, industry and services) and also labor force participation rates, total and by sex.

Other tables in the section give data on components of population change (i.e. fertility, births, deaths and rate of natural increase), infant mortality rates, and life expectancy at birth, access to social infrastructure (sanitation, safe water and health services) and school enrolment ratios for primary and secondary levels.

Table 3.1. Labor Force by Sector

The labor force includes economically active persons aged 10 years and over. It includes the unemployed and the armed forces, but excludes housewives, students and other economically inactive groups. The agricultural sector consists of agriculture, forestry, hunting and fishing. Industry comprises mining and quarrying, manufacturing, construction, electricity, gas and water. Services include all other branches of economic activity and any statistical discrepancy in the origin of resources.

Table 3.2. Labor Force Participation Rates

The table shows the percentage of the population within each sex and age group that participates in economic activities (either employed or unemployed) from ILO data. Figures shown are ratios of the total economically-active population to the total population of all ages. Activity rates for females may be difficult to compare among countries because of the difference in the criteria adopted for determining the extent to which female workers are to be counted among the "economically active".

Table 3.3. Components of Population Change

Total fertility rate indicates the number of children that would be born per woman, if she were to live to the end of the child-bearing years; and bears children during those years in accordance with prevailing age-specific fertility rates. The crude birth rate represents the annual live births per thousand population. The crude death rate is the annual number of deaths per thousand population. Rate of Natural increase of the population is the difference between Crude Birth and Crude Death rates expressed as a percentage. The data in the table are obtained mainly from the United Nations Population Division, UNICEF and the World Bank.

Table 3.4. Mortality Indicators

The variables presented in this table - namely infant mortality rate and life expectancy at births - are as defined in Table 1.1. The sources of data are also the same.

Table 3.5. Population with Access to Social Infrastructures

The percentage of people with access to sanitation is defined separately for urban and rural areas. For urban areas, access to sanitation facilities is defined as urban population served by connections to public sewers or household systems, such as pit privies, pour-flush latrines, septic tanks, communal toilets, and other such facilities. In the case of the rural population,

the definition refers to those with adequate disposal, such as pit privies and pour-flush latrines. Applications of these definitions may vary from one country to another, and comparisons can therefore be inappropriate.

The population with access to safe water refers to the percentage of the population with reasonable access to safe water supply (which includes treated surface water, or untreated but uncontaminated water such as that from springs, sanitary wells, and protected boreholes). The threshold for the distance to safe water in urban areas is about 200 meters, while in rural areas it is reasonable walking distance to and from sources where water can be fetched.

The population with access to health services refers to the percentage of the population that can reach appropriate local health services by local means of transport in no more than one hour. Data in this table are obtained from the World Bank.

Table 3.6. School Enrolment

The primary school enrolment ratio is the total number of pupils enrolled at primary level of education, regardless of age, expressed as a percentage of the population corresponding to the official school age of primary education. School enrolment ratios may be more than 100 per cent in countries where some pupils' ages are different from the legal enrolment age. Data in this table are obtained from UNESCO.

The secondary school enrolment ratio is the total number of pupils enrolled at secondary level of education, regardless of age, expressed as a percentage of the population corresponding to the official school age of secondary education.

Data Sources

1.	**Basic Indicators**	Food and Agriculture Organization: FAOSTAT Database, 2003. United Nations Population Division: The 2000 revision. World Bank: African Development Indicators, 2001/2002. Regional Member Countries, ADB Statistics Division.
2.	**Macroeconomic Indicators**	
2.1 - 2.4	National Accounts	United Nations: National Accounts Yearbook, various years. World Bank: Africa Live Database, February 2003. IMF: World Economic Outlook data files, September 2002. ADB Statistics Division. Regional Member Countries.
2.5 - 2.6	External Sector	IMF: World Economic Outlook, Data files, September 2002.
2.7 - 2.10	Money Supply, Exchange Rates and Prices	IMF: International Financial Statistics, February 2003, and International Financial Statistics, Yearbook, 2002. ILO: Yearbook of Labor Statistics, various years. ADB Statistics Division, Regional Member Countries.
2.11	Government Finance	IMF: World Economic Outlook Data files, September 2002.
2.12 - 2.13	External Debt	IMF: World Economic Outlook, September 2002. ADB Statistics Division.
3.	**Labor Force and Social Indicators**	
3.1 - 3.2	Labor Force	ILO: Labor Force Statistics, various years. World Bank: African Development Indicators 2001/2002 ADB Statistics Division.
3.3 - 3.6	Social Indicators	UNICEF: The State of the World's Children, various years. World Bank: African Development Indicators, 2001/2002. UN: Human Development Report, 2002. UN: Population Division, The 2000 Revision. Regional Member Countries. ADB Statistics Division.

This publication was prepared by the Bank's Development Research Depart (PDRE). Other publications of the Department are:

AFRICAN DEVELOPMENT REVIEW
A semi-annual professional journal devoted to the study and analysis of development issues in Africa.

ECONOMIC RESEARCH PAPERS
A working paper series presenting the research findings, mainly by the research staff, on topics related to African development policy issues.

COMPENDIUM OF STATISTICS
An annual publication providing statistical information on the operational activities of the Bank Group.

GENDER, POVERTY AND ENVIRONMENTAL INDICATORS ON AFRICAN COUNTRIES
A Biennial publiation providing information on the broad development trends relating to gender, poverty and environmental issues in the 53 African countries.

SELECTED STATISTICS ON AFRICAN COUNTRIES
An annual publication, providing selected social and economic indicators for the 53 regional member countries of the Bank.

AFRICAN ECONOMIC OUTLOOK
An annual publication jointly produced by the African Development Bank and the OECD Development Centre, which analyses the comparative economic prospects for African countries.

Copies of these publications may be obtained from:

Development Research Department (PDRE)
African Development Bank

Headquarters	**Temporary Relocation Agency (TRA)**
01 BP 1387 Abidjan 01, COTE D'IVOIRE	15 Rue du Ghana, Angle Av. Hedil Nouira et
TELEFAX (225) 20 20 49 48	Pierre de Coubertin
TELEPHONE (225) 20 20 44 44	BP 323 – 1002 TUNIS BELVEDERE
TELEX 23717/23498/23263	TUNISIE
Web Site: www.afdb.org	TELEPHONE (216) 71333511
EMAIL: afdb@afdb.org	Web Site: www.afdb.org
	EMAIL: afdb@afdb.org